9/06

D0065388

MORMON AMERICA

MORMON AMERICA

THE POWER AND THE PROMISE

RICHARD N. OSTLING AND JOAN K. OSTLING

HarperSanFrancisco
A Division of HarperCollinsPublishers

HarperCollins books may be purchased for educational, business, or sales promotional use. For information please write: Special Markets Department, HarperCollins Publishers, 10 East 53rd Street, New York, NY 10022.

HarperCollins Web Site: http://www.harpercollins.com
HarperCollins®, ☐®, and HarperSanFrancisco™ are trademarks of
HarperCollins Publishers Inc.

FIRST EDITION
Designed by Joseph Rutt

Library of Congress Cataloging-in-Publication Data

Mormon America : the power and the promise / Richard N. Ostling and
Joan K. Ostling. — 1st ed.
p.   cm.
Includes bibliographical references and index.
ISBN 0–06–066371–5 (cloth). — ISBN 0–06–066372–3 (pbk.)
1. Church of Jesus Christ of Latter-day Saints—United States.
2. Mormon Church—United States.   I. Ostling, Joan K.   II. Title.
BX8635.2.O88   1999
289.3'73—DC21   99–28516
CIP

99 00 01 02 03 ❖/RRDH 10 9 8 7 6 5 4 3 2 1

ALASKA

Edmonton
Cardston   Regina
                    Toronto
                      Montreal
UNITED   Halifax
STATES

HAWAII

Hermosillo
Colonia Juarez
    Ciudad Juarez   Monterrey
    Mexico City   Tampico
       Oaxaca   Merida
              Villahermosa
Tuxtla Gutierrez Guatemala
    San Jose   City
                        Caracas
          Bogota

     Guayaquil

■ Apia
   ■ Papeete
■ Nuku'alofa

                                    Recife

                        Lima
                            Cochabamba

                                 Campinas
                                      Sao Paulo
                    Santiago   Porto Alegre
                          Montevideo
                    Buenos Aires

Santo Domingo

**United States
(announced)**
Birmingham, AL
Nauvoo, IL
Louisville, KY
Baton Rouge, LA
Harrison, NY
Oklahoma City, OK
Medford, OR

Preston ■
London
         Zollikofe

Madrid ■ ■

                      Acc

**United States
(under construct**
Fresno, CA
Kona, HI
Boston, MA
Detroit, MI
St. Paul, MN
Billings, MT
Raleigh-Durham
Bismarck, ND
Albuquerque, NM
Palmyra, NY
Columbus, OH
Columbia, SC
Memphis, TN
Nashville, TN
Houston, TX
Spokane, WA

United States (existing)

Anchorage, AK	Dallas, TX
Mesa, AZ	American Fork, UT
Los Angeles, CA	Bountiful, UT
Oakland, CA	Logan, UT
San Diego, CA	Manti, UT
Denver, CO	Monticello, UT
Orlando, FL	Ogden, UT
Atlanta, GA	Provo, UT
Laie, HI	St. George, UT
Boise, ID	Salt Lake City, UT
Idaho Falls, ID	South Jordan, UT
Chicago, IL	Vernal, UT
St. Louis, MO	Seattle, WA
Las Vegas, NV	Kensington, MD
Portland, OR	

■ **Temples of the Church**
● **Announced Temples**
□ **Temples under Construction**

As of April 4, 1999

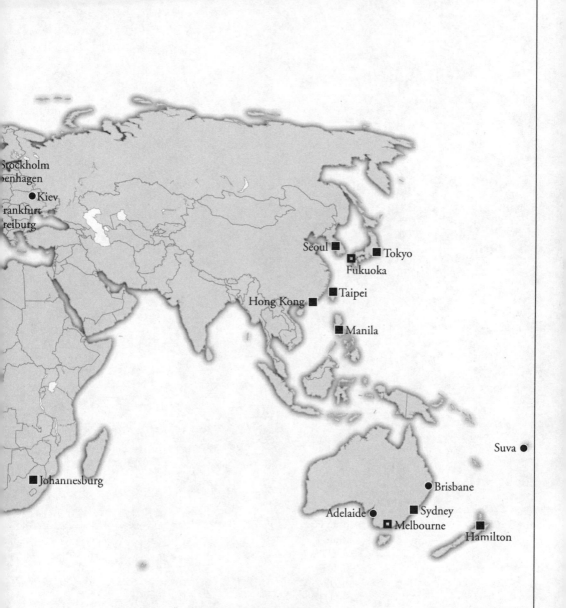

Stockhom
enhagen
●Kiev
rankfurt
reiburg

Seoul ■
■ Tokyo
Fukuoka
■ Taipei
Hong Kong ■
■ Manila

Suva ●

■ Johannesburg

● Brisbane
Adelaide ● ■ Sydney
Melbourne
■ Hamilton

Mormon Temples
Around the World

CONTENTS

PREFACE

SHOULD NON-MORMONS WRITE A BOOK ABOUT MORMONISM? THE COAU-thors are, admittedly, conventional Protestants. Sometimes it seems as though adherents of the faith would prefer to see depictions only by fellow believers. But we were encouraged during this project when a distin-guished faculty retiree at Brigham Young University remarked that perhaps *only* outsiders could produce the sort of book we had in mind—namely, a candid but nonpolemical overview written for non-Mormons and Mormons alike, focusing on what is distinctive and culturally significant about this growing American movement. If we have succeeded, the out-siders will find some fascinating information and want to learn even more. And the insiders will see themselves portrayed fairly while learning some things they would not have known otherwise.

The idea for this book originated when Richard N. Ostling and S. C. "Sam" Gwynne were fellow *Time* correspondents doing the field reporting for the 1997 "Mormons Inc." cover story. Ostling covered the spiritual side and Gwynne the temporal aspects of the Church of Jesus Christ of Latter-day Saints, especially its fabled wealth. Though their magazine reportage was the starting point, almost all of the material was newly developed dur-ing the preparation of this book, which is coauthored by Richard with his wife, Joan K. Ostling.

Ostling, now a religion writer for the Associated Press, has frequently covered the faith during three decades of specializing in this field, includ-ing in-person interviews in Salt Lake City with church presidents Spencer

Kimball (1978) and Gordon B. Hinckley (1997). Gwynne brought special credentials to his work investigating the money side, perhaps the most controversial topic in the cover story and the book. An international banker turned journalist, he has been editor-in-chief of *California Business* magazine and the senior editor managing *Time's* business section. His career as a *Time* correspondent, including coauthorship of the book *The Outlaw Bank* (1993), has won him the John Hancock and Gerald Loeb Awards for financial writing and the Jack Anderson Award for investigative reporting. (The latter is named in honor of the most famous Mormon in journalism.) The coauthors gratefully acknowledge his contributions.

A note about terminology. The church officially informs media personnel that the use of "Mormon Church" and the "Mormon" nickname for members is "both incorrect and confusing." The word is supposed to appear only in the scriptural name, the Book of Mormon. The organization also directs writers to shun "LDS" and "LDS Church." It prefers the church's full nine-word name in the first reference, and after that "the Latter-day Saints" or "the Church."

Here the church is attempting to make water run uphill, so ingrained are these terms in modern usage. Normally it is good journalistic practice to call people what they call themselves. Not all conservatives like to be known as Fundamentalists, for example. But "Mormon" carries no particular animus, nor does the useful shorthand "LDS" for the church's full name, and both are used often in conversation by members who are unashamed of their affiliation. To the general public the faith's best-known ornament, after all, is the Mormon Tabernacle Choir. "Mormon" is also useful in distinguishing the larger Utah-based church from the Missouri-based Reorganized Church of Jesus Christ of Latter Day Saints (with a capital D and no hyphen, the sort of detail that keeps copy editors alert) and other groups with related names.

Our practice, then, will be to use the church's full name here or there, "Saints" occasionally (and always with a capital S since all other churches employ this term generically), and "Mormon" or "LDS" much more frequently.

The LDS scriptures are listed by full name (the Book of Mormon, Doctrine and Covenants, Pearl of Great Price [and subsections of the latter: the Book of Moses, the Book of Abraham, Joseph Smith—Matthew, Joseph Smith—History, and the Articles of Faith]). LDS scripture citations are named in full (since the titles are unfamiliar to general readers) except for the Doctrine and Covenants, abbreviated to D&C. Another frequently used abbreviation is BYU for Brigham Young University.

We express our warm personal appreciation to: the Mormons who reviewed the manuscript prior to publication and who shared their faith journeys with us; the anonymous sources who provided financial information and copies of the 1988 and 1999 *General Handbook of Instructions,* with essential information not available to the church's membership or the general public; the church officials and other sources who granted us interviews; and Michael R. Leonard and other staff members of the church Public Affairs Department who patiently fielded our numerous queries. As prefaces always state, the sins of omission and commission herein are ours, not theirs. And special thanks to our colleagues at HarperSanFrancisco, including John Loudon and Mark Tauber. We are also grateful for old-fashioned public and academic libraries, and for modern interlibrary loans, (800) book orders, superstores, the World Wide Web, faxes, and CD-ROMs.

Those readers who are immersed in this complex field will immediately recognize how much this book draws upon the prior expertise of specialists in the LDS community, who have produced a truly remarkable range of works. We freely acknowledge that indebtedness. Rather than footnotes within the text, there are notes at the end of the book listing important source references for each chapter. Many important contributions are credited in the text as well as in the suggestions in the section "For Further Reading."

INTRODUCTION
A NEW WORLD FAITH

CRADLED ON ALL SIDES BY THE SNOW-GLAZED PEAKS OF THE WASATCH Range, Salt Lake City, Utah, at the turn of the millennium awaited the invasion of the 2002 Winter Olympic Games: some 3,500 athletes and coaches, 10,000 media personnel, and 70,000 daily visitors. These guests, and the billions watching the telecasts beamed to 160 countries, would quickly learn that this is a city like no other in the United States.

There are arcane liquor laws to navigate. In most hotels an unfamiliar volume of scripture is carefully placed in the bedside drawer of each room. The geography of the town centers on a ten-acre complex known as Temple Square, with every address determined by how far a block radiates from this sacred center. By the dictate of its founding prophet, the town's layout has 132-foot-wide streets, broad enough for turning a train of four oxen and a covered wagon. The centerpiece, a multi-spired block of gleaming marble topped by a gilded trumpet-blowing angel, is a temple of secret rituals with precincts forbidden to tourists and TV cameras.

Diagonally across the street from Temple Square is the large, fashionable ZCMI Center Mall. The initials stand for Zion's Cooperative Mercantile Institution. The majority stock in this company is held by the city's dominant institution, the Church of Jesus Christ of Latter-day Saints (LDS), known to all as the Mormon Church. Inside, beyond the beehive-imprinted sidewalks and near the usual chain boutiques and food court, is the huge Deseret Book outlet. It is stocked with thousands of titles, conference tapes, and pictures of church officers, but there is no Starbucks coffee bar. That would violate an unbreakable church tenet. Along with Mormon titles, surprisingly, the store carries Billy Graham's autobiography *Just as I Am* and many titles by the twentieth century's best-known apologist for orthodox Christianity, C. S. Lewis. A stack of survival kit boxes with emergency essentials, including first aid and water purification supplies for use in time of disaster, stands prominently displayed near the cash registers. Deluxe version: $181.50. Down the hall a small shop features temple souvenirs, white slippers, and simple, long, white, part-polyester dresses for temple wear, bearing labels like "For Eternity," "Forever Yours," and "Angelique."

The majority of the shoppers, like 70 percent of Utah citizens, are Mormons. This is their headquarters city, their Olympus, their Zion. Mystery continues to surround their church. Though it is hard to imagine when contemplating this placid valley with its prosperous metropolis, no religion in American history has aroused so much fear and hatred, nor been the object of so much persecution and so much misinformation. Mormons are intensely patriotic Americans; they even believe the Constitution and the democracy it enshrines were divinely inspired. Yet their own church is rigidly hierarchical, centralized, authoritarian, and almost uniquely secretive. It is also, relative to size, America's richest church, with an estimated $25 to $30 billion in assets and something like $5 or $6 billion in annual income, mostly from members' tithes.

The church began in upstate New York in 1830 with six members. By 1844, when a lynch mob assassinated its thirty-eight-year-old prophet, Joseph Smith Jr., the flock had already grown to over 26,000. During the past quarter-century it has moved up to seventh place among America's church bodies, bypassing the Presbyterians, the Episcopalians, and the Lutheran Church—Missouri Synod. Heading into the twenty-first century, the church's membership had surpassed the 10 million mark internationally, with more than half the members living outside the United States. The faith is expanding so rapidly that the non-Mormon sociologist Rodney Stark projects that during the coming century—with something like 265 million members by 2080—it will become the most important world religion to emerge since the rise of Islam some fourteen centuries ago.

Salt Lake's founder hardly had the Olympics in mind when he viewed the Great Basin in 1847 and supposedly declared that "this is the right place" for his bedraggled band of pioneers to dig in and settle. But somehow one suspects Brigham Young might have enjoyed the sixteen-day party and have been grateful for all the attention focused on the city he built. The church made no direct contributions to the International Olympic Committee, but church-owned businesses, including radio and TV stations and the *Deseret News* newspaper, gave about $211,000 to the bid committee and helped with media projects. The head of the local committee until 1997 was LDS member Thomas Welch. Churchgoers were prominent among the 15,000 local Olympic volunteers who signed up.

The city had tried for more than two decades to land the Olympics; Utahns were eager to update the city's image as a cow town populated by bland religionists. But the years preceding the Olympics carried reminders that the Salt Lake area, with a population now over 1.2 million and growing fast, home to biotech industries as well as church office buildings, can escape neither the problems endemic to contemporary urban life nor the controversies of its colorful Mormon past. The city has smog, sprawl, and Tongan-Samoan gang wars. Bribery scandals over the Salt Lake bid for the Games sullied the clean-cut image of both the Olympics and Salt Lake City. And polygamy hit the national news again as the activities of some splinter Mormons became a joke on late-night TV. Mainline Mormons were keenly sensitive about all that.

The nineteenth-century pioneers who came to this arid and seemingly unpromising valley did so because they had nowhere else to turn. They came on horseback, in covered wagons, the wretched poorest on foot dragging handcarts. They had been hounded in turn out of New York State, Ohio, Missouri, and Illinois. Their leaders had been tarred and feathered, jailed, and even shot to death. Again and again the believers had lost their homes. At the time Young assumed command and led them into the wilderness, their destination was a gathering place outside the organized United States where they could develop their faith under church protection, in security and peace.

Some 80,000 Mormons crossed the plains into Zion in the twenty-two years before the Transcontinental Railroad arrived to open up the region. It is estimated that as many as 6,000 pioneer Saints died getting there. Utah passed from territorial status into statehood in 1896, after a virtual civil war with the federal government over polygamy had largely been settled. But Mormonism began as, and still is, a uniquely American faith. Mormons, of course, were a major factor in settling the American West. "Go West, Young Man," for freedom, opportunity, and a fresh start, has long been the classic American myth.

For Mormons, though, the American myth is also scriptural. The Garden of Eden was literally located around Independence, Missouri; after expulsion from the Garden, Adam and Eve moved north, not far from present-day Interstate 35. And someday, they believe, the Lord will return to Independence, seventy miles to the south. Unfortunately, the venue for the Second Coming, the "temple lot" dedicated long ago by the prophet Joseph Smith, is owned by the splinter Church of Christ (Temple Lot), a 2,300-member group also known as the Hedrickites. The 10-million-member Utah church can only view the site from its property next door. The headquarters of another claimant commands a third corner of this millennial intersection, the Reorganized Church of Jesus Christ of Latter Day Saints (RLDS), with 250,000 members. The RLDS, established in 1860 by Smith disciples who did not follow Brigham Young west and never believed in polygamy, fought the tiny Temple Lot church through the Missouri courts a century ago for right of possession of the sacred site, and lost.

The New World is not just a special place in God's design for the future. Looking to the past, too, Mormonism believes in an American prophet who received from the hand of God New World scriptures that recorded a sacred history of the ancient Americas, with a chosen people who carried out divinely ordained activities and were eventually ministered to by Jesus Christ himself, who literally came in the flesh to preach to them after his resurrection. It teaches that God reestablished his church beginning in upstate New York and granted it the only priesthood authority that exists on earth—a church based from then until now on U.S. soil and governed at the top almost exclusively by U.S. citizens.

In the Book of Mormon, the scriptures on golden tablets given to Smith by the Angel Moroni, God's biblical work was extended to the Americas, by one leading apostle's reckoning, in the period from 2247 B.C. to A.D. 421. The book tells about the Lamanites, Native Americans who are considered by Mormons to be part of the Ten Lost Tribes of Israel. Jesus Christ came to preach to these Indians, the book declares, and for some time, many centuries before Columbus, an American church flourished, then fell into apostasy until the truth and the true church were restored through Joseph Smith. The tablets foretold the prophet's name, Joseph Jr. (II Nephi 3). Besides giving these new scriptures, God commissioned his American prophet to revise significant portions of the Bible that Smith taught had been corrupted by Jews and Christians.

Mormonism, as the movement was quickly nicknamed, provided nationalistic Americans with a very American gospel. Despite demanding claims on the lives of believers, it was from the beginning optimistic and upbeat, a reaction against the establishment New England Calvinism. It denied original sin and stressed individual moral choice, proclaiming that every human could progress toward godhood. It was a religious version of the American dream: Everyman presented with unlimited potential. Its theology provided a highly idiosyncratic blend of biblical literalism and strict moralism, a characteristic emphasis on disciplined self-reliance, and post-Enlightenment liberalism on the nature of man and God.

A church without professional clergy, but with a highly centralized and authoritarian structure, the Church of Jesus Christ of Latter-day Saints is ruled top-down by a self-perpetuating hierarchy that is ritualistically "sustained" by unanimous vote at church conferences in Salt Lake City. Atop the pyramid is the current president, prophet, seer, and revelator, who chooses a first counselor and second counselor and acts with them in a collective First Presidency. Next comes the Quorum of the Twelve Apostles, who hold lifetime positions and are always ranked by seniority of attaining that rank, then echelons of lower authorities and officeholders. There is neither a forum for public debate nor a church legislature to set policy. Obedience to tenets and administrative minutiae as defined by the General Authorities at Temple Square is the only allowable response. Despite the religion's global ambitions and non-U.S. majority, the denominational bureaucracy in Salt Lake, like the top echelon of the hierarchy that commands it, is overwhelmingly American.

The church's *General Handbook of Instructions,* which covers everything from church discipline and governance to instructions on how to dispose of worn-out holy underwear, is a confidential document issued in numbered copies distributed to a specified list of officials. The church's biennial almanac is odd as denominational yearbooks go. It gives extensive statistics on members, baptisms, missionaries, wards (congregations), stakes (geographic subdivisions similar to presbyteries or dioceses), and the like, but no financial statistics. It provides pictures and biographies of church authorities, but few clues as to their functions. Unlike other such reference works, it contains no directory of the organization's bureaucracy. It does, however, meticulously list every LDS believer who ever participated in the Olympics, beginning with an athlete adorned with a Mormon scriptural name: Alma Richards (gold medal, high jump, 1912).

Mormons of every stripe are obsessive about their image. Headquarters was delighted when President Gordon B. Hinckley was interviewed by Mike Wallace on CBS's *60 Minutes* in 1996 and by Richard Ostling on the PBS *NewsHour with Jim Lehrer* in 1997, when he appeared on *Larry King Live* in 1998, and when the church was profiled in a mostly respectful *Time* cover (August 4, 1997) honoring the Utah pioneer trek's sesquicentennial. Such intense interest is not confined to headquarters. The independent magazine *Sunstone,* a stylish outlet for liberals and dissidents, prints a regular "Mormon Media Image" column. When the American Muslim Council finds that only 35 percent of Americans have a favorable image of Mormons, or Finnish Lutherans rate Mormons almost as negatively as they rate Muslims and just a tad better than Jehovah's Witnesses, or the Evangelical periodical *Christianity Today* devotes a cover story to Rodney Stark's projections (in 1998), or a network TV sitcom takes a "cheap shot at Mormons and their beliefs" (ABC's *The Hughleys,* 1998), these critiques are duly reported in *Sunstone.*

Mormons are deeply concerned that their church appears to outsiders as a "cult," that slippery and all-purpose slur aimed at marginal faiths. The perception was cruelly and famously reinforced in 1997 during basketball playoffs with the Utah Jazz when Dennis Rodman of the Chicago Bulls was fined a record $50,000 by the National Basketball Association for saying he didn't like playing around the "f——ing Mormons." Many sophisticated Mormons found the incident amusing and, in any case, did not mind having the Tattooed One as an adversary. The real Mormon wincing came when, in a disingenuous defense of his wayward star, Coach Phil Jackson told a national audience that "Dennis did not understand that Mormonism was some type of cult or sect." The phrase resounded against Mormon sensibilities like fingernails on a blackboard.

Michael Austin, a West Virginia college professor whose hobby is tracking popular literature with a Mormon theme, observes that negative Mormon images have been fixed since the nineteenth century. He told a Sunstone Symposium in Salt Lake City that "the frequency with which these stereotypes appear in contemporary fiction suggests that they have never really disappeared from America's collective cultural memory." Austin lists seventy-six such pulp westerns, historical romances, science fiction novels, horror stories, true crime novels, and mystery fictions currently in print with such themes as blood atonement murders, maidens held hostage, underground financial power, fanaticism, hierarchical dictatorship, conspiracy, and vengeance by secret members of "Danite" brigades, an unofficial but legendary Mormon vigilante group.

The nineteenth-century pedigree behind these literary attacks included the very first Sherlock Holmes mystery, Sir Arthur Conan Doyle's *A Study in Scarlet* (1887). The book came complete with Mormon villains, the captive maiden, and Danites described as sinister Avenging Angels:

> Fuller knowledge of the organization which produced such terrible results served to increase rather than to lessen the horror which it inspired in the minds of men. None knew who belonged to this ruthless society. The names of the participators in the deeds of blood and violence done under the name of religion were kept profoundly secret. The very friend to whom you communicated your misgivings as to the Prophet and his mission might be one of those who would come forth at night with fire and sword to exact a terrible reparation. Hence every man feared his neighbour, and none spoke of the things which were nearest his heart.

Doyle had never visited Utah, but Mark Twain, writing irreverent travel pieces a dozen years earlier in *Roughing It,* had. His oft-quoted passage about polygamous wives:

> My heart was wiser than my head. It warmed toward these poor, ungainly and pathetically "homely" creatures, and as I turned to hide the generous moisture in my eyes, I said, "No—the man that marries one of them has done an act of Christian charity which entitles him to the kindly applause of mankind, not their harsh censure—and the man that marries sixty of them has done a deed of open-handed generosity so sublime that the nations should stand uncovered in his presence and worship in silence.

Twain further described Brigham Young as "the only real power in the land. He was an absolute monarch—a monarch who defied our President—a monarch who laughed at our armies when they camped about his capital—a monarch who received without emotion the news that the august Congress of the United States had enacted a solemn law against polygamy, and then went forth calmly and married twenty-five or thirty more wives." Twain's famous Book of Mormon exegesis ("chloroform in print") in *Roughing It* is either vicious or viciously funny, depending on the reader's point of view.

With all that, LDS public relations obviously had its work cut out. After statehood arrived, so did tourists, and with them the first official public relations gesture in the form of a small information booth planted in Temple Square. More important than the booth was the Mormon Tabernacle Choir, which was already bringing the church positive worldwide recognition. To this day it is the one aspect of Mormonism that virtually everyone has heard about. The choir first performed just twenty-nine days after Young's first pioneers reached the valley. By 1893 it had grown to 350 singers and received an invitation to the Chicago World's Fair choral festival, even though the related World Parliament of Religions snubbed the Saints. Salt Lake City's businesses, both Mormon and non-Mormon, were as excited as Utahns would be a century later about their Olympics bid, and they raised money to send 250 of the singers to Chicago. With typical

Mormon attention to detail, and a consciousness of not wanting to look like crude hicks, choir members were given extensive written instructions in manners:

> Never eat with your elbows sprawled on the table. Between courses, one elbow, not both, may be leaned upon.
>
> Never dunk in public. At home go ahead.
>
> Never place a whole piece of bread on the palm of your hand and slap butter on it with a house-painting technique. Bread should be broken enough for one mouthful at a time, buttering each piece as you break it. Rolls and butter the same way.

With choral technique at least as impeccable as their etiquette, they won second place in the competition. Since then the choir has made many international tours, sung at four U.S. presidential inaugurations, and compiled a distinguished catalog of recordings, including hot-selling discs on which its thick choral sound blends beautifully with the legendary rich strings of the Philadelphia Orchestra under Eugene Ormandy's baton. Many a non-Mormon eye has moistened at the strains of the choir's trademark Mormon hymn, William Clayton's 1846 "Come, Come Ye Saints," with its closing testimony of faith in the face of hardship, "All is well! All is well!"

Since 1929 the choir has sung in weekly broadcasts from the Tabernacle on Temple Square, the longest continuous program in American radio history. Unlike the temple, the Tabernacle is open to the public, and tourists regularly pack the auditorium for the live broadcast. Today *Music and the Spoken Word* is beamed to some 1,500 radio, TV, and cable stations. The format has been invariable for decades: choir numbers, some organ music from the 206-rank, 11,623-pipe instrument, and, about twenty-two minutes into the program, a brief inspirational talk. Notably, the words are carefully void of anything that would distinguish Mormonism from conventional Christianity. As the historian Jan Shipps, a non-Mormon expert, puts it, the broadcast is a "presentation of an acceptable image of Mormonism."

With Utah's statehood, and two church pronouncements disavowing the practice of polygamy (1890 and 1904), Mormons began swimming in the American mainstream. Despite nineteenth-century persecutions, and the U.S. House of Representatives' refusal to seat the polygamist B. H. Roberts after his landslide election victory in 1898, Mormons have always been intensely patriotic. They fought bravely in every twentieth-century war. With their emphasis on self-reliance during the Depression 1930s, they won widespread respect for their efforts to take care of their own through their unique church welfare system.

In the last third of the current century, the Mormon diaspora began in earnest. The Mormon is no longer merely a resident of the Mountain West. He might be your neighbor, the one most likely to help in a time of crisis, not at all strange. More than anyone else on the street, he might seem honest, reliable, hardworking, and earnest—all the Boy Scout virtues. His children are obedient, his family close-knit. If he delivers a prayer on a community occasion, it is in unremarkable, evangelical-sounding language, complete with the old-fashioned *thee* and *thou*.

This is the flip side of the Mormon image edging into the third millennium: Mormons as a model minority, a hardworking people with more education than the American average, deeply committed to church and family. That image moved to the fore perhaps in the 1950s and 1960s, when media attention to scruffy beatniks and hippies made clean-cut Mormon youths look appealing to most Americans. The church's emphasis on family values seems to bespeak stability in a culture of turmoil. Since the 1980s the church has poured a constant stream of press releases into the media marketplace, conveying information about new temples, new stakes, increased missionary activity, mass rallies in places like Madison Square Garden, international humanitarian activities, and the placement of its vast genealogical archives on the Internet for all to use.

Since World War II liberal Protestant divines have held well-publicized seminars seeking to define the least common denominator of faith for a secular age or to sift the authentic deeds of Jesus in the Gospels from the many supposedly fictional ones. Some few have even declared the "death of God." Contradicting this strategy is the thesis of Dean Kelley's *Why Conservative Churches Are Growing* (1972) and subsequent scholarship by religion sociologists. According to them, churches that demand real commitment and a distinctive lifestyle are the ones that grow.

And the Mormon Church does demand unusually heavy commitment, along with a highly distinctive lifestyle. Members in good standing—those with a "recommend" permitting admission to temples—are required to "tithe," that is, to donate to the church 10 percent of their gross annual income. They also forgo two meals each month so that the money saved can be given to an internal welfare system that assists fellow members in need. They abstain from alcohol and tobacco, as many other groups do, but also from caffeinated beverages. Their young men are expected to donate two years of their lives to full-time missionary work when they turn nineteen, and they and their families pay their own way for this privilege. It is not uncommon for devout Mormons of both sexes to spend up to twenty hours a week in unpaid church service and activities.

In an irony of history, these radical Mormon communitarians of the nineteenth century assimilated into the American economy and are now commonly right-wing capitalists and respectably Republican (though the church is officially nonpartisan). The LDS ranks are filled with prominent politicians, including members of the U.S. House and Senate, captains of industry, and achievers in many other fields. Just as surely, the Mormon people have sought to blend into the nation's moral and spiritual economy. The onetime believers in plural marriage, considered a dire threat to Victorian probity and the entire nation, have become the exemplars of conservative monogamous family values. Perhaps the greatest irony is that their core allies in political fights for the family in recent times have been Protestant Evangelicals, whose forebears crusaded in tandem with the Republican Party to crush the polygamous church and whose theologians today still see the Utah-based faith as doctrinally dangerous.

Are Mormons Christians? Mormons and non-Mormons frequently debate this complex issue. To the Saints the very question is offensive. The Mormons themselves, with their unique body of doctrine, believe that they are not only Christians but the only *true* Christians, or at least that theirs is the only true Christian church. That tenet is infallible, for it stems from the original calling of the founding prophet. Indeed, this is Mormonism's very reason for existence.

Many books have been written about Mormonism. They tend to be defenses or polemics. Often they are by specialists writing for other specialists. The most readable books for general audiences are usually limited by topic or confined to the fields of history or social science. This book is designed to introduce Mormonism to interested outsiders as well as to insiders, who often have things to learn as well. It examines this growing American subculture's colorful history, unique beliefs, and penchant for secrecy, its lifestyle and finances, its place in the religious and secular world today, and its growth and prospects for the future. This is a real faith and must be understood in those terms, without caricature. As Jan Shipps observes, Mormonism can no longer employ special pleading for itself as a protected minority. What occurs inside Mormonism is no longer merely an internal matter, and what Mormonism does is becoming vitally important to the larger culture. The Mormon people are multidimensional and entering the third millennium as full-fledged citizens of an important new world religion.

CHAPTER I
SEALED WITH BLOOD

Nauvoo, Illinois, today sits at a picturesque bend in the Mississippi River, a tourist attraction and state historical park with visitor centers operated by competing churches at opposite ends of the restored town. The Church of Jesus Christ of Latter-day Saints (LDS) owns the imposing brick Heber C. Kimball house and the Masonic lodge. The Reorganized Church of Jesus Christ of Latter Day Saints (RLDS) owns Joseph Smith's grave and his two homes. Relations are polite. The visitor can take the LDS tour in a cart pulled by Amish-raised draft horses and admire the cornfields and soybeans, the rushing creek, the restored shops, and the old Masonic building. There is no sign of the once mosquito-infested malarial swamps, and neither church has restored any of the cramped wooden hovels in which most of the Saints actually lived during Nauvoo's brief moment of glory.

Today as one breakfasts at Grandpa John's Café in the backwater country town perched on the high bluff above the river, it is hard to believe that in its day—five years of growth and fame before it became a ghost town—Nauvoo rivaled Chicago. Nothing like this theocratic principality in the heart of America had been seen since Pilgrim and Puritan days. Here the prophet Joseph Smith maintained a militia of 3,000 to 4,000 men under arms, at a time when the full U.S. Army had only 8,500 soldiers. At its height the population of Nauvoo proper reached 12,000 citizens; several thousand more Saints tilled the ground in nearby Hancock County or across the river in Iowa. These were frontier days, and the white limestone temple rising 160 feet high on the crest of the hill was an imposing sight for miles around.

Praise for Nauvoo's impressive achievements appeared in the newspapers of Boston, New York, and elsewhere. A steady stream of visitors came in 1843 and 1844 to admire the town, visit the strange exhibit of Egyptian mummies in its little museum, and sample Smith's hospitality. They included Charles Francis Adams, son of former president John Quincy Adams, and Josiah Quincy Jr., son of Harvard's president and later the mayor of Boston. Quincy was impressed with Smith's charisma and how he "won human hearts and shaped human lives." But Quincy also sounded a somewhat ominous cautionary note when he observed that Joseph Smith was far more than the entrepreneurial mayor of a successful, if unique, frontier town: "His influence, whether for good or for evil, is potent today, and the end is not yet."

That influence had begun in Palmyra, New York, fifteen years earlier with the translation of the golden plates that Smith testified had been lent him by the Angel Moroni. These latter-day scriptures described the migration of Israelites to the New World—where they became ancestors of Native Americans—and the risen Christ's ministry on American soil. Smith translated these writings into the Book of Mormon, a revelation that Mormons would place alongside the Bible. The influence continued as a band of six followers incorporated a new church and multiplied into a movement of thousands willing to follow their prophet anywhere. And it did not end when a mob left Joseph Smith's bullet-ridden body propped against a well outside the jail at Carthage, Illinois.

The assassination of their prophet left the Saints grief-stricken and dispirited. Nevertheless, as in Quincy's prediction that "the end is not yet," from that bloody atrocity there emerged the most successful faith ever born on American soil, a church regarded by some today as a major emerging world religion.

In the spring of 1844 matters were spinning out of control for the prophet. He was charged as an accessory to attempted murder and faced an extradition warrant to Missouri, where a thug had pumped buckshot into the head of Governor Lilburn Boggs, who had cruelly mistreated the Saints. Amazingly, Boggs survived. It was rumored that the assailant, never caught, had operated at the behest of Smith. Despite vigorous denials by church officials, talk also abounded of something unthinkable—that the prophet and other top church officials were secretly taking multiple wives. Accusers also said Smith was profiting from land speculation over the miseries of poor Saints. Some of his closest colleagues were beginning to regard him as a fallen prophet.

Never passive, Smith responded with a frenzy of political activity. First he declared himself a candidate for president of the United States. Shortly thereafter he organized the secret Council of Fifty to plan an ambitious political future, and he had that body anoint him as "King, Priest and Ruler over Israel on Earth." He petitioned Congress for authorization to raise and lead a 100,000-man army, personally loyal and answerable only to him, that would subdue the western territories from Texas to Oregon. He proposed that anyone who would "attempt to hinder or molest the said Joseph Smith" in this design was to be liable to two years' imprisonment. Congress did not oblige.

In the midst of all this, Smith preached the most important sermon of his career. The doctrines he presented in this discourse—a multiplicity of gods, eternal progression, a heavenly Father who had a body and used to be a man, denial that God created the cosmos "out of nothing"—departed radically from Christian orthodoxy.

Joseph Smith once said, "A religion that does not require the sacrifice of all things never has power sufficient to produce the faith necessary unto life and salvation." The Saints' readiness to sacrifice all things had already been well tested. Just five years earlier the Mormons had arrived in Illinois, fleeing east across Missouri up into Iowa and across the frozen Mississippi. Missouri's Governor Boggs had thrown them a threat: get out or face extermination. Joseph Smith was in jail in Liberty, Missouri, that winter of 1838–39, under threat of execution for a trumped-up charge of treason. His loyal wife, Emma, trudged across the icebound river on foot with a babe in arms, several little ones clinging to her skirt, and the prophet's papers in a bag tied to her waist. A senior apostle by the name of Brigham Young was emerging as a leader, shuttling back and forth to shepherd the refugees in the harrowing evacuation from Missouri.

The refugees, thousands of them, were welcomed into Quincy-area homes by sympathetic Illinois natives who recognized the Saints as victims of religious persecution forced to leave land and possessions behind. Illinois was still frontier country; it had been a state for only twenty years, and settlers were scattered. A few months later, possibly because the prophet had become something of an embarrassment in Missouri, Joseph Smith was allowed by guards to escape. In the late spring of 1839 Smith bought on credit property on both sides of the river fifty miles north of Quincy from the land speculator Isaac Galland. By June, late for the planting season, the town was platted in a gridiron of one-acre lots, and the prophet was already at work promoting it as the site of the gathering, the new Zion where his tribe should live. Smith called the settlement Nauvoo, inspired by a name he said came from Hebrew and meant a beautiful place of rest.

Nauvoo, then as now, is divided between an upper and lower town. Smith's city was on the lower flats, a marshy wetland the Saints soon worked to drain—but not before malaria, typhoid fever, and dysentery were added to the Saints' miseries. The epidemics in 1839 and 1840 were so sweeping that there were hardly enough well to care for the ill. Diaries and journals are full of tales of prayer, anointings, and miraculous healings, but the same writings also reveal constant grief over fresh graves. The prophet himself lost his father and a brother.

Astonishingly, Smith chose at this point to send eight of his apostles to England on a mission. Through the work of an earlier mission in 1837, some 1,400 English converts had already been baptized into the church. When Brigham Young left in September 1839, he parted from his wife and a ten-day-old infant and was so weak from fever that he could barely walk without help. An outside observer might have called such a mission foolhardy fanaticism, but the mission was to succeed and have an enormous impact on the church.

The English converts were mostly poor and working-class. A severe depression, the displacements of the Industrial Revolution, high food costs, and general unrest made them open to promises of a new kingdom of God on earth. Zion on the Mississippi might provide land, food, and sanctuary. London was not particularly responsive, but Liverpool, Manchester, and other places seemed to provide a steady supply of discontented Methodists ready for the Mormon gospel.

The Mormon hallmark of practical attention to detail is evident in an August 1841 edition of the *Millennial Star,* founded by Brigham Young, a newspaper for the English Saints. They were advised about the cost of passage and freight, how and what to pack, when to report for sailing. They were told their first shelter in Nauvoo might be tents that could be devised from thirty or forty yards of good calico. In their kingdom city they could raise their own pigs and chickens and collect wood from the nearby wilderness for cheap fuel. Elder Parley Pratt advertised to English converts that life in America would cost one-eighth as much as in England and described Nauvoo as a true promised land:

> Millions on millions of acres lie before them unoccupied, with a soil as rich as Eden, and a surface as smooth, clear, and ready for the plow as the park scenery of England. Instead of a lonely swamp or dense forest filled with savages, wild beasts and serpents, large cities and villages are springing up in their midst, with schools, colleges, and temples. The mingled noises of mechanism, the bustle of trade, the song of devotion, are heard in the distance, while thousands of flocks and herds are seen grazing peacefully on the plains, and the fields and gardens smile with plenty.

By the time the prophet was murdered, almost 5,000 English Saints had emigrated to Nauvoo, most intensely loyal to Young and soon willing to move on with him to Utah. For several years after Smith's death that emigration virtually stopped, to be resumed after the church had settled in Utah. By 1870 some 38,000 English citizens had joined the Mormon gathering in the United States; another 13,000 Europeans, mostly Scandinavians, had also come to the American Zion.

The earliest shelters in Nauvoo, tents and lean-tos, were gradually supplanted by wooden structures and finally by frame and brick houses. It is estimated that by 1844 Nauvoo, counting the upper and lower parts of town, had about 1,500 log homes and shops, 650 frame houses, 350 brick buildings (including the Masonic lodge and Seventies Hall), and about 200 masonry houses. Cut limestone curbs bordered gravel paving for many of the roads in Nauvoo. Construction was the biggest industry in town. Joseph Smith had two homes in Nauvoo: first a block log house fronting on the river, followed in 1843 by the frame Mansion House, which had a hotel wing. An ambitious masonry hotel, the Nauvoo House, was never completed.

The Saints were also encouraged to till the "soil as rich as Eden" to produce a green and fertile landscape, planting mulberries and grapevines, peach trees, and raspberry bushes. Most had flower and kitchen gardens, perhaps a cow and a few chickens in their yard. Landscapers advertised their skill in pruning trees.

Nauvoo had a surprisingly active cultural life. The press was an important institution in any American town, and the Mormons, who had published their own newspaper since their Ohio sojourn years before, began publication of a church newspaper from Nauvoo in late 1839, the *Times and Seasons*. There were schools, choirs, bands, and theatricals in which Young himself enjoyed taking part as an actor; debate societies and cotillion dancing; and a lending library of 200 volumes. Pastimes included corn-husking contests and quilting bees, swimming and horsemanship. Beginning in 1841 most of Nauvoo's leading male citizens became active in the Masonic lodge. The following year the prophet organized the Relief Society for the women, recognizing their similar need for mutual aid and social interaction; he installed his wife Emma as president.

Protection for the Saints was a pressing concern for the prophet, due to the depredations in Missouri. In the fall of 1839 Smith traveled to Washington, D.C., for two interviews with President Martin Van Buren, hoping for the redress of grievances, including property losses, that the Saints had suffered. The Saints' problems, he was advised, were properly a matter of state rather than federal governance. Congress, too, rebuffed his petitions. At this point, the prophet undoubtedly decided that the necessary power and means for protection had to reside with the Saints themselves.

In December 1840 the new city received its charter from the state legislature, which granted Nauvoo such unique powers that it very nearly created an independent city-state, or as the RLDS historian Robert Bruce Flanders calls it, *Nauvoo: Kingdom on the Mississippi*. Political expediency was doubtless also part of the process, since the state was eager for development and the Mormons were a desirable bloc of settlers, disciplined and industrious. And they had a pivotal potential in early 1840s Illinois politics, since the state population was closely divided between the Democratic and Whig Parties. According to Flanders, the Illinois legislature was also distracted by severe state fiscal problems and charter applications from other budding municipalities. Nauvoo's charter, technically modeled on the city charter of Springfield, was lobbied through by Smith's counselor, John Cook Bennett.

Nauvoo's charter provided for no effective separation of powers. The mayor, first Bennett and later Smith himself, was head lawmaker and judge. The mayor served on the city council and was also chief justice of the municipal court. With the oligarchic nature of Mormon church government and the installation of church officials in many government posts, civic and religious power overlapped, and the newborn city functioned effectively as an independent theocracy within Illinois. Though religious minorities were granted their freedoms, there was no separation of church and state of the sort envisioned in the U.S. Constitution. Controversy over the charter grew quickly in 1842 until the clamor led to its repeal in 1845, after Smith's death.

Under the charter, Nauvoo was allowed to establish a militia with state-authorized commissions. The state also helped to equip the legion by providing 250 small arms and three cannons. Later it was reported that the Nauvoo Legion had several thousand small arms and thirty heavy pieces as well. (The latter figure was probably an exaggeration.) Smith and Bennett, commissioned as lieutenant general and major general, respectively, established the Legion with delight: dressed in blue-jacketed officer uniforms resplendent with gold braid, they organized troops with regular drills. Military parades with fluttering silk flags highlighted civic ceremonies, which were climaxed by the punctuation of booming cannons. Military lore and mock war games fascinated the prophet.

The charter had a unique provision on writs of habeas corpus that could free arrested persons if the municipal council chose to protect them. That made Nauvoo an island of safety for legal refugees. It may in some cases have been legitimate protection for some of the Saints, including the prophet himself, but it was also open to considerable abuse. This provision became a contentious matter with area "Gentiles"—that is, non-Mormons—who were angry that river pirates, thieves, and counterfeiters could run to Nauvoo, placing themselves beyond the reach of outside law. According to Flanders, "the habeas corpus clause of the charter and the cavalier fashion in which the Mormons used it generated much popular fear and hatred, and were the points upon which legal attacks on the whole charter finally focused."

Land speculation was another contentious matter. Illinois largely opened up after the War of 1812 when Congress gave war veterans land grants in lieu of pay. Veterans sold their land to speculators, who in turn sold to other speculators, each time with an increase in price despite the paucity of homesteaders. The price balloon finally burst. Many parcels of land were sold for taxes; titles became increasingly cloudy. The church bought its parcels on credit and in turn sold lots to incoming Saints. The justification for the hefty city lot prices was that the profit benefited the community as a whole. It was impossible, however, to separate church business from private Smith finances, a murky situation that was replicated later in Brigham Young's Salt Lake City.

Competition arrived in the form of upper-town development, largely in the hands of private entrepreneurs such as William Law, second counselor to Smith in the church's three-man First Presidency. The competition was for labor as well as for land sales. Smith wanted workers to speed up construction on Nauvoo House and the temple, tithing one workday in ten. Other work was paid in scrip redeemable for goods at the church's tithing warehouse. Law and other private developers in the bluff-top area paid workers in cash. Conflict was inevitable.

Beneath its busy, prosperous exterior, there were serious economic problems. Nauvoo had a bubble economy built on optimism, the promise of expansion, land speculation—and credit. One unfortunate fact about Nauvoo, despite some pretty brick buildings and neat gardens, was that it had very little cash. People had shaky title to their land and lived on scrip and barter and their kitchen gardens, bearing faith in their prophet, living with hope for the promised millennial future, and sharing charity with fellow believers.

To some degree, expansion meant work. Houses needed to be built; necessary service crafts and shops were kept busy. But most of the English immigrants, by 1844 one-third of the city's population, came in poor and without cash. Absorbing them proved difficult; the Nauvoo economy could not support its population. There might be some livestock and skills for barter, but there was precious little capital. The railroad did not go through Nauvoo, and an ambitious project to build a millrace through the center of the city failed when it ran into a stratum of solid limestone. Instead, the site became a quarry for the temple. Although there were many skilled artisans in Nauvoo, only cottage industries and home shops developed, none with goods marketed far beyond Hancock County.

The prophet himself opened a small red brick general store. "The trouble with the store was the trouble with the whole Nauvoo economy," writes Flanders. "Business was brisk, but there was too much credit and too little cash. The steady flow of goods from the shelves and bins suggested that the enterprise was prospering, when in fact it was approaching insolvency." Flanders thinks Smith was probably more interested in supplying goods to Nauvoo citizens than in profit. There was faith that "debts were to be paid eventually out of the increment of the kingdom." Unfortunately, what actually happened was that Mormons declared bankruptcy and repudiated their debts. Smith himself declared bankruptcy in 1842, hardly leaving Nauvoo in any shape to attract outside capital.

Doctrine and ritual matured during the Nauvoo years. Smith taught that only through the priesthood in his church, available to all male believers, could ordinances be performed that would result in the "exaltation" of the Saints, that is, the highest reward in heaven. First came vicarious baptism for the dead, in accord with an 1841 revelation by which living proxies would undergo the ordinance in place of dead loved ones, giving their forebears in the afterlife the opportunity to choose for or against the salvation that was uniquely available in the restored true church. The Mississippi River served as the first baptistry for the proxy ordinance. In November 1841 a temporary pine baptistry resting on the backs of a dozen wooden oxen was dedicated for this use in the temple-in-progress.

The lengthy temple revelation, apparently inspired by the Old Testament concept, is part of Doctrine and Covenants (hereafter D&C), which, like the Book of Mormon, has scriptural status in the LDS Church. It commanded Smith to build not only the temple for ordinances but the Nauvoo House. The hotel was to be "a delightful habitation for man, and a resting-place for the weary traveler, that he may contemplate the glory of Zion," and the revelation specifies in great detail just how the stock was to be apportioned and paid.

The next important ritual Smith introduced was the "endowment," first performed in May of 1842 with a small group of male church leaders on the second floor of the prophet's store, and the following year extended to women. This ceremony included washings, anointings, secret hand-shakes and sacred names, penalty oaths, a creation drama, and symbols with many similarities to the Masonic rituals that the prophet had just learned. The most important devotional elements were solemn covenants of obedience to God, fidelity in marriage, and consecration of worldly goods and personal talents to the Lord's service.

Saints often met in each other's homes for prayer and simple devotional services; once the partially completed temple had room for a temporary auditorium, members often gathered there for sermons. But from the ear-liest days of Nauvoo a grove of trees that formed a natural amphitheater provided the best-loved backdrop for sermons when the weather was good. On April 7, 1844, in that outdoor theater, Joseph Smith delivered his most important doctrinal oration, the King Follett Discourse, which opened with a eulogy for a friend of that name who had recently been killed dig-ging a well.

Mormonism's radical departure from traditional Christian beliefs is clear in the Follett address. Much of this had been previously pronounced and taught by Smith, including the 1843 revelation (D&C 130:22) of the startling belief that God "the Father has a body of flesh and bones as tan-gible as man's." But in the Follett sermon, preached just two months before his death, Smith's doctrines reached their final expression. The Utah-based LDS (but not the Missouri-based RLDS) treats the discourse with a special status and has used it as an authoritative source, carrying forth its teaching ever since it was delivered.

"God [the Father] himself was once as we are now, and is an exalted Man, and sits enthroned in yonder heavens!" he declared to his listeners. "If you were to see him to-day, you would see him like a man in form— like yourselves, in all the person, image, and very like a man in form; . . . I am going to tell you how God came to be God." God the Father is therefore not the unchanging creator of traditional theology. He exists as a being in progress, with men and women progressing similarly.

Explaining the idea of heavenly exaltation, Smith proclaimed that "you have got to learn how to be Gods yourselves, and to be kings and priests to God, the same as all Gods have done before you,—namely, by going from one small degree to another, and from a small capacity to a great one,— from grace to grace, from exaltation to exaltation, until you attain to the resurrection of the dead and are able to dwell in everlasting burnings and to sit in glory, as do those who sit enthroned in everlasting power."

The exalted believer's reward will be "to inherit the same power, the same glory, and the same exaltation until you arrive at the station of a God and ascend the throne of eternal power, the same as those who have gone before." Smith was fascinated to learn that *Elohim,* a Hebrew word in the Old Testament referring to God, is plural. (Traditional scholars generally treat that usage as indicating a royal "we" or an intensifier of God's magnitude, not plurality in number.)

Creation, Smith preached, is not the *ex nihilo* of orthodox Christianity and Judaism. Matter is eternal, and God, acting as head god in a council of gods, organized chaotic matter into the world we know. Intelligence is also eternal, and the "mind or the intelligence which man possesses is coequal with God himself." Salvation of the dead is man's greatest responsibility, along with the "sealing power" through which we can "seal our children and our dead for the fulness of the dispensation of times."

Then came his famous valedictory: "You don't know me; you never knew my heart. No man knows my history, I cannot tell it: I shall never undertake it. I don't blame any one for not believing my history. If I had not experienced what I have, I could not have believed it myself. I never did harm any man since I was born in the world. My voice is always for peace."

Peace might have been possible if the prophet had been as gifted in politics as in oratory. He was not. Nor was he a good judge of men. His inner circle was in constant turmoil, with frequent turnover and alienation among his closest colleagues. Of the eleven official witnesses who testified that they saw the Book of Mormon's golden plates, two had soon died (the Whitmer brothers in 1835 and 1836), and among the nine who lived on, six at one time or another quit the prophet's church or were excommunicated, though three later returned. Only Smith's own father and two brothers remained steadfast in their commitment.

As fear mounted among Gentiles over the growing power of the Mormon bloc vote, the meteoric rise and fall of Smith's chosen colleague, the flamboyant scalawag John Cook Bennett, was a disaster for the Saints. Supposedly a bachelor, Bennett had actually deserted a wife and three children back in Ohio. He arrived on the scene at Nauvoo in 1841. Urbane, capable, and a physician by apprenticeship training, Bennett soon became Joseph Smith's closest adviser, though Emma Smith never trusted the smooth talker. Besides shepherding the Nauvoo charter through the legislature, Bennett helped supervise drainage of the swamps and treated fevers with the new medicine, quinine. He soon became "assistant president" with the church's First Presidency, the mayor of Nauvoo, chancellor of its "university," and leader of the Nauvoo Legion.

Things deteriorated rapidly in 1842 with an unseemly exchange of immorality charges between the two men. The catalyst was their competition for nineteen-year-old Nancy Rigdon as plural wife. Pretty Nancy was not interested, and her father, First Counselor Sidney Rigdon, opposed plural marriage, at the time an inner-circle secret. Smith excommunicated Bennett.

Bennett retaliated. He wrote lurid exposés of life in Nauvoo, a series of letters that were first published at intervals in Springfield's *Sangamo Journal*, picked up by newspapers around the country, then later in 1842 issued as a book called *The History of the Saints: or, An Exposé of Joe Smith and Mormonism.* The sensationalist letters were filled with bawdy details of the sex life in Nauvoo and of a secret organization of men called Danites whose inner group of "Avenging Angels" were to spy on and assassinate dissenters and enemies of the church. (The Danites were never an official arm of the church; it is not clear the extent to which church leaders had unofficial knowledge or gave unofficial approval to their activities.)

Many in and out of Illinois recognized Bennett for the oily opportunist that he was. But there was just enough of a kernel of truth to arouse internal suspicion and whip up anti-Mormon sentiment elsewhere. The editorial voice of the nearby *Warsaw Signal* grew increasingly shrill. With the rumors of plural marriage and violence, uneasiness over the visible prowess of the Legion at drill, jealousy over the successes in Nauvoo, fear of the political powers of the Mormon bloc, irritation over the land speculation, and anger over Nauvoo's use of habeas corpus, relations between the citizens of Nauvoo and surrounding Hancock County turned sour. Perhaps the local Gentiles also harbored a certain resentment against what they perceived as the confident self-righteousness of the Saints. As the author Wallace Stegner puts it, "A chosen people is probably inspiring for the chosen to live *among;* it is not so comfortable for outsiders to live *with.*"

Smith embarked on an astonishing round of political activity in early 1844. With the backing of the Quorum of the Twelve Apostles, he declared himself an independent candidate for the U.S. presidency on January 29, running on a progressive platform of religious rights, purchase of freedom for slaves, emptying of the jails, and overhaul of the economy in a populist mode. In February he organized the apostles and hundreds of other missionaries to fan out across the country in support of his candidacy. On March 11, the strictly secret Council of Fifty was formed as a theocratic policymaking body, a "shadow government," as Flanders calls it, that functioned sporadically in Utah into the 1870s. The Council originally had fifty-three members, including three non-Mormons, two of whom apparently were known counterfeiters.

Treating Nauvoo as a sovereign city-state, Smith and the Council sent ambassadors to England, France, Russia, and the Republic of Texas. He was exploring the possibility of planting Mormon colonies somewhere in the West—Texas, Oregon, Mexico, and California were possibilities—and attempting to tilt competing political powers toward Mormon benefit. Then came Smith's rebuffed bid to Congress for an army of 100,000.

The next step, on April 11, was to have the Council ordain Smith as "King, Priest and Ruler over Israel on Earth." According to the LDS historian D. Michael Quinn, what occurred that day was clearly different from the second anointing ordinance that elevated a man to be a "King and Priest" in heaven. The RLDS historian Flanders notes that when Smith declared, "I am above the kingdoms of this world, for I have no laws," he was speaking apocalyptically rather than politically. But Smith did believe by 1844 that the "government of God" must eventually replace the governments of the world, including that of the United States.

Opposition to Smith intensified inside and outside of Nauvoo. The most important inner dissident was William Law, Smith's second counselor in the church's First Presidency. Scholars generally agree that Law was no Bennett; a man of integrity and substance, he was respected in the Mormon community. Some of the issues between Law and Smith were economic: Law was one of the private developers who controlled the upper town and paid workers in cash, while Smith operated on scrip, credit, and tithed labor. But the deeper antagonism was religious. Law was loyal to Smith's older conceptions of God and unalterably opposed to plural marriage. Publicly the polygamy doctrine was denied, but Smith and other high church officials were practicing it in secret. Rumors spread, and dissension spread as well.

Through 1843 the Smiths and Laws met together regularly for private prayer. Their disagreement over plural marriage became increasingly acrimonious. Smith arranged for spies to report to him on the activities of Law and Law's close associate Robert D. Foster. On January 3, Law confronted Smith, the Nauvoo police, and a former Danite named Daniel Carn, charging that they were plotting to kill him. Carn defended the Danites and criticized Law for opposing plural marriage. Two days later Law again met with Smith and the Nauvoo police, reporting that he and three other dissidents felt they were in mortal danger. Smith denied the charge and three days later released Law as second counselor. The issue was personal as well: there is evidence that at some point Smith propositioned the wives of both Law and Foster.

Smith kept most of his plans for a new world order secret, but four days after receiving kingship he told the non-Mormon press about his dream of "theo-democracy," whatever that might mean. Uneasy questions were spreading; on April 15, Law received an offer of reinstatement. He rejected it unless Smith would agree to "public acknowledgement and cease from his abominations." Smith did not back down.

Three days later the Council of Fifty, supposedly a civic body, took ecclesiastical action: Law was excommunicated, along with his brother Wilson Law and colleague Robert D. Foster, an odd action for a nonecclesiastical body, "not for a court-martial but for religious delivery to the torments of hell," according to Quinn. A trial was supposed to be granted Foster, but when Smith learned that Foster had more than forty witnesses, he realized that a trial might be turned into a spectacle against himself and thought better of it.

Despite Masonic-type oaths to bind secrecy, defectors from the Council of Fifty told Law about the prophet's anointing as king, and Law and other dissenters began making plans. A new press arrived in town, and on May 10 the dissenters published a prospectus for a newspaper, the *Nauvoo Expositor.* The prospectus pledged to "exercise the freedom of speech in Nauvoo, independent of the ordinances abridging the same." It argued for repealing the city charter and referred to Smith as a "self-constituted Monarch." On May 12, some 300 people met to establish the "Reformed Church of Jesus Christ," with Law as its leader.

One day later Sidney Rigdon visited Law to offer a second negotiation for reconciliation. Again Law stipulated his condition: Smith would have to apologize publicly for teaching and practicing plural marriage. Hardly likely. Four days after this meeting Smith held a public Nauvoo nominating convention to validate his candidacy for president.

The *Expositor* appeared in Nauvoo on June 7. In the context of the times, and for dissidents who had been denied a public forum, its writers were relatively restrained in their wording. The paper advanced a desire for a "reformation in the church," "hazarding every earthly blessing, particularly property, and probably life itself, in striking this blow at tyranny and oppression." It argued against polygamy, political intrigue, "false doctrines" such as the "doctrine of many Gods" preached in the Follett sermon, the habeas corpus provision of the city charter, Smith's participation in Nauvoo land speculation, and acknowledgment of "any man as king or law-giver to the church, for Christ is our only king and law-giver." Robert Foster and William and Jane Law included signed affidavits that they had read the text of the prophet's secret revelation on plural marriage, and that Joseph's brother Hyrum had introduced the revelation in secret council.

An emergency meeting of Nauvoo's city council was called for June 10. Since polygamy was not legal in Illinois (and not publicly acknowledged by the church until 1852 from the safe vantage point of Utah), Hyrum Smith blandly reaffirmed past official denials of plural marriage, assuring the council that his brother's 1843 revelation was not for modern times; it referred only to ancient days. Therefore, the *Expositor* had libeled Smith. The *Expositor,* of course, was a clear threat to the prophet's control of Nauvoo. In addition to the publicly denied polygamy, some of Smith's political activities represented a radical break from the normal parameters of Jacksonian democracy. Smith knew that someone from the Council of Fifty, despite the secrecy oaths, had betrayed him by giving information to Foster and Law. According to Quinn, "He could not allow the *Expositor* to publish the secret international negotiations masterminded by Mormonism's earthly king." But Joseph, as mayor of Nauvoo, declared action was essential because the *Expositor* faction would "destroy the peace of the city" and foment a "mob spirit."

With the backing of his Council, Smith ordered that the new press be smashed and all possible copies of the press run destroyed. The spirit of the Bill of Rights may thus have been grossly violated, but technically, under Illinois law at the time and Nauvoo's charter, the only crime committed by Smith on June 10 was a violation of property rights. The following day Law was informed that there was a murder plot against him and his associates. Aware of the prophet's security forces and the well-armed Legion, Law and Foster fled with their families from Nauvoo.

Events escalated rapidly. Press hysteria came from nearby Warsaw, where the *Signal* screamed, "War and extermination is inevitable! CITIZENS ARISE, ONE AND ALL!!! Can you *stand* by, and suffer such INFERNAL DEVILS! To ROB men of their property rights, without avenging them. We have no time for comment! Everyman will make his own. LET IT BE WITH POWDER AND BALL!" Mormons feared anti-Mormon retaliation. Local non-Mormons feared the Nauvoo Legion. Smith also feared for his life. On June 18, he declared martial law and mobilized the Legion. Non-Mormons pressured Governor Thomas Ford to mobilize the state militia. Everyone had good reason to be afraid; civil war was a very real possibility.

At Ford's request, Smith ordered his Legion to disarm. The governor, promising safety to Smith and his companions, wanted the prophet to turn himself in to face charges in Carthage, the county seat. On June 22, Smith fled across the Mississippi into Iowa, accompanied by his loyal brother Hyrum in spite of the prophet's wish that Hyrum remain behind. "I want Hyrum to live to avenge my blood, but he is determined not to leave me," he wrote in his personal journal. That night messengers brought Joseph a letter from Emma telling her beleaguered husband that some of the Saints felt the prophet had abandoned them out of cowardice. Joseph crossed back into Illinois the next day, aware that he faced death. "I am going as a lamb to the slaughter," he said. Since someone slipped a six-shooter into his cell that he later fired into the attacking mob, "lamb" was not an exact metaphor, but he conducted the waning days of his life with dignity and courage.

Smith surrendered on June 24 and was taken to Carthage Jail, where he was imprisoned along with Hyrum and apostles John Taylor and Willard Richards. The jailer treated the prisoners kindly, but Ford had left the anti-Mormon Carthage Grays guarding the jail. Inside, the prisoners passed the time in prayer and talk and wrote brave notes to their families. Joseph asked Taylor to sing a popular song that he liked, "A Poor Wayfaring Man of Grief."

Late in the afternoon of June 27, a mob of men disguised with black-ened faces approached the jail. The Grays fired weapons preloaded with blanks. One gang bounded up the stairs and fired through the door where Smith's party was held. The bullet that passed through the door struck Hyrum Smith in the face, killing him instantly, but the mob kept firing. As attackers burst into the room, Joseph Smith discharged his gun all six times with three misfires and wounded three. While the assailants contin-ued to fire away, Smith leaped or fell through the window, beginning the Masonic cry for help, "Oh, Lord, my God," but not living to complete the words: "Is there no help for the widow's son?" Some of the attackers pumped more bullets into Joseph's body by the well before the crowd dis-persed. Richards was uninjured; Taylor was wounded seriously but sur-vived to become the church's president decades later in Utah. Hyrum and Joseph Smith lay bloodied and dead.

Sixty-one years later, speaking at Brigham Young University, one of Joseph's plural wives, Mary Elizabeth Lightner, remembered him saying, "I am tired. I have been mobbed, I have suffered so much from outsiders and from my own family. Some of the brethren think they can carry this work on better than I can, far better. I have asked the Lord to take me away. I have to seal my testimony to this generation with my blood. I have to do it, for this work will never progress until I am gone for the testimony is of no force until the testator is dead." At the age of thirty-eight, the prophet had sealed his testimony with blood.

An uneasy peace settled on Hancock County. All sides feared violence; there was none. The Saints were grief-stricken. The bodies were transported from Carthage back to Nauvoo in an open wagon. Some reports say that as many as 20,000 filed past the bodies on June 28 as they lay in state in Nauvoo House. After a public burial, Emma Smith had the bodies disinterred and moved to a secret location for fear the graves might be desecrated. (They lay in that secret place until 1928, when the RLDS reburied the bodies next to Emma's in a marked grave by the river.)

If the *Warsaw Signal* viewed the murders with satisfaction, a number of other papers, even in Illinois, recoiled at the assassination. Nationally many newspapers connected the Smith murders with the bloody anti-Catholic mob riots that had occurred in Philadelphia in May and July 1844, seeing both as expressions of religious bigotry and dangerous symptoms of mob law. A murder trial was held nearly a year later in Carthage, but there were no convictions.

For a time peace prevailed. Construction on the temple resumed at an accelerated pace. Young and others added to their homes. With uncertainty about the leadership succession, the Quorum of the Twelve directed affairs for the church and Nauvoo. By the end of the summer Young was in command. That fall harassment against the Saints, encouraged by the editorial voice of Thomas Sharp in the *Signal,* resumed with sporadic mob burnings of barns, outbuildings, and crops in outlying areas. The state legislature repealed the Nauvoo city charter in January 1845.

The leadership knew the Saints had to go and began plans to abandon Nauvoo. Saints tried to divest themselves of their property, taking what little they could get. In the winter of 1845–46, thousands of endowment rites were carried out in the new temple. The first contingent of Saints left Nauvoo in February, just five days after a vane in the shape of an angel had been placed atop the tower on the temple. By the time summer arrived Nauvoo was largely empty. Thomas L. Kane, traveling through shortly thereafter, described the scene in his 1850 book *The Mormons:*

> I looked, and saw no one. I could hear no one move; though the quiet everywhere was such that I heard the flies buzz, and the water-ripples break against the shallow of the beach. I walked through the solitary streets. The town lay as in a dream, under some deadening spell of loneliness, from which I almost feared to wake it. For plainly it had not slept long. There was no grass growing up in the paved ways. Rains had not entirely washed away the prints of dusty footsteps. Yet I went about unchecked. I went into empty workshops, ropewalks and smithies. The spinner's wheel was idle; the carpenter had gone from his work-bench and shavings, his unfinished sash and casing. Fresh bark was in the tanner's vat, and the fresh-chopped lightwood stood piled against the baker's oven. The blacksmith's shop was cold; but his coal heap and ladling pool and crooked water horn were all there, as if he had just gone off for a holiday. . . . I could have supposed the people hidden in the houses, but the doors were unfastened; and when at last I timidly entered them, I found dead ashes white upon the hearths, and had to tread tiptoe, as if walking down the aisle of a country church, to avoid rousing irreverent echoes from the naked floors.

Once again the Saints had abandoned their homes and possessions. This time it was for a trek outside the United States. The city of Joseph Smith was dead, and Zion was no longer in Illinois. Perhaps it could be reborn in Utah.

CHAPTER 2

BEGINNINGS: A VERY AMERICAN GOSPEL

BECAUSE MORMONS IN FLIGHT ABANDONED THEIR TEMPLES IN OHIO AND Illinois, the oldest temple now in use by the Latter-day Saints is in Utah, a graceful sandstone structure in St. George that was completed in 1877 during pioneer days. The church's one hundredth temple, by a 1999 decree of President Gordon B. Hinckley, is being erected at the place where it all began, the western New York hamlet of Palmyra.

Just before Mormonism emerged in the nineteenth century, Palmyra and the surrounding region were pioneer territory. Settlers had begun to migrate to the Mohawk River Valley in significant numbers in the 1790s, and a boom area of some sophistication had developed to the west by 1817, when construction began on the Erie Canal. In Palmyra and other small towns there were schools, lending libraries, newspapers, debating societies, and cheap printing presses. The newcomers had to work hard to clear the land and fell trees, but the soil was more fertile than the unyielding, boulder-filled acreage of New England.

That same tract of upstate New York was fertile ground for religious excitement, so much so that it became known as the "Burned-Over

District," subject to repeated fires of revival. Itinerant preachers working there included the likes of wild-eyed Lorenzo Dow (sort of a Methodist), whose asthmatic eccentricities earned him the nickname of "Crazy Dow" as he traveled up and down the East during the first several decades of the century. Odder yet was Isaac Bullard, a believer in free love and communism who wore only a bearskin and taught that it was a sin to wash. Bullard planted himself in Vermont, but his disciples went forth into New York and Ohio. The more respectable Charles G. Finney, a revivalist in a style similar to that of Billy Graham in the twentieth century, began his preaching career in upstate New York in 1824 and 1825, later becoming an abolitionist crusader as well.

In the early phase of the Republic, the old denominations—Congregational, Presbyterian, Episcopal—had to struggle to spread their coastal hegemony into the frontier. There was no shortage of new sects and communitarian experiments during the period when the Mormons created their kingdom on earth. Mother Ann Lee, the foundress of the Shakers and preacher of celibacy and spiritual perfectionism, landed in Watervliet, New York, in the late eighteenth century. Her followers came to regard her as a female Second Coming of Jesus Christ. By 1825 one of the spreading Shaker communities had been established thirty miles from Palmyra. John Humphrey Noyes advocated a "biblical communism" as well as "complex marriage" (a sanctified free love), announced that the kingdom of God had come, and established the Oneida Community in upstate New York by 1848. Religions of every stripe seemed to flourish, from spiritualism to liberal rationalism to socialist utopianism to Swedenborgianism, with its concepts of eternal marriage and a three-tiered heaven.

Millennial expectations and the restoration of a pure, primitive form of New Testament Christianity were two major strains in the nineteenth-century religious flux. In this period of economic, social, and religious uprootings, people fastened their attention on the end times. "The first generation of United States citizens may have lived in the shadow of Christ's second coming more intensely than any generation since," writes the historian Nathan O. Hatch. Revivalists and social reformers preached that people should prepare their hearts, their lives, and their society for the

Second Coming. Best of all, God's chosen people might build his king-dom, the New Jerusalem, right at home on American soil.

William Miller, an upstate New York farmer, determined after studying the scriptures that the Lord would return in 1843; later he changed the date to 1844. His movement enlisted a following of 30,000 to 100,000, and one contemporary estimate put it as high as a million—at a time when the nation's population was only 17.3 million. But the Lord did not meet the timetable in 1844, and many believers filtered away. Ellen G. White rede-fined 1844 as an event in heaven, preached that Christ's earthly return was imminent, and rallied Millerites into what became the Seventh-day Adventist Church, which today rivals the Mormon Church in worldwide expansion. Despite its innovations, Seventh-day Adventism perpetuated traditional, core Christian theology.

The desire to restore the purity of early Christianity was equally power-ful for many Americans. Alexander Campbell, a Scotch-Irish immigrant of Presbyterian background and some university education, succeeded in turning that mood into a movement between 1811 and 1832. A good public debater, he cofounded the era's "Restoration Movement" with his father Thomas. The movement, progenitor of today's Disciples of Christ, Christian Churches, and Churches of Christ, rejected creeds but did not devise novel doctrines. The Campbellites concentrated in the frontier country of Ohio, Kentucky, Indiana, Tennessee, and West Virginia but had nationwide influence, numbering 22,000 by 1832 and 118,000 by 1850.

Stir into this restless stew a bit of folk religion, including a few pinches of magic and the occult, and personal visions, and one has the mixture that was simmering in upstate New York just as the Erie Canal opened up in 1825, providing a highway from Albany to Buffalo and the western frontier.

What most of these new popular religious movements shared was "a passion for expansion, a hostility to orthodox belief and style, [and] a zeal for religious reconstruction," according to Hatch in *The Democratization of American Christianity*. Moreover, "they all offered common people, especially the poor, compelling visions of individual self-respect and col-lective self-confidence." As the sociologist Thomas F. O'Dea observes in his classic study *The Mormons*, because the older Calvinist churches were associated with the rising business class and the university-educated professional elite of the day, including the clergy, disadvantaged groups had been left by the wayside.

The family of Joseph Smith Jr. was counted among the disadvantaged class when they moved to western New York in 1816. Like two-thirds of the new arrivals, the Smiths were poor farmers leaving behind, they hoped, the rocky soil and depression economy of western New England. The future prophet was eleven years old then, one of eight children.

Joseph Smith Sr. had had a bad run of luck. At the start of his married life in 1796, his father had given him part ownership of a farm, and his bride Lucy brought a substantial $1,000 cash wedding gift to the marriage. Some investments turned sour, and by 1803 Smith had to sell his land to pay debts. After that he earned his living as a tenant farmer, teaching school in the winter to make ends meet. Between 1803 and 1816 the family moved seven times around Vermont and New Hampshire, then finally into New York. After two years working at odd jobs ranging from masonry to tapping for maple sugar, he was able to make a down payment on a parcel of land. Unfortunately, he bought the land at the height of a price speculation bubble.

Like so many Americans of the time, Smith was suspicious of institutional religion and remained aloof. Palmyra had Presbyterian, Quaker, Baptist, and Methodist churches, but he never joined any of them. For a time Lucy and two of the sons became Presbyterian. Joseph Jr. seemed interested in Methodism but was confused by the churches' competing claims. The Smiths were a deeply religious family; all of them prayed and studied the Bible.

The Smiths could not afford tuition, so none of the children had much formal education; their father probably taught them at home. Lucy later wrote that Joseph Jr. was not as bookish as his brothers, but his description of his boyhood "First Vision" clearly shows that he was steeped in the Bible and biblical language. Joseph was also obviously a highly imaginative and intelligent young boy, interested in the Indian culture hinted at by the burial mounds in the area. Some said the mounds contained evidence of a lost race.

Lucy, in her *Biographical Sketches* of 1853, described Joseph Jr.'s youthful fascination with Indians in the years just prior to his translation of the

Book of Mormon: "During our evening conversations, Joseph would occasionally give us some of the most amusing recitals that could be imagined. He would describe the ancient inhabitants of this continent, their dress, mode of travelling, and the animals upon which they rode; their cities, their buildings, with every particular; their mode of warfare; and also their religious worship. This he would do with as much ease, seemingly, as if he had spent his whole life with them."

In the religious excitements of the Burned-Over District, many people were susceptible to mystical experiences and visions; Joseph Sr. was among them. Lucy wrote about seven of these dream-visions of a person on a quest seeking salvation, relating all of them in biblical style and five in first-person language.

Joseph Jr.'s First Vision occurred when he was fourteen. In the church's canonized version of it, written in 1838, two embodied personages appeared in a bright pillar of light in the "Sacred Grove," now owned by the church in Palmyra. One of the figures, God the Father, pointed to the other and said, "This is my beloved Son. Hear Him!"

The boy asked guidance on what church to join, and the all-important answer became enshrined in the LDS scriptures. "I was answered that I must join none of them, for they were all wrong; and the Personage who addressed me said that all their creeds were an abomination in his sight; that those professors were all corrupt."

Smith's Second Vision came three years later, when the Angel Moroni visited, identifying himself as a member of an ancient race and a messenger sent by God to tell the seventeen-year-old boy that there "was a book deposited, written upon gold plates, giving an account of the former inhabitants of this continent, and the sources from whence they sprang." This book, said Moroni, had the "fullness of the everlasting Gospel." Deposited with these plates were the Urim and Thummim, transparent stones in silver bows fastened to a breastplate, which were to be used to help translate the book.

Joseph told his father about the vision, then went to find the plates in a stone box buried in the nearby Hill Cumorah, just as the angel had said. But the angel warned him that he was not spiritually mature enough to take custody of the plates. He instructed Joseph to make annual return visits to the spot on that date. On September 27, 1827, he was allowed to have temporary custody of the plates and the spectacles to translate the Book of Mormon. Moroni's plates were said to be thin golden sheets about eight inches square, bound with three large rings, a "gold Bible" that soon became the object of widespread rumors around Palmyra.

Joseph had been busy in the years between the visions. He was a part-time but active participant in folk magic, using divining rods and "seer stones," or "peep-stones," to find buried treasure. Both father and son, from about 1819, were active in such treasure-digging and achieved something of a mysterious local reputation in the profession—mysterious because there is no record that they ever found anything despite the readiness of some local residents to pay for their efforts. Joseph Jr. had several seer stones; after placing them in a hat, he would gaze at them, rather like looking at crystal balls to guide in seeking treasure. Such activity was illegal, and in 1826 young Smith was hauled into a Bainbridge, New York, court and found guilty of disorderly conduct for his money-digging.

In his own scriptural history, Smith was less than forthright, depicting himself as a day laborer hired to locate an old mine, and stating that this gave rise to the "prevalent story" of magic treasure-digging. But Mormon historian D. Michael Quinn has carefully detailed Smith family activities in ritual magic and ownership of various occult objects and talismans, documenting the influence of this folk religion in early Mormonism. The evidence is too well documented to deny. Another Mormon historian, Columbia University's Richard L. Bushman, has written, "There has always been evidence of it in hostile affidavits from the Smiths' neighbors, evidence which Mormons dismissed as hopelessly biased. But when I got into the sources, I found evidence from friendly contemporaries as well, Martin Harris, Joseph Knight, Oliver Cowdery, and Lucy Mack Smith. All of these witnesses persuaded me treasure-seeking and vernacular magic were part of the Smith family tradition, and that the hostile witnesses, including the 1826 trial record, had to be taken seriously."

In early 1827 Joseph Jr. had to elope with Emma Hale because the bride's father, Isaac Hale, objected strenuously to his future son-in-law's disreputable occupation of looking for treasure with magic stones rather than working the land like a respectable farmer. Smith's work with seer-stone magic and treasure-seeking soon shifted to translation of the Book of Mormon. And in spite of Isaac Hale's objections to Smith's seer-stone activities, he allowed the newlyweds to return for a time and live in his home in Harmony, Pennsylvania, where Smith began his translation of the plates.

A blanket was hung to divide the room. On one side of the blanket, Smith would work with the Urim and Thummim as a kind of magic spectacles, his favorite seer stone, the golden plates, and the hat, while the scribe worked on the other. Smith would bury his face with the seer stone in the hat and then dictate words to the scribe. Serving as scribes in the early days were both Emma and Martin Harris, a prosperous farmer from the Palmyra area who, excited by the prospects of Smith's golden Bible, had followed him to Harmony.

Somewhat to Emma's distress, Joseph never allowed her to see the naked plates. Eventually eleven witnesses testified that they had actually seen the plates. Three—Harris, David Whitmer, and a Whitmer in-law, the new local schoolteacher Oliver Cowdery—said that an angel appeared and showed them the engraved golden plates. Later eight others—including four more Whitmers, another Whitmer in-law, and the prophet's father and two brothers—testified that they had "seen and hefted" the plates. The two testimonies are printed in every copy of the Book of Mormon. Smith's scriptural account said that when the translation was done, "according to arrangement" he returned them to the custody of the angel.

Harris was willing to subsidize publication of the amazing book, but he wanted scholarly validation first. Smith transcribed some characters from the plates in a language he called "reformed Egyptian," and in early 1828 Harris took the facsimile to Professor Charles Anthon, a famous classicist at Columbia University. Harris said that Anthon verified the authenticity of the document; Anthon later wrote a letter denying that he had said the document was genuine and declaring it a hoax.

Whatever happened, Harris's faith was confirmed by the experience, but he wanted his wife to see the production of several months' labor, the literary work for which he was willing to mortgage their farm. Lucy Harris was skeptical. Smith lent Harris the first 116 manuscript pages in June 1828 to take back to Palmyra to show his wife. The manuscript became a popular neighborhood exhibit, but one day the pages disappeared. The distraught Smith could not be completely sure the pages would ever surface, and it would be impossible to rewrite another verbatim copy. He received a timely revelation, however, instructing him to proceed without retranslating the lost pages. The lost portion of the story, he was told, was also embedded elsewhere in abbreviated form; Smith could pick up that version when he arrived at that section of the plates.

So the work proceeded. Eventually Oliver Cowdery assumed the scribal chores, and the job was completed at a furious pace. Back in Palmyra, arrangements were made with E. B. Grandin's print shop to produce 5,000 copies of the Book of Mormon. The completed book was copyrighted in June 1829, and the printed copies were bound and ready for sale in March 1830. The devoted Martin Harris had to sell his farm to raise money for the $3,000 printer's bill. He would lose his unhappy wife as well as his farm.

The book was highly controversial from the beginning. Mormons, of course, believe the book has a divine origin, and LDS apologetics from the beginning stressed that an uneducated farm boy could not have produced such a complex book. Non-Mormons generally assume that Joseph Smith wrote it, though few writers today accuse him of having been a blatant and consciously calculating fraud. Various theories have been floated on the contemporary sources that Smith might have used.

O'Dea, a Catholic scholar, sees a commonsense, naturalistic explanation: "Joseph Smith was a normal person living in an atmosphere of religious excitement" that, "through a unique concomitance of circumstances, influences, and pressures, led him from necromancy into revelation, from revelation to prophecy, and from prophecy to leadership of an important religious movement and to involvement in the bitter and fatal intergroup conflicts that his innovations and success had called forth." Non-Mormon scholars as diverse as Harold Bloom and Rodney Stark regard Smith as a man with a creative and inspirational genius in religion. All scholars generally agree that Smith became a remarkable, charismatic religious leader, and that the Book of Mormon as it flowed from his pen has taken its place among the world's most influential religious books.

The original edition was 588 pages long, with diction resembling King James English. To the average non-Mormon, many passages seem tedious, and Mark Twain had fun with the fact that the phrase "and it came to pass" recurs some 2,000 times. Extensive portions of the Bible appear verbatim, or nearly so, and there are almost 300 biblical-sounding names. The story is a complex one, LDS defenders point out, involving migrations, family feuds, battles, good versus evil. The tantalizing aspect of the book is its planting of sacred history right in the heart of the New World. Smith's startling doctrinal innovations, such as the multiplicity of gods, were to come later.

The Book of Mormon tells of two ancient seaborne migrations from the Holy Land to the Americas, by Hebrew peoples who are assumed to be ancestors of Native Americans. The older migration, by the Jaredites, occurred after the Tower of Babel incident around 2200 B.C., and the later one around 600 B.C., just before the Babylonian captivity of the Israelites. In the second, more detailed narrative, Lehi, a descendant of the biblical patriarch Joseph, builds a ship. Guided by a compass, he sails by way of the Indian and Pacific Oceans to the Americas, landing possibly in Central America. Two of Lehi's sons become wicked and rebellious, so God curses them with a dark skin. Many American Indians, traditionally called "Lamanites," are supposed to have descended from them. Nephites are the descendants of Lehi's faithful son.

Nephite history develops the story with faithful prophets, persecutions of the righteous, the construction of cities and temples, Lamanite wars, two Almas as hero priests, and revivalist preachers. The most crucial episode occurs in III and IV Nephi. After his resurrection in Jerusalem, Jesus Christ comes to preach his message to Lamanites and Nephites and to establish his true church in the Western Hemisphere. A united Christian commonwealth flourishes in peace and prosperity for several centuries. Then come sin and apostasy and a great division between the Lamanites and Nephites climaxing with a great battle. That battle, in which the Nephite forces number 230,000, takes place at Hill Cumorah in A.D. 400. Moroni, the last survivor and son of the great Nephite general Mormon, stores the golden plates that will be revealed to a latter-day prophet fifteen centuries later.

For the Mormon, the Book is evidence of God's revelation, too complex a production for an ill-educated, unsophisticated young man. Critics point to it as a product of nineteenth-century religious excitement. Speculation about the Hebrew origin of the Indians was a commonplace of the time. One book Joseph Smith likely knew was Ethan Smith's *View of the Hebrews,* published in Vermont in 1825 and containing considerable material on the subject, as well as a description of ancient Central American Indian ruins.

Smith's new church took its first step on May 15, 1829, when he and Cowdery said that John the Baptist appeared and instructed them to baptize and ordain each other into what he called the Aaronic priesthood. Shortly thereafter they reported that Peter, James, and John appeared to initiate them into the Melchizedek priesthood and to instruct them on organizing a new church. The Church of Christ (later renamed twice) was officially incorporated on April 6, 1830, in the Whitmer log home at Fayette, New York. About thirty believers were present, with six of them serving as legally required organizers.

From the beginning leaders taught that every member was a missionary. Groups of believers began to develop in several towns. The question of religious authority had to be settled at the outset when Hiram Page claimed that he, too, received revelations through seer stones. Joseph Smith issued a divine revelation to make it very clear that he alone held "the keys of the mysteries" and that only his utterances carried authority for the church (D&C 28). So the concept of continuing revelation through the prophet as a source of authentic authority in doctrine and governance reached back to the beginnings. Soon Joseph directed Emma to compile a hymnbook and made plans to collect his post–Book of Mormon revelations in the Book of Commandments, subsequently called the Doctrine and Covenants. He also launched his own version of the King James Bible, rewriting passages to make it conform more closely to his own teachings.

In the fall of 1830, following a revelation to Smith, four missionaries set off to convert Indians. Two of them, Cowdery and the former Campbellite Parley Pratt, visited the fiery Campbellite preacher Sidney Rigdon in the village of Kirtland, near Cleveland. Rigdon converted to Mormonism, bringing his 127-member congregation with him. Soon the branch grew to 1,000 believers, and in 1831 Joseph Smith received a revelation to move the church headquarters from New York to a more hospitable Ohio.

Missouri entered the picture in 1831 when a band of Latter-day Saints left Ohio to migrate farther to evangelize the Indians on the frontier and establish a new gathering place for the kingdom of God in Jackson County, Missouri, a much rougher place than either western New York or northeastern Ohio. If upstate New York is the locus of the first latter-day revelations, western Missouri is forever enshrined in Mormon scripture as the arena of God's future dealings with mankind. When Smith visited in 1831, he proclaimed Jackson County the "land of promise, and the place for the city of Zion," with the town of Independence the "center place" (D&C 57). Smith also taught that this was the site of the biblical Garden of Eden.

This site was to be the focus of the Lord's millennial promises and Christ's Second Coming, and in accordance with God's instructions, Smith laid a cornerstone on the exact location for the temple where Jesus will one day reign. Then there is Adam-ondi-Ahman, seventy miles to the north in Daviess County, the place where Adam went after God expelled him from Eden. Adam is a hero in Mormon theology, and this gently undulating prairie valley, otherwise an unremarkable piece of American midwestern real estate, is the place where Adam will return to prepare for Christ's Second Coming (D&C 116).

Smith's attention for the next several years was split between Ohio and Missouri, but he lived in Kirtland until financial debacle hastened his departure for points west. As ever, life had its jarring moments for the Saints in Ohio, climaxing on March 24, 1832, when a bunch of hoodlums led by a fallen-away Mormon tarred and feathered Smith. Emma cleaned him up, and he managed to preach the next day. The next several years in Ohio were relatively peaceful, though it was a poor community; many newcomers had sold their farms to join the prophet or had few assets at the outset. In an idealistic attempt to resolve the problem, Smith established the "Law of Consecration," also called the "United Order of Enoch," as a sort of communistic redistribution. The idea was to dedicate material goods and property to the church, working the land in stewardship, with the surplus given to the bishop for redistribution to the poor. This plan apparently caused dissension and did not work very well.

The Kirtland Saints worked and sacrificed from 1833 to 1836 to build a big stone temple, fifty-five feet wide and sixty-five feet long, somewhat resembling an enlarged New England chapel with a steeple. It was designed with two floors, one for worship and the other for a school. Laborers were to donate one workday in seven to the construction. When dedicated, it was the site of outpourings of speaking in unknown tongues, trances, and visions—charismatic activities of religious excitement not typical of Mormonism afterward, though these expressions of religious excitement were taken up by Pentecostal Protestant sects at the turn of the century. The Kirtland temple today is owned by the rival RLDS denomination, which claims to be Joseph Smith's true heir.

From 1831 on, as Saints arrived in Kirtland by its eastern door, others continually exited to Missouri by its western door. The population reached one or two thousand, many living in temporary log dwellings before departing westward. But Kirtland had a surprisingly active cultural life, with its fledgling School of the Prophets (adult higher education) and a variety of publications spilling from the press, including a newspaper, a journal, and books for the church. Dozens of Saints, including the prophet, studied the Hebrew language for a time.

It was in Kirtland in 1835 that Smith bought some papyri and four Egyptian mummies from the traveling showman Michael Chandler. Smith enjoyed displaying the mummies. The papyri were to become the basis for another part of his work of spiritual translation, the Book of Abraham, which was later recognized by the Utah church as part of a third added book of LDS scripture, the Pearl of Great Price. The Book of Abraham was to become in the midtwentieth century one of the most difficult challenges for Mormon apologetics, in terms of both its historical authenticity and its use as a justification for the church policy of making blacks ineligible for the priesthood until 1978.

Economic problems spelled the end of Kirtland. Smith left his financially troubled church for Salem, Massachusetts, at summer's end in 1836, hoping one last time that the use of his seer stone might produce treasure that he had been told lay under a house (D&C 111). The seer stone failed again, and his money-digging was no more successful than before.

The Kirtland bank he tried to establish fared no better. One way of getting lots of money is to print it, and Smith tried that. Since he did not have the capital to establish a licensed bank, he took the pile of notes on which he had already had printed "the Kirtland Safety Society Bank" and instructed the printer to add the prefix *anti-* and the suffix *-ing* to the word *Bank* on each note. For a brief while in early 1837 everyone seemed to have lots of money, but it soon became clear that the notes were worthless paper, and merchants in places like Cleveland were not amused. Failed land speculation and failed banks elsewhere in the nation added to the general economic malaise. Since Smith's society could not redeem the notes with coin, and land values had collapsed so that real estate also failed to secure the notes, a predictable string of lawsuits followed. There was even an unseemly brawl in the temple itself. When a warrant was issued on January 12, 1838, on a charge of banking fraud, Smith and First Counselor Rigdon fled on horseback in the middle of the night, one step ahead of the law. Their horses were pointed toward Missouri.

But trouble lay ahead. Missouri may have been specially sanctified as the kingdom of God, but non-Mormon neighbors could not have appreciated such revelations of entitlement as "ye shall assemble yourselves together to rejoice upon the land of Missouri, which is the land of your inheritance, which is now the land of your enemies" (D&C 52:42, proclaimed in June 1831). A more ominous note was sounded three months later: "And the rebellious shall be cut off out of the land of Zion, and shall be sent away, and shall not inherit the land" (D&C 64:35, 36b).

By 1833 the prophet was citing a parable to recommend attack if necessary to possess the land. The Saints were to "redeem my vineyard; for it is mine; . . . break down the walls of mine enemies; throw down their tower, and scatter their watchmen. And inasmuch as they gather together against you, avenge me of mine enemies" (D&C 101:56–58). By February 1834 the revelations spoke of revenge: "And my presence shall be with you even in avenging me of my enemies, unto the third and fourth generation of them that hate me. Let no man be afraid to lay down his life for my sake; for whoso layeth down his life for my sake shall find it again. And whoso is not willing to lay down his life for my sake is not my disciple" (D&C 103:25–28).

What was happening in Jackson County at this time?

Converts began to arrive by the dozens and then hundreds; at first they tried to live communally by the Law of Consecration. A town was laid out similar to the plat Smith had drawn in Kirtland, and a cornerstone laid for the millennial temple. Converts arrived from missionary activity all over the United States and from overseas as well. This was to be Zion, the gathering place for the Saints to build the kingdom of God.

The Saints' theology of entitlement was not the only irritant. Many residents were suspicious of the Mormons for having never held slaves and for being friendly to the Indians. Their group solidarity and communal land holdings represented a threat to the political balance of power between the Whig and Democratic Parties. By 1833 there were 1,200 Saints in Jackson County, and their number was increasing so rapidly that it appeared that soon they would be the majority.

Organized opposition led to confrontation, then mob action. A church printing office was destroyed in retaliation for a pro-abolitionist newspaper article, and two church leaders were tarred and feathered in July of 1833. Three days later another mob appeared, armed with handguns, clubs, and whips, and forced church leaders to sign an agreement to leave Jackson County. Church leaders told their men it was time to arm themselves for protection; before the Saints left Jackson in November ten homes had been destroyed by vigilantes in a confrontation that resulted in the deaths of one Mormon and two assailants.

Most of the Saints moved on into Clay County in November, temporarily living in anything from tents to huts to abandoned slaves' cabins. The following May, in 1834, the prophet dispatched from Kirtland a militia of 205 men carrying both arms and a banner emblazoned with the single word *Peace.* Called "Zion's Camp," the militia lasted for two months while Mormons tried to negotiate Jackson County property problems. The soldiers began to succumb to cholera, and when the threat of serious armed conflict mounted, Smith recalled the militia to Ohio. One of Smith's military colleagues on the Zion's camp trek was the newly converted Brigham Young.

Clay County was a two-year resting place for the Saints before some of the same resentments that had developed in Jackson County began to reappear. Two new counties were carved out of the sparsely settled northern Missouri frontier, Caldwell and Daviess, with the unwritten understanding that the Mormons could settle there. The most important settlements were

Caldwell County's Far West, which had nearly 5,000 Saints in the vicinity by 1838, and Daviess County's Adam-ondi-Ahman, which had about 1,500 the same year as Joseph's relocation from Ohio.

Trouble began to simmer again, inside and outside the church. Some Saints, able to sell their Jackson County properties, were regarded as treasonous by other believers who held on to their titles. The sellers included some important church leaders, such as Oliver Cowdery and David Whitmer, who were excommunicated. Around this time the soon-to-be-legendary Danites were formed by Sampson Avard. Also called the "Avenging Angels," this group was a highly secret society bound by penalty oaths; originally formed for retribution against internal dissenters, it later shifted its mission to include retaliation against anti-Mormon mobs. The group was pledged to plunder, lie, and even kill if deemed necessary. It is not clear to what extent the church leadership bestowed its backing or was aware of Danite activities.

The fiery Rigdon sparked a tinderbox in a July 4 speech when he thundered, "And that mob that comes on us to disturb us; it shall be between us and them a war of extermination; for they will have to exterminate us: for we will carry the seat of war to their own houses, and their own families, and one party or the other shall be utterly destroyed."

The "Mormon War" of August to October 1838 was the inevitable result of the incendiary challenge. Mob violence went back and forth. Some Mormon homes were burned; reports, probably exaggerated, of Danite activities reached Governor Lilburn Boggs, who echoed Rigdon's words with his famous order of October 27 that the Mormons "must be treated as enemies and must be exterminated or driven from the state, if necessary, for the public good."

The brutal result of Boggs's order came three days later with the bloody massacre at Haun's Mill on October 30, 1838. About 200 armed militiamen marched into the Haun's Mill settlement on a fine day with children at play while their fathers worked at crops or guarded the mill. Joseph Young, older brother of Brigham, watched as the militia approached and people scattered, some seeking safety in the blacksmith shop, others running to hide in the nearby thickets. The horror was over quickly, and when the mob was gone, there were seventeen dead, including several in the blacksmith shop and ranging from an old man hacked to death to a ten-year-old boy mortally shot. Several others died within days. Most of the bodies were buried by tossing them down a new and dry twelve-foot-deep well. Artemisia S. Myers Foote, a nineteen-year-old girl, never forgot the horror of each body sliding down the plank into the well: "Every time they brought one, and slid him in I screamed and cried, it was such an awful sight to see them piled in the bottom in all shapes."

The Haun's Mill Massacre to this day retains a special place in the Mormon catalog of persecutions. At the time, it was painfully clear that the Mormons would once again have to evacuate and place their Zion, their kingdom plans, in another location. Also at the time, their beloved prophet was incarcerated in Liberty, Missouri, on a fabricated murder charge, and in that winter of 1838–39 he was unable to lead the evacuation of the Saints to Illinois.

Why were the Mormons so hated? Was it pure religious bias? D. Michael Quinn writes that "religious belief, as non-Mormons understood it, had little to do with anti-Mormonism." But by the mid-1830s Mormons had embraced a religion that claimed priority in all aspects of life. Conflict was inevitable. "Fear of being overwhelmed politically, socially, culturally, economically by Mormon immigration was what fueled anti-Mormonism wherever the Latter-day Saints settled during Joseph Smith's lifetime."

Similarly, as the LDS historians Leonard Arrington and Davis Bitton point out, the Mormons' worldview and lifestyle were far more encompassing than those of their contemporaries. They included not only theology and morality but "also an eschatology, an economic philosophy, and a goal of community-building that inevitably meant political and economic tension with their neighbors." LDS assumptions and goals were "inconsistent with American pluralism" in some fundamental ways. With the Mormon determination to gather into a cohesive community, there were only three solutions: protection by the government to set up an independent theocracy, extermination, or expulsion. In the end nineteenth-century Mormons had the western frontier as a safety valve. In Utah they were to be the majority, the "old settlers."

The persecutions, as Arrington and Bitton point out, did not involve mass murders. The total Mormon loss of life from Missouri vigilante

murders was about forty, far fewer than the number killed in the
Philadelphia anti-Catholic riots of 1844. Any lynching or vigilante murder is one too many, of course. But suffering came more often from noise,
threats, and property damage than from actual violence, "a far cry from
unrestrained massacres." The Arrington–Bitton analysis continues:

> Usually the targets were selective: the houses of the leading men,
> printing establishments, or stores. When outlying settlements were
> hit, it was with a view to forcing the Mormons to pull back and
> reverse their outward expansion. Women and children were usually
> allowed to flee for their lives. Men were humiliated by beatings but
> not—except at Haun's Mill—indiscriminately slaughtered. The
> fatalities, with few exceptions, occurred when Mormon defensive
> units were functioning as troops in the field.

All of this, of course, should not minimize the suffering. No one wants
to live with his family in an atmosphere of insecurity and fear. That atmosphere of defensiveness, as well as the call to a geographic gathering place,
helped forge the Mormon identity, the consciousness of their own peoplehood. It fostered such characteristics as communal cooperation, loyalty,
discipline, and a certain wary paranoia.

Mormons like to call themselves a "peculiar people," taking the term
from verses in both testaments: "For thou art an holy people unto the Lord
thy God, and the Lord hath chosen thee to be a peculiar people unto himself, above all the nations that are upon the earth" (Deuteronomy 14:2).
"But ye are a chosen generation, a royal priesthood, an holy nation, a peculiar people; that ye should shew forth the praises of him who hath called
you out of darkness into his marvellous light" (I Peter 2:9).

In the twentieth century being a "peculiar" people has become a matter
of meeting the distinctive demands of a highly disciplined LDS lifestyle
rigorously centered in the church, since "Zion" is no longer interpreted as
a geographic gathering place. But in the rude experiences of the 1830s and
1840s the Mormons developed their sense of being a chosen people
through persecutions, communal solidarity, millennial expectations, and

commitment to building the kingdom of God on earth for the faithful. That tribal identity forged in the holy experiments of Missouri and Nauvoo was carried with the Saints as they embarked on a remarkable hegira into the wilderness of Utah.

CHAPTER 3
THE AMERICAN EXODUS

Requirements of Each Family of Five for the Journey Across the Plains
Each family consisting of five adults, will require 1 good strong wagon,
well covered. 3 good yokes of oxen between the ages of four and ten.
Two or more cows. One or more good beeves, some sheep if they have
them.

THE LIST WENT ON TO INSTRUCT THE EMIGRÉS TO PREPARE A YEAR'S SUPPLY
of food for each family, including one thousand pounds of flour in sturdy
sacks, a bushel of beans, cured meat and dried fruit, a good musket or rifle
for each man with powder and lead, one hundred pounds of sugar, twenty-
five pounds of salt, between ten and fifty pounds of seed and farm tools,
cooking utensils, "a few goods to trade with the Indians," and other supplies to total one ton for each wagon.

Although there had been an uneasy peace for a time in Hancock
County, Illinois, after the murder of the prophet in 1844, marauding mobs
soon became active again. Arsonists destroyed more than two hundred
homes as well as haystacks, barns, and other buildings on farms scattered
beyond Nauvoo. After anti-Mormon gangs committed several murders
and some rapes in outlying areas, terrified farm families began to take
refuge inside the borders of the city itself. The Saints wanted to finish their

beloved temple, to honor the wishes of their dead prophet, and to carry out their long-desired holy ordinances. But the leaders were already planning to transplant the kingdom somewhere west, on a new frontier.

By October 1, 1845, the Quorum of the Twelve Apostles had agreed with a committee sent by Illinois Governor Thomas Ford to leave the following spring as soon as grass was ready to provide forage for their animals along the way. Trustees were appointed to remain behind and help dispose of property, but as a sign of their readiness to leave, the Mormons refrained from further planting of winter wheat.

By early December the temple was completed sufficiently to begin sacred ceremonies, and working around the clock for several months, more than 5,600 endowments were rushed through, along with family sealing rituals. The temple that they had sacrificed so hard to build would survive Mormon Nauvoo only briefly; it was severely damaged by arson two years later and then destroyed by a tornado two years after that. (In 1999 it was announced a private donor has given funds to rebuild the Nauvoo temple, a replica of the original, righting a 150-year-old wrong.)

During the last few months of Joseph Smith's life several destinations for Zion had been considered, including Texas, California, and Oregon. In the year after the assassination the apostles and the Council of Fifty focused on the Salt Lake Valley, which at the time belonged to Mexico. The church authorities wanted a location far enough in the wilderness that the Saints could be isolated from other settlers and the outside world, a gathering place where the church could develop a cohesive community. The other options were too attractive to other settlers.

The Nauvoo evacuation was carefully planned. The families were to be grouped along military lines in groups of ten, fifty, and one hundred, each with an officer reporting to an authority further up the line. Shops in Nauvoo were busy forging wheels and sewing canvas canopies; families attempted to divest themselves of their property and organize supplies for the road. Their livestock was to go with them, some 30,000 head of cattle, flocks of sheep, mules, and horses. Pigs and poultry were to travel in coops attached to the wagons.

Brigham Young took a nose count before Thanksgiving: 3,285 families planning to trek west, with 2,508 wagons ready and another 1,892 in preparation. Two new threats precipitated the carefully prepared move into a premature and hasty winter exit: a warrant was issued to arrest Brigham Young on a charge of sheltering counterfeiters, and a false rumor circulated that federal troops were planning a raid. With flatboats and skiffs, the first group of Saints left the wharf at Nauvoo and crossed the Mississippi River on February 4. That first cold night in Iowa nine women gave birth. Young's own extended family left Nauvoo on February 15, a group of fifty with fifteen wagons. Hundreds more, then thousands of the Mormon refugees followed over the next weeks as the river froze to form a solid walkway, and a temporary camp was set up at Sugar Creek, nine miles into Iowa.

The American Exodus was under way, with Young as the latter-day Moses.

Figures vary on the size of the 1846 emigration from the United States. Some scholars say that as many as half may have drifted away from Young's church or decided to stay on in the Midwest, to be replaced by converts. At Smith's death there were 26,000 Mormons worldwide, and by some estimates, in the late spring of 1846 there were as many as 16,000 Saints on the road headed toward the Great Basin. Brigham Young called his people the "Camp of Israel." Ever conscious of history, many kept diaries, as Mormons then and now are encouraged to do, and the diaries show that the Saints were deeply conscious of the biblical parallels to their wandering through the wilderness toward the promised land.

At Sugar Creek rules were drawn up that would govern the wagon trains in camp and on the journey ahead. These included the time to rise and pray (up at 5:00 A.M. and ready to roll by 7:00 A.M.); regulations for wagons on the road; the length of the lunch hour; how to circle the wagons at night; how to guard the livestock; the time for evening prayers and bed (8:30 P.M.); and punishments for such infractions as swearing or beating animals. The principle of organized cooperation along the route was established with a string of camps set up en route, each planted with crops to be harvested by Saints traveling through later.

The first destination was Winter Quarters, near what is now Omaha, Nebraska, about 300 miles from Nauvoo. Some Saints, without money for outfits, had remained in Nauvoo until the end of the summer. Others, apparently unmolested by non-Mormons, had simply decided to remain in Illinois or had drifted back; still others went to St. Louis first for outfits and supplies and joined the Saints later on the road. In the first months road progress was painfully slow—an agonizing six miles on a good day. The wagons were hampered by the torrents of an unusually rainy spring; wheels clogged with sticky, thick mud slithered through increasingly deep ruts on the trail until sometimes the wagon bed sank all the way down to the mud. Those Saints who left in February took four months to reach their destination. Some lucky ones who waited until late May to leave Nauvoo needed less than three weeks to cover the same territory.

At Winter Quarters land was cleared, over 620 log cabins were built and fenced, and crops were planted. A grist mill was constructed and put into operation. Winter Quarters continued to serve as a semipermanent staging area; over several years some 20,000 people lived there for a time before undertaking the next 1,000 miles to Utah. It was platted like a town, with the temporary residents—3,200 families or so at a time—divided into 22 wards. They worked hard, but there was time for cheerful play as well; comic readings were staged, and a brass band accompanied singing and dancing.

From Winter Quarters Brigham Young sent a letter to President James K. Polk:

> The cause of our exile we need not repeat; it is already with you, suffice it to say that a combination of fortuitous, illegal and unconstitutional circumstances have placed us in our present situation, on a journey which we design shall end in a location west of the Rocky Mountains, and within the basin of the Great Salt Lake, or Bear River valley, as soon as circumstances shall permit, believing that to be a point where a good living will require hard labor, and consequently will be coveted by no other people, while it is surrounded by so unpopulous but fertile country.

Who was Brigham Young, the man who seized leadership to plan the successful migration of such a mass of people?

Like the first prophet, Young was a dirt-poor New Englander born in 1801 to a large Vermont farming family. Like Joseph Smith, Brigham grew to maturity under the influence of the religious activities in upstate New York's Burned-Over District; his youngest brother was named after the itinerant revivalist Lorenzo Dow. When Brigham was fortunate enough to own a pair of shoes, he wore them inside church services but carefully carried them during the walk. Brigham's mother died of tuberculosis when he was fourteen.

As Young matured, he acquired the typical skills of a rural boy, from hunting and trapping to farming and tapping for sugar. Lacking formal education, though literate, he learned through apprenticeship the skills of the construction trades, including carpentry and paint-mixing. He also mastered the crafts worked in a forge, and his industry and initiative won him a high local reputation. In 1823 Young moved west, lured by better opportunities in the boomtowns along the Erie Canal. In 1824, the year he married his first wife, Miriam Works, he briefly became a Methodist. Miriam died in 1832 of tuberculosis, leaving him with two small daughters.

Brigham Young's brother Phinehas was introduced to the Book of Mormon by Joseph Smith's brother Samuel in 1830. Brigham took his time, studying the new scripture carefully, evaluating the Mormons he met. In the spring of 1832 he, all his brothers and sisters, and other family members were baptized, and all would remain loyal Mormons. The next year Young moved to Kirtland and in 1834 joined Joseph Smith's Zion's Camp militia expedition to Missouri. For the rest of his life he cherished the memory of those two months spent close to the prophet, learning about the faith and becoming a trusted insider.

Smith named Young to the original Quorum of the Twelve Apostles in 1835, and he became president of the Quorum in 1840. After the assassination there were competing claims for leadership of the church, including those of several Smith family members. There is historical evidence that Joseph Smith blessed his son, Joseph III, with the intention that the boy would become his successor, but the boy was only eleven when his father was murdered. There were other claimants, the most aggressive being Sidney Rigdon, the only surviving member of the First Presidency. But on August 8, 1844, Brigham Young asserted the claims of the Quorum of the Twelve to govern the church and was supported by the vote of a church General Conference. Joseph Smith had been a charismatic leader, full of creative ideas and doctrinal innovations. Brigham Young was a genius organizer and shrewd administrator, a colorful orator little given to intellectualizing or revelations. He was just the right man to lead his people to their promised land.

Young's leadership skills had become apparent in the 1839 Missouri evacuation to Illinois while Smith was imprisoned in Liberty, Missouri. This time the Saints fully accepted the leader who cajoled, ordered, harangued, organized, loved, and led them. He was, writes Wallace Stegner, a "terrible and rewarding man to be scolded by. There has never been a people that so dearly loved a scolding," and Young understood them "to the ground." There were to be no rules that could not be kept, but there would be order in camp, Young told his followers.

Federal help of a sort arrived in June 1846 when President Polk authorized General Stephen W. Kearny to raise a battalion of Mormon volunteers to help fight the war against Mexico. By July 20, after Young had coaxed and pressured the beleaguered families for three weeks, 526 of the menfolk marched off in the battalion. Their clothing allowance of $21,000, left with Young at Winter Quarters, was an important source of hard cash for the refugee church. Another $50,000 in battalion salaries was eventually funneled back into church funds. None of the battalion actually fought; most were mustered out and returned to their families in six months after marching to California. Another eighty or so reenlisted for another six months.

By April 7, 1847, more than 70 wagons were outfitted and ready to roll toward Iowa, the first contingent to cover the 1,031 miles to Salt Lake. The lead wagon carried the precious bell from the tower of the Nauvoo temple (now on display in Temple Square in Salt Lake City). The initial wagon train included 143 men, 3 women, 2 children, a boat, a cannon, 93 horses, 52 mules, 66 oxen, 19 cows, 17 dogs, and some chickens. Along the way they would have to cope with illness, exhausting work, hostile Indians, and wild animals. They forded streams and crossed rivers in homemade rafts. They learned that the bumpy wagon ride churned their butter for them, and that buffalo dung made good fuel.

The mosquitoes thickened as the party made its way across the Rocky Mountains in late June and early July, and a number of the travelers, including Young, became very ill with what was probably Colorado tick fever. On July 20, a small advance group went ahead into the Salt Lake basin, glimpsing their first view of the valley two days later. In good Mormon fashion, two hours after entering the valley they set to work, organizing the first planting of potatoes and other crops. Mountain streams tumbled down nearby canyons, promising fresh water for domestic use and irrigation. This was semidesert country, treeless and with sandy soil, but the high grass could sustain grazing. The area had been traversed by traders and trappers, but not by white settlers. The Ute Indians were further south. Two days later a weak but recovering Brigham Young entered the valley. According to legend, he surveyed the valley and said, "This is the right place, drive on." That date, July 24, is now marked by the big annual Pioneer Day celebration, a state and Mormon holiday in present-day Utah.

Laboring six days a week and observing Sunday as a day of rest, the advance party began to build cabins, using adobe because of the wood shortage, and to lay out streets according to a plat drawn up by Young four days after entering the valley. All streets were to be 132 feet wide, enough space for an ox train to turn around, and to be numbered and named from the temple lot reserved in the center. The streets were to have twenty-foot sidewalks; lots were to be one and a quarter acres, with eight lots to the block and houses set twenty feet back from the street. Natural resources were to be developed for the common good. A church General Conference was held in the fledgling Salt Lake City, and in late August, after setting policies for government and trade, Young and a small party headed back to Winter Quarters. They passed other emigrant trains heading into the valley, groups of Saints from Colorado and Mississippi as well as points to the east. By the time winter settled into Salt Lake more than 2,000 Saints had arrived in the basin, and their leader was back at Winter Quarters, where he was named president of the church at the end of 1847. Fully in charge of his people, Young prepared the larger movement to head west in the spring.

Food shortages haunted the earliest residents of the valley before the snows melted in the spring of 1848. The first potatoes had been the size of grapes and were gone too soon. Some of the livestock disappeared in the wake of Indian and wolf raids. By early spring farmers were desperately eating anything from roots to crows. Just as spring crops were ready for harvest, hordes of crickets swarmed over the fields and chomped the corn and wheat. Whole families tried to burn them out, smoke them out, beat them out with brooms—to no avail. Still the crickets came. The people knelt and prayed. At the height of a plague of biblical proportions, when some considered packing up and moving on to California, large white flocks of seagulls soared in from the Great Salt Lake and devoured the crickets. For several weeks the birds gorged on the black crickets, regurgitated the indigestible parts, and went back to eat more. Faithful Mormons honor this as divine intervention, the "Miracle of the Seagulls," and a monument to the event stands today near the temple.

When Young left Winter Quarters in May 1848, there were 2,000 Saints ready for the trail. His own contingent had 397 wagons, 1,229 people, 74 horses, 1,275 oxen, 699 cows, 184 loose cattle, 411 sheep, 141 pigs, 605 chickens, 37 cats, 82 dogs, 3 goats, 10 geese, 2 beehives, 8 doves, and one crow. Families took seriously the prophet's instructions to write their own journals and histories. They were experiencing sacred history.

One important safety rule was that all wagons should keep rolling without a stop, because a break in the train would make it vulnerable to Indian attack. Shortly after Young's train rolled out Lucy Groves, a young mother weak from childbirth, fell out of her wagon, breaking three ribs and a leg as the wagon's front wheels rolled over her body. Her husband barely managed to pull her out of the path of the rear wheels. Young set her leg, but it was rebroken several days later when a child stumbled over her. This time the young woman screamed every time her wagon bumped, and she begged Young to leave her behind. Young refused and, ever practical and ingenious, fashioned a hammock from her mattress, swinging it from the bows of the wagon. He blessed her and for several days rode next to her to monitor her condition.

Young himself became the father of male twins born en route. His own section of the wagon train entered the Salt Lake Valley on September 20, after 122 days on the road, averaging twelve miles each day of travel. This time Young was home for good; he lived his remaining twenty-nine years in the valley, building the kingdom and shaping his people.

Some evidence implies that Young wanted to establish a sovereign empire in the West, but there is more evidence that church authorities wanted the territory to be part of the United States. They carried an American flag with their first 1847 caravan and planted it in their new town. In 1848 the United States gained possession from Mexico with the Treaty of Guadalupe Hidalgo, which ended the Mexican War, and the area was formally organized as a territory in 1850, with Brigham Young appointed as governor. The Mormons wanted their land named Deseret, after a Book of Mormon word meaning "honeybee," to symbolize cooperative industry. The beehive today is on the state's official seal, but Congress chose to create a territory and name it Utah after the Ute Indians.

Gathering all the Mormon Saints to the new kingdom in the Great Basin was Young's first priority. By the end of 1848 another 3,000 settlers had made it to the Salt Lake Valley, and Young began to assign groups of them to establish a string of other settlements north and south in the valley, and then later in a wider range and into Nevada, eastern Utah, Arizona, New Mexico, southern Colorado, and San Bernardino, California. Emigrés continued to arrive at a pace of 3,000 to 4,000 newcomers every year. After 1852, when the midwestern Saints were largely relocated in the Great Basin, immigrants began to arrive in large numbers from overseas, especially England and Scandinavia, about 3,000 each year, challenging the ability of the land and the economy to absorb them. By 1857 the Mormon population in the Great Basin was about 35,000; by 1869 that figure had swollen to 75,000; and by 1877, the year Young died, the new Zion was home to about 135,000 souls.

Many of the overseas Saints arrived with the assistance of the Perpetual Emigrating Fund (PEF), established in 1850 to help poor converts come to the Great Basin. Some paid their own way, of course; others paid a portion; and the rest were expected to repay the fund later with goods, cash, or labor. They usually came by ships chartered from Liverpool, landing in New Orleans. Again, in typical Mormon fashion, the Mormon passengers were carefully disciplined and organized into small groups with leaders. There were prayers and cleaning duties, choirs and classes. Many of the poorest ate better on board ship than they had at home. The next leg was by riverboat up the Mississippi to Missouri, then the overland journey to

Utah. A family might leave Liverpool in January and arrive in Salt Lake City by October.

Immigrant wagon trains were greeted at Emigration Canyon with an escort; when they arrived in Salt Lake City, they were met with ceremony and fanfare—brass bands and a cannon salute—as they passed Temple Square. After celebrations with special dinners, singing, and dancing, they would attend placement meetings to receive their housing and work assignments. Often Saints who were already established would temporarily house newcomers and help their guests find employment.

The PEF was an expensive program for the church, so in 1856 church leaders hit on the idea of handcarts to provide a quicker, cheaper solution to the overland journey. Under ideal conditions, the handcart companies could move faster than oxen-drawn wagon trains. The carts were like oversized wheelbarrows with two wheels and a pair of long handles that one or two adults could lift to pull the carts while they walked overland. The carts could be loaded with several hundred pounds of the most essential food and supplies. One drawback, of course, was that this strategy limited the journey to those with enough physical stamina to walk and haul; moreover, the travelers had no real shelter. Another problem was that some dishonest suppliers used green wood, so the carts sometimes fell apart before they reached their destination. From 1856 to 1860 more than 3,000 Saints walked from Iowa through Nebraska and into Utah pulling these handcarts.

In 1856 the first three handcart companies left Iowa City in June and safely walked 1,300 miles to Utah, arriving in September. They were followed by a tragedy that lives as a landmark in the trek saga. There are graves in Winter Quarters, in all the supply camps en route, in early Salt Lake City, and in the other early settlements. Many died from cholera, tuberculosis, and other diseases that took their toll in the nineteenth century. Babies and young children died, as did women in childbirth, and others succumbed to the dangers and privations common to pioneers on the American frontier. But none are more poignant than the deaths in the Willie and Martin handcart companies en route to the Great Basin.

Bad luck dogged the companies from the start. Their suppliers delivered the carts later than scheduled, and it was late in July 1856 before the emigrants were ready to head for the Great Basin. Those experienced in the ways of the Rockies advised them to wait until spring, but they were eager to reach their promised land. The 500-person Willie company and 576-person Martin company left the Nebraska staging area in late August. Their carts, shoddily thrown together with green wood, began to stick and wobble. The travelers tried to grease the axles with tallow; this proved to be disastrous since the tallow attracted sand, which ground the joints down. The carts began to collapse. A freakishly early blizzard blanketed the emigrants with snow, which became thicker as they ascended the Rockies. Supplies began to run out. News of the impending disaster, of more than 1,000 Saints facing an early winter trapped on the trail, reached Salt Lake City in October. Young appealed for donations, and a mule train of rescuers reached the handcart travelers, but not before more than 200 had frozen to death or died of exhaustion. The companies finally reached Salt Lake City in early December. Many of the survivors had to undergo amputation of frozen fingers and feet. Mary Goble Pay, a survivor, wrote in her diary:

> We arrived in Salt Lake City nine o'clock at night the 11th of December 1856. Three out of four that were living were frozen. My mother was dead in the wagon.
>
> Bishop Hardy had us taken to a home in his ward and the brethren and sisters brought us plenty of food. We had to be careful and not eat too much as it might kill us we were so hungry.
>
> Early next morning Bro. Brigham Young and a doctor came. The doctor's name was Williams. When Bro. Young came in he shook hands with us all. When he saw our condition—our feet frozen and our mother dead—tears rolled down his cheeks.

On the great day in May of 1869, when America's Transcontinental Railroad was completed with the driving of the golden spike at Promontory Summit near Ogden, Utah, the pattern of emigration changed permanently. From that point on traveling to Utah was no more arduous than any train trip. From the church's point of view, of course, the ease with which the Great Basin was linked to the rest of the country was a double-edged sword. With rapid travel and communication—a transcontinental telegraph had gone through a few years before the railroad—the Mormon kingdom was clearly linked with the rest of the United States. The Saints were no longer isolated. The challenge increasingly posed to church authorities was to strengthen group loyalty and solidarity in the face of the encroachments of the outside world.

From the first Young's goal was to attain economic self-sufficiency for the Saints. In the earliest years the pressing need was simple survival while absorbing a constant stream of new arrivals into a fragile economy. Some of Young's colonizing decisions were flawed. Occasionally there was needless suffering when newcomers were sent off too late to provide for themselves before winter closed in. But most settlers answered the call obediently, and the sheer need to survive allowed plenty of scope for individual initiative. Mormons blended a sturdy emphasis on self-reliance, part of their theological as well as their pioneer heritage, with a strong culture of mutual help. The dream of building God's kingdom in such an inhospitable environment required cooperation through authoritarian organization as well as the impulses of private neighborliness and charity. Food was often rationed, but through cooperation the pioneers avoided starvation. Young's sermons, bristling with earthy language and colorful illustrations, make it clear that not all the sharing was cheerful and voluntary, and individual members were sometimes not above a bit of corner-cutting in their tithing contributions.

Agriculture was the first priority for Utah's settlers, and before arriving in the Great Basin the leaders were well aware that farming there would differ greatly from raising crops in humid climates. Water control and irrigation were planned from the outset, with access and distribution a clear matter of church regulation. Crop yields were often marginal. Land, however, was available for the taking, unlike in Ohio, Missouri, and Illinois, where it required cash or credit. Only one white settler resided in the basin when the Saints arrived, a trapper named Miles Goodyear who claimed to own a large portion of the valley near present-day Ogden. About $2,000 of good Mormon battalion cash bought him out. The emerging kingdom economy mixed cooperative venture with private ownership. Land was often assigned by lot; a small farm in a new village might often be a ten-acre allotment, with extra plots for polygamous families. Homes were often grouped around a village meetinghouse to create a communal village, with farmers traveling to their fields outside of town.

Saints were regularly exhorted not to import nonessential items. They were to make their own clothes, make do, or do without. Incoming freight was to concentrate on necessary manufactured items such as machinery. Young attempted to establish industries that would serve the Saints' needs and possibly produce goods for sale outside the Great Basin: sugar, wool, cotton, silk, iron. For a variety of reasons—including distrust of importing skilled Gentile administrators, insufficient capital, daunting environmental problems, and sometimes sheer bad luck—none of the early ventures was particularly successful. Most production was confined to cottage industries.

But expanding contact with the Gentiles had an upside. As thousands of non-Mormon emigrés passed through the basin on their way to California—some in the gold rush of 1849, some ordinary settlers—they were willing to pay inflated prices for supplies the Saints were willing to sell. The Saints were discouraged from participating in the gold rush, but some did, and gold dust began to trickle into church coffers, too. For a while Utah minted its own gold coins. In the late 1850s, with a federal military fort established not far from Salt Lake City, the Saints discovered that a military base, then as now, could be a profitable project for the local residents. The army brought with it good cash for a cash-starved economy. When the soldiers were withdrawn in 1861 to fight the Civil War, they left behind a bonanza in military surplus. The Saints were able to buy about $4 million worth of goods for $100,000: food, livestock, animal feed, iron, tools, and equipment.

Contracts for the transcontinental telegraph and railroad lines were made through the church and provided employment for many in the 1860s. Mining was increasingly important as significant mineral deposits were discovered in the basin, and it became profitable once the railroad made it practical to ship large quantities of ore. Young, however, was suspicious that mines and miners would attract more unwanted Gentile influence into the basin, and he pressured the Saints to avoid the industry and stick to agriculture.

In the early 1870s an attempt was made to establish cooperative communities, stores, and factories partly to avoid doing business with non-Mormons. The School of the Prophets, named after the early Kirtland educational enterprise but in Utah more of a governing council, was established by Young in 1867 to guide these activities. This council and its branches included about 5,000 priesthood holders who met to study religious questions as well as to guide economic activities for the church.

In 1874 the School of the Prophets was absorbed into the United Order of Enoch, an idealistic experiment in localized cooperative enterprise and communitarian living that took as inspiration the early church ideas of conservation and stewardship. With the railroad's entry into the desert, the idea was partly to keep the outside world at bay and avoid absorption into eastern big business. About one hundred of these communities were formed, mostly in southern Utah. There were several types: (1) A commune in which all economic property was owned in common and differential wages were paid depending on the participant's original property contribution and his work skills and assignment. (2) Extension of various cooperative activities already begun, in existing settlements or wards of cities, using "increase" to establish a variety of enterprises ranging from sawmills to cheese production. (3) Strictly communal cooperatives, much like the twentieth-century kibbutz in Israel.

Some of these cooperatives fell apart quickly through member disagreements. Others became increasingly complex as they branched into a wide variety of ventures. Some lasted until the 1880s, when they fell victim to the pressures of antipolygamy campaigns. The historian Leonard Arrington, in his classic study *Great Basin Kingdom,* writes that there is much evidence to indicate that these cooperatives were designed to be temporary, but that they "helped to keep Utah economically independent of the East longer and more completely than would otherwise have been the case."

A more centralized cooperative venture was Zion's Cooperative Mercantile Institution (ZCMI), which was founded in 1868 and lives on as a major commercial institution in today's Intermountain West. Young wanted Mormons to boycott Gentile merchants, so ZCMI was established, originally as a wholesale operation; retail was added later. Two men,

Young and William Jennings, together owned nearly 80 percent of ZCMI shares. The signs at ZCMI stores had the words "Holiness to the Lord" emblazoned over the All-Seeing Eye of Jehovah. ZCMI immediately controlled the wholesale business of the area and soon dominated retail activities as well. Spies allegedly reported on disloyal Mormons who patronized Gentile merchants. Over this same period Mormons established other significant large-scale cooperative enterprises in banking and textile manufacture and expanded agriculture-related production.

Internal opposition to the cooperatives arose in a movement later known as the Godbeite heresy. William Godbe, a leading merchant and friend of Young, and other intellectuals of the day wanted the Mormons to end their social and economic insularity and founded the *Utah Magazine* to argue their case. They believed that Utah's future economic growth and prosperity depended in considerable part on developing its mineral resources and practical interaction with Gentiles. In the long run Utah's agriculture could not possibly compete with that of places like California.

Astute as those perceptions may have been, expressing them was considered to constitute heresy because one was not supposed to disagree openly with the policies of church authorities. The Godbeite leaders were excommunicated, but not before launching the *Salt Lake Tribune,* originally a fervently anti-Mormon publication and today a nonpartisan daily competitor of the church-owned *Deseret News.* The Godbeites also founded a political party to resist the church's hegemony and generally stretched the limits of dissent in Mormon country at a time when no law was made or action carried out without the approval of a shadow government operated by the church. The Godbeites founded a small, short-lived splinter, the Church of Zion, which developed spiritualist tendencies. It was telling that the only significant church schism during Young's reign essentially involved economics, not doctrine. Young's main importance to the later church was organizational rather than intellectual or theological.

In 1877, after years of isolation and with Young's decades of rule coming to an end, the church was again increasingly embroiled in anti-Mormon difficulties, this time at the federal level. As in Illinois, the issues were the recurring ones of theocratic control and polygamy. A shared heritage of persecution and pioneer hardships, in addition to shared beliefs, had developed a powerful sense of group identity. Joseph Smith's church polity has been hierarchical and authoritarian from the beginning. This was naturally reinforced by the pioneer experience in which survival depended on community cooperation that flowed necessarily from a clearly defined authority structure.

All that was clear enough. What was less clear was how Mormon ideals could play themselves out within the American conception of church-state relations. Shortly before Smith was assassinated, he claimed that "the whole of America is Zion itself from north to south." At the same time his revelations regarded American institutions, and especially the U.S. Constitution, as divinely inspired. Young, like Joseph Smith before him, always allowed for untrammeled private freedom of worship for non-Mormons. The problem lay in how to balance their territorial claims for the kingdom of God against those of American secular society. The separatism of Mormonism, Thomas O'Dea writes, "was not only theocratic in church government but also totalitarian, in the sense of encompassing the totality of human activity within its orbit and under the leadership of the church."

Beginning in 1850 the Mormons repeatedly applied for admission as a state to the Union, a goal not achieved until nearly two decades after Brigham Young's death. Strands of separatism always mingled with patriotism in the Mormon attitude toward the Union, and after territorial status was achieved, relations with federal officials were edgy. When Young's term as provisional governor ended in 1854, he was not about to move over easily and cede the office to a federal appointee. Through a mixture of Mormon truculence and ineptitude in Washington, a federal governor was not seated until after the "Utah War" of 1857–58, another episode that looms large in the Mormon collective memory, although it was a war in which no shot was fired.

Utah's success at keeping its own affairs in church hands became an embarrassment to the U.S. government. In 1856 the national Republican candidates campaigned with a promise to rid the country of the "twin relics of barbarism," slavery and polygamy. In 1857 President James Buchanan, convinced by false reports that the Mormons were in rebellion, sent a military contingent to Utah to install his appointee, Alfred Cumming, in the territorial governor's seat.

Rhetoric grew increasingly apocalyptic as the church prepared for the federal government's Utah Expedition. Young's response was to plan the Great Move. This was a dramatic gesture in which 30,000 Saints temporarily abandoned their homes and farms, in and around Salt Lake City, with Mormon men instructed to torch any settlements the army attempted to occupy. The idea was in part to demonstrate true Mormon solidarity, and perhaps also to win some sympathy back east. For several weeks, as many as 600 wagons a day rolled out of Salt Lake City. In the end the soldiers marched peaceably through Salt Lake City, on June 30, 1858, under strict instructions not to tamper with anyone's property; they set up camp thirty miles south of the city. Governor Cumming assumed office without further trouble. And all the Saints came back home. The episode, say Arrington and Bitton, had "something of the incongruity of comic opera. The President of the United States had dispatched the largest peacetime army in the nation's history to oversee the installation of half a dozen officials in a minor territory."

The worst episode during the Utah War period had nothing to do with U.S. soldiers. This was the infamous Mountain Meadows Massacre of September 11, 1857, in which Mormon settlers in southern Utah led Indians in attacking disarmed non-Mormons in the Fancher wagon train that was passing through, murdering more than one hundred. This tragic affair has to be understood in the context of the hysteria of the time, as well as the vigilante culture that sometimes operated on the raw frontier. Mormons had apparently refused to sell supplies to the Fancher train, and the emigrés had responded by taunting the Mormons on sensitive pressure points like the Haun's Mill Massacre and the murder of their prophet. The careful research in Juanita Brooks's 1950 book *The Mountain Meadows Massacre* shows that the Mormons acted from a mixture of motives, including fear of war and invasion as well as a desire for revenge.

Brooks's research also makes it clear that Young was not part of the plot to wipe out the Fancher train, but the same research implicates the church in attempting to cover up the role played by Mormons in the slaughter. The nation at the time of the murders reacted with horror, and the church feared that its negative image was impeding the attempt to achieve statehood. Nearly twenty years after the massacre one Mormon was executed by the territorial government as a scapegoat made to carry the whole blame for the tragedy. Amends were not made until four decades after Brooks's book when the church erected a monument dedicated to the victims of the massacre. The church's current president, Gordon B. Hinckley, then first counselor in the First Presidency, attended.

Three years after the federal soldiers built their base, they abandoned it to fight the Civil War. Utahns were largely ignored during the war, a turn of events much to Young's liking. Mormons sent T. B. H. Stenhouse to Washington, who reported that President Abraham Lincoln had said: "Stenhouse, when I was a boy on the farm in Illinois there was a great deal of timber on the farm which we had to clear away. Occasionally we would come to a log which had fallen down. It was too hard to split, too wet to burn, and too heavy to move, so we plowed around it. You go back and tell Brigham Young that if he will let me alone I will let him alone."

But not long after the Civil War the winds changed as Utah's period of isolation ended. The waning years of Young's life were spent shoring up the Saints' insularity by the cooperative movement and protecting the promised land from the encroachments of Gentile business and secular culture. In the years after his death the church had to deal with the largest barrier to statehood, the inflammatory issue of plural marriage.

When Brigham Young died on August 29, 1877, the legacy he did leave behind was clear. Under his presidency, the church had grown from 26,000 to 135,000 members. Major persecutions lay just ahead, but the resiliency to meet the challenges was also in place. The church was what he had hoped it would be: large, growing, and with a healthy sense of its own unique peoplehood. He died of peritonitis following a ruptured appendix, and a daughter reported that he perished with the name of Joseph on his lips.

CHAPTER 4
POLYGAMY THEN AND NOW

POLYGAMY LIVES. CONSERVATIVE ESTIMATES PLACE THE NUMBER INVOLVED at 30,000—clandestinely in metropolitan Salt Lake City, more openly in southern Utah, adjacent Colorado and Arizona, and some other scattered points west. Some think the actual number is several times that.

They are not hard to find, although in Salt Lake City they live discreetly. An intellectual being interviewed in Salt Lake mentions that a clerk at his favorite Mormon bookstore is a polygamous wife. A desk clerk at the Travelodge across the street from Temple Square says that she regularly sees polygamous wives shopping at supermarkets near her home in Sandy. They are the ones filling their carts with institutional-size boxes of everything, a dozen gallons of ice cream or ten watermelons at a shot. Everyone knows who they are, says the desk clerk, herself a faithful LDS member, but no one makes it an issue, and they keep to themselves.

Every now and then polygamy flashes into national headlines: the occasional murder, barely pubescent brides, abuse of a wife or child. The Church of Jesus Christ of Latter-day Saints shudders at such stories and solemnly hastens to emphasize the difference between the Temple Square church and the outlanders. Any LDS member caught practicing polygamy is excommunicated. Polygamous converts in the African missions must become monogamists or they are denied baptism, making Mormonism more conservative on that point than many other churches today. Most people call the modern polygamists Mormon Fundamentalists. The LDS church resents the term. They are not Mormons, headquarters insists. They are not members, and they do not follow the leaders or their dictates, so how can they be called Mormon Fundamentalists?

But the Mormon Fundamentalists, to call them by the term they and scholars studying them use, do exist. And though they embarrass the LDS authorities, they are an awkward part—and by all accounts a growing part—of the Mormon Church's nineteenth-century legacy that lives on into the new millennium.

Polygamy and slavery were the "twin relics of barbarism," thundered the first Republican Party platform of 1856, which pledged to stamp out both. The identification of polygamy with Mormonism had become a national issue by then, and it inflamed Americans for decades as Utah repeatedly applied for statehood. California made it into the union by 1850, and Nevada in 1864, but it took Utah until 1896. Tired of territorial restrictions, Mormons were eager for the greater freedom to govern their own affairs that would come with statehood. Outside of Utah, other Americans were suspicious of the church, its economic power, and its theocratic control.

But above all there was the explosive matter of polygamy. Smith and his successors in Utah managed American history's only wide-scale experiment in multiple wives, boldly challenging the nation's entrenched family structure and the morality of Western Judeo-Christian culture. The practice greatly aggravated the persecution of the Restored Church, that is, the true church restored through the Book of Mormon and the latter-day prophets.

At first it was hard for even Brigham Young to swallow. When Smith first inducted him into the secret commandment of plural marriage, Young later recalled, "it was the first time in my life that I desired the grave, and I could hardly get over it for a long time. And when I saw a funeral, I felt to envy the corpse its situation."

But get over it he did. By his death in 1877 Young had married twenty wives (by the conservative count of the semiofficial *Encyclopedia of Mormonism*) and fathered fifty-seven children by sixteen of them. When the famous editor and social reformer Horace Greeley interviewed Young in 1859 for the *New York Daily Tribune,* he asked, "Does not the Apostle Paul say that a bishop should be 'the husband of one wife'? [I Timothy 3:2]"

"So we hold," answered Young. "We do not regard any but a married man as fitted for the office of bishop." Somewhat disingenuously he added, "But the apostle does not forbid a bishop having more than one wife."

Joseph Smith started it all, and the number of his wives is a matter of some scholarly dispute. Fawn Brodie, in her classic biography of Joseph Smith, *No Man Knows My History,* puts the number at forty-eight. Brodie, raised Mormon, was a niece of David O. McKay, then an apostle of thirty-nine years' standing and later church president. The book's tone is irreverent, and its research, though largely substantiated by later scholarship, infuriated church authorities. She was expelled from the church in 1946. "I was excommunicated for heresy—and I was a heretic—and specifically for writing the book," she cheerfully said later.

Smith's biography in the *Encyclopedia of Mormonism* mentions that he took "at least" twenty-eight plural wives. Stanley Ivins puts the number at eighty-four in unpublished research in the 1950s, but many of these were clearly only sacred "sealings" for eternity. D. Michael Quinn counts forty-six. Todd Compton, in his exhaustively researched *In Sacred Loneliness: The Plural Wives of Joseph Smith* (1997), comes up with a list of thirty-three well corroborated by affidavits and other written evidence, plus eight "possible" wives with more problematic evidence, and a further eight documented by posthumous sealings conducted shortly after Smith's death. There were also at least five known cases of women who rejected his polygamous proposals.

Compton devotes a biographical chapter to each of the thirty-three well-documented plural wives. It is an intriguing list. There were at least eleven polyandrous unions in which the wife was already married to another man. There were four sister pairs (Huntington, Partridge, Johnson, Lawrence) and one mother-daughter pair (Sessions) on the list. Although some Mormon apologists have attempted to justify polygamy in part because it sheltered single women beyond marriageable age, the facts show otherwise. The vast majority of plural wives were younger than the first wife, often nubile teenagers. In addition, there typically was a shortage of women on the frontier. Of Smith's thirty-three well-documented wives on Compton's list, only three were significantly older than Smith, and those three already had husbands. Other brides of Joseph were as young as fourteen, which was the minimum age for marriage in Utah law until 1999, when it was raised to sixteen or fifteen with court permission.

In these and other Smith marriages, polygamy—the church prefers the term "plural marriage"—covered both polygyny, more than one wife per husband, and polyandry, more than one husband per wife. Polygyny was the usual pattern, apart from Smith himself and possibly a few exceptional early cases involving his closest associates taking wives who already had husbands. Smith, and Young after him, readily granted divorce to either men or women for polygamous marriages that were having difficulty. (Although the divorce rate for temple marriages today is quite low, divorce in Mormonism did not and does not carry the stigma found in Catholic or Evangelical Protestant culture.)

Polygamy wove an intricate web of personal ties in Nauvoo. It became "one of the chief tests of the total loyalty that Smith was coming to demand of his closest followers," according to the historian Lawrence Foster. Since polygamy "vastly expanded the network of personal loyalties and the range of possible relationships," it greatly strengthened social cohesion in a time of tribal persecution. Smith often asked close friends for their wives and daughters. Compton reports that in some of the eleven polyandrous marriages in which the wives remained living with their first husbands, the first husbands stood as witnesses as their wives were eternally "sealed" to Smith.

Early Mormon polygamy, with the complexities of its social and theological justifications, clearly involved far more than rationalization for inflated male libidos. Still, some of the activities seemed decidedly nonclinical. A number of Smith's plural wives were dependent orphans or young women employed and living in his home. Some of the marriages were the result of pressure or spiritual coercion from the prophet: he told prospective wives, especially those who were daughters of his inner circle, that "such relationships would insure their salvation and link their families indissolubly to [himself] and the faith to which they were so committed," writes historian Lawrence Foster. Emma did not much cotton to the principle, so mostly the marrying was done behind her back, though over the years it became harder for Smith to conceal his activities.

Evidence of Smith's unconventional ideas about marriage dates back to 1830, when his hasty exit from Harmony may have been because Emma's cousin, Hiel Lewis, "accused Joseph of improper conduct with women." Mary Elizabeth Rollins Lightner wrote that Smith approached her in 1831 when she was only twelve, telling her privately that he had been told in a vision that she was the first woman God commanded him to take as plural wife. Lightner actually became a Smith plural wife eleven years later, after she had married another man.

There is also evidence that brothers participating in the 1832 mob that tarred and feathered Smith in Kirtland, Ohio, were inflamed by the possibility that Smith had proposed to their sixteen-year-old sister, Marinda Nancy Johnson, who eventually did become a plural bride of the prophet. The assailants threatened to castrate Smith, but the doctor brought along by the mob refused to carry out the procedure.

The comely sixteen-year-old Fanny Alger, a hired girl living with the Smiths in Kirtland, became the prophet's plural wife in 1833 when he was twenty-seven. In a pattern that was to be repeated several times, Emma suspected a relationship and threw Fanny out of her house. Rumors were circulating with increasing intensity in Kirtland.

While Smith was away visiting Michigan in August 1835, W. W. Phelps introduced an antipolygamy resolution in Cowdery's handwriting that was adopted unanimously by a church assembly: "Inasmuch as this church of Christ has been reproached with the crime of fornication, and polygamy; we declare that we believe, that one man should have one wife; and one woman but one husband, except in case of death, when either is at liberty to marry again."

This became a scriptural revelation in the Doctrine and Covenants, appearing in all editions through decades of polygamous practice until it was removed by LDS church authorities in 1876 and replaced by D&C 132, which permits a plurality of wives. It is still published as section 112 of the Reorganized LDS church's edition of the D&C. The resolution was passed on August 17; Fanny, who later married monogamously, was probably gone from Kirtland by the time Smith returned to Ohio on August 23.

A rift was developing between Smith and Cowdery, the loyal scribe and Book of Mormon witness. Cowdery, probably never a polygamist, apparently had witnessed the sexual relationship between Fanny and Joseph and regarded it as adultery; "the circumstantial evidence is strong that Cowdery's respect for Joseph diminished after that point," writes Compton. In early January 1838 Cowdery wrote to his brother about the "dirty, nasty filthy affair of [Smith] and Fanny Alger's," and a public reconciliation with Smith was very short-lived. After Cowdery sold his property in Independence, Missouri, at a time when the Saints were encouraged to keep their Missouri land holdings, he faced charges of disloyalty. On April 12, 1838, he was tried and excommunicated for this and for "seeking to destroy the character of President Joseph Smith, Jun., by falsely insinuating that he was guilty of adultery."

The prophet's defiance of marital law and convention was emboldened beginning in November 1835, when he conducted a wedding for his friend Newell Knight. Smith had been forbidden by a court to conduct marriages, and Knight's bride was not yet divorced from her non-Mormon husband. Knight's journal recalled that Smith said, "The Gentile law has no power to call me to account for it." Over the succeeding two months Smith conducted at least five other illegal weddings.

Smith's polygamous activities continued in Nauvoo in 1841, with most of his marriages taking place in 1842 and 1843. His youngest bride, in some ways typical, was fourteen-year-old Helen Mar Kimball. In her early teens Helen fell in love with Horace Whitney, who was three years older, but the young lovers were fated to be separated in eternity because Smith intervened. Helen was the daughter of Apostle Heber C. Kimball, a close colleague of Smith's. The prophet first asked Heber for his wife, Vilate. Heber agonized over the situation for three emotionally tortured days; then, "with a broken and bleeding heart," he led Vilate to Smith. The prophet backed off, saying it had merely been a test of loyalty. A year later, in 1843, Smith returned and asked for the Kimballs' young daughter Helen.

Helen's feelings are well documented, since nearly four decades later she wrote a first-person memoir for her children. When her father approached her about the prophet's proposal, she was shocked, for she had never heard of polygamy. In addition, she already had a sweetheart and a young girl's dreams.

Smith often put pressure on such decisions by imposing a tight deadline. Helen had twenty-four hours to digest the situation and capitulate. The pressure included a heavy-duty religious component. Smith told her, "If you will take this step, it will ensure your eternal salvation & exaltation and that of your father's household & all of your kindred." Helen's mother bore anguish "none but God & his angels could see."

Helen wrote a poem expressing the lonely isolation of a young girl's heart, watching her "youthful friends grow shy and cold," withstanding "poisonous darts from sland'rous tongues" while aching "like a fetter'd bird with wild and longing heart, / Thou'lt dayly pine for freedom and murmor at the lot." The poem continues with a tribute to Joseph Smith and eternal glory, and another tribute to her father. Her own writings and other evidence indicate that she felt rebellious at times, and that it is possible she had not grasped before the ceremony that the marriage was to have a sexual component.

With Smith's death in 1844, Helen was free to return to the normal life of a teenager and did so, enjoying girlfriends and parties. On February 3, 1846, a few days before fleeing Nauvoo, Helen was married to her real sweetheart, Horace Whitney, "for time" because she was already sealed to Smith for eternity. Horace, in need of an eternal companion, was sealed to an already-deceased female Saint.

Lucy Walker was another teenager who found coping with spiritual coercion difficult. After Lucy's mother died in early 1842, her younger siblings were scattered in various homes. Smith sent Lucy's father on a mission and took Lucy into his own home to work for Emma. Lucy was horrified when, probably in late 1842, Smith approached her with a polygamous proposal. She wrote, "No mother to council; no father near to tell me what to do, in this trying hour. Oh let this bitter cup pass. And thus I prayed in the agony of my soul." Smith backed off for a while.

The prophet resumed his quest in April 1843, telling Lucy, who was now sixteen, that it was a "command of God" and damnation would be her reward if she refused: "I will give you untill to-morrow to decide this matter. If you reject this message the gate will be closed forever against you." She told Smith that God had not revealed to her that she should become his wife. Smith responded: "You shall have a manifestation of the will of God concerning you; a testimoney that you can never deny. I will tell you what it shall be. It shall be that peace and joy that you never knew." In response to that pressure, Lucy had the requisite vision and married Smith several days afterward. Later she said, "It was not a love matter, . . . but simply the giving up of myself as a sacrifice to establish that grand and glorious principle that God had revealed to the world."

Sarah Ann Whitney, sister of Helen Mar Kimball's second husband, Horace, was another reluctant teenage plural wife. Helen described her friend and later sister-in-law as "proud and somewhat eccentric; but the influence that she seemed to hold over one was almost magnetic." The intellectual and artistic Whitney family was part of Mormonism's elite leadership circle, so this marriage was clearly another dynastic linkage of the prophet with a prominent family of Saints. Smith told Sarah's father that the reward for him would be "honor and immortality and eternal life to all your house." Smith feared that Horace Whitney would oppose his sister's polygamous union, so he removed that obstacle by sending Horace off on a mission. Helen Mar Kimball wrote of her friend, "Sarah felt when she took this step that it would be the means of severing her from the happy circle in which she had moved as one of their guiding stars."

Some months after Sarah's plural union with Smith he arranged a cover marriage to help protect the polygamous secret. Sarah married the widower Joseph C. Kingsbury in a civil "pretended marriage." Smith then sealed Kingsbury to his deceased first wife.

In the busy spring of 1843 Smith married another pair of fatherless daughters who were living in his house. Sarah Lawrence, seventeen, and her nineteen-year-old sister Maria were legal wards of Smith's, and the prophet had also been named guardian trustee of their rather sizable estate. There is some evidence that Smith borrowed from estate funds. William

Law, second counselor to Smith in the First Presidency and a longtime Lawrence family friend, filed suit in Hancock County charging Smith with living in adultery with Maria. A week before Law and his friends published the *Nauvoo Expositor* in 1844, Smith flatly denied the charge of polygamy in a public declaration: "What a thing it is for a man to be accused of committing adultery, and having seven wives, when I can only find one." Law, who believed Smith had defrauded the sisters' estate, and aware that Emma was strapped for money, repaid the sisters' missing funds himself after Smith's death.

The most famous of Smith's plural wives undoubtedly was Eliza Snow, who was close to Smith's own age when she married him in 1842. She moved into the Smith home and began teaching school. Her presence in the Smith household aroused Emma's jealousy, and in February 1843 Emma threw her out into the snow. There is one account claiming that Emma actually kicked Eliza down a staircase and that Eliza miscarried Smith's child as a result.

After Smith's death, Heber Kimball and Brigham Young offered to marry the prophet's plural wives to take care of them as proxies for time. Most accepted the offer and moved west; Eliza became a wife of Young's. In Utah she became the most famous Mormon woman and was active as an intellectual, poet, essayist, president of the women's Relief Society— and defender of polygamy as a doctrine central to "the Gospel of the Son of God." She traveled widely from Europe to Israel, lectured, and died at age eighty-three in her own apartment at Brigham Young's Lion House.

The number of Smith's polygamous offspring is a bit of a mystery. There was only one child from a plural marriage generally acknowledged as such: Josephine, daughter of Emily Dow Partridge. Several sources indicate there were others, raised in other families and under other names. Such children had, of course, been conceived in secrecy.

Rebuffing a prophet who was capable of yoking the proposal to a choice of salvation or damnation was tough. But at least five women did spurn the prophet's bid for marriage. The best known was probably the spirited nineteen-year-old Nancy Rigdon, daughter of First Presidency counselor Sidney Rigdon, in an 1842 episode that soured Smith's relationship with her father in much the same way that the prophet's association with Cowdery had suffered a decade earlier.

Smith invited Nancy into a private room at a printing office, locked the door behind them, and presented her with his proposal, including the usual appeal that God had revealed to him that she was to be his wife. Nancy had been forewarned by Mayor John C. Bennett, who also found her attractive. (She did not respond to Bennett either.) Nancy threatened to raise a ruckus if Smith did not unlock the door and let her go.

The next day Smith sent Nancy a letter attempting to coax her with the argument that "happiness is the object and design of our existence." The letter continued, "That which is wrong under one circumstance, may be, and often is, right under another." Furthermore, "our Heavenly Father is more liberal in his views, and boundless in his mercies and blessings, than we are ready to believe or receive." After Nancy showed the letter to her father, Sidney Rigdon confronted Smith, who denied the proposal until Rigdon produced the letter. At that point Smith acknowledged that Nancy's story was true.

The letter was soon published by Bennett, whose motives may have been suspect but whose knowledge of Smith's polygamy has been shown to be accurate if sensationalized. Nancy's story is corroborated not only by the letter and her father's testimony but by her brother John, her brother-in-law George W. Robinson, and Orson Pratt. Smith loyalists responded with a campaign of character assassination. Bennett continued to publish exposés that posed a threat to Smith. Emma stood by her husband, writing the Illinois governor that Bennett was a "most consummate scoundrel."

Smith's steadfast denials that he engaged in polygamy were necessary in order to perpetuate a practice that violated the law. (Apologists point out that plural marriages involved religious ceremonies and should not be confused with bigamy or simple adultery.) In the October 1, 1842, issue of the church newspaper *Times and Seasons* Smith wrote: "We have given the above rule of marriage [monogamy] as the only one practiced in this church, to show that Dr. J. C. Bennett's 'secret wife system' is a matter of his own manufacture." With the prophet's denial, most Nauvoo citizens believed Bennett had made up the stories. But the rumors were getting stronger.

Most historians today agree that there was an unpublished revelation on plural marriage as early as 1831. Yet the Book of Mormon, published in 1830, was conventionally monogamous:

And it came to pass that Riplakish did not do that which was right in the sight of the Lord, for he did have many wives and concubines (Ether 10:5).

Behold, David and Solomon truly had many wives and concubines, which thing was abominable before me, Saith the Lord. . . . Hearken to the word of the Lord: For there shall not any man among you have save it be one wife; and concubines he shall have none" (Jacob 2:24, 27).

Behold, the Lamanites, . . . they have not forgotten the commandment of the Lord, which was given unto our fathers—that they should have save it were one wife, concubines they should have none, and there should not be whoredoms committed among them (Jacob 3:5).

Biblically, the justification for polygamy lay in the practices of some Old Testament patriarchs. The compassionate biblical Levirate concept of marrying and caring for a dead brother's wife is apparent in Joseph Smith's taking Agnes Coolbrith Smith, the widow of his younger brother, Don Carlos, as a plural wife in 1842. Something similar may be seen in the marriages of Heber Kimball and Brigham Young to Smith's plural wives after the assassination.

Polygamy is not countenanced in later Judaism or the New Testament, though Smith was capable of some creative exegesis. While trying to induce Benjamin Johnson in 1843 to act as go-between in convincing his sister Almera to join his polygamous roster, Smith told Johnson to listen closely to a sermon he would preach that evening. The prophet's text was the Gospel parable of the talents, presented as a "radical critique of monogamy as something inherently inferior and less than sacred." If a man had lots of talents—that is, wives—God would bless him, but subtract blessings if a man had only one.

Other new religions in that era developed unorthodox sexual practices, including the celibate Shakers and the "complex marriage" of the Oneida Community. The Swedish scientist and seer Emanuel Swedenborg, whose ideas were discussed in Smith's hometown newspaper, taught a "spiritual wifery" in which marriage was for eternity. (The polyandrous husband of one of Smith's plural wives was a Swedenborgian from upstate New York.) And Smith was at least aware of Islam, a polygamous faith, since he included it in the list of religious groups promised freedom of worship in Nauvoo.

Characteristically Smith's revelations put a special spin on the idea. Nowhere in the Old Testament is polygamy related to salvation, nor does glorification intensify from sheer quantity. It is also not yoked to the idea of eternal marriage in heaven, as in Mormon doctrine. Although in today's Mormon Church the idea of celestial exaltation and eternal marriage is separate from the doctrine of polygamy, in nineteenth-century Mormonism the tenets were clearly linked. And equally clearly, elite status in heaven had a great deal to do with family quantity. This "celestial marriage" doctrine was strictly patriarchal. A woman could be sealed eternally to only one male, but a male could be sealed eternally to any number of women. Smith's own multiple marriages, along with those of his closest circle, produced an extensive, interlocked dynasty connected throughout eternity.

In nineteenth-century Utah church authorities were under pressure to practice polygamy and produce large families. The *Encyclopedia of Mormonism* says that an estimated 20 to 25 percent of adult Mormons were involved in polygamous families, but "among Church leadership plural marriage was the norm for a time." This linkage of exaltation and quantity survived into the twentieth century only in the notion that a good Saint's spiritual duty included providing earthly tabernacles for souls-in-waiting, that is, to have families with a lot of children.

For a long time Smith dodged the issue of polygamy with Emma. The church's 1842 *Times and Seasons* declaration of monogamy was signed not only by an unknowing Emma but also by two of Smith's secret plural wives, Eliza Snow and Sarah Cleveland. Newel K. Whitney and John Taylor, already polygamists, were also signatories. Years later, asked how she could have signed the statement, Eliza used a casuistry typical of the issue: "We made no allusion to any other system of marriage than Bennett's. His was prostitution, and it was truly *his*. . . . In those articles there is no reference to divine plural marriage." The use of legalistic, deliberately evasive code words here and elsewhere sometimes became a defense for what less sympathetic critics might call lies.

After the confrontation between Emma and Eliza in February 1843, Joseph could no longer duck the issue on the home front. Now he had to win Emma over to his new concept of marriage. Until Emma relented, Joseph refused to grant her his new endowment ritual, which he taught was essential to heavenly exaltation. When at last she did relent, he rewarded her on May 18, 1843, sealing them for time and eternity, and later bestowed the endowment.

In theory, the first wife was to be consulted to approve plural wife additions, but the practice was often breached. Now Emma gained the privilege of endorsing plural wives for Joseph. She chose a sister pair, Emily and Eliza Partridge, unaware that they were already plural wives of her husband. To conceal this, Smith performed a second sealing ceremony with the Partridge women. Emma chose another sister pair, the Lawrences; William Law later charged that Emma had her eye on the girls' inheritance.

For a while the Partridge and Lawrence women lived in the Smith household, with Emma in charge, but it obviously was a rocky relationship. The biographers Newell and Avery write that "the evidence seems clear that Emma gave her permission for plural marriage and immediately regretted that they had been performed. Emma began to talk as firmly and urgently to Joseph about abandoning plural marriage as he had formerly talked to her about accepting it."

The household situation of the plural wives varied. Those who were polyandrous lived with their first husbands; others lived with their parents, with each other, or with other families of the church's inner circle that were aware of plural marriage. Unlike polygamous husbands later on in Utah, Smith did not support his plural wives. Saints apart from the insider group continued for the most part to be unaware of the practice.

In July 12, 1843, Smith received and wrote the official revelation on plural marriage. It contained a warning to the rebellious Emma: "But if she will not abide this commandment she shall be destroyed" (D&C 132:54). The revelation also commanded her to forgive Joseph of all his trespasses. Emma, however, continued to use her position as Relief Society president to oppose polygamy; Joseph responded by suspending the organization in March of 1844. It was not revived until more than three decades later in Utah when Brigham Young ordered it reorganized—with Eliza Snow as president.

It seems clear that, in his way, Smith continued to love and be loyal to his first wife. He once told a critical plural wife, "If you desire my love, you must never speak evil of Emma."

After Smith's assassination, Emma remained in Illinois. Quarrels with Brigham Young over the distribution of her husband's estate led to a permanent breach. Her son Joseph III eventually became president of the rival Midwest branch, the Reorganized Church of Jesus Christ of Latter Day Saints. Neither she nor Joseph III were willing to admit that Joseph had been polygamous, as denial erased earlier painful memories. In an 1879 interview shortly before she died, Emma claimed, "He had no other wife but me," and added, "He did not have improper relations with any woman that ever came to my knowledge." She also testified, "I know Mormonism to be the truth; and believe the Church to have been established by divine direction."

In pioneer Utah any man who aspired to become part of Mormonism's power structure became a polygamist, so any American Mormon whose heritage includes pioneers from prominent Mormon families has polygamous forebears. First wives generally had a higher status than plural additions. The typical polygamous family had two wives; three was uncommon. More than that was rare and generally seen only in the highest ranks of the church.

Men varied in how they handled their polygamous homes. Each woman was usually responsible for her own children. Men tried to provide separate homes, or at least separate apartments, for each of their wives and families, and attempted to rotate their time and attention. Polygamous wives did the work common to pioneer women of their day; often their emotional and social lives centered on their children and, sometimes, fellow "sister" wives.

The church taught that marriage was for eternity, not for romantic love. Sensationalist press accounts to the contrary, Utah was not filled with bawdy licentiousness. Within the premise of plural marriage, the typical polygamous home was strictly moral, deeply religious, and hardworking, and many devout women were among the defenders of the polygamous principle.

But the rest of the country's reaction against polygamy rose to a crescendo of near hysteria. As some writers point out, this was the Victorian age, the era when the monogamous family became enshrined as the bulwark of civilization. "Mormonism was referred to as the 'plague spot' in the Rocky Mountains," writes the historian B. Carmon Hardy. "Bracketed with slaveholders as barbarians in the antebellum period, after the Civil War Utah polygamists were cast with blacks as animal and profligate."

Congress provided the first legal challenge with the Morrill Anti-Bigamy Act of 1862. The law was written to prohibit bigamy and adultery; Mormons complained that neither category fit the "celestial marriage" of church doctrine. Enforcement, in any case, depended on local judges and juries that were, of course, Mormon, so the law was ineffective in Utah. In 1872 Brigham Young was indicted on a charge of adultery, but the U.S. Supreme Court threw this out on technicalities, along with other indictments pending under that law.

The Poland Act of 1874 stiffened the Morrill Act by placing court jurisdiction in the hands of federal appointees rather than local probate courts. LDS Church authorities asked George Reynolds, husband of two wives and a secretary in the First Presidency, to volunteer for a test case. The Supreme Court issued the final *United States v. Reynolds* decision in 1879, and it was the turning point. A unanimous court found against Reynolds despite arguments made on his behalf under the religious freedom clause of the Bill of Rights. The decision, rendered by Chief Justice Morrison R. Waite, said that polygamy was "odious" and that, while laws "cannot interfere with mere religious belief and opinions, they may with practices." The decision cited human sacrifice as another example of a religious practice that could justify governmental interference.

All that was left was open defiance. The *Deseret News* editorialized vigorously. Polygamous families began to move to other places, including

Arizona, Colorado, Wyoming, Nevada, and northern Mexico. Huge demonstrations took place in Salt Lake City. In 1882 Congress responded with the Edmunds Act, which strengthened the Morrill Act by making "unlawful cohabitation" grounds for criminal prosecution.

Church President John Taylor in 1886 said he had received a revelation confirming polygamy: "I have not revoked this law nor will I for it is everlasting and those who will enter into my glory must obey the conditions thereof, even so amen." This revelation was never elevated to scriptural status, but today's Mormon Fundamentalists use it to support their continued polygamy.

Taylor added to his own polygamous family on December 19, 1886, by marrying twenty-six-year-old Josephine Roueche. He was seventy-eight years old. Taylor and a number of other polygamists went underground, some hiding in their own homes. Federal agents combed the area and imprisoned a number of the men. It is a tribute to Mormons that there were no violent standoffs or deaths in this period. Mormon families are full of stories of "cohabs" in hiding. Federal agents would burst into a house to check the closets and bedding. One bishop hiding in a store escaped in a box, crated up as an organ marked "Handle with Care." President Taylor died in hiding on February 27, 1887.

The federal government continued to pursue the church and in 1887 passed the tougher Edmunds-Tucker Act, which dissolved the church corporation, putting its properties and funds into receivership. Plural marriages continued to be performed, but the church began to hedge. "Celestial marriage," which had meant achieving the highest degree of glory in heaven through polygamous marriage, gradually began to be redefined as simply eternal marriage. Hardy writes that one church lobbyist working to persuade Congress to grant Utah statehood insisted that "celestial marriage meant nothing more than being sealed to a single partner for eternity. This shift, taken as one of several moves designed to lessen hostility toward the Saints, would be confirmed after the turn of the century when, again, the church labored with its public image."

For the Saints, all of this was also exacerbated by a certain millennial fervor. In Joseph Smith's *History of the Church,* the prophet in 1835 had predicted that "56 years should wind up the scene," which brought one to about 1891. He had published as scriptural revelation that God had told him, "Joseph, my son, if thou livest until thou art eighty-five years old, thou shalt see the face of the Son of Man" (D&C 130:15). But that revelation is hedged: "I believe the coming of the Son of Man will not be any sooner than that time" (D&C 130:17).

Mormons never backed themselves into official commitment to a certain date the way the Millerites did, but many Saints understood the polygamy crisis in terms of apocalypse. If the kingdom of God was at hand, it was especially important to live according to the highest spiritual principle, which meant polygamy.

Religious authority, in Mormonism, includes the concept of continuing revelation through the current church president, who holds the titles of seer, prophet, and revelator. Earlier doctrine may evolve, but a previous prophet, though superseded, is not "wrong." The idea of continuity is stressed in interpreting doctrine. Accordingly, when President Wilford Woodruff announced the official end of polygamy on October 6, 1890, he did not teach that Joseph Smith's D&C 132, the revelation on polygamy, was an error or that it was no longer regarded as doctrine. Woodruff's proclamation simply said: "We are not teaching polygamy or plural marriage, nor permitting any person to enter into its practice, and I deny that either forty or any other number of plural marriages [as reported since the past June] have during that period been solemnized in our Temples or in any other place in the Territory." The text was added to the Doctrine and Covenants as an "official declaration."

As one might expect of any change to such a deep-seated principle, the declaration did not immediately stick. For more than a decade some leaders in the Mormon hierarchy quietly continued to add polygamous wives. For instance, Abraham Owen Woodruff, son of the church president who issued the declaration, became an apostle in 1897 and took a second wife in 1901. The historian D. Michael Quinn lists about ten polygamous marriages that received the private approval of Joseph F. Smith, nephew of the founding prophet, who became church president in 1901. Smith was simultaneously assuring the apostles and the public that new polygamous marriages were not being authorized. He issued the "Second Manifesto" declaration against polygamy in 1904 but personally authorized plural marriages in 1906 and 1907.

Writes Quinn, "The murkiness and ambiguities of these authorized polygamous marriages after 1890 (and especially after 1904) guaranteed the growth of a polygamous underground that continues today in opposition to church policy." Because of the church's sensitivity to the issue of post-Manifesto polygamy, Quinn, at the time a tenured Brigham Young University history professor, was denied access to related archival materials in the First Presidency vault in 1982. In a 1981 speech, Quinn said, "One of the most obvious demonstrations [of "faith-promoting" church history that conceals the controversies and difficulties of the Mormon past] is the continued spread of unauthorized polygamy among Latter-day Saints during the last seventy-five years, despite efforts of church leaders to stop it. Essential to this church campaign is the official historical argument that there were no plural marriages authorized by the church or First Presidency after the 1890 Manifesto. This official position adds that whatever plural marriages occurred between 1890 and the so-called 'Second Manifesto' of April 1904 were the sole responsibility of two renegade apostles, John W. Taylor and Matthias F. Cowley."

Quinn states that more than 250 polygamous marriages took place between 1890 and 1904 with authorization from the First Presidency. For Quinn, the denial of this "in LDS church statements and histories has actually given credibility to Fundamentalists in their promotion of new plural marriages after 1904 in defiance of the First Presidency." Faced with research by Quinn and other historians in recent years, the *Encyclopedia of Mormonism* of 1992 mentions in passing that unofficially there were some post-Manifesto marriages, but it avoids mentioning that any post-Manifesto marriages were authorized by members of the First Presidency.

To the present day polygamy claims validation from a secret 1886 revelation supposedly delivered by President John Taylor while he was living underground. And if Mormon Fundamentalists dissemble, they have plenty of precedent in the church's nineteenth-century casuistry. Writes Hardy, "Mormon Fundamentalism is at least partially a consequence of such tactics." These Fundamentalists "defend the propriety of reticence and false denial when dealing with the things of God, especially plural marriage. The use of codes and ciphers when threatened by hostile laws is approved." Dorothy Allred Solomon, who was raised in a prominent contemporary Fundamentalist home, said the resort to distortion was called "Mormon logic." She remembers her father justifying such evasions with the familiar saying, "We must sometimes disobey a lesser law to keep a higher one."

Polygamy, of course, is still illegal. The most infamous twentieth-century law enforcement incident was the 1953 raid on a polygamous community at Short Creek, Arizona. The raid, following smaller raids in 1935 and 1944, was covered by 25 cars full of reporters and photographers. The nation was treated to pictures of 263 children torn from their mothers and placed in foster care. Fathers went to prison; mothers were pressured to sign antipolygamy statements. The LDS-owned *Deseret News* applauded the action. Within two years all the families had been reunited and were still committed to living "the principle" that had once been central to Mormonism. No one has since then had the stomach to mount another major raid. The late twentieth century has had a very different sexual culture: live and let live.

But polygamy continues to break into the news every now and then. Some of the polygamous sects have a tendency to schism and violence. J. Gordon Melton's *Encyclopedia of American Religions* lists a dozen polygamous denominations, the largest being the United Order of Colorado City, Arizona. By Melton's count, at least seventeen polygamous leaders were murdered in the 1970s, mostly members of the LeBaron clan or its rivals. Additional lurid murder cases were splashed into the headlines in the 1980s and later, regarding the Singer-Swapp clan, the LeBarons, and others—the stuff of pulp fiction.

Ours is a time of "alternative lifestyles." On December 11, 1997, the "Living Arts" section of the *New York Times* ran a glamorous spread, two pages including color photos, of wealthy plural marriage family houses, titled "A House, 10 Wives: Polygamy in Suburbia." The piece treated the subculture affectionately, as a mildly odd variant of an ever-expanding American normalcy, ignoring the soaring welfare caseload that is a more typical symptom of modern-day polygamy.

But at century's end another twist entered the polygamous picture: wife and child abuse, including charges of pedophilia and incest. In July of 1998 polygamy again made national headlines when a sixteen-year-old plural wife ran away from the Kingston clan and pressed charges against her uncle and father. In June 1999 the uncle was convicted of incest; the father who allegedly performed the ceremony making her a fifteenth wife had earlier pled no contest to a charge of third-degree felony child abuse. Through a support group of former plural wives called Tapestry of Polygamy, stories began to surface about arranged marriages and virtual imprisonment. It's part of a past that Utah would like to forget.

Fourteen months after the warm lifestyle story, the *New York Times Magazine* ran a quite different piece, "The Persistence of Polygamy," by Timothy Egan, telling of dusty intermountain towns and young women with limited options. "For the women who brought polygamy out of Utah's closet, the 2002 Olympics remain the trump card," predicts Egan. "More than 10,000 visiting journalists will be deluged with information about the world's greatest snow, the glowing city in the Wasatch, the spotless facilities. And then, when they grow tired of the luge and the Tabernacle Choir stories, the press will have no trouble finding the women of Tapestry, who will tell them about Utah's other heritage."

There are many deeply loyal Mormons, descendants of polygamists, who wish the church would grow beyond its embarrassment about the polygamist past and come to terms with its history. Looking pained during a private discussion of the subject, one of Brigham Young University's most distinguished faculty members said, "I wish they would deal more honestly and openly with the polygamy which is part of our heritage. They always react with embarrassment, almost denial. I am the descendant of a second wife. Except for polygamy I wouldn't be here—or my line is illegitimate."

Tourists visiting Temple Square can see a beautifully photographed film, *Legacy,* which tells the story of Mormon persecutions and the epic trek to Utah. The central character is a composite figure based in large part on the journal of Mary Elizabeth Rollins Lightner. The movie gives not the slightest hint that Lightner was a polyandrous wife of Joseph Smith. In fact, there is no mention at all of polygamy in *Legacy.*

CHAPTER 5
REDEFINING THE KINGDOM OF GOD

In 1887 THE UNITED STATES CARRIED OUT AN ASTONISHING ACT. A NATION founded upon the principle of religious freedom, which had enshrined that principle in its Constitution's Bill of Rights, passed a law that dissolved a church. The denomination involved, the LDS Church, was, as the historian Martin Marty has written, "safely describable as the most despised large group" of the day.

That year the Edmunds-Tucker Act added teeth to the 1862 Morrill Act, which had first raised the threat of suspending the church and limited its property holdings to $50,000. But that act was not enforced. The Edmunds Act of 1882 took direct aim at ending polygamy, and the Edmunds-Tucker Act of 1887 went far beyond authorizing "polyg hunts": it set out to destroy the church's temporal kingdom. The 1887 law provided for the dissolution of the corporation of the church under direction of the U.S. attorney general, with its property to be disposed of by the secretary of the Interior Department.

Ironically Edmunds-Tucker also abolished woman's suffrage in Utah. (Utah women received the franchise again with passage of the state's first constitution in 1895.) The territory's women had originally won the right in 1870 and were the first in the nation allowed to cast votes. According to the scholars Claudia and Richard Bushman, "the *New York Times* had suggested that granting suffrage to women, enabling them to vote out polygamy, would solve the Utah problem." In fact, it made no difference; support of LDS polygamy doctrine was certainly not limited to the men.

Early Mormonism had spawned some powerful, independent women. Martha Hughes Cannon, for example, worked her way through the church's University of Deseret setting type for an early Mormon feminist publication, the *Woman's Exponent.* She went on to graduate from the University of Michigan School of Medicine. A plural wife and mother of three, she later became the first woman state senator in the United States, and she would sniff saltily in an 1896 *San Francisco Examiner* interview that a plural wife most certainly was not enslaved by her husband. "If her husband has four wives, she has three weeks of freedom every month." A Democrat, she had just defeated her Republican husband and other candidates for a seat in the first Utah state senate.

In the crises developing a decade before statehood, church authorities had seen the escheat coming. Earlier still, Brigham Young had sometimes secretly arranged for leaders to hold church properties to avoid the threat of government confiscation. Now President John Taylor worked to circumvent Edmunds-Tucker, passing title of properties to members who would hold them as trustees for the church, to specially created separate nonprofit organizations, or to ward and stake organizations, and selling or transferring other holdings to individuals or associations on the understanding that they would retain them for later church use.

President Taylor had been severely wounded by the mob that murdered the prophet Joseph Smith at Carthage Jail in 1844, and to his dying breath Taylor, living in hiding as an outlaw, held fast to the spiritual necessity of the founder's polygamous ideal in the face of persecution. The Edmunds-Tucker law went into effect the day after Taylor was placed in his grave in 1887. A court receiver was appointed, and intense legal maneuvering followed as a legal challenge was fought to the Supreme Court. In *Church of Jesus Christ of Latter-day Saints v. the United States,* the high court passed down a 5–4 decision on May 19, 1890, in support of the government action. The majority opinion stated: "Congress had before it—a contumacious organization, wielding by its resources an immense power in the Territory of Utah, and employing those resources and that power in constantly attempting to oppose, thwart and subvert the legislation of Congress and the will of the government of the United States."

The Edmunds and Edmunds-Tucker Acts had disenfranchised all polygamists. In addition, the territorial government of Idaho passed a law requiring voters to take an antipolygamy oath: they had to swear that they did not belong to any organization that believed in or taught the principles of polygamy. The *Davis v. Beason* case from Idaho, also decided by the Supreme Court in 1890, upheld that law despite LDS arguments grounded in the First Amendment's clause guaranteeing the "free exercise" of religion. The Court called polygamy and bigamy "crimes by the laws of the civilized and Christian countries." The polygamy cases (the two 1890 rulings plus the 1879 *Reynolds* decision) were the Supreme Court's first limitation on religious liberty and thus affected the legal prerogatives of all denominations.

Polygamy was the catalyst for change in the LDS Church, and the issue that rallied the country, but for some the deeper issue was political. Senator Frederick T. Dubois of Idaho wrote in his autobiography, "Those of us who understand the situation were not nearly so much opposed to polygamy as we were to the political domination of the Church. We realized, however, that we could not make those who did not come actually in contact with it, understand what this political domination meant. We made use of polygamy."

The United States could not accept a quasi-independent nation-state in its midst, an independent theocratic kingdom, or a secular government on paper behind which stood a shadow church government that determined its laws and lawmakers, or a court system in which religious authority decided secular disputes. Gentiles in Utah were outsiders, and if they were vigorously critical, they were suspect. "LDS publications applauded physical attacks on anti-Mormons until 1889, the year the First Presidency also publicly abandoned its ideals of a political theocracy," writes D. Michael Quinn.

The key word, perhaps, is "publicly" abandoned. The church wanted statehood in large part because Utah would essentially run its own affairs as a state, whereas the federal government and its appointees had considerable latitude in running a territory. Gentiles in the Intermountain West and across the country fought statehood, fearing that with a clear Mormon majority obediently following the church's direction, the church would control the secular affairs of Utah as well as those of nearby areas with a significant LDS population. Mormons, after all, had followed the commands of Joseph Smith and then Brigham Young in politics as well as belief, and it was not unreasonable to assume they would continue to obey their leaders' dictates.

But if the jails were full of polygamists, LDS leaders were imprisoned or underground, and the church was threatened with loss of its property, how long could the church withstand the pressure? With Edmunds-Tucker, the LDS Church had been brought to its knees. Even many non-Mormons felt that some of the act's punishments were unfair. In his private journal, Taylor's successor, President Wilford Woodruff, wrote, "I am under the necessity of acting for the temporal salvation of the church." A year and a half after he assumed office Woodruff announced an "official declaration" accepting obedience to federal law and announcing the end of the polygamy practice. This declaration of September 25, 1890, soon known as the "Manifesto," was unanimously "sustained" by General Conference vote on October 6, but the legal wrangling over it was to continue for years.

Historian Klaus J. Hansen maintains that "the Manifesto clearly was primarily a tactical maneuver to save not only the church but if possible the political kingdom as well." The church was in the process of giving up not only polygamy but economic and political separatism, and in return it was poised to swim toward the American mainstream. Signaling the shifting political ground, Woodruff, the church's fourth president, was the first to refrain from having himself anointed theocratic "King over Israel on the Earth." In 1894 Utah began to form a state government, and statehood arrived at last in 1896.

Between 1894 and 1896 the church received its properties back, or what was left of them after the dispersal. Obviously church finances had taken a severe beating, worsened by the prolonged national depression of the 1890s. Tithing income from members, of which only one-third had been paid in cash rather than goods, had been worth about $500,000 annually through the 1880s but dropped by more than one-third in 1890. At the same time the church had high legal expenses and was also trying to assist the families whose heads were imprisoned; about 1,300 were serving sentences ranging from several months to several years. An additional complication had been the necessity of running the church from the underground, using trusted nonpolygamists as go-betweens.

During the years of receivership Temple Square was leased by the church from the federal government at a token $1 a month. The great Salt Lake Temple, forty years in preparation, held an open house for non-Mormons on April 5, 1893, and was dedicated for Mormon use the next day. It served as a great symbol of unity and triumph for an institution undergoing a difficult period of transition. At the same time the national organization was borrowing funds from regional and local divisions, such as stakes, to stay operational. By 1898 it had $3.36 million in obligations, much of that owed to bankers outside of Utah. Lorenzo Snow, who succeeded to the church presidency in 1898, resolved to put the church on a firm financial footing. When the prophet's nephew Joseph F. Smith became church president in 1901, he continued Snow's policies by reemphasizing the importance of the tithe and moving toward cash rather than in-kind contributions, issuing $1 million in bonds to pay indebtedness, and divesting the church of some unprofitable business ventures.

Rudger Judd Clawson, the first polygamist convicted and imprisoned by the federal government, was ordained an apostle in 1898 and served as the church's accountant over this period. Clawson had originally earned his living as a bookkeeper for his brother's wholesale dry goods business. While serving his prison sentence he earned money by teaching bookkeeping classes to fellow inmates at $.25 a lesson or sixty lessons for $15, earning $500 toward the support of his own family. (He considered this a bargain: he had paid $45 for the same course.)

Clawson reported to President Snow: "Deducting the entire active assets of the Church at that time . . . left a balance of indebtedness of $1,222,475.89. . . . It would have been a clear case of bankruptcy but in the providences of the Lord, the possible did not happen." Stake presidents and bishops were called to Salt Lake City for an April 1899 conference with one topic on the agenda: tithing. It was estimated that in 1890 only 17.2

percent of members were tithe-payers. President Snow traveled around preaching and exhorting members to tithe, and by 1901 the number had jumped to nearly 30 percent. The early years of the twentieth century were prosperous, and with the increased tithing receipts, which now were arriving mostly as cash, the divestiture of some church business ventures, and conservative fiscal policies, the church had paid off every dollar of its indebtedness by 1905. Tithing had for some time been officially linked to temple recommends, the required permission in order to participate in sacred temple activities; in 1910, under President Joseph F. Smith, that tithing requirement began to be strictly enforced.

The economy of the region, meanwhile, was changing significantly. The railroad, as expected, brought in non-Mormon influences, commercial and otherwise, and firmly tied the Great Basin economy to the nation at large. Edmunds-Tucker had dissolved the Perpetual Emigrating Company and seized its assets, but emigration had already slowed to a trickle. Economic conditions in England and Scandinavia had improved relative to Utah, and church authorities began to encourage Saints to build the Lord's Zion wherever they already lived rather than to gather in the Intermountain West. Discouragement of foreign immigration began in the 1890s and became official policy with a 1907 First Presidency pronouncement, which was reiterated in 1921 and again in 1929. There was also some out-migration within the United States among Saints seeking economic opportunity beyond the Great Basin.

Mining, largely in non-Mormon hands, increased in economic significance, as did other non-Mormon commercial interests. Church authorities lifted their boycott against Gentile businesses in 1882; the communal cooperative movement had largely died or been turned over to private interests. An increasing number of enterprises were independently owned and operated for profit by private Mormon members, ordinary businesses not directly controlled by the church.

The church's principal divestitures, begun by Snow and continued by Smith, included the sale of the Deseret Telegraph System to Western Union; the Utah Sugar Company (although the church retained the majority stock interest); Utah Light and Railway Company (later part of the Utah Power and Light Company); the Saltair resort and recreational companies; and various mining properties, including iron and coal claims near Cedar City. The church retained some basic activities in hydroelectric power, transportation, and beet sugar manufacturing, as well as some mining ventures. Certainly the church continued as an economic influence in the Intermountain West through the twentieth century and eventually became an institution of quite considerable wealth. But the balance between sacred and secular had permanently shifted by the turn of the century. As Leonard Arrington puts it in *Great Basin Kingdom:*

> With these sales, and with the abolition of tithing in kind in 1908, the self-sufficient Kingdom may be said to have been brought to an end. A more acceptable adjustment between spiritual and secular interests was attained. And with this adjustment, the church no longer offered a geographic and institutional alternative to Babylon. Faith became increasingly separated from community policy, and religion from society. Individualism, speculation, and inequality— once thought to be characteristics of Babylon—were woven into the fabric of Mormon life.

No longer an economically self-sufficient kingdom or a controlling regional monopoly, the church began to reinvest in businesses after 1907 once it was out of debt. It regained control of the Provo Woolen Mills, the Utah-Idaho Sugar Company, and the Beneficial Life Insurance Company, constructed the elegant Hotel Utah in downtown Salt Lake City, reacquired ZCMI stock, and maintained control of Zion's Savings Bank & Trust Company, the *Deseret News* newspaper and bookstore, and the Salt Lake Theater, as well as stock in some other companies. The times were prosperous, and it seemed that a conservative investment policy could help ensure church income in leaner times.

After President Woodruff's Manifesto, the church also prepared for the adjustment to secular politics. In 1891 the church dissolved the People's Party, the Mormon vehicle that had dominated Utah politics for two decades. Members were told to choose between the national Republican and Democratic Parties. Initially people felt more affinity for the Democrats, since the Republicans had launched the polygamy wars and had more frequently placed obstacles in Utah's road to statehood. Grover Cleveland, a Democrat, had signed the 1896 act that gave Utah statehood. But President Joseph F. Smith was a Republican, as was Utah's first powerful U.S. senator, Reed Smoot. Through the twentieth century Mormons increasingly have felt more at home with the Republicans' business-oriented economic policy, resistance to centralized federal government, and conservative social philosophy. Though typically Republican, LDS voting patterns were no longer simplistically monolithic, and the church's lobbying was limited largely to issues on which it felt its religious interests were directly at stake.

But there were some early bumps in the political road. In the early years, predictably, the church wanted a say in the choice of men who would be sent to Washington. In June 1895 the Democrats nominated B. H. Roberts, a third-echelon General Authority as a member of the First Council of the Seventy, to be the first Utah congressman, and Moses Thatcher, one of the Twelve Apostles, for U.S. senator. At the October General Conference Joseph F. Smith, then the second counselor in the First Presidency, openly rebuked his two lesser colleagues for not having cleared their candidacies in advance with the church. Both men lost the November election five weeks later.

The following February the First Presidency issued a "political manifesto" requiring General Authorities to sign a statement that they would seek church approval first before seeking public office. Both Roberts and Thatcher refused to sign and were suspended from ecclesiastical office. Roberts, believing such a requirement was a basic infringement of his civil rights, capitulated just hours before a deadline of March 24, 1896, signed the manifesto, wrote a letter of apology to the First Presidency, and was reinstated. Thatcher was more stubborn: he refused to sign, was expelled from the Quorum of the Twelve, and barely evaded excommunication.

Roberts, probably the most interesting intellectual ever to achieve appointment as a General Authority, ran for the U.S. House of Representatives again two years later, this time with church clearance, and won with a 7,000-vote margin. But he never was allowed to take his seat in the House. A polygamist who openly continued to cohabit with three wives, one of them possibly married after the Manifesto, Roberts aroused anti-Mormon, antipolygamist emotions to a new fever pitch around the country. Opposition groups ranged from the Protestant Ministerial Alliance of Utah to the League for Social Service.

William Randolph Hearst's *New York Evening Journal* conducted an effective anti-Roberts crusade, including a serial publication of Arthur Conan Doyle's first Sherlock Holmes mystery, *A Study in Scarlet,* retitled *Mormons: The Curse of Utah.* The paper also ran an extensive series of non-fiction articles filled with research by the flamboyant Charles Mostyn Owen. Underlying the furor was the suspicion that church authorities were hiding new, post-Manifesto marriages. In fact they were, as shown by the well-documented research of recent historians, including B. Carmon Hardy and D. Michael Quinn.

A petition that claimed to have seven million signatures protesting the seating of Roberts was presented to the speaker of the House—twenty-eight scrolls wrapped in an American flag (and probably including some duplicate signatures as well as the signatures of children). When a vote was taken after hearings, Roberts lost 268–50. A monogamous Mormon Democrat, William H. King, later took his seat. Roberts continued to speak out and over the years frequently took Democratic stands not popular with Mormon leadership.

The next case splashed in national headlines was that of Reed Smoot, a member of the Quorum of the Twelve Apostles, who was elected to the U.S. Senate in 1903. Clergy have occasionally won seats on Capitol Hill, but to this day Smoot is the only person to serve simultaneously in the Congress and as a high governing authority of a major religious body. As with Roberts, organized opposition spread from the Salt Lake Ministerial Association and other non-Mormon Utahns across the country, with charges that Mormons, possibly including Smoot himself, were still practicing polygamy. The claim was true for Mormonism, but false for Smoot. Hearings dragged on until 1907, with more than 3,000 pages of testimony, though Smoot was allowed to occupy his seat throughout those years.

The church itself was on national public trial along with Reed Smoot. The Manifesto itself had said nothing about whether cohabitation with pre-Manifesto wives would continue. Five days after publishing the declaration, Woodruff had told his apostles, "This Manifesto only refers to future marriages, and does not affect past conditions. I did not, could not and would not promise that you would desert your wives and children. This you cannot do in honor." Whatever the law provided, many Americans felt that was reasonable, and pre-1890 polygamists were rarely prosecuted.

In March of 1904 Church President Joseph F. Smith was called to testify. He was an open polygamist with six pre-Manifesto wives (one divorce) and an eventual total of forty-eight children, thirteen of them post-Manifesto. He assumed the tacit amnesty toward pre-Manifesto commitments, though in 1906 he was to be convicted of unlawful cohabitation and fined $300.

Before Congress Smith was candid about his own continuing cohabitation but flatly denied all new post-Manifesto marriages by the church: "I know of no marriages occurring after the final decision of the Supreme Court of the United States on that question . . . and from that time till today there has never been, to my knowledge, a plural marriage performed in accordance with the understanding, instruction, connivance, counsel, or permission of the presiding authorities of the church, or of the church, in any shape, or form."

Asked directly if he had personally performed or known of post-Manifesto plural marriages, Smith responded, "I never have." Pressed by the chairman about reports of such LDS marriages being conducted in Mexico, Smith responded, "Nowhere on earth, sir." The chairman repeated, "Do you know of any such?" Smith replied again, "No, sir; I do not."

Enough was known about post-Manifesto plural marriages that Smith's testimony and the evasiveness, contradictions, and inconsistencies of other church leaders' appearances before the Senate committee left many Mormons queasy, Smoot discouraged, and non-Mormons more convinced than ever that the dissembling of LDS leaders amounted to outright deceit. According to Hardy, Apostle John Henry Smith's memory losses on the stand were unusually impressive, and "Apostle Marriner W. Merrill, who took a plural wife in 1901, risked charges of perjury by submitting an affidavit in which he swore that he had taken no additional wives since the Manifesto."

Some high church authorities suspected of post-Manifesto polygamy refused to respond to Senate requests to appear. One tired investigator, obviously a cynical Washington realist, finally declared he would prefer a "polygamist who doesn't polyg" over all the "monogamists who don't monog." The Senate committee voted seven to five against seating Smoot. When the issue reached the full Senate floor for debate, Senator James H. Berry of Arkansas dragged in the Mountain Meadows Massacre as an argument against seating Smoot. Smoot, so the implication ran, was a product of and responsible for an organization capable of horrors such as that. To Berry it mattered not at all that the tragedy had occurred four years before Smoot was born.

But the Utahn had some important non-Mormon supporters, including President Theodore Roosevelt, who let it be known that he thought Smoot should retain his seat. In the end the Senate could not muster a two-thirds majority vote to depose him, and Smoot went on to a thirty-year Senate career, rising to become the influential chairman of the Senate Finance Committee.

Entering the twentieth century, the church obviously wielded considerable political influence on its own turf, among its own people. But it was no longer a unified force across the board as its people struck out on their own in the secular political world and the give-and-take, locally and nationally, of political issues worked out in the real world of Babylon.

The polygamy issue that trailed Mormons into the twentieth century— and still does, owing to the continuing activities of the schismatic Mormon Fundamentalists—did not, could not, disappear instantly with Woodruff's 1890 Manifesto. Mormon polygamy had been neither an alternative lifestyle nor a countercultural statement; it had been a commitment to the highest divinely revealed ideal. Those practicing the ideal were Mormonism's elite. A church cannot change a central paradigm overnight. With the post-Manifesto writings of the theologically influential apostle James E. Talmage and others, "celestial marriage" has been redefined to mean "eternal marriage" and is completely divorced from plural marriage.

Continuing revelation is a central Mormon belief. The president of the church is sustained as its prophet, seer, and revelator. Some historians believe that Joseph Smith Jr.'s sure sense of his own religious authority, and his undeniable charisma, were key factors in the new church's growth. People in a rootless, rapidly changing culture yearn for the security of an identity, of belonging to a cohesive community. The Mormon Church proclaimed certainty, the sure keys to eternal truth, and for decades polygamy had been one of those keys.

Each church president since Smith has also been a prophet whose revelations are authoritative. Most of the revelations are not sustained by the church General Conference to enter the "Standard Works" that carry permanent scriptural status along with the Bible, that is, the Book of Mormon, Doctrine and Covenants, and the Pearl of Great Price. Though Mormon doctrine has evolved over the years and the prophets are never officially overruled or declared wrong, the church's current president and prophet, Gordon B. Hinckley, may have come close to doing just that in a September 8, 1998, interview on the *Larry King Live* television show. Despite the authority of both D&C 132 and the 1890 Manifesto in the Mormon scriptures, when asked about polygamy, Hinckley responded, "I think that it is not doctrinal."

But was Woodruff's declaration considered a revelation in 1890? There was nothing in the document itself to indicate its level of inspiration, no first-person voice of the Lord. It did not proclaim any doctrine, nor did it disavow previous doctrine. It simply stated that the practice was suspended under the circumstances. Significantly, the LDS leadership did not propose Woodruff's 1890 Manifesto as a scriptural addition to Doctrine and Covenants until 1908, well after that omission had been repeatedly remarked on at the Smoot hearings and by journalists writing hostile magazine and newspaper articles. The critics were well aware that, at the same time, D&C 132, the revelation authorizing polygamy, remained a part of Mormon scriptures (and still is).

The first three of the Manifesto's five short paragraphs were a denial of newspaper stories reporting on the Utah Commission's forthcoming annual report. Woodruff, aware that a negative commission report could hamper the progress toward statehood, took pains to refute the press dispatches claiming there had been forty or so new plural marriages in the preceding months. The concluding two paragraphs asserted that "nothing in my teachings to the Church or in those of my associates, during the time specified . . . can be reasonably construed to inculcate or encourage polygamy," and so church members should follow his example in submitting to the law.

He concluded, "I now publicly declare that my advice to the Latter-day Saints is to refrain from contracting any marriage forbidden by the law of the land."

Among the apostles Woodruff consulted about the Manifesto before releasing it to the press were Franklin D. Richards and Marriner W. Merrill. During the time span discussed in the declaration, which denied that new plural marriages had taken place, Richards had performed ten of these ceremonies, and Merrill himself had taken a new plural wife.

The Manifesto and post-Manifesto activities left a large credibility gap noticed by non-Mormons as well as Mormons. Top church authorities themselves were divided. A number of apostles took post-Manifesto wives, four of them during Lorenzo Snow's brief presidency alone (1898–1901). In the first three years of his presidency Joseph F. Smith helped plan the continuation of plural marriage, sending apostles to Canada and Mexico to establish avenues for plural sealings to be performed in those countries and advising apostles on how to duck subpoenas to testify in the Smoot hearings.

Eventually the uproar became so great that John W. Taylor (son of the late church president), who was Smith's Canadian emissary, and Matthias Cowley, sent to oversee plural marriages in Mexico, were made scapegoats and resigned from the Quorum of the Twelve Apostles in 1905. In 1911 Cowley was stripped of the right to exercise his priesthood privileges, and Taylor was excommunicated. Cowley's full membership was restored in 1936 shortly before he died, and Taylor's posthumously in 1965.

According to Quinn, the last post-Manifesto plural marriages known to and personally authorized by Joseph F. Smith took place in 1906 and 1907. In October 1907, not long after Smoot's seat was validated by vote of the Senate, Anthony W. Ivins, who had conducted dozens of post-Manifesto plural marriages in Mexico, was sustained as apostle. Altogether, according to Hardy's count, 262 documented plural marriages involving 220 LDS men were solemnized and sealed between October 1890 and December 1910. The last child born of these unions arrived in 1931. Joseph F. Smith served as president of the church until 1918 and was followed by the last polygamous president, Heber J. Grant, who died in 1945. Grant's three marriages were pre-Manifesto; his first and third wives died in 1893 and 1908; he continued living with his second wife, Hulda, who died in 1951. Grant pursued a fervid antipolygamous policy during his years as president.

Beyond the tight world of the General Authorities, Mormons and non-Mormons in Utah had problems reconciling contradictory public statements, denials, and observable facts, the latter including babies. The Gentile press, including the *Salt Lake Tribune,* and the church press, including the *Deseret News,* spilled rivers of ink in response to the issue, and the ink spilled across the print media nationwide.

From 1909 to 1911 the *Tribune* ran 119 articles on post-Manifesto polygamy, and the articles named (mostly accurate) names. As Hardy puts it, "Much of the *Salt Lake Tribune's* ferocity in those years was fueled by disgust that Mormon leaders would, while claiming their church to be the Lord's special vessel of truth, so frequently corrupt it."

If secrecy and false denials helped fuel the Mormon Fundamentalist movement, it also fed a negative media image. Aware of continuing plural marriages in the Mormon leadership, Protestant ministers in Utah rallied anti-Mormon support across the nation. Some of the attacks were largely accurate. In *McClure's* magazine, Burton Hendrick described the use of Mexico and Canada for plural marriage ceremonies. Some of the articles were lurid and sensationalist. Sarah Comstock told her readers in *Collier's* that in southern Utah the practice of polygamy was so widespread that letters were addressed "Brother L— and wives." A piece by Alfred Henry Lewis for *Cosmopolitan* suggested that Mormons imported European female converts to become white polygamous slaves. When word of that reached Europe, Mormon missionaries faced some nasty mob action.

Post-Manifesto Mormons were in a situation analogous to that in Nauvoo. Polygamy was again secret, denied in public, and causing division inside the church itself. The high authorities, as well as the rank and file, included members who were uncomfortable with contorted evasions of truth. But what Hardy calls "pretzled language" became common public discourse on the subject of plural marriage. Matthias Cowley could say in one breath, "I am not dishonest and not a liar and have always been true to the work and to the brethren," and in the next breath, "We have always been taught that when the brethren were in a tight place that it would not be amiss to lie to help them out."

Such deceit in the name of a higher perceived good was not invented by Mormons. Mental reservation in lying for a higher cause is probably as old as human history, but a heavy price is paid for it in terms of credibility. And Mormon tradition itself is contradictory on that point. D. Michael Quinn uses the term "theocratic ethics" for the concept that truth as ordinarily conceived has a lower priority than obedience. He sees Joseph Smith Jr.'s first written statement of this in his fruitless letter courting Nancy Rigdon: "That which is wrong under one circumstance, may be, and often is, right under another. . . . Whatever God requires is right, no matter what it is, although we may not see the reason thereof till long after the events transpire. . . . But in obedience there is joy and peace unspotted." On the other hand, in 1990 Gordon B. Hinckley, then first counselor in the First Presidency, wrote a piece entitled "We Believe in Being Honest" for the church's *Ensign* magazine, warning that when one uses falsehood and deception even in a worthy cause, it can spread "like a disease that is endemic."

The credibility problem and the reality of post-Manifesto polygamous activities fueled anti-Mormon flames up to World War I. Mormons were as concerned about public relations then as they are now. The *Improvement Era,* precursor to the *Ensign,* rejoiced in 1904 when a major eastern trade publisher, G. P. Putnam & Sons, issued *Scientific Aspects of Mormonism* by N. L. Nelson, a Brigham Young University professor. Church authorities were less happy with the negative pieces published in 1910 and 1911 in such major national magazines as *Pearson* and *Everybody's Magazine.* Pulp fiction had a heyday featuring sensationalized stock Mormon characters. From 1910 to 1915, however, *Americana,* which had printed earlier critical material on Mormonism, printed a series on church history by B. H. Roberts that was published later by the church as its six-volume *Comprehensive History of the Church.*

Tours of the Mormon Tabernacle Choir, starting with its appearance at the 1893 Chicago World's Fair, became a positive public relations vehicle for the church. In 1911 the choir toured the country, singing at Madison Square Garden in New York for ten days, performing concerts in twenty-five cities, and singing at the White House at the invitation of President and Mrs. William Howard Taft.

Back in Salt Lake City the first tourist kiosk opened on Temple Square in 1902; an octagonal building twenty feet across, it provided volunteer-guided tours and dispensed tracts and pamphlets. That first year about 150,000 non-Mormon tourists visited Temple Square to admire the great temple, visit the Tabernacle, and, perhaps, hear its famous choir and organ. The next year a larger tourist bureau was built; by 1906 free organ recitals in the Tabernacle had become a daily summer feature. The number of visitors grew each year; today it is in the millions.

By the time World War I approached, Mormons had more than tiptoed into Babylon, and Babylon had come to them. Within a decade of statehood, federal agencies operating in Utah included the Army and its Corps of Engineers, the Soil Conservation Service, the Bureau of Land Management, the Forest Service, the National Park Service, the Geological Survey, the Reclamation Service, the Fish Commission, the Biological Survey, the Bureau of Agricultural Engineering, and the Smithsonian Institution. The federal government began to finance and construct vast irrigation projects beyond the capacity of the church's resources. All this was in addition to private Gentile economic activities.

After statehood the patriotism of Utahns was so enthusiastic that Mormons were regarded as model Americans by the time World War I arrived. By then, authorized, new post-Manifesto marriages really were no longer being performed, and active press antagonism had faded. Mormon volunteers had participated in the Spanish-American War, and in World War I Mormons fulfilled more than their quota for enlistments, with over 24,000 men in uniform, of whom 544 died. Mormons also oversubscribed their goal in Liberty Bond sales. Gradually, except in cheap fiction, the polygamous past was being forgotten.

As Mormons blurred into the multicultural American landscape, their kingdom paradigm shifted. In the nineteenth century the claims had been territorial, prescribing a geographic gathering to Zion. The Mormons had never been able to balance those territorial claims for the kingdom of God against the American secular society with its church-state separation. The problem, writes Thomas O'Dea, was that "the Mormons never worked out consistently the political implications of their religious philosophy." The separatism of Smith's original nineteenth-century Mormonism, as in the O'Dea analysis, went beyond theocratic church government. It placed all areas of human activity within church control, under the all-encompassing authority of ecclesiastical leadership.

Joseph Smith's scriptures had taught that the U.S. Constitution is divinely inspired ("And for this purpose have I established the Constitution of this land, by the hands of wise men whom I raised up unto this very purpose" [D&C 101:80]). His kingdom of God claimed America for Zion, but Smith and Brigham Young never provided for the ambiguities and conflicts inherent in a theocratic kingdom that had to function somehow under a democratic umbrella.

Another major shift during this period was the waning of latter-day millennialism. Smith's predictions had inspired Second Coming expectations among the Saints around 1890. The LDS scriptures also teach that the final judgment and salvation will come in the 7,000th year of earth's "continuance, or its temporal existence" (D&C 77:6, 12). And Smith had told an 1843 General Conference that "there are those of the rising generation who shall not taste death till Christ comes."

More recently, that logically led Apostle Bruce R. McConkie to figure in the 1979 edition of his influential *Mormon Doctrine* that the Second Coming of Christ "is not far distant." But the millennial hope is muted among most of today's Mormons and no longer tied to an expectation of the Lord's return by a particular time. Former experiences like tongues-speaking are explained away and visions have become less frequent. The kingdom of God is the church, and before the Lord does return there will be chaos on earth and all earthly kingdoms will disintegrate. Then the church will be there, ready to provide order amid chaos. The survivalism in Mormon culture today—food storage and emergency kits—reflects the continued smoldering of some of the millennial embers.

Asked about this aspect of the faith, President Hinckley explains: "We've always been a practical people dealing with the issues of life. We've said that a religion that won't help people in this life won't do much for them in the life that comes. We believe that. And we don't spend a lot of time talking about or dreaming about the millennium to come. We hope we're preparing for it. We hope we'll be prepared when it comes. We don't know when it will happen. We're not spending a lot of time on it. We're doing today's job in the best way we know how to do it."

Still, millennial fascination survives into the twenty-first century, as evidenced by BYU professor Daniel C. Peterson's 1998 book *The Last Days*, with commentary on 550 end times teachings of the General Authorities. And devoutly Mormon Columbia University historian Richard Bushman remarked that Hinckley plays down the theme precisely because it is relevant, "not because it's dying. If the President were to blink an eye toward Jackson County, Missouri, people would flow there. The belief is still potent, but it's latent. That's still our view of history. All that nineteenth-century stuff is still in our culture. The church could, in a flash, constitute a complete society."

During the pre-statehood years in Utah, the Mormons' identity as a people specially set apart was seasoned through shared beliefs and a sense of having lived through sacred history. But as the twentieth century progressed, the kingdom of God was no longer a geographic enclave, a theocratic political kingdom, or a nation-state within a nation. And at the dawn of the twenty-first century the kingdom increasingly is Mormonism as it exists in the diaspora outside the United States. Mormons are not just in Utah; they and their temples are everywhere. The kingdom is a church, a denomination with a very distinctive history, culture, and theology, but a denomination like any other, accepting the life of a normal religious group functioning within the ordinary boundaries of the secular world.

CHAPTER 6

ALMOST MAINSTREAM

ONCE ISOLATED IN THEIR INTERMOUNTAIN GHETTO AND DESPISED BY THE broader American society, the Latter-day Saints by the mid-1970s were becoming established as an accepted element in American life. Ezra Taft Benson had served in the Eisenhower cabinet as Secretary of Agriculture, a Smoot-like apostle-cum-politician. The 1974 dedication of the ostentatious 160,000-square-foot temple outside Washington, D.C., provided visible evidence of the Mormons' eastward march. In 1976 Donny and Marie Osmond began a three-year network TV run that enhanced the Saints' image of squeaky-clean respectability. The Mormon Tabernacle Choir was as American as, well, the Mormon Tabernacle Choir. And the church membership was steadily expanding in the United States and around the world.

With one conspicuous exception. Blacks were not a part of the normal Latter-day kingdom. Thus, there was a revolution in the making when the warm-hearted old church president Spencer W. Kimball decided to erect a temple in São Paulo, Brazil. The São Paulo project, as the first temple to serve the surging populations south of the Rio Grande and only the fourth outside the United States and Canada, exemplified the great twentieth-century theme of Mormon missionary advance. But Kimball's move also led inexorably to an ideological change that was vital for the church's prospects in Latin America and Africa, and for its acceptability in a United

States that had recently ended a shameful history of Jim Crow laws. Kimball was to bring Mormonism into the modern world.

For well over a century the LDS prophets had taught that God did not allow a person with any black African blood to be admitted to the priesthood. Many major American institutions, churches among them, had struggled to overcome prejudice in their midst. The nation's religious denominations still tended to be largely segregated by race as a matter of choice and custom, but no other body had instituted such a sharp racial preference or placed it at the level of divine revelation. Apart from the racial offense that the priestly apartheid caused, as a practical matter it was an especially difficult tenet to apply in Brazil, a country of hopelessly complex racial admixtures. In fact, until World War II LDS proselytizing in Brazil was aimed mostly at German-speaking immigrants, who were all white. The decision to open a Brazilian temple forced the top leadership to reconsider racial theology in the light of worldwide opportunities.

The teaching imposed a severe disability on Saints of black African descent, since in the Mormon system the priesthood is everything. The first level of the priesthood is normally entered by all boys at age twelve through an LDS equivalent of the Jewish bar mitzvah, or by adult male converts shortly after baptism. Without priesthood many routine forms of church participation are beyond reach, such as distribution of the sacrament. Black men were shut out of mission assignments, an important rite of passage for aspiring LDS lads, much less leadership posts at the local, regional, national, and international levels later on. Moreover, in Mormon belief the office carries eternal consequences. Priesthood is the necessary condition for men receiving temple endowments and eternal sealings of marriage that admit its holders to the highest tier in heaven and potential godhood.

The long-embedded black priesthood prohibition was suddenly toppled with a dramatic announcement from Kimball's First Presidency dated June 8, 1978, less than five months before he was to dedicate the São Paulo temple. In 1981 the words became LDS scripture as a "declaration" included along with the antipolygamy Manifesto at the end of Doctrine and Covenants:

He [God] has heard our prayers, and by revelation has confirmed that the long-promised day has come when every faithful, worthy man in the Church may receive the holy priesthood, with power to exercise its divine authority, and enjoy with his loved ones every blessing that flows therefrom, including the blessings of the temple. Accordingly, all worthy male members of the Church may be ordained to the priesthood without regard for race or color.

The late Leonard Arrington, then the official historian for the church, heard of the announcement from his secretary. Five minutes later his son called from New York City bursting with the news. "I was in the midst of sobbing with gratitude for this answer to our prayers and could hardly speak with him. I was thrilled and electrified," Arrington recalled. Merrill Bateman, now president of Brigham Young University, well remembers the day. During several trips to Africa as a Mars candy executive he had learned of people attracted to the Latter-day gospel, but obviously the church could not promote missions in black Africa. In June 1978 Bateman, by then dean of BYU's business school, was driving in Provo, Utah, when he heard the report on his car radio. "Tears began running down my face. It was a great day. I had many, many friends in Africa, and black friends in this country."

In the 1950s Kimball had pioneered a controversial but well-meaning program to place American Indian youths with LDS families in order to evangelize them and provide them with educational opportunities. He had long struggled with the black policy and was perhaps the only General Authority in that period who would have taken the lead in ending it. Shortly after the "long-promised day," Kimball, in typically low-key fashion, told this book's coauthor Richard Ostling in an interview for *Time* magazine: "I spent a good deal of time in the temple alone, praying for guidance, and there was a gradual and general development of the whole program, in connection with the Apostles." Further complexities surrounding the historic revelation have since been filled in by various insiders.

Kimball had been mulling the policy with American black friends, and when the cornerstone was laid for the São Paulo temple, he met a prominent black Brazilian believer, Helvecio Martins. Martins had faithfully saved funds to send his son on a mission, only to learn that the lad could not serve because of his race and consequent lack of priesthood. By one account, Kimball privately advised Martins that he should prepare himself to receive the priesthood. (Martins soon did, and he would later be the first Saint of African descent to become a General Authority, serving in the Second Quorum of the Seventy from 1990 to 1995.) Around that time Kimball began a systematic personal plan of prayer and fasting, asking God for change. In the weeks leading up to the revelation Kimball faithfully went to the Salt Lake Temple each day to pray alone. Meanwhile, Kimball and his two counselors in the First Presidency discussed the issue over several weeks, then informed the Twelve Apostles about their deliberations and asked them to pray over the matter. Apostles provided Kimball with written materials giving their thoughts and background on the policy, and Kimball talked with a number of them individually. On May 30 Kimball drafted a statement about removing the barrier and showed it to his two counselors.

The pivotal day was June 1, when all of the General Authorities held a regularly scheduled meeting in the fourth-floor "upper room" of the Salt Lake Temple where the First Presidency and the Twelve confer each week. When the three-hour session was concluded, Kimball asked the first and second counselors and the apostles to remain behind. (Two apostles were absent.) The thirteen men discussed the priesthood problem for more than two hours. Kimball then suggested that the group form a circle to pray and asked consent to act as their collective "mouth." But as Kimball began to pray, apparently the words that came forth were not expressed as Kimball's words to God but as God's words to the church.

To those in the room, it was like another Pentecost. Apostle David B. Haight recalls, "I was there with the outpouring of the Spirit in that room, to such a degree that none of us could speak afterwards. . . . It's difficult to even explain." According to the late apostle Bruce R. McConkie, a strong exponent of the ban on blacks, Kimball "heard the voice, and we heard the same voice. All doubt and uncertainty fled. He knew the answer, and we knew the answer. . . . I was there; I heard the voice." As Apostle (now President) Gordon B. Hinckley remembers it, "No voice audible to our physical ears was heard. But the voice of the Spirit whispered into our minds and our very souls." McConkie quoted his fellow conservative, the late apostle (and later president) Ezra Taft Benson, as saying he had never experienced anything of such spiritual power during his half-century in the hierarchy. McConkie quashed rumors circulating among the Saints that God or the Prophet Joseph or an angelic messenger was personally manifest in the upper room that day. "These things did not happen."

On June 7 Kimball told his two counselors he had decided to announce the elimination of the ban and asked three apostles to draft a public statement. At the regular weekly temple meeting on June 8 the First Presidency and the Twelve reaffirmed the inspiration they had received on June 1 and agreed on the wording of the official statement. The next day all the General Authorities who were in town met to give their consent to the announcement, which was made later that day.

To non-Mormons the leadership's struggles over this question are perplexing. Why did such a policy ever exist, and why did it take so long to eliminate it, and with such difficulty? The explanation is that the teaching was entangled with the church's scriptures and the authority of its prior prophets. The Mormon situation was similar to the Catholic Church's struggle in the 1960s over another widely criticized teaching, that the natural or "rhythm method" is the only licit means of birth control. Catholic scholars were urging liberalization, and a special Vatican study panel agreed, but Pope Paul VI felt bound by precedent. In a 1968 encyclical, he famously proclaimed that the prohibition as defined by his predecessor popes still applied in the era of the Pill.

In Joseph Smith's first scripture, the 1830 Book of Mormon, skin color is a motif, though it pertains to Native Americans (Hebrew "Lamanites" in the LDS understanding) rather than blacks. The book does say that "all are alike unto God," who "denieth none that come unto him, black and white, bond and free, male and female" (II Nephi 26:33). However, passages in five of the fifteen scriptural books (I Nephi 12:22–23; II Nephi 5:21–25 and 30:6; III Nephi 2:14–16; Jacob 3:5–9; Alma 3:6–9) teach that the Lamanites' dark skin is a direct curse from God for sinfulness, or that dark peoples are shiftless and loathsome, or that white skin is desirable.

The first of the II Nephi 5 passages, for example, teaches that God caused a "cursing" to come upon the American Lamanites, accompanied by "a skin of blackness" so that they were no longer "white, and exceedingly fair and delightsome." God's purpose was to make the Lamanites "loathsome unto thy people" and to prevent intermarriage. "Cursed shall be the seed of him that mixeth with their seed; for they shall be cursed even with the same cursing. And the Lord spake it, and it was done."

Mormon teaching against race-mixing remains in force. The 1978 package about the black revelation in the weekly *Church News* supplement of the *Deseret News* carried a sidebar that quoted three speeches from Kimball admonishing Saints not to "cross racial lines in dating and marrying." However, the Kimball quotations framed this as practical direction to enhance compatibility and avoid marital stress, not as a scriptural commandment. In 1981 the Kimball administration rewrote II Nephi 30:6 to say that righteous Indians would again become "pure" and delightsome, rather than "white." But the other scriptural references to blessed whiteness and accursed darkness remain unaltered.

Black skin as a sign of unrighteousness arose later in the 1830s with the Book of Moses and Book of Abraham, Smith revelations that are part of the scriptural Pearl of Great Price. Moses is a selection from Smith's own revision of the Old Testament, while Abraham is a miraculous rendition of ancient Egyptian manuscripts that Smith believed were written by the ancient biblical patriarch. In Moses 5:24–31, Cain is depicted as "Perdition" and the malevolent Master Mahan who makes a secret pact with Satan. "The seed of Cain were black" and among Cain's descendants "a blackness came upon all the children of Canaan, that they were despised among all people" (Moses 7:8, 22). Abraham 1:21–27 recounts that the heirs of the Canaanites and Noah's son Ham "preserved the curse in the land" and that Noah "cursed him [Ham] as pertaining to the Priesthood." This is the only passage linking the divine curse to the priesthood, but it is important because many Mormons today believe they literally perpetuate the very priesthood line that traces back to Noah and Adam.

Defenders of Joseph Smith, and those who argued for black priesthood before 1978, noted that one African American was ordained while Smith was alive, and possibly two. So, they reason, he must not have applied the ancient priesthood curse to these latter days, even though he shared the white racial folklore of the time and considered blacks the offspring of the biblical Ham, cursed to servitude.

The chief contradictory evidence is shaky. During a reexamination of the black ban in 1879, two of Smith's contemporaries claimed that the prophet had told them verbally in the 1830s that Negroes could not hold the priesthood. Smith and his close associates were expressing pro-slavery views at a time when the Mormons faced dangerous hostility from Missourians due to suspicion of abolitionist sympathies. But by 1844 Smith was campaigning for the presidency on an enlightened platform calling on the government to buy slaves their freedom.

Whatever the founder understood his scriptures to teach about race, the twentieth-century church faced the additional reality that all of Smith's prophetic successors until 1978 enforced the black ban as God's will. The staunchest of them all was the first, Brigham Young. Defenders of the ban contended that Young would not have enunciated the policy unless it expressed the will of his mentor Smith, and Smith's penchant for secret teachings made that claim all the more plausible. Young and other authorities apparently practiced the priesthood ban as early as 1847, but Young's earliest explicit enunciation came in 1849 when he told Apostle (and later President) Lorenzo Snow that "the Lord had cursed Cain's seed with blackness and prohibited them the Priesthood."

Young legalized black slavery in the Utah of 1852, and his noteworthy racism—alas, not unusual at that time—came to the fore in an 1859 discourse. Young specified that the biblical "mark" God put on Cain was "the flat nose and black skin." He further characterized descendants of Cain as "black, uncouth, uncomely, disagreeable and low in their habits, wild, and seemingly deprived of nearly all the blessings of the intelligence that is generally bestowed upon mankind." The president also said that the line of Cain was cursed with servitude, and that "the Abolitionists cannot help it, nor in the least alter that decree." That curse, and the curse of priesthood denial, would not be lifted "until all the other descendants of Adam have received the promises and enjoyed the blessings of the priesthood and the keys thereof." An 1854 address had clarified that the curse would be ended after "all the other children of Adam . . . have received their resurrection from the dead." After 1978 church critics spotted this as a theological inconsistency, since the black priesthood is being permitted prior to the end times.

Young was also Mormonism's harshest foe of miscegenation: "Shall I tell you the law of God in regard to the African race? If the white man who belongs to the chosen seed mixes his blood with the seed of Cain, the penalty, under the law of God, is death on the spot. This will always be so."

The Book of Abraham was added to the LDS scriptures in 1880, thus providing a proof-text for the priesthood ban. Another later development was the explanation of the ban in terms of Smith's teaching that all humans have an unremembered, heavenly preexistence before they are born on earth. Smith himself never drew the connection, but this, for some LDS authorities, especially Apostle (later President) Joseph Fielding Smith, produced a racial law of karma, according to which God consigns souls who are spiritually inadequate in the preexistence to be born into the black race.

The black policy was assumed, and consistently applied, but never officially articulated until August 17, 1949, after a liberal LDS sociologist had challenged the authorities to reexamine the basis for the doctrine. The official statement on the "Negro Question" from the First Presidency attributed the teaching to the founder Smith and the will of God: "The attitude of the Church with reference to negroes remains as it has always stood. It is not a matter of the declaration of a policy but of direct commandment from the Lord, on which is founded the doctrine of the Church from the days of its organization, to the effect that negroes may become members of the church but that they are not entitled to the priesthood at the present time."

As for when that time would come, the First Presidency quoted Young's millennial teaching that those "cursed with a skin of blackness" will be eligible after all other people have received their priesthood.

"Why the Negro was denied the Priesthood from the days of Adam to our day is not known," the First Presidency declared. But the church's position "may be understood when another doctrine of the Church is kept in mind, namely, that the conduct of spirits in the pre-mortal existence has some determining effect upon the conditions and circumstances under which these spirits take on mortality," although "the details of this principle have not been made known." Once that is understood, "there is no injustice whatsoever involved." And since God punishes individuals for their own sins, this "would imply that the Negro is punished or allotted to a certain position on this earth, not because of Cain's transgression, but came to earth through the loins of Cain because of his failure to achieve other stature in the spirit world."

The black policy was unremarkable enough prior to the civil rights movement that in 1957 sociologist Thomas O'Dea's *The Mormons* did not even mention it. But the succeeding years brought continual grief for the church, including athletic boycotts of Brigham Young University, picketing of Mormon buildings and conferences, religious brickbats when the Mormon George Romney ran for president, cancellation of a Mormon Tabernacle Choir tour, a New York City protest over the LDS visitors' center, an embarrassing public squabble with the Saints' partner in youth work, the Boy Scouts of America, and a hassle with black members of Congress and the U.S. Bureau of the Census over the church's use of public genealogical records. A 1966 book by the *New York Times* correspondent Wallace Turner branded the LDS Church "a political and social cancer" and "one of the most influential organs of racial bigotry in the United States."

In 1969, a matter of days before President David O. McKay died, his two counselors in the First Presidency issued a softened version of the 1949 teaching combined with an endorsement of civil rights in the secular realm. But those who know the Mormon hierarchical culture say that, unlike with the polygamy emergency, the church would never have announced a racial revelation under political pressure. It seems that 1978 was the right moment because the public outcry had died down.

After 1978, remembrance of the racial past was soon treated as an embarrassment and a hindrance to multiracial evangelism. The Church Educational System's current "seminary" high school level text on church history tosses ten words about the revelation into a laundry list on the Kimball administration, never mentioning race or the long-standing ban. Brigham Young University's Jessie L. Embry reports that a missionary to Newark, New Jersey, advised workers in black areas to "razor out" the page dealing with the Lamanite curse of dark skin in a children's Book of Mormon reader. But the past is not so easily excised. And because the 1978 statement and subsequent instruction have not addressed the theological background, some Mormons believe there is considerable mopping up yet to do.

Consider the reaction of Apostle Bruce R. McConkie, who felt the Spirit move through the upper room in 1978 and later advised Saints to "forget everything that I have said" defending the priesthood ban. Nevertheless, the next year the revised version of his *Mormon Doctrine*—widely influential and still on sale today in church-owned bookstores—mingled the words of the new black revelation with the older race theology. McConkie writes that "the race and nation in which men are born in this world is a direct result of their pre-existent life." Citing Moses 5, he states that by God's infinite wisdom there is a "caste system" involving racial segregation. "Cain, Ham, and the whole negro race have been cursed with a black skin, the mark of Cain, so they can be identified as a caste apart, a people with whom the other descendants of Adam should not intermarry."

In 1992 McConkie's book and the scriptures and teachings it cites came to the attention of a black Saint, A. David Jackson of Rancho Santa Margarita, California, after the regional stake president asked him to prepare a church talk on blacks and Mormonism. Jackson was shaken, and offended. A commercial real estate agent and former Baptist, he had converted in 1990 knowing nothing about the LDS racial issue. He researched the matter, raised his objections with his congregational "home teacher," the lawyer Dennis Gladwell, and finally went to the top, sending President Hinckley a twelve-page appeal in 1995. It was a remarkable act in such a hierarchical and authoritarian church. Jackson said that Hinckley should order the removal of *Mormon Doctrine* from church stores and libraries. And citing the Book of Moses, Brigham Young, and the First Presidency's 1949 decree, he asked Hinckley to issue a follow-up racial "declaration" for addition to Doctrine and Covenants "repudiating any interpretation of doctrine that ties racial characteristics of any kind to spiritual conditions or spiritual worthiness in this life or in the pre-existence."

The First Presidency's office replied through an exceedingly cautious procedure. It sent a letter of response to Jackson's ward bishop. The ward bishop then recited the authorities' letter to Jackson but did not give it to him, apparently because that would have put headquarters on the record. The letter assured Jackson that current official teaching was free of racism, but it did not meet his demands about publicly clarifying this in light of the past authorities. However, his friend Gladwell was energized by Jackson's research and asked an acquaintance and fellow attorney, Marlin K. Jensen, for help. Jensen was a respected LDS General Authority in the First Quorum of the Seventy and assigned to the headquarters public affairs committee. (He has since been elevated to the Presidency of the Seventy.) Gladwell sent Jensen a thirty-four-page survey of LDS racial theology, lamenting that "none of these theories or views have ever been disavowed or qualified officially." In 1997 Jensen and a public affairs staff member, William Evans, conferred with Jackson, Gladwell, and Armand L. Mauss, a Mormon sociology professor at Washington State University who is an expert on LDS racial teaching. Mauss provided extensive research on offensive publications and concepts that are still common among the Saints.

In July of 1997, at Jensen's request, Jackson, Gladwell, and Mauss drafted and sent a formal proposal hoping that Jensen would raise it with the First Presidency and the Twelve. The paper said that white Mormons think the 1978 revelation resolved everything, but that black Mormons react differently when they learn the details. The church "cannot overlook or simply ignore the statements set forth explicitly in the 1949 declaration" and related materials. Mormons believe that "almost anything said by a General Authority is quasi-scripture and inspired, especially when expressed as doctrine or principle. . . . Hence, the absence of any official correcting statement by the Church regarding these issues will perpetuate a belief system in these unfortunate and pejorative views." The paper repeated Jackson's plea to Hinckley for a scriptural declaration in Doctrine and Covenants explicitly repudiating such tenets and implications.

In 1998, however, Jackson told Larry Stammer of the *Los Angeles Times* about his behind-the-scenes efforts. Given well-known sensitivity of the hierarchy about acting under the glare of publicity, Mauss laments, that disclosure killed any prospect that officialdom would act on remaining racial issues any time soon. The day the *Times* story appeared the First Presidency stated that it and the Twelve had not discussed the matter, and that there was no need to. The 1978 declaration "continues to speak for itself." Hinckley later told the *Times,* "I don't see anything further that we need to do." He explained, "I don't hear any complaint from our black brethren and sisters. I hear only appreciation and gratitude wherever I go."

Indeed, Jackson has found little success in seeking public backing from fellow LDS blacks. He says that with most black Mormons, "when they find out about this, they exit"; he estimates that thousands have become inactive, although few have formally resigned. "You end up with the passive African Americans in the church," he says. "Those who remain tell me, you go ahead and do this, but don't use my name. They all want the change, but few want to take direct responsibility."

Catherine Stokes, an African American who is assistant deputy director of health care regulation in the Illinois state health department, buttresses Hinckley's viewpoint. At the time of the 1978 revelation Stokes, a former Protestant, was a follower of the Unity School of Christianity. That summer she viewed the Hawaii temple and filled out a visitor's card. Some weeks later "these two little white boys came to my door" and initiated the standard series of proselytizing sessions. Stokes was baptized in April 1979, and her daughter soon thereafter. Her ex-husband and many black friends thought she was crazy to join a "white" church. "I came to this conclusion, not to let racism—mine, yours, or somebody else's—get in the way of what I believe is true." Brigham Young? He "said some harsh words," but "I don't think he asked God. He was acting on his own."

In the late 1980s the oral history program at Brigham Young University managed to compile a list of 500 American blacks who were active in the LDS church and persuaded 201 of them to respond to a mail survey. The results lend support to both Jackson's worry about black dropouts and Hinckley's contention of contentedness. Embry summarizes: "Most black Americans who have joined the LDS church experience genuine and heartfelt acceptance; at the same time they have concerns over the past priesthood exclusion and latent forms of racism and prejudice exhibited by some white members." A solid 81.5 percent "agreed" or "strongly agreed" that they were hopeful about their own future as Mormons. But that left nearly one-fifth who were not, a potentially worrisome statistic since virtually all were recent converts still involved in church life and thus members one would expect to be upbeat. And there is the unanswered question of whether the attitudes of the 60 percent who did not answer the survey would have resembled those of the 40 percent who did.

As for opinion among the coming generation of white LDS leaders, Eugene England, a BYU English professor emeritus, warns that "false ideas that were invented to rationalize our earlier racist practices are still with us." From occasional surveys he has made in his classes, England reports that "a majority of bright, well-educated Mormon students say they believe that blacks are descendants of Cain and Ham and thereby cursed and that skin color is an indication of righteousness in the premortal life. They tell me these ideas came from their parents or seminary and Sunday school teachers, and they have never questioned them."

Mauss believes that "the residue of racialist teaching still found in LDS literature, whether glorifying some lineages or denigrating others, can only get in the way of bringing the world unto Christ." Mormons may wonder why the Lord "permitted" a discriminatory policy, he writes, but it seems plausible that it had a "strictly human origin. An open admission of this realization may be the best way to start dealing with the black issue in Mormon history. There is no reason for even the most orthodox Mormon to be threatened by the realization that the prophets do not do everything by revelation and never have."

Conversion and retention may be a looming difficulty among U.S. blacks, but the church has taken steps to stress inclusivity—for instance, by giving new attention in denominational publications to African American believers. In 1998 President Hinckley made a breakthrough appearance, speaking on race relations at a regional conference of the NAACP.

Internationally, the church has been making up for its century-plus of lost time. Weeks after the 1978 revelation, BYU's Bateman took time off to return to Africa on special assignment, helping to establish the pioneer LDS congregations in Nigeria and Ghana. Many others pitched in to reach the formerly untouched black populations overseas. Today there are 112,000 baptized Saints in Africa, 97,000 in the Caribbean, and 640,000 in multiracial Brazil. In 1998 Hinckley conducted the first tour of black Africa by an LDS president (not counting South Africa) and announced that a temple would be built in Ghana in addition to the one in Johannesburg dating from apartheid days.

The progress of twentieth-century missionary endeavors otherwise is also mapped by the geography of temples, whose rituals are essential to the temporal and eternal lives of believers:

1919 The dedication of the first temple outside the continental United States (Laie, Hawaii)

1923 The first temple outside U.S. territory (Cardston, Alberta, Canada)

1955 The first temple outside the United States and Canada (Zollikofen, near Bern, Switzerland)

1956 The first U.S. temple outside the traditional Mormon region (Los Angeles, the site thirty-three years earlier of the first regional stake in the U.S. diaspora); and temples for both England and New Zealand

In 1983 Hinckley dedicated temples in Western Samoa, Tonga, and Tahiti in the Pacific Islands, the arena for the faith's biggest foreign success story. Much credit belongs to David O. McKay, who had served as president from 1951 to 1970. McKay was a mission-minded, forward-looking leader who had taken a 56,000-mile world mission trip as a young apostle in 1921 and 1922. His administration had quietly settled confusion and decided that skin color and black features were not the criteria for priesthood exclusion but rather African parentage, thus opening the offices to dark-skinned Fijians. (Darker racial groups also granted priesthood in that era included the Negritos of the Philippines, tribes in New Guinea, and Australia's Aborigines.) McKay also decided to shift the burden of proof so that dark-hued priesthood applicants were no longer required to prove their lineage; instead, it was up to church officials to raise any questions.

Though LDS work in the Pacific dated back to the nineteenth century, once McKay's First Presidency opened the priesthood for good, regional stakes began sprouting across Polynesia. Today there are 156,000 members in the church's Pacific Islands Area. LDS penetration of the United States, at 1.8 percent of the national population, is overshadowed by the percentages in Tonga (40 percent), Western Samoa (25), American Samoa (22.6), Nieu (15), Kiribati (7.1), Tahiti (6.3), the Marshall Islands (5.4), Rarotonga

(4.5), Micronesia (2.4), and Palau (2.2). McKay also replaced the wing-and-a-prayer preparation for young missionaries with a language training school, established in 1961 in Provo, Utah, which developed into today's booming Missionary Training Center (MTC).

Kimball, also a missionary strategist, made a shrewd maneuver in 1974, enlisting David M. Kennedy, the suave former Secretary of the Treasury and U.S. Ambassador to NATO, to be the church's "special consultant for diplomatic affairs." D. Michael Quinn interprets that as a step toward the theocracy of old, reminiscent of Joseph Smith's 1844 dispatch of foreign ambassadors from his Illinois city-state. But Kennedy's chief task—one at which he excelled, by all accounts—was to win friends in the Washington diplomatic corps and overseas in order to smooth the path for missionizing. LDS advances were especially notable in the Communist bloc countries. The church won legal recognition in Poland in 1977 and erected a temple in the former East Germany in 1985. A recalcitrant Russia warily granted post-Communist legality in 1998.

If Quinn miscast the Kennedy assignment, he and other authors are more on target in depicting the church's post-theocracy political involvements within the United States. The twentieth-century LDS record has not always been what simple stereotypes might suggest, nor have Mormons automatically followed the leader. The powerful U.S. senator and church apostle Reed Smoot defied the church president by voting to override President Taft's veto of an immigration bill, and the First Presidency favored the League of Nations while Smoot was vocal on the successful negative side. Smoot opposed Prohibition, which was backed by fellow apostles. In 1933 the teetotaling First Presidency and Twelve Apostles decided the church would not campaign against the repeal of Prohibition because it was a partisan political issue, although they quietly hoped that good Mormons would vote dry. As it turned out, Utah was the state that put the constitutional amendment repealing Prohibition over the top. Some thirty-five years later the LDS authorities repealed their past nonpartisanship on alcohol and ardently fought a "liquor by the drink" proposal in Utah.

Church leaders left little doubt about their opposition to Franklin D. Roosevelt in 1932 and 1936, but Utah gave him lopsided majorities anyway.

In 1940 the General Authorities drafted a joint anti-FDR statement but never issued it. Hostility to Roosevelt's New Deal as an affront to economic gumption and individualism produced a benign by-product. In 1936, after a survey showed that 88,000 Saints were on welfare, the church turned a Salt Lake stake program into the elaborate, nationwide Church Security Program (later the Church Welfare Program) to supply needy believers with food and work. Martin Marty writes that this system to "take care of their own" caused anti–New Deal Americans to look on the separatist Saints with new respect. There was much mythology; it was hardly true that all Mormons went off the government dole. But neither was the program "fictitious," as one FDR agent claimed. Rather, church welfare was the most ambitious religious effort to do what could be done to help during the Depression, and it remains in full operation today as a singular achievement of the Latter-day religion.

Senator Smoot lost his longtime seat in the 1932 FDR sweep and never forgave the authorities for not doing more to boost his reelection. But the authorities apparently never quite forgave the Senate candidate who drove Apostle Smoot into retirement. Elbert Thomas, a University of Utah political scientist, was a faithful Mormon, like the majority of Utah politicos. But he was also a liberal, a Democrat, and a New Dealer, so the hierarchical chill set in. It took until 1950, but conservative Mormon Republicans finally whipped Thomas with one of their own, Wallace F. Bennett (the father of current Utah Senator Robert Bennett). Bennett was a central casting Mormon politician, a prominent business executive, son-in-law of the deceased church president Heber J. Grant, a longtime Sunday school board member, and author of the 1958 testimonial book *Why I Am a Mormon.*

The dominant LDS Republican celebrity of this period, however, was not Bennett but Ezra Taft Benson. He had been an apostle for a decade when he received President McKay's permission to serve in Eisenhower's cabinet. Inside the LDS community things got interesting after the fiery right-winger returned from Washington to resume his full-time church work. Addressing a church conference, Benson declared that "no true Latter-day Saint and no true American can be a socialist or a communist." He later allowed that it was hard to imagine a Mormon being a Democrat, either. Other church authorities expressed a different view, especially

Apostle Hugh B. Brown, one of McKay's counselors, and that was the pattern throughout the Benson controversies. Benson next endorsed the John Birch Society, an extremist anti-Communist group for which his son Reed was Utah coordinator and later the national spokesman. Robert Welch, the founder of the ultra-right-wing group, then published his notorious book stating that Benson's former colleague Eisenhower was guilty of "knowingly receiving and abiding by Communist orders, and consciously serving the Communist conspiracy, for all of his adult life."

In January 1963 McKay's First Presidency publicly deplored the John Birchers' attempts to associate the church with their viewpoint, without naming Benson. The apostle thereafter spoke to a large Birch meeting in Los Angeles and praised Welch. Eventually, the First Presidency announced that Benson was being assigned to supervise the European mission, and officials made no effort to hide the fact that he was being sent into exile overseas. In the twentieth century apostles in good standing may travel the world, but they are based in Utah. Taking no hints, Benson gave yet another talk to a church meeting in New Orleans, praising the John Birch Society and attacking Presidents Eisenhower and Kennedy for using federal troops to enforce school integration. Just before departing for Europe, Benson told a Utah church audience that the civil rights movement was "part of the pattern for the Communist takeover of America." The hierarchy's political infighting went on for years thereafter.

Benson had political ambitions as well as opinions. In 1965 he asked McKay's permission to run for U.S. president. McKay directed Benson not to campaign actively, but he also did not require that Benson decline a draft. There was then a brief boomlet for an anti–civil rights third party with South Carolina's Senator Strom Thurmond running for president and Benson for vice president. A more serious effort took hold in early 1968 when Alabama Governor George Wallace wrote McKay asking permission for Benson to be his third-party running mate. McKay wisely refused.

The Benson years told much about the church's modern sociopolitical role. Despite his apostolic stature and national prominence, Benson never carried the church membership or leadership with him. The First Presidency consistently prevented any association of the faith with either partisanship or extremism. And when Benson became church president through automatic seniority succession in 1985, he did not use that power-ful estate to push his political opinions. There were probably three reasons for that. First, the president must foster the good of the entire world church, not partisan American agendas. Second, Benson was aged and lacked vitality by the time he took charge. Third, the collective leadership custom, in which the president usually acts with his two counselors and often with the Twelve Apostles as well, tends to moderate what one person might do alone.

Though the church opposed Communism in principle and holds the American nation to be a unique part of God's plan, it has not held a sim-ple militaristic stance. Officialdom discourages conscientious objection to armed service but allows it as an option after consultation with local church authorities. In a significant 1939 policy statement, the First Presidency said that the biblical command "thou shalt not kill" applies to political entities as well as individuals and condemned war as an instru-ment of national policy. In 1940 and 1942 the leadership combined calls for patriotism with disavowal of church support for war as a self-righteous jus-tification for genocide and mass destruction. Apostle J. Reuben Clark, the first Mormon to be a U.S. ambassador, became as extreme on the left as his colleague Benson later was on the right, pleading for an unarmed and neu-tral United States in World War II and the early Cold War years. At the beginning of the Reagan era (1981) the First Presidency opposed deploy-ment of the MX missile in western Utah and neighboring Nevada and urged the government to seek "viable alternatives" to nuclear conflict.

As the century wore on Mormons in the state of Utah and elsewhere became among the most lopsidedly loyal elements in the conservative Republican coalition. So much so that it created ripples when Marlin Jensen, a Democrat, told the *Salt Lake Tribune* in 1998 that the last thing the authorities wanted was "a church party and a non-church party. . . . It's not in the best interest to be known as a one-party church." He spoke weeks after the First Presidency issued an election-year encyclical urging Saints to seek public office and apply "gospel principles" to government.

On matters relating to religious tradition, individualism, and personal morality, the LDS leadership has taken resolutely conservative stands. Issues that the hierarchs have addressed over the years include right-to-work laws, Sunday closing laws, gambling, abortion, pornography, divorce, the Equal Rights Amendment for women, and homosexuality. Increasingly in the past two decades the Mormon people, with the implicit or explicit sympathy of the leadership, have become proponents of the "Religious Right" agenda alongside the Evangelical Protestants, who were their bitterest foes in polygamy days and remain their main critics in matters of religious doctrine.

A significant episode was the 1998 U.S. House of Representatives vote on a constitutional amendment stating that government shall not hamper "people's right to pray and to recognize their religious beliefs, heritage or traditions on public property, including schools." The amendment, backed by the Christian Coalition and a phalanx of Evangelical organizations, was introduced by Oklahoma Representative Ernest Istook, a Republican Mormon. And in the roll call, every LDS member of the House, Republicans all, voted yes. (The 224–203 vote fell short of the required two-thirds majority.)

Within Utah hardly anything of importance happens without consideration of church sensibilities. Salt Lake's *Deseret News,* one of three U.S. daily newspapers operated by a religious body (along with the *Christian Science Monitor* and the *Washington Times,* owned by a Unification Church entity), provides a daily index of the range of acceptable LDS political thinking. On the national scene the post-theocratic Mormon Church, like all religious denominations in the democracy, has lobbied on behalf of its institutional interests and advocated what it regards as the good of society. Some Americans may agree, and others may disagree.

The LDS church has emerged as a slightly exotic but prosperous and perfectly acceptable piece of the multicultural national mosaic. What difference does it make that Mormons eschew coffee and alcohol if yuppies sip herbal tea and Perrier, or that Mormons wear sacred underwear if Muslim and Hindu robes dot Middle American shopping malls? At the turn of the twenty-first century the remaining barriers between Mormonism and the rest of society are no longer political. The uniquely Mormon distinctives are almost wholly theological, in an American culture where theology now carries only modest importance and seems to matter less with each passing year.

CHAPTER 7
MORMONS, INC.

LIKE A STURDY SENTINEL IN THE FINE, FRAGILE SUNSHINE AT THE southern edge of Salt Lake City, an enormous, multistory grain elevator rises, with fifteen barrels painted pure white. Inside is 400,000 pounds of wheat that is not to be moved, sold, or given away. The goal is to have in storage at this and other locations 100 pounds of grain for every LDS man, woman, and child worldwide, a church guide says proudly. It is supposed to be rotated every four years. This is a reserve to be used only in time of need.

What sort of need? "If things got bad enough so that the normal systems of distribution didn't work," says a friendly bishop at Welfare Square. "If those other systems broke down, the church would still be able to care for the poor and needy." The "bad enough" relates to the church's millennial teaching that before the imminent return of Christ there will come a time of terrible worldwide chaos. That same belief is enshrined in many sectors of conservative Protestantism, minus grain elevators. But "bad enough" can also refer to an ordinary disaster such as flood, earthquake, or even just plain poverty.

Around the corner from the enormous grain silo is something called the "Bishop's Storehouse." It looks a bit like a supermarket except that the shelves are filled with products carrying the brand label of Deseret, referring to the special Mormon synonym for honeybee. Deseret Industries is a far-flung organization owned by the LDS Church that produces goods to take care of poor people, its own and others. There are Deseret-brand hand soaps and laundry soaps, canned peaches from the church's cannery in Boise, beans from the church's bean farms in southern Idaho, spaghetti sauce from the church's plant in Mesa, Arizona, peanut butter from the church's peanut butter facility in Houston, apples from church-owned orchards in Idaho, and bread, cheese, milk, pudding, cottage cheese, fruit drinks, and butter, all from yet another facility just a few blocks away.

These goods come from the 87 canneries and the extensive network of ranches and farms owned by the church. The products are transported by a large fleet of trucks, also owned by the church, and distributed at 106 Bishop's Storehouses and 48 Deseret Industries stores belonging to the church around the country. Some of the beef is from cattle born on Mormon land, fattened on Mormon farms, slaughtered in Mormon slaughterhouses, and packed in Mormon packinghouses before being shipped to Mormon storehouses. The goods become part of the church's own private welfare system, staffed largely by volunteers from church wards who in a typical year log almost 270,000 man-days of labor. All of this is consumed daily in massive quantities by tens of thousands of Mormons and non-Mormons alike who have fallen on hard times.

Welfare Square is really just a tiny cell in a much larger organism, the church's mixture of for-profit, nonprofit, charitable, and ecclesiastical holdings. This just might be the most efficient churchly money machine on earth. The welfare plan is one of the Mormon Church's most intriguing sectors, unique in concept and scope among the religions of America.

Also unique is the broader economic pattern of the Mormon empire. What makes the LDS Church distinctive is not just the amount of money coursing through its congregations each week—though that is also singular for the size of the denomination—but the church's heavy investments in corporate enterprises. The research for this book produced an estimate that its investments in stocks, bonds, and church-controlled businesses were worth $6 billion as of 1997, and that church-owned agricultural and commercial real estate had a value of an additional $5 billion. Asked for guidance, one insider told us that those figures "do not appear unreasonable." The worth of other categories of assets: U.S. meetinghouses and temples, $12 billion; foreign meetinghouses and temples, $6 billion; schools and miscellaneous, $1 billion. The estimated grand total of LDS assets, by a conservative reckoning, would be $25–30 billion. If assets have appreciated as much as they should have in recent times, the figure could go well beyond that.

Yet another LDS trademark is the system of membership tithing that brings in what we project as offerings of $5.3 billion a year, though one knowledgeable source thinks $4.25 billion might be a safer estimate. Stocks and directly owned businesses produce perhaps $600 million more in cash income. The estimated yearly annual revenues total $5.9 billion, or by the more conservative reckoning, just under $5 billion. Per capita, no other religion comes close to such figures. (The method for reaching all these estimates is explained in appendix B.)

Several factors underlie the LDS Church's prosperity. It has a form of sacred taxation like no other: members are obliged to give a tithe (10 percent) of their income to the church in order to gain access to temples and to participate in the holiest ordinances of salvation and exaltation. The salaried staff is not large, and the performance of most duties by part-time unpaid volunteers cuts operating expenses to the bone. The highly centralized control and flexibility of the system enable leaders readily to modify money flow and alter policies so that current income matches programs. Finally, by all accounts the businessman-apostles maintain effective administrative controls that minimize waste and maximize efficiency.

The strict secrecy with which the hierarchy guards the financial facts is unique for a church of this size. Officials refuse to divulge routine information that other religions are happy to provide over the phone to donors or inquirers. Outsiders' money estimates always raise disclaimers from officialdom, presumably because of the danger that fat-looking figures might weaken members' tithing compliance. This has led to a cat-and-mouse game with various journalists who have attempted over the years to unveil the vast empire of corporate Mormonism.

When the estimates given here were first sketched out in a 1997 *Time* magazine cover story, the managing director of the public affairs department at LDS headquarters made this formal reply: "Leaders of the church were disappointed that you created a false impression of the church's income and wealth. Your estimates were greatly exaggerated. The church's income is not nearly what was reported. Also the church's assets are primarily money-consuming assets and not money-producing." Of course, this spokesman did not provide even the vaguest hints as to what was wrong and what the truth might be, either then or in response to a further inquiry for this book.

It was not the first time the church had reacted swiftly, and negatively, to a money piece, nor was *Time* the first to make such an attempt. In 1962 *Esquire* magazine ran a cover story that put church income at $1 million a day. In 1974 two reporters at the *Idaho Falls Post Register* took a stab at it. In 1978 the Los Angeles–based reporter Jeffrey Kaye tried to expose the western ranges of the Mormon financial empire for *New West* magazine in a piece titled "An Invisible Empire: Mormon Money in California."

A few years earlier Kaye had interviewed N. Eldon Tanner, the man credited by observers with dragging the church into the era of modern finance after a liquidity crisis in which bank balances hit a dangerously low level. (It was at that point that the church stopped giving its members summary financial reports.) The interview, recounted by Robert Gottlieb and Peter Wiley in *America's Saints* (1984), became an unavoidable enticement to investigative journalists looking for a challenge. Church money figures are "never disclosed," said Tanner. They used to be, said Kaye. "Yes, years ago." Why not now? "We just didn't think it was necessary." How do you respond to critics, then? "We don't respond!" "You don't respond?" Tanner concluded, "We respond by silence."

By the early 1980s the researcher John Heinerman, then Mormon, and the sociologist Anson Shupe mounted what remains the most detailed attempt. Using extensive material provided by church insiders (in one incident, Mormon security tossed Heinerman out of an archive), the two published their account in *The Mormon Corporate Empire* (1985). Understandably this book was deeply resented by the church, not only for its financial disclosures—which in most cases were probably quite accurate—but for its conspiracy theory according to which the church wanted nothing less than to take over America in preparation for the 1,000-year reign of Jesus Christ.

In 1991 the daily *Arizona Republic* threw half a dozen reporters at the problem for more than six months, and while the effort produced a major newspaper series, the reporters could only scratch the surface. Though lacking Heinerman's internal records, the team unearthed lots of interesting material as they combed property records in 120 counties and 22 states. The result was a finely detailed look at many properties and commercial developments the church holds.

It is simply impossible to tally Mormon assets or income with accuracy, just as it would be to try to figure out the finances of a multibillion-dollar multinational corporation without access to inside accounts. The only writers to get such a glimpse were Heinerman and Shupe, who clearly got some of the goods on such specifics as church bond holdings but provided only a partial view of the Mormon entity. Today Shupe says the book's estimate of $8 billion in church assets as of 1983 was intentionally very conservative. "We were easily 30 percent low," in which case a better estimate back then might have been $11 billion or more. Shupe thinks church assets today might be in the "$20–30 billion range," but admittedly he has not worked on the topic in years.

The data that investigators do get their hands on, as *Arizona Republic* editors told the *New York Times,* can be "incomplete, partly outdated and sometimes contradictory." When reporters locate what they think is a solid number, it has often turned out to be wrong. *Esquire* ran with a wild guess by the non-Mormon mayor of Salt Lake City, who put church income at $1 million a day, or $365 million a year, as of 1962. D. Michael Quinn saw the actual figure for that period—$100 million—so *Esquire* was off by 350 percent.

The church vigorously denounces and discredits any attempt to estimate its finances. When the *Arizona Republic* estimated income from tithing and other sources at $4.7 billion, of which $4.3 billion came from the tithe, the church public affairs department said this was "grossly overstated," just as *Time* had "greatly exaggerated" six years later. Quinn, who spent many years poking around Mormon archives during his years on the BYU faculty, said it's hard to see $4.3 billion as a gross exaggeration. Using the known tithing revenues from 1952 to 1962 as a baseline, Quinn writes that "the church's tithing revenues for 1990 would be far in excess of $4.3

billion. From this perspective that estimate seems conservative." Adjusting for inflation from Quinn's account, *Time*'s $5.3 billion in tithing revenue is nearly reached or even seems low, and that assessment is made *without* even considering the huge membership growth—assuming, of course, that most of the converts remain steadfast in the faith and in making the expected contributions to it.

To gauge the unusual nature of LDS investments, consider a denomination of almost identical U.S. membership, the Evangelical Lutheran Church in America. The ELCA holds only the portfolio of stocks and bonds that covers employee pensions, and in 1997 that amounted to only $152 million, compared with the billions in direct Mormon investment. Like most large denominations, the ELCA spends most of the contributions it receives on a combination of charity, real estate maintenance, and staff salaries. "Our stewardship is not such that we grow the church through business ventures," remarked the ELCA's Pastor Mark Moller-Gunderson when told that his church was being compared with the LDS Church. Typically churches spend most of what they take in and maintain modest "rainy day" margins.

Not so the Mormons. Their enterprises range from a $16 billion insurance company to perhaps $6 billion in stocks and bonds, if not more. There's a $172 million chain of radio stations (seventh-largest in the country). The church's more than 150 farms and ranches, including America's largest cattle ranch, make it one of the largest landowners in the nation. The farms and ranches encompass somewhere in the neighborhood of one million acres, roughly equal to the size of the state of Delaware.

The talented church managers run a tight and profitable financial ship and can spend the cash any way they choose. They are not held accountable to the unquestioning flock in any way. The officials make their investment decisions in secret and report no dollar figures to anyone outside of the group of white-haired, life-tenured gentlemen at the top. One thing, however, is known. The church is on a building binge of historic proportions, part of an attempt to match its burgeoning global membership. It is building 350 meetinghouses or chapels each year and has more than a hundred of its trademark temples in operation, under construction, or announced. Large temples cost $18 million or so a pop. All of this is financed with cold, hard cash. The church tells its members to avoid debt, and it practices what it preaches.

Thoughtful Saints might wonder whether the church should spend more of its assets on programs that benefit the membership rather than further enriching an already huge financial base. The Hinckley-era campaign for new temples and meetinghouses is a step in that direction.

The scars of history lie behind much of the church's management system, which from the beginning was secretive, hierarchical, and authoritarian. It had brushes with bankruptcy in Ohio in the late 1830s, in Utah at the end of the nineteenth century, and—unknown to the membership—that hidden crisis shortly after the church released its last public accounting of expenditures in 1959. Although the subsequent cutoff in financial information was never explained, there was no grumbling from the compliant membership.

The church's leaders may be amateurs in theological training, unlike top bureaucrats of other churches, but many of the highest authorities were successful businessmen before becoming full-time church officials and are fully able to provide professional financial guidance. And then, too, in the Mormon system there is that large amount of free administrative and mundane labor from lay volunteers at the lower levels, which remains a huge cost-saving factor.

The heritage of pioneer self-reliance remains significant. Brigham Young once said, "The kingdom of God cannot rise independent of Gentile nations until we produce, manufacture, and make every article of use, convenience or necessity among our people." Present-day President Hinckley echoes this: "Our commercial properties are largely the outgrowth of our pioneer enterprises. . . . In the early days of the church, the church had to step in to fill a void that existed." Says Republican Senator Robert Bennett of Utah, whose grandfather was a church president, "In Brigham Young's day the church was the only source of accumulated capital in the territory. If anything was built it had to be built by the church because no one else had any money."

Accordingly, the church owned virtually every enterprise of any size, and the cultural byword was, even then, self-reliance. In the nineteenth century this took the form of cooperative communitarian economics.

What emerged often looked very much like complete vertical integration, with the church owning every step of the production process. So busily did it involve itself in the economy of the pioneer West that, by Quinn's estimate, during the first century of corporate Mormonism the ranking General Authorities were partners, officers, or directors in over 900 different businesses, ranging from banks (48) to lumber companies (34), newspapers and magazines (60), mining firms (55), railroads (55), and hotels (9). A conglomerate from its first such opportunity, the church has always preferred to marshal and invest its own capital—with varying degrees of success—for reasons related both to pioneer survival and to its heritage of millennial and apocalyptic theology.

Church officials extended a degree of cooperation to the *Time* correspondent S. C. Gwynne when the magazine was producing its 1997 cover story. Though authorities would disclose neither specific amounts invested in enterprises (unless regulatory requirements had made this information publicly available) nor total assets, tithes and other contributions, or investment income, they did agree to talk about how many enterprises of what type they managed. They also discussed the church's internal structure and what bodies or persons controlled which companies and investments.

Gwynne was generally impressed by the scrupulous integrity as well as business acumen of those guiding church finances. Of course, the wall of secrecy would tend to prevent outsiders from divining any lapses of fraud or ineptitude that can occur in a large organization in which administrators manage large sums of money and decisions are affected by fraternal trust. As with other denominations, the top LDS leaders have a modest lifestyle compared with executives holding secular corporate responsibilities.

It is unfair to characterize corporate Mormonism as a runaway beast with a voracious appetite for gobbling up as many American assets as possible, as some have suggested. The truth is that, despite its expanding membership, the LDS Church has been steadily divesting itself of various businesses since World War II. In the past four decades the church has bailed out of banking and hospitals and sold off manufacturing operations.

That is not to say that the church is not in a mild expansionary mode. It is growing assets like its radio stations cautiously and conservatively. It is acquiring new farm and ranch land, also cautiously. Nevertheless, Hinckley has ordered the General Authorities, who used to acquire a handy form of personal income by sitting on many corporate boards, to relinquish these posts, a major change in how the church relates to the business community around it. In effect, the General Authorities have shifted focus to concentrate on managing the global growth of the church.

A perfect example of the church's business professionalism is Rodney H. Brady, president and CEO of Deseret Management Corporation, a holding company for virtually all of the church's commercial enterprises. Like many other high-ranking church officials, Brady has both extensive experience as a Mormon-style lay clergyman and an extensive worldly background. Holder of a Harvard business doctorate, he is former vice president of Hughes Tool, executive vice president of the pharmaceutical giant Bergen Brunswig, and onetime assistant secretary of the Department of Health, Education, and Welfare.

The businesses Brady now oversees employ about 2,500 people (more during harvest). No church tithe money flows into these enterprises. Agribusiness functions under two other Deseret holding companies, AgReserves and AgriNorthwest; about 150 farms and ranches are owned by the church. Of these, about 100 serve its welfare system while 50 operate on a for-profit basis, though Deseret reported in early 1999 that there were then only 25 commercial operations. (The exact number of for-profit properties varies as land is shifted between welfare use and commercial use.) The for-profit operations pay government taxes as well as a 10 percent tithe on operations that is given back to the church.

All this adds up to a sizable operation. One holding is the 312,000-acre Deseret Ranch outside of Orlando, Florida, the largest cattle operation in the United States, larger even than the famous King Ranch of Texas. Based on recent real estate transactions in Brevard County, the land is worth $858 million. The church owns one of the largest potato producers in the country, is the largest producer of nuts through its farms in California's San Joaquin Valley, and has extensive orange and grapefruit holdings in Florida and corn and apple production in the Northwest. One of the church's many cattle ranches in the West, Deseret Ranch on the Utah-Wyoming border, exceeds 200,000 acres.

Life insurance sold exclusively to Mormons is a vestige of an earlier era when the church set up companies to provide services no one else would or could. Deseret Management owns several smaller insurance companies as well, including Beneficial Life, Continental Western Life Insurance Company, the Pacific Heritage Life Insurance Company, the Western Life Insurance Company, and the Utah Home Fire Insurance Company. Beneficial Life is by far the largest, with $16 billion in insurance in effect and assets of $1.6 billion. Beneficial is now run as a purely commercial concern and insures many non-Mormons.

The church's media holdings include Bonneville International Corporations, which owns fifteen radio stations and two television stations. It has consolidated its holdings into four major markets: Washington, D.C., Chicago, San Francisco, and Salt Lake City. Bonneville sales in 1996 were $172 million. Bonneville donated an impressive $35 million to community services in 1996, according to the *Radio Business Report*.

Presiding Bishop H. David Burton, the top LDS financial officer despite his pastoral-sounding title, sees these media outlets as giving the church a voice in the community, not only to disseminate ordinary news and information but also to speak on moral issues. "We have had a number of opportunities to pick up Howard Stern and dismissed them immediately," he says. "That's just not our style of broadcasting."

Bonneville also owns Salt Lake City's 65,000-circulation *Deseret News,* a daily that recently built itself a fancy new building using $15 million of its own reserves (no tithe funds). Church authorities formerly ran the paper with an iron fist but no longer even sit on its board, and the new editor, John Hughes, former editor of the *Christian Science Monitor,* is non-Mormon. Through Deseret Management the church operates thirty-three bookstores in the United States, sixteen of them in Utah.

Through a number of subsidiaries, the church is quite active in real estate apart from temples, chapels, ranch, and farm land. In Salt Lake City the Hotel Temple Square Company owns several pieces of real estate in and around Mormon headquarters buildings; other property is held through Zions Securities, a real estate management and development company. The *Arizona Republic* in 1991 estimated the church's Salt Lake

City holdings at over $137 million. The church also owns various properties in other states, including office buildings in California, Florida, and Arizona and 24,000 acres of land in places like Jackson County, Missouri—where Mormons believe Jesus Christ will return and reign—held for what Brady calls "special purposes."

A company called Hawaii Reserves manages extensive LDS real estate development in Hawaii that includes the Polynesian Cultural Center (PCC); the 2,000-student Brigham Young University/Hawaii (BYUH); and Hawaii Resources, Inc. (HRI), a development company in Laie. HRI, a subsidiary of Deseret Management, operates a shopping center, has some business and residential real estate holdings, and provides the 7,000 residents of the Laie community with road and utility services.

Together these church-owned companies have a profound impact on the economy of the island. The LDS Church was expected to spend over $1 billion there in the 1990s, a projection made by the church in 1995 based on the $100 million invested in 1994 alone. They provide more than 3,400 jobs in Hawaii. The Polynesian Cultural Center provides 1,100 jobs, 600 of which are held by BYUH students. According to the church, the non-profit PCC has contributed more than $150 million to BYUH since 1963, making it one of the country's leading corporate supporters of education.

The Polynesian Cultural Center is one of the more intriguing Mormon investments, in part because it demonstrates so clearly how the church chooses to use its temporal investments to further its religious goals. Located thirty-two miles from Waikiki, this forty-two-acre park contains replicas of seven different types of Polynesian villages and attracts one million visitors a year, making it one of Hawaii's premier attractions. Like some latter-day Disney, the church also owns the Laniloa Lodge resort as well as a significant amount of residential housing and the local sewer and water systems.

Working through BYUH, next door to the park, the center provides legal employment for student converts from the Pacific Rim who lack U.S. green card residency work permits. Adults visiting the park spend on average between $44 and $59 a day; children spend $30 to $39. Official earnings are not published, but this suggests revenue in the range of a minimum $40–45 million a year.

The rest of the church's holdings, outside of Deseret Management, consist of its stock and bond investment portfolio; its meetinghouse and temple real estate; its educational holdings, including BYU in Utah and Hawaii, the two-year Ricks College in Idaho, a BYU center in Jerusalem, the LDS Business College in Salt Lake City, hundreds of seminary and institute buildings, and a smattering of secondary schools in places like Fiji and Samoa; the church's 52 percent holding in ZCMI, the largest department store chain in Utah, a publicly traded company; the ranches and farms in its welfare system; miscellaneous real estate holdings around the country; and "special purpose" real estate such as its genealogical archives, libraries, and historical properties.

If the LDS Church were a U.S. corporation, by revenues it would rank number 243 on the *Fortune* 500 list. (Revenues are the best standard of measurement. Ranking a religious body by assets has little meaning since so much is locked into purely religious-use real estate.) Mormons, Inc., lands somewhere between Paine Webber ($5.7 billion) and Union Carbide ($6.1 billion), a tad smaller than Continental Airlines ($6.4 billion), and about twice the size of *Reader's Digest* ($3.1 billion). The church's gargantuan assets dwarf anything in that revenue class. If one were to add in the gross revenues of all church-controlled business entities (more in keeping with the *Fortune* 500), the total would be vastly higher.

As for comparison with religious bodies rather than corporations: the Seventh-day Adventists, with a similar global membership, reported total revenues of $1.6 billion. The Evangelical Lutheran Church in America, with a similar U.S. membership, had $1.7 billion in revenue for 1995 versus the Mormons' estimated $4.9 billion in U.S. income the same year, making the LDS Church nearly three times as rich on a per-member basis.

How does the church spend its money? Assets were not revealed in the last financial accounting to be issued, but Arrington and Bitton summarized 1958 expenditures in *The Mormon Experience:* ward and stake buildings and activities, $28,313,005; schools and education, $15,508,502; missions, $13,034,893; welfare, $6,881,667; construction and operation of temples, $2,756,550; general administration, $2,264,940; central church buildings, $1,242,913; genealogy, $1,748,831; men's and women's auxiliaries (spending from their funds), $664,625; other, $378,380. Total expenditures for 1958: $72,794,306.

Though conditions have changed markedly since 1958, the breakdown of major priorities might be somewhat similar today. The cost of church-wide administration remains low, as is typically true for religious denominations.

President Hinckley is emphatic in pointing out that most of the church's assets are "revenue-consuming and not revenue-producing." True enough. Like other religions, the LDS Church spends its money largely on buildings for worship and fellowship, education, missionary programs, maintenance of existing structures, and welfare for its own members and others. But as it invests in temples and meetinghouses, the church shores up its potential base of tithing income. And then there's that investment portfolio. Church doctrine encourages members to set aside money and food reserves, and "the church practices what it preaches," says David Burton. "Do we net to zero? No, we don't net to zero."

The main source of revenue, the tithes, comes directly into Salt Lake City. Says *Sunstone* editor Elbert Eugene Peck, "All dollars go to headquarters, and then headquarters disburses it. The collections are taken on Sunday, and by Monday the church knows every cent it has collected and calls go out to bishops to make sure the money has been deposited in banks." Burton confirms this, saying that all Mormon finance is "centralized" in Salt Lake City. Fast offerings stay a bit more local: they are collected and used for the welfare needs of local stakes.

A tithing dollar raised in the Philippines becomes just part of the church's general funds. As a practical matter, of course, some of that tithe money raised in Philippine pesos will be spent in Philippine pesos, and therefore the church would have local currency accounts in Manila. Tithes go into a number of consolidating bank accounts around the world, from which the Mormon financial managers can make money go where they need it to go. That is partly because the church is growing at such a breathtaking pace, and this growth has put enormous strains on the Mormon financial and organizational structure.

The church has handled this growth by, in effect, completely retooling itself as though it were a multinational corporation. President Hinckley, faced with the exponential growth of the church, shifted local-level financial decisionmaking, including especially building projects, to headquarters in Utah. More recently part of the burden of local maintenance funding has been returned to the wards.

This global growth, of course, transfers much church wealth from the developed world to the developing world, especially Latin America, where the expansion is particularly successful. The wealth moves generally in the form of building projects and not, as one might expect, in welfare from congregations in the United States to congregations overseas. Since welfare fast offerings are retained at the local level, this means that fast offerings in the Philippines are made to help Filipinos. Furthermore, converts to Mormonism may not be middle-class, but they think they are middle-class and are usually literate, so their self-reliance and belief in work are not altogether different from the beliefs held by a Mormon in Bountiful, Utah.

Perhaps the most interesting problem the church faces is how to maintain such a far-flung multinational organization and still control its home base. After all, this was a church that for years was largely located in Utah and a few western states. It had a very homogeneous membership.

"They've got a couple of problems," says the venture capitalist Bradley Bertoch. "First, the church needs to recruit labor to drive their business growth beyond the borders of Utah and the United States. But at the same time they have to make sure they don't lose control of the home ground. If you are a multinational company, you face the same problems of resource allocation in new markets. The difference, of course, is that it's all much easier if you have the tether of brotherhood."

One of the guiding principles of Mormonism is self-reliance, and nowhere is this more apparent than in the church's remarkable welfare system. The church teaches that if a person encounters hard times, his first duty is to solve the problem himself. If he cannot solve the problem, he is directed to look to his extended family for help. If he still cannot solve his problem, he is to ask his bishop for the church's help. By church precept, only as a last resort is he to go to the federal government, understood as a sometimes necessary evil. Avoiding outside help as much as possible applies to good times and lean. It is the reason the church maintains those huge grain silos. No matter how hard times get, it can still feed its own. In this sense, it can seem as militantly self-sufficient as any militia-survivalist with a bunker in his backyard—except that Mormons believe in sharing rather than guarding a hoard with a gun.

When a person comes to the church for help, a large and highly efficient church-run system kicks in. Facilities have paid professionals as necessary, but most of the labor in the storehouses, all those canneries, and even some of the agricultural operations, the sixty-one social service centers, and the well-patronized Deseret Industries thrift stores, comes from Mormon ward volunteers. Many Mormon couples joke about having furnished their first homes with "Early DI."

Volunteer labor not only stretches the philanthropic dollar but solidifies church ties as members work together. And possibly most important, it helps the church remain truly independent of any government or corporation. It can grow its own food, process it, can it, ship it. There are, of course, some items it does not produce, such as plastic garbage bags, but these are not deemed necessary for survival. Anyone interested in survival should check out the church's prodigious bean-growing and -processing capabilities.

Does the Mormon welfare system actually work? The best assessment an outsider can make is that, yes, it seems to. A recipient of Mormon welfare may be paid in cash or may be given coupons he or she can use in a Bishop's Storehouse for some of those Deseret-brand foods. All Mormons are supposed to receive monthly visits from ward "teachers," an office in the lay priesthood, and these teachers can help bishops and relief society presidents assess member needs. Everything a welfare recipient receives is controlled by the bishop, who has complete flexibility to deal with the church member as he sees fit. It is not unusual for the church to help a church member finish an education or receive vocational training if that is deemed the problem.

Above all, what is stressed are permanent, not temporary solutions, and welfare recipients are almost always asked by the church to do something in exchange for the help they receive. The church's 99 employment offices are another important part of this system. In 1996 they placed 47,239 people in gainful employment.

According to Keith McMullin, a General Authority who oversees the welfare system, "the average recipient gets aid for two and a half to three months. The average cash value of the aid is $300. A good portion of that comes in the form of commodities." McMullin adds that less than 5 percent of the church's membership in the United States and Canada uses the system today; 25 percent did so during the Great Depression, when the system was started.

In its stress on self-reliance and meticulous attention to detail there may be no charitable organization on earth to match the Mormon Church, pound for pound, volunteer for volunteer. It works as well as it does in part because of its unusually high degree of vertical integration. The Mormons grow the peaches, can the peaches, ship the peaches, distribute the peaches, and, yes, eat the peaches, but not before actually working in the store to help pay for their welfare by, among other things, stacking the peaches. Another reason the Mormon welfare system works so well is that, though the goal is not profit but philanthropy, it is run very much like a business.

The welfare system is funded out of the fast offerings, in lieu of eating two meals, that Mormons give the first Sunday of each month in addition to their tithe. These funds stay local until they meet the needs of the ward. Once local needs are met, they flow to higher levels to be used elsewhere. "Elsewhere" could be humanitarian aid virtually anywhere in the world. Some production takes place on church property outside the United States. Zimbabwe, for example, is home to church-owned farmland, and there is a spanking-new cannery in Yerevan, Armenia, for the use of church members and volunteers. Half of Armenia is unemployed.

Nonfood items are packaged in south Salt Lake City's Humanitarian Sort Center to be shipped for international humanitarian aid: reconditioned medical equipment and sewing machines, school supplies and blankets, thousands of tons of secondhand clothes for poor people and disaster relief. As with other charities, the Sort Center seeks donated goods from businesses as well as individuals for these projects. Once largely dependent on distribution networks of other churches and charities outside the United States, the LDS Church is increasingly developing its own channels.

In the fourteen years from 1984 to 1997, the church says, it made a total of $30.7 million in cash donations to non-Mormon humanitarian aid (not counting the worth of commodities and goods shipped) in 146 countries, including the United States. Its efforts have included responses to flooding in the U.S. Midwest (1993), the earthquake in Kobe, Japan (1995), and the Korean crop failure (1996–97). In 1997 there were 1,272 welfare (as opposed to evangelistic) missionaries serving two-year terms in the United States and abroad. LDS cash donations for humanitarian aid in 1997 totaled $4.6 million. Additional humanitarian aid channeled through the church in 1997 included 3,338 tons of clothing, 4,023 tons of food, 220 tons of educational materials, and 351 tons of medical equipment and supplies.

All churches, of course, perform charity and mercy work, but it is difficult to compare those efforts with LDS humanitarian programs. In 1997 U.S. congregations of the similarly sized Evangelical Lutheran Church in America raised $11.8 million in cash donations for worldwide hunger. The same year it raised $3.64 million for domestic and international disaster response, for a one-year humanitarian cash total of $15.44 million, more than half the amount the LDS provided over fourteen years. Then there were the Lutherans' many assistance programs apart from simple cash donations. Like the Lutherans, many Protestant and Catholic agencies at home and abroad do extensive—and expensive—medical and educational work. The LDS Church no longer maintains hospitals, and its short-term missionaries concentrate on proselytizing for converts.

Nevertheless, in their commodity production and welfare systems, the Latter-day Saints have created and maintained a remarkably massive and efficient mechanism for meeting human needs of their own members. No other religious denomination has attempted to follow in their path.

CHAPTER 8

SOME LATTER-DAY STARS

THE OCCASION BOTH DISPLAYED AND CELEBRATED THE LATTER-DAY
Saints' presence in the firmament of American celebrityhood that encom-
passes personalities in all realms of achievement and, yes, a rogue or two.
Some 200 scholars, members of the Mormon History Association, including Leonard Arrington, the dean of the twentieth-century LDS historians,
were gathered in a well-marbled reception room at the Dirksen Senate
Office Building on Capitol Hill. Their hosts that evening in 1998 were no
less than three LDS members of the U.S. Senate: Robert Bennett and
Orrin Hatch of Utah and Gordon Smith of Oregon. The thoughtful
opening prayer was led by Hatch, who in 1976 had defeated fellow
Mormon Frank Moss, the last Utah Democrat in the Senate. (Hatch eventually became chairman of the powerful Senate Judiciary Committee and
announced a long-shot bid for the U.S. presidency in 1999.) The group
was then greeted by Admiral Paul Yost Jr., the retired commandant of the
U.S. Coast Guard and the second Mormon in history to achieve four-star
rank in the American military.

The courtly Bennett took the floor to highlight the Mormons' changing status in the capital. Early in the century, he reminisced, Reed Smoot
had been forced to fight for three years to be given his Senate seat. He had
been "on trial; so was the church." After his victory, Smoot and his family

had still been snubbed socially until the night when President Theodore Roosevelt, leaving a party, turned, and said, "Good night, Mrs. Smoot." That broke the ice. In those days the only LDS worship in town had been the Sunday afternoon gathering in the Smoot living room. Bennett described "the acceptance we have in the capital" as "light years" away from that of the Smoot days, but also markedly better than during the period when his father, Wallace Bennett, served in the Senate between 1951 and 1975.

A few years before, Bennett recalled, when he had been asked to preside over the annual Presidential Prayer Breakfast, someone had expressed surprise: "I thought it was some *Christian* sort of thing." The scholars in Bennett's audience responded to that theological slight with an in-group chuckle. Currently, Bennett pointed out, there were four "temple recommend" senators, the three Republicans in the room that night plus Nevada's Harry Reid, who shortly thereafter was to become the Senate's number-two Democrat (minority whip). Nowadays, said Bennett, "no one thinks it extraordinary" to have Mormons in the Senate and House.

Mormon presence in celebrity circles has come so far that no one thinks it extraordinary, either, to find a Mormon testimony bearer in such places as professional football (quarterback Steve Young of the San Francisco 49ers) or baseball (Dale Murphy, late of the Atlanta Braves) or to learn that certifiably wholesome entertainers (the Osmonds) are Mormon. There are best-seller authors (such as Stephen Covey), distinguished academics (prize example: Kim B. Clark, dean of the Harvard Business School), wildly successful businessmen (the Romneys, Marriotts, and Huntsmans), and even famous scientists (the late Philo Farnsworth, inventor of electronic TV transmission and the picture tube).

But nowhere is the Mormon presence more solidly expressed as a voice in the American mainstream than in the world of politics. After the 1998 elections a record sixteen Mormons were seated in Congress, signifying their people's secure place in the American establishment. (The Evangelical Lutheran Church in America, with a similar U.S. membership, boasted eighteen seats.) A fifth LDS senator had been added, former Congressman Michael Crapo of Idaho. There were eleven Mormons in the House of Representatives: all three of Utah's representatives, Christopher

Cannon, Merrill Cook, and James Hansen; John Doolittle, Wally Herger, Howard "Buck" McKeon, and Ron Packard of California; Matt Salmon of Arizona; Mike Simpson of Idaho; Ernest Istook of Oklahoma; and Tom Udall of New Mexico. Udall was the only Democrat. (The nonvoting delegate from American Samoa, Democrat Eni F. H. Faleomavaega, was also LDS. Democratic Representative Leonard Boswell of Iowa was a member of the separate Reorganized Church.)

During the twentieth century's closing phase the two Utah Republican senators became the toast of the Washington news shows, enmeshed in the Bill Clinton impeachment, while back home in Utah other Mormon celebrities were caught up in the country's other moral pageant of the period, the Salt Lake City Olympics scandal. For his part, sober-sided Judiciary Chairman Hatch veered between judiciousness and moralistic contempt for the impeached president. He told Salt Lake's Mormon daily, the *Deseret News,* "These offenses were committed by the chief executive of our country, the individual who swore to faithfully execute the laws of the United States." The nation can tolerate a president who makes a mistake, he said, but not one "who makes a mistake and then breaks the law to cover it up. Any other citizen would be prosecuted for these crimes."

Hatch voted to oust Clinton on both the perjury and obstruction of justice counts. So did Senator Bennett, who was simultaneously the object of considerable press attention as chairman of the special Senate committee examining the threat of a Y2K computer meltdown and of the Republican team handling issues in the technology industry. Bennett said it is dangerous for the nation to have a president who lies, whether under oath or not. "We cannot trust his word, whatever the issue. We will always be fearful of where that trait of his could take us, and we should be." Bennett told the Senate he had a clear conscience. "I would vote the same if the president's name were Ronald Wilson Reagan." In the waning days of the trial Bennett was in the spotlight working fruitlessly with California Democrat Dianne Feinstein, seeking to revive his plan for a Senate censure of the errant president.

Another LDS impeachment player was Congressman Christopher Cannon, one of the House Republican managers who prosecuted Clinton before the Senate. An attorney, Cannon was first elected in 1996 to represent Provo and part of the Salt Lake area. After cataloging Clinton's deeds before the Senate, Cannon declared: "All these acts obstruct justice. All these acts are federal felony crimes. All these acts were committed by William Jefferson Clinton." Like almost everyone, the LDS senators voted strictly along party lines on the two counts against Clinton, as the Saints in the House had done on all four of the impeachment articles.

Indeed, it's hard to find any ideological Mormon bloc across party lines on Capitol Hill. Senator Reid, as a rare Mormon Democrat, has urged federal and Nevada state legislation requiring insurance companies to cover birth control, hardly a mainstream Mormon viewpoint. And he spoke to an organization of gay and lesbian constituents shortly after Clinton became the first U.S. president to do so. But sometimes church interests attract bipartisan help. Democrat Reid, whose son served a term as a missionary to Argentina, coaxed his friend Vice President Al Gore into asking Russia's President Boris Yeltsin about legalizing the LDS Church in that country. Republican Senator Gordon Smith went further, advocating an amendment that could have cost the recalcitrant Russians $200 million in foreign aid. That "got everyone's attention," commented Jeffrey Holland, the apostle overseeing the newly legalized Russian mission.

Early in his Senate tenure, Hatch discussed the church's role in politics at length in a *Sunstone* interview. He said, "I have yet to have any General Authority give me any instructions concerning how I should vote back in Washington, and I would be shocked if one did." On the other hand, "if a church feels strongly that a moral issue has been acutely violated, then I think that church is obligated to do its best to stand up for its belief." After all, he noted, that's what the pope does. That probably summarizes the outlook of most Mormons in politics to this day.

Throughout the twentieth century Mormons have naturally dominated among the top officeholders in Utah. B. H. Roberts, who was refused a seat as an early Utah member of the U.S. House of Representatives after statehood, and Senator Smoot were both General Authorities in the church hierarchy. So was the controversial Ezra Taft Benson, who was simultaneously an LDS apostle and secretary of agriculture.

Utah has had a Mormon governor for all but twenty of the years since achieving statehood in 1896. The incumbent, Michael Leavitt, was the only LDS governor among the fifty states as of 1999. He is a practicing church member and onetime missionary who set a state record by winning reelection in 1996 with a margin of 75 percent. But the boy wonder image enjoyed by Leavitt, in line to be chairman of the National Governors Association, was tarnished by the Olympics bribery scandal. He had served on the controversial Salt Lake bid committee, but he insisted that he had been a mere figurehead who did not attend the meetings. The Olympics misconduct, he declared during the agonizing cleanup phase, violated the community's moral standards and had occasioned "relentless soul-searching."

Leavitt and his colleagues scoured the ranks of Mormon business celebrities to find a Mr. Clean to be the new president of the Salt Lake Organizing Committee. They ended up recruiting Mitt Romney, a millionaire venture capitalist, cofounder of the Staples office-supply chain, heir of Utah pioneers, onetime missionary, church lay official in Boston, and member of an LDS political dynasty. His father, George Romney, was president of American Motors Corporation and served as governor of Michigan beginning in 1962. Even more than Ezra Taft Benson, George Romney placed Mormonism in the nation's political consciousness through a failed try for the 1968 Republican presidential nomination. He then served in the Nixon cabinet as secretary of the Housing and Urban Development Department. His wife, Lenore, ran for the U.S. Senate in 1970 but suffered a crushing defeat by the incumbent Phillip Hart.

Both of the Romneys' sons carried on the family interest in politics. In 1998 Scott Romney had the governor's backing for the Michigan attorney general nomination, but the state Republican convention picked someone else. Mitt Romney gave Massachusetts' senator-for-life Ted Kennedy a bit of a scare as his Republican opponent in 1994. Ted injected religion into the race, demanding to know whether Mitt supported the LDS policy of denying blacks full participation until 1978. Mitt coolly reminded voters that Ted's brother John had had to face anti-Catholic questioning when he ran for president.

There's also a Democratic LDS political dynasty, the Udalls, who are said to have held more offices in Arizona than any other family. Stewart Udall, whose grandfather David had come to Arizona as a Mormon missionary and whose father, Levi, had been a state supreme court justice, won three terms in the U.S. House. He then served as the Interior secretary under President Kennedy; he continued work as a lawyer and environmental activist after leaving Washington. His younger brother and law partner, the late Morris "Mo" Udall, succeeded him in the House and served for fifteen terms. Morris ran for the Democratic presidential nomination in 1976 but lost to Jimmy Carter. Stewart's son Tom, New Mexico's attorney general, ousted an incumbent to win a U.S. House seat in 1998. (Morris's son Mark was also elected to Congress from Colorado, but he does not identify as LDS.) Oregon's Republican Senator Smith is also related to the Udall clan.

Another colorful Washington personality, though briefly, was Paula Hawkins, the crusading housewife who was elected to the U.S. Senate from Florida in 1980. Hawkins was the first and as yet only LDS woman in the Senate, the first woman to be elected a U.S. senator without being the wife or daughter of a politician, and the first well-known LDS woman to report suffering sexual abuse as a child. Hawkins complained that male chauvinists refused to take her seriously; after just one term she was defeated for reelection by Florida's popular governor, Bob Graham. Another Mormon, Democrat Jean Westwood, in 1972 became the first woman to chair a major U.S. political party. Angela "Bay" Buchanan, a Catholic who converted to Mormonism as an adult, was named treasurer of the United States by President Reagan, the youngest person to hold that office. She was campaign manager in her brother Pat's presidential runs of 1992 and 1996 and then became cohost of *Equal Time* on CNBC television.

Prominent LDS appointees to high federal office besides Benson, Udall, and Romney have included Secretary of the Treasury David M. Kennedy (named in 1969), later the church's ambassador; Secretary of Education Terrel H. Bell (1981); U.S. Education Commissioner Sterling McMurrin (1961); Assistant Secretary of Labor Esther Peterson (1961); Assistant Attorney General Rex Lee (1975); and Lieutenant General Brent Scowcroft, named national security adviser by President Ford in 1975 and again by President-elect Bush in 1988.

The nation's highest civilian honor, the Presidential Medal of Freedom, was given to Esther Peterson in 1981 for her consumer advocacy. The same honor went in 1988 to the late LDS hotel magnate J. Willard Marriott, who had begun with a nine-stool root-beer stand in 1927, and in 1996 to Morris Udall. Benson was granted the Presidential Citizens Medal in 1989 while he was president of the church. The Congressional Medal of Honor, the highest military honor, has been given to at least eight Mormons.

Then there are the public figures who didn't win medals. Arizona Governor Evan Mecham was the first prominent LDS politician to be impeached and removed from office, though he was acquitted on criminal charges stemming from a campaign loan. And Mormon Richard Miller blotted the church's long reputation for producing FBI agents in 1991 when he became the bureau's first accused spy; he was sentenced to twenty years.

Even more than FBI agents, Mormons are thought of as businessmen, and they have produced an impressive number of successful ones since the pioneer struggles. D. Michael Quinn has compiled a list of 140 corporations, outside the Intermountain West and not controlled by the church, that have had LDS executives in one of the top positions. The *Latter-day Herald,* an independent monthly based in Leesburg, Virginia, publishes a mythical "Mormon Stock Exchange" of publicly traded companies with top executives who are active church members. Listings for 1999, in order of market capitalization: Albertsons (President Richard L. King), Marriott International (Chairman J. W. Marriott Jr.), Zions Bancorporation (Chairman Harris H. Simmons), Black & Decker (CEO Nolan Archibald), Times Mirror (Chairman Mark Willes), First Security Corp. (Chairman Spencer Eccles), Ryder System (CEO Tony Burns), Iomega (Chairman David J. Dunn), Hollywood Ent (CEO Mark J. Wattles), ASARCO (President Francis McAllister), Franklin Covey (Chairman Stephen R. Covey), Fonix (Chairman Steve Studdert), Geneva Steel (President Robert Grow).

To the general public, the most famous of the breed is J. W. "Bill" Marriott Jr. of Bethesda, Maryland, his father's successor as head of the billionaire family's enterprises. Besides hotels, the Marriott companies have holdings in real estate, restaurants, airline and dormitory food, and assisted living for seniors. But nary a casino. The Mormon ethic is also reflected in the corporation's global outlook and commitment to selling service, cleanliness, consistency, and assiduous attention to detail. In 1998

Fortune named Marriott International one of the one hundred "best companies to work for in America," praising it for, among other things, providing child care for low-income workers and a twenty-four-hour phone hotline for employees with personal problems.

Bill Marriott is generous with time and money when it comes to the church. And he puts the Book of Mormon beside the Gideons Bible in the nearly 200,000 hotel rooms of the Marriott, Ritz-Carlton, Courtyard, Fairfield, Residence Inn, Renaissance, and Towne Place Suites chains. Why? The LDS book is "the word of God" and "clarifies a lot of the teaching of the Bible and a lot of things we read in the Bible," he says. Marriott also professes, "I know that in this day and age we are led by a prophet of God, President Gordon B. Hinckley, and that God talks to him and reveals to him what he wants him to do."

If anything, Jon M. Huntsman of Salt Lake City is even more the paragon of LDS piety among businessmen. He is chairman of Huntsman Chemical, a corporation that he owns outright. With some 10,000 employees, it is the largest privately held chemical firm in the world, a ranking further solidified by a $2.7 billion purchase of four British firms in 1999, doubling annual sales to the $7.4 billion range. Huntsman's personal net worth has been estimated by *Forbes* at $2.2 billion. In 1997 *Fortune* ranked him among the twenty-five most generous Americans in personal philanthropy apart from corporate foundations. Huntsman has pledged $100 million to a cancer institute at the University of Utah and built a concrete plant to provide housing for victims of the earthquake in Armenia. In 1998 he presented his alma mater, the University of Pennsylvania business school, with $40 million, no strings attached. He gives generously to a Salt Lake homeless shelter and, of course, to the LDS Church.

Like many others among the LDS lay "clergy," Huntsman estimates that he devotes fifteen to twenty hours per week to church duties. He once dropped company responsibilities and moved his wife and nine children to Washington, D.C., to serve as the mission president. "I find it impossible to separate life and corporate involvement from my religious convictions," he says. Relief of human suffering has been added to mere profit-making as an explicit corporate goal, and as a result, employees at Huntsman "have had a far greater spirit of accomplishment and motivation" and "our unity and teamwork and corporate enthusiasm have never been higher." He tells employees, "I feel the Lord has blessed us in this company."

Huntsman is equally devoted in his support for church doctrine. The Book of Mormon "allows us to understand how a civilization existed on this the American continent and what the role of the Savior was in coming forth to this continent." He says that "there has never been a question in my mind that Jesus Christ established this church at this point in time so that men and women could derive happiness and could prepare themselves for his second coming and perform the ordinances necessary in this mortal state."

President Hinckley's own nephew, Mark Willes, is a more controversial Mormon executive who moved from vice chairman of General Mills to CEO of the Times Mirror newspaper company in 1995. He was also publisher of the flagship *Los Angeles Times* from 1997 to 1999. There he earned the office nicknames of "Cap'n Crunch" and "the Cereal Killer" by quickly shutting down *New York Newsday* and cutting jobs at the *Times* and his other papers, which include the *Baltimore Sun, Hartford Courant,* and *Long Island Newsday.* Distinguished figures in American journalism complained that Willes was marketing newspapers as a product like Cheerios when he blurred the traditional line between the editorial and business sides in favor of a teamwork approach. And there was considerable turnover in the executive ranks. In 1999 the *Columbia Journalism Review* commented that it was "not hard to find staffers who'll tell you that the [*Times*'s] content has been dumbed down to further his goal of increased circulation." But investors were more sympathetic toward his campaign to remake American newspapering.

The Utah native David Checketts, president and CEO of New York's Madison Square Garden, utilized that position to host President Hinckley's 1998 rally there and offered the opening prayer. In that year's ranking by the *Sporting News* of the one hundred most powerful people in sports, Checketts ranked seventy-fifth, just behind the joint chairman of the Chicago Bulls and White Sox and just ahead of the Turner Sports president. Checketts, formerly president of the Utah Jazz basketball team and then vice president of the National Basketball Association, is part of the ownership group for basketball's New York Knicks, and his company operates such entities as New York's Radio City Music Hall and the MSG Network. The latter responsibility put Checketts in a peculiar spot for a devout Mormon when he hired Marv Albert to call Knicks games on radio and to host a nightly sports show on cable TV. Albert's sportscasting career had seemingly died less than a year earlier after he halted a lurid trial by admitting misdemeanor assault on a former girlfriend. NBC-TV said it had no plans to rehire Albert, but Checketts explained, "We consider Marv part of the family, and loyalty is important to us."

The most famous Mormon in the sports world, by far, is Steve Young, quarterback of the NFL's San Francisco 49ers and great-great-great-grandson of Utah's founder, Brigham Young. Steve Young was a star player for Brigham Young University's veteran coach LaVell Edwards, who has sent a series of quarterbacks to the NFL, including the 1990 Heisman Trophy winner Ty Detmer. Detmer was Young's understudy with the 49ers until he was traded to the Cleveland Browns.

Remarkably, Steve Young's career only got in gear when he was nearing thirty-one. He first earned a law degree, then spent two years in the now-defunct U.S. Football League (after a $40 million signing deal), two years with hapless Tampa Bay, and four seasons on the bench as backup for the 49ers quarterback Joe Montana. But since 1991 there's been no stopping him. He was the league's most valuable player in 1992 and 1994, MVP for the 1995 Super Bowl, and a Pro Bowl player for six consecutive years. Despite his abbreviated career, he has run for more touchdowns than any quarterback in the history of the National Football League.

More significantly, the sports statistician Allen Barra contended in the *New York Times Magazine,* Young is the best quarterback in football history. By the NFL's complex statistical measure for overall performance, Young's career average of 96.2 puts him in first place, and his 1994 season rating of 112.8 is the highest anyone has ever achieved. His pass efficiency rating (yards per throw adjusted for interceptions) is number one in NFL annals, edging out Otto Graham and Young's teammate Montana. In the 1998 season, during which he turned thirty-seven, Young posted 62 percent in pass completions, 4,641 yards gained, and an overall rating of 97.3.

Young is also a charity champion, concentrating on helping children. "If you can effect change for a child," he reasons, "you're effecting change for sixty or seventy years and many generations." He continually raises money for his Forever Young Foundation, which provides a wide range of medical, academic, and athletic opportunities to sick and underprivileged youngsters.

He puts the emphasis on youth appeal in his frequent testimonial talks for the LDS Church. And he's as devout as they come, deviating from Mormon expectations only by remaining unmarried as of 1999. Since his job requires Sunday work during the season, he receives permission from his bishop to hold weekly sacrament meetings on Saturday nights, in his hotel if the team is playing an away game.

"I've found myself many times trying to make decisions in my life, career decisions, decisions about my personal life, which direction I should go. I've struggled over many decisions and the Book of Mormon has had a great soothing effect on me many times, trying to find the right thing to do." As Young sees it, religious faith is the great leveler, and fame counts for nothing in God's eyes. "I don't have to do anything other than live righteously, follow the teachings of my parents and the prophets that are on earth today, and the prophets of old." He finds comfort in the well-fixed habits of the Mormon lifestyle. "You don't have to wake up every morning and say I'm not going to drink today or I'm not going to smoke today or I'm going to be a man of integrity today. I've made decisions so often they become a part of you."

Dale Murphy, former star outfielder for the Atlanta Braves, is equally committed. Raised Presbyterian, he converted to the LDS Church after the witnessing of a teammate while he was playing minor league ball in South Carolina. Murphy belted 398 career home runs and was the National League MVP for two consecutive years (1982, 1983), league RBI champion for two consecutive years (1982, 1983), and a seven-time member of the all-star team. He had a remarkable season start in 1985, with an RBI in each of the first seven games and a team record of 29 RBIs for the month of April. He seems destined to enter the Baseball Hall of Fame alongside fellow Mormon Harmon Killebrew, who ranks fifth in all-time career home runs (573) and was American League MVP in 1969.

Upon retiring from athletics, Murphy agreed to serve a church mission presidency. Of the Book of Mormon, he testifies, "I know that it's the

Word of God and it's what Joseph Smith said it was." The father of eight believes that marriage in the Mormon temple for time and all eternity is one of his faith's most important benefits: "The most important duty we have is to our families. And to be able to go to the temple and have that blessing of being sealed together forever is the greatest blessing you can receive." Murphy also walks the walk. For his humanitarian work, he was named to the Sports Humanitarian Hall of Fame in its second year of existence.

Other star LDS athletes have included the golfers Billy Casper and Johnny Miller (both in the PGA Hall of Fame); Jack Dempsey and Gene Fullmer (both in the Boxing Hall of Fame); and the lineup of twenty-one Olympic medal winners listed in the LDS *Church Almanac,* including the gymnastics gold medalist Peter Vidmar.

Some Mormons are stars of the best-seller lists, applying their religion's Middle American values and inspiration in a winning formula. Consider Stephen R. Covey, who taught organizational behavior at Brigham Young University and in 1983 set up his own Covey Leadership Center to make available his hugely successful speeches and seminars on management techniques. His reported fee for personal appearances runs from $50,000 to $60,000. In 1989 Covey published *The Seven Habits of Highly Effective People,* which has sold in the millions in twenty-eight languages. Since then he has turned out other motivational and organizational titles, including *The Seven Habits of Highly Effective Families,* a classically Mormon theme from a father of nine children.

Covey's books and seminars do not preach Mormonism in any overt way. And his company sent clients an apology, denying any political agenda, following one untypically ideological Covey speech. He agreed to appear at a fund-raiser for Hawaii's Save Traditional Marriage organization, part of the successful movement to ban same-sex marriage in Hawaii. Covey had been quoted in the Honolulu papers as stating that the bar to homosexual coupling was "a natural law" and that he supported the movement against it. The Covey organizational gospel was subjected to a 1998 *New Republic* analysis that was equally hostile toward Covey's writings and the entire Mormon religion. Both were branded suspect, "deeply authoritarian," and patriarchal.

Interviewed by Apostle M. Russell Ballard on a video used for evangelistic home meetings, Covey said, "You can pretty well trace almost all the social problems in the world to the breakdown of the family. So the family is part of God's plan of eternal happiness for his children." Covey borrowed an image from C. S. Lewis to explain his own faith: "I believe in Christ as I believe in the sun at noonday, not that I can see it, but by it I can see everything else. First of all, he's my personal Savior. I'm not qualified to save myself." Covey has offered heartfelt testimony to the restored gospel at such church events as the dedication of the new stake center in Ashburn, Virginia.

Covey has the same literary agent as Richard and Linda Eyre, who are also LDS parents of nine. Drawing on their church's old-fashioned family values, they have scored in the booming self-help genre with such titles as *Teaching Your Children Responsibility, Teaching Your Children Joy, Teaching Your Children Values, How to Talk to Your Child About Sex,* and *Three Steps to a Strong Family.*

Richard Paul Evans has the touch for the generic pop inspirational market. As a young advertising executive in Salt Lake City, he wrote *The Christmas Box,* a fable about the death of a child and "the true meaning of Christmas" that he said came to him through early-morning divine guidance. When no publishing house (not even LDS publishers) showed interest, he printed and marketed the book on his own. *Box* was a word-of-mouth publishing phenomenon. The church-owned Deseret Books chain sold 6,000 copies in the 1993 Christmas season, then 70,000 the next year. After sales hit 250,000, Simon & Schuster paid $4.2 million for the rights to *Box* and a sequel. Critics loathe Evans's writing; ordinary readers love it.

Though she never mentions her own religious affiliation, there are elements of LDS theology as well as New Age spirituality woven into Betty J. Eadie's surprise 1992 inspirational best-seller, the coauthored *Embraced by the Light.* It tells of Eadie's near-death experience during a 1973 operation in which she says she was taken up to heaven and met Jesus. Raised on a South Dakota Indian reservation and at a Catholic boarding school, with some Methodist influence, Eadie is an adult convert to Mormonism. That shows in *Embraced,* which describes a vision of Jesus and God the Father as two visible, embodied beings. In an ABC-TV interview, Eadie said she learned through her heavenly ascent that people who died in the Nazi Holocaust had chosen their fate prior to birth, a personal riff on the Mormon theology of premortal existence. Mormon members snapped up the book, but Apostle Boyd K. Packer reportedly called it "bunk" at one stake meeting and the Evangelical Protestant polemicist Douglas Groothuis accused her of promoting what he regarded as Mormon heresies. Undaunted by critics, she wrote another best-seller, *The Awakening Heart,* in 1996. In 1999 she made her first appearance with New York's Seminar Center, a prime showcase for mediums, New Age gurus, and self-help advisers "to the stars."

Though Mormons are not as well known for high-end literature, they can claim two winners of the Pulitzer Prize for historical writings (Merlo Pusey in 1952 and Laurel Thatcher Ulrich in 1991) and three winners of the Bancroft Prize in history (Pusey, Ulrich, and Richard Bushman). Pulitzers in journalism have gone to Mormons John M. Hightower, Robert D. Mullins, and the investigative reporter Jack Anderson. Steve Benson, Ezra Taft's grandson, won the 1993 Pulitzer for editorial cartooning, but he is no longer a church member.

One best-selling book writer whom devout Mormons might rather forget is the rough-edged, Emmy-winning TV personality Roseanne Barr. She has written a sarcastic account about being raised by Jewish parents in Salt Lake City but with an involvement in Mormonism for ten years during her girlhood, along with her mother, after a Mormon's prayer appeared to cure her of childhood palsy. Barr was also in a state mental hospital for a year, gave birth out of wedlock, and in 1991 accused her mother of physical abuse and her father of sexual abuse. Both parents flatly denied the charges.

For Mormons, and Mormon watchers, the paragons of Saintly showbiz would be Donny and Marie Osmond. Donny broke in as a boy, singing at age six with his brothers as The Osmonds on TV's *Andy Williams Show* as an LDS version of The Jackson Family. The Osmond brothers, minus Donny, are still performing in Branson, Missouri. From 1976 to 1979 the teenage Donny cohosted a network TV variety show with younger sister Marie. During those years they won a Grammy and the various Osmond acts racked up ten gold singles and fourteen gold albums. After assorted entertainment ventures, and a divorce and remarriage for Marie, the toothsome siblings reunited in 1998 for a G-rated TV talk show. Donny asked *Details* magazine, "Why is goodness looked upon as trite? . . . Mormonism has given us a sense of stability, a moral code, and sexual purity."

The church can claim another entertainment superstar, Gladys Knight, but she earned her fame long before her children persuaded her to be baptized into the Mormon Church in 1997. Her third marriage has broken up, and she is now on her third religion, having been raised Baptist and with a later conversion to Catholicism. Knight is Mormonism's one and only African American celebrity, a singularity reflecting the church's long-standing racial barrier. Knight is honored in the Rock and Roll Hall of Fame and was costarred in a short-lived TV sitcom with Flip Wilson. Her soul classic with the Pips, "Midnight Train to Georgia," was the nation's number-one record. But her latest album, *Many Different Roads,* testifies to nondenominational faith. She says, "I know my purpose, which is to further God's message and to shine his light a little more brightly."

Other Mormons who have made their mark include the actor Dean Jagger (an adult convert); the classical pianist Grant Johannesen; and the artificial heart surgeon William DeVries. Noted Mormon academicians include David P. Gardner, former president of the University of California system; E. Gordon Gee, president of West Virginia, Colorado, Ohio State, and Brown universities; and Harvard Business School's dean, Kim B. Clark.

Clark reminisced in an interview about how church growth has changed Mormon life in Boston since his arrival as a green Harvard freshman in 1967, a western public school graduate "without connections" mingling with eastern preppies. At that time all Mormons within the Route 128 belt met as one small, closely knit ward. In that "terrible first year," socially and academically, Clark found that his church congregation "was my salvation." There are now nine hundred Mormon students in the Boston area, about forty of them at Harvard. With two special wards for students and other young singles, and a large and well-established institute program, LDS parents no longer feel so reluctant to send their youths east to college.

Clark himself soon gave up his original goal to become a doctor but went on to graduate from Harvard cum laude, earn two more Harvard degrees, marry, father seven children (coaching youth basketball teams along the way), and produce a steady stream of scholarly books and articles. He was invited to join Harvard's faculty in 1978, the year he earned his Ph.D. The church, he says, is "like an anchor." It gives him a "clear sense of values" while helping to "handle conflicts in how I spend time, how to balance my life while living a full life." Knowing "where my priorities are has helped me academically, meeting my needs for achievement, because it makes me put first things first."

And there are those beauty queens. Assiduous as ever, D. Michael Quinn has compiled a listing of forty-nine pageant winners, starting with the 1951 Miss America, Colleen Hutchins. Mormon lasses have been named Mrs. America, Miss USA, Mrs. USA, Miss Universe, Miss World, Miss Teenage America, Miss Indian America, Miss Chinatown USA, Miss Rodeo America, Miss Drill Team USA, Miss Cheerleader USA, and, appropriately enough for the daughters of Deseret, the American Honey Queen of 1995. Amy Osmond, niece of Donny and Marie, was America's Junior Miss 1994, bearing the crown once worn by Kathie Lee Gifford, Deborah Norville, and Diane Sawyer.

Entering the twenty-first century, Mormon star achievers are standouts who fit easily within the ordinary matrix of American life. Given certain characteristics of the cohesive Mormon culture, its stress on discipline, hard work, and obedience, it is not surprising that Mormon achievements would be especially noticeable in certain fields: business, law, politics, the military and government work, medicine, athletics.

Weaker areas of achievement are equally predictable. A characteristically literal turn of mind combined with dogmatic Mormon ideals and a certain cultural isolation results in highly sentimentalized representational visual arts. LDS sculpture, paintings, even typography and graphic arts, appear rather like orphans from the late nineteenth century. Something similar undercuts Mormon efforts in the high arts in general; art is confused with propaganda, never with a quest; preconceived answers precede questions. In Mormon culture art is inspiration or entertainment, not exploration. As a result, Mormons—like those in some other American sectarian groups—are largely absent from the highest levels of achievement in the fine arts, literature, and the humanities in general. History is something of a special case (see chapter 15).

But as Senator Bennett noted, the public achievements of Mormons in American life are no longer extraordinary. The "peculiar people," both celebrity achievers and ordinary believers, are fully a part of America's mainstream.

CHAPTER 9
THE POWER PYRAMID

We thank thee, O God, for a prophet
To guide us in these latter days. . . .

THE WORDS OF WILLIAM FOWLER'S NINETEENTH-CENTURY MORMON hymn reverberated through Madison Square Garden on a Sunday morning in 1998 as 74,000 believers spontaneously broke into song to salute Gordon B. Hinckley. The president of the Church of Jesus Christ of Latter-day Saints had come to address the first such mass "Fireside" ever held in the New York City area. The gathering place was appropriately Mormon, since the Garden's president and CEO is the devout church member David Checketts. Thousands waved white handkerchiefs in greeting, and the bespectacled, avuncular Hinckley waved his in response. There was palpable excitement in the air, as there always is during a Mormon president's visitations out among the flock.

In some ways the church does not create a personality cult around its leadership. For instance, believers are told not to request autographs from any of the General Authorities. There was no ring-kissing or genuflection when selected believers were given a chance to meet Hinckley at a reception prior to the rally. But the presidential mystique has been enhanced in recent decades through a renewed emphasis on the church president's special title as prophet. "President" is a common enough designation for a chief executive, religious or secular. But as Fowler's hymn signifies, he is also the church's "Prophet, Seer, and Revelator." No spiritual leader of any other sizable denomination, not even the pope of Rome, carries such a status as God's direct spokesman on earth combined with such thoroughgoing control over a religious organization.

Hinckley is identical to Pope John Paul II in one regard, however. From the start of his reign he has notably strengthened his office and the bonds of his church through widespread worldwide travels. In just the first two years after his 1995 ascent to the top job, Hinckley visited twenty-two states in this country, twenty-eight other nations, and all the continents except Africa, which he reached soon thereafter. As part of his extensive travels in the years before becoming president, he personally dedicated half the LDS temples currently in use. More than any of his predecessors during the decades of church expansion, he is a personal presence for believers worldwide.

Besides overall vigor, the Hinckley regime has featured missionary advance, an unprecedented temple-building blitz, continuing erection of meetinghouses at a 350-a-year clip, tight administrative efficiency, and a more expansive approach to public relations. The last effort is no surprise. Gordon Hinckley is the godfather of Mormon publicity. In 1935 the University of Utah English major had completed a missionary stint in England and, at age twenty-five, was named the first executive secretary of the Church Radio, Publicity, and Mission Literature Committee. Except for time off helping run railroads during World War II, he was responsible for Mormon promotions in all media until he became executive secretary of the missionary committee in 1951. As church president, Hinckley has held an unprecedented number of open press conferences from New York to Albuquerque to Seoul to Tokyo, and he has granted interviews to newspapers, magazines, and TV's Mike Wallace and Larry King. In these appearances, ever the professional publicist, he conveys an upbeat philosophy and smoothes over the more controversial LDS teachings.

Born on June 23, 1910, Hinckley is entering the twenty-first century as a surprisingly spry octogenarian who arrives at church headquarters around 7:00 A.M. on the typical weekday and leaves perhaps eleven hours later, toting a briefcase stuffed with evening homework. He keeps fit through a nightly workout on an exercise treadmill, economizing his time by simultaneously watching the *NewsHour with Jim Lehrer* on TV. He jested, "I don't jog. I speak at the funerals of those who do." He and his wife Marjorie, wed in 1937, head a picture-book Mormon clan of five children, twenty-five grandchildren, and eighteen great-grandchildren.

People think of revelations to the Mormon president and hierarchy in terms of blockbusters such as the cessation of polygamy (1890) and the opening of lay offices to males of African descent (1978). But in LDS belief, the hierarchy is divinely directed in more mundane matters as well.

In an interview, Hinckley emphasized that the leadership seeks such guidance collectively: "Now and again a serious problem arises on which we do need direction and understanding. What do we do? We counsel together as brethren. We pray. We even fast. It's a very sacred thing. An answer comes; I'm satisfied of that. And the results that are achieved from what comes bear out the fact that it was done under inspiration, under revelation. It works. Now, it isn't a constant everyday thing. No. It comes as needed, according to need and opportunity."

He added that such occurrences "are very sacred and they're personal, and I don't like to talk about them very much, but they're very real."

Hinckley cited the examples of deciding to build a temple or selecting a General Authority or regional leader. He revealed that special divine guidance was also sought when the hierarchy discussed the idea of centralizing at headquarters all spending for construction and the other special needs of meetinghouses and cessation of local fund-raising drives. "We considered it. We prayed about it. We fasted about it. And the answer came that we should do it. No, we didn't hear a voice, but we received a perception, strong and clear."

Looked at in less spiritual terms, Hinckley and his colleagues instituted a new managerial strategy at a time when growth was already putting severe strains on the church and planning for ever greater expansion was essential. With some 25,000 congregations spread across 160 nations and territories, the top executives decided to end the previous role of local believers in participating in some financial matters, centralizing all strategy, funding, and construction planning at church headquarters. With every penny of members' offerings flowing to Salt Lake City, a smaller group of managers would be able to plan global expansion more efficiently.

But the Hinckley strategy is simultaneously moving in the opposite direction, too, pushing more ecclesiastical authority out into the field. Observers consider this to be Hinckley's most significant administrative tactic. Formerly, regional presidents overseas had to, in effect, "call in" to Salt Lake. But the Hinckley-era hierarchy has taken the unprecedented step of adding the new office of Area Authority, with such powers as creating new regional stakes and appointing their leaders. For the first time some key decisions are made in foreign countries, and occasionally by foreign nationals, always subject to review from Salt Lake as necessary.

Tony Burns, a Mormon who is chairman of the $6 billion Ryder Systems, Inc., of Miami, says he patterned some of his own corporate reorganization on the Hinckley design. "I learned from what the church did, and that helped me set up our new consumer business units," says Burns, who employs 45,000. "I think it is truly inspired as a model for growth." Joseph Cannon, CEO of Geneva Steel in Orem, Utah, is another managerial admirer. "What's fascinating about Hinckley is his sense of history. He's a huge history buff. He's got one foot in the nineteenth century and one foot in the twenty-first."

When an LDS president takes office, he chooses seasoned churchmen to be his first counselor and second counselor, and these three men then operate as a collective trio known as the First Presidency. The president sometimes acts on his own but almost always in the collective name of the First Presidency, and often the First Presidency takes a step together with the Quorum of the Twelve Apostles as the "Council." At meetings in the paneled boardroom at church headquarters, the presidential troika is placed at a shorter head table while the Twelve, placed by seniority, are seated along a longer table to create a T formation, subtly signifying their slightly lower status. (The fifteen men also meet weekly in the temple nearby.) In the inner sanctum the power dynamics between the First Presidency and the Quorum have shifted over the decades. But as far as outsiders are concerned, these fifteen men atop the Mormon hierarchy are a unitary force that rules with unchallenged—and virtually unquestioned—authority.

The institution of the collective First Presidency has come in handy. Like the popes, LDS presidents serve until they die; there is no tradition of resignation or removal of a president for cause. Unlike members of Catholicism's College of Cardinals, who lose voting power at age eighty, the same rule of life tenure holds for the Twelve Apostles. The first three times the LDS presidency fell vacant, there were politically convoluted gaps of two to three years before the next president took office. To avoid confusion and delay, a curiously rigid succession system took hold that could be altered in theory but never has been. The Quorum of the Twelve always chooses as new president the apostle who has served the longest, regardless of circumstances. That means the president of the church is old, often very old, not infrequently infirm when chosen, and sometimes non compos mentis during his tenure.

It was an open secret that owing to this system Hinckley often served as the de facto leader of his church, filling in for ailing superiors, long before he became the president in name. Thus, he came into the presidency well prepared for the task and doubtless determined to use his years of vigor to revitalize the top office.

There was serious presidential incapacity from 1942 until 1945, when Heber J. Grant died at age eighty-eight. The same problem developed in 1965-70 during the final years under President David O. McKay, who died at ninety-six, and once again during much of the reign of Joseph Fielding Smith, who became president in 1970 at the age of ninety-three and died in 1972.

Hinckley himself was named an extra counselor to President Spencer W. Kimball in 1981 because the first and second counselors (eighty-three and eighty-four years of age, respectively) were both incapacitated. Not long afterward Kimball himself, then eighty-six, became seriously disabled following a third brain operation. Hinckley (who soon became second counselor when the incumbent died) was effectively in charge of the church for four years until Kimball died in 1985.

Kimball's successor, Ezra Taft Benson, took office at eighty-six with signs of memory loss and physical frailty, and by 1989 was so handicapped that First Counselor Hinckley, along with Second Counselor Thomas S. Monson, had become the de facto leaders. Benson's condition was the topic of a minor flap in 1993 involving his grandson Steve Benson, a Pulitzer Prize–winning editorial cartoonist with the *Arizona Republic* (who soon left the church for other reasons). The younger Benson stated publicly that his grandfather had long struggled with increasing senility. "I believe the church strives mightily to perpetuate the myth, the fable, the fantasy, that President Benson, if not operating on all cylinders, at least is functioning effectively enough" to still be regarded as the "living, functioning prophet."

The following year Benson died and was succeeded by Howard W. Hunter, eighty-six and frail, who was able to function during only the first six of his nine months as president. When Hunter died in March of 1995, the shadow president became the actual president, and the Hinckley era began in earnest.

Like all incoming presidents, Hinckley was "sustained" in office by vote of the members attending the next church General Conference in Salt Lake City. But these are ritual occasions, not elections. God has already extended the call through his anointed leaders, and it is the duty of the membership to recognize this. The conferences have no elective or legislative role whatsoever. Some other hierarchical church bodies reserve doctrinal matters to the leadership and allow delegated assemblies to supervise temporal aspects, but not Mormonism. The conference does not even function in an advisory role or as an open forum. Nor does the hierarchy decide on certain policies through open discussion at national meetings, as the U.S. Catholic bishops do. The information that an LDS conference receives or does not receive—for instance, on finances—is totally the prerogative of the top leadership.

In the tightly managed Mormon kingdom, information, policy, planning, the appointments and removals of all regional and local officials, organizational minutiae—everything flows from the top down.

The inner workings of Mormonism appear to follow closely the structure and outlook of the modern American corporation, with thoroughgoing commitment to obedience and secrecy regarding internal operations, and an external strategy that combines well-calibrated public relations and commitment to sales (that is, conversions). The top of the hierarchy functions under a myth of unanimity; by policy, all disagreements must be hammered out in private and then presented with a united front. The unanimity is also chronological. When current leaders abrogate the policies and teachings of predecessor prophets, the change must not be admitted lest the church's infallibility appear to be in question. Some of these tendencies appear in other religious denominations, but rarely in such exaggerated form.

Like some Protestant groups, notably the Churches of Christ, the LDS Church takes pride in the fact that it has no "clergy class." But of course, LDS lay officers fill the same sort of role that clergy do and are ceremonially installed in office. What is largely unique to the Mormon way is the degree to which the clergy-type tasks are filled by appointees who work part-time and without pay. Leaders of regional and local units are volunteers who hold down secular jobs and squeeze in their demanding church workloads in off hours. They lack the sort of formal schooling for the pastoral vocation that most denominations require.

Even at the highest levels of doctrinal authority, oversight is the responsibility of leaders who are typically former business executives rather than intellectuals, and who rarely have academic training in religion, philosophy, or ancient languages. It is hard to imagine Catholic cardinals, Eastern Orthodox metropolitans, Episcopal bishops, or Lutheran district presidents—much less ordinary parish clergy in those groups—holding office without graduate-level theological training.

Along with the unpaid part-timers, the LDS hierarchy is assisted by a large, salaried headquarters bureaucracy in Salt Lake City. These employees administer all programs under the direction of their superiors, but anonymously. Their names and their functions are largely unknown to the wider church membership. The level of their practical influence in shaping the church can only be guessed at.

At the top of the pyramid of officialdom known as the General Authorities stand the First Presidency and the Twelve, who all receive the same (never revealed) salary. These fifteen men supervise their appointees at all the lower levels. One category is the presiding bishop and his first and second counselors, who together form the Presiding Bishopric, which is responsible for the church's temporal matters.

Men in the rank known as "Seventies" oversee the geographic regions. (This term stems from Moses' call to seventy elders and Jesus' commissioning of seventy itinerant disciples.) The seven-man Presidency of the Seventy supervises all Quorums of the Seventy (who do not actually number seventy, though they may someday), full-time salaried executives who ordinarily retire at age seventy. The Second Quorum of the Seventy (also not yet seventy in actual number) are full-time but unsalaried officials who serve five-year terms.

Hinckley has created three new levels, not considered among the General Authorities, to accommodate the geographic expansion. These part-time regional overseers live in their home countries and retain secular employment: the Third Quorum of the Seventy (for Europe, Africa, Asia, and Oceania), the Fourth Quorum (Latin America), and the Fifth Quorum (North America).

The ritual of members sustaining their assigned leaders, the top-down control, and the three-in-one leadership structure continue down to the regional and local levels and even to the auxiliary organizations for women and youth. The church's regional unit is called the "stake" (similar to a Catholic diocese), and the local congregation is the "ward" (similar to a Catholic parish).

The term "stake" refers to the poles that held up the sacred tabernacle in which biblical Israel worshiped. By the Book of Mormon account, Jesus used the term when he preached in the Western Hemisphere. An LDS stake has roughly 3,000 or more members. Stakes are usually made up of five to a dozen geographic wards, with ward membership determined by one's address. "Ward" was a common term for the subdivisions of a municipality when Joseph Smith organized his city of Nauvoo, where secular and religious government were combined. Brigham Young continued the system in pioneer Utah.

Where the Mormon population is thin and not yet strong enough to produce its own leaders, the church is organized into geographical missions (with districts parallel to stakes) and branches (parallel to wards). In the United States the stake and mission regions often overlap.

A stake president is chosen and approved by a regional Seventy, as assigned by headquarters. The stake president then chooses his two counselors, also subject to approval from a Seventy. The head of a local ward is called a "bishop," and he is recommended by the stake president and then approved directly by the First Presidency and Quorum of the Twelve in Salt Lake. The bishop chooses two counselors to form a three-man "bishopric," subject to approval by his stake presidency and stake high council. Within the ward, the auxiliary organizations (the women's Relief Society, Young Women, Young Men, Primary, Sunday School) do not function independently or choose their own leaders as they would in most denominations. Rather, the Bishopric appoints the heads and then approves the leaders' choices for counselors who form the usual LDS leadership trio. The bishop also controls virtually every routine congregational post (such as assistant librarian, choir president, denominational magazine representative). All very controlled, all very top-down.

Except in special cases (young singles, foreign languages, students), the members are assigned to wards, and hence to bishops, strictly on the basis of where they live. With typical Mormon thrift, it is common for two or three wards to share the same meetinghouse with staggered Sunday schedules. Bishops hold a great deal of discretionary power over the members, especially the granting or withholding of temple recommends and other disciplinary actions. For instance, a bishop could bar a father from the privilege of baptizing his own son, or parents from giving the customary talk at the farewell service for a departing missionary child. And through the close-knit hierarchical system, the top leadership can keep close tabs on troublesome free spirits at the local level. (For more on this, see chapter 21.) To reinforce this culture of control and personal fealty, the church requires the leader of the local congregation to interview each member annually regarding his loyalty to church leaders as a prerequisite for receiving a "temple recommend." Without it, a Latter-day Saint is a second-class citizen and cannot enter church temples to perform the central rituals of the faith.

Mormon micromanagement extends into all sorts of ward business that other hierarchical churches leave up to the local clergy and laity. Wards are required to fill out and send in a blizzard of reports. The General Authorities control not only the spending and fund-raising within a ward but the ward's choice of name and the architectural design of its building. Headquarters specifies that videos may not be shown during the Sunday sacrament meeting, and that wards need permission from above to switch

TV satellite transponders or to record non-LDS television shows on church equipment. No athletic events not sponsored by the church can be held on ward premises.

The church hierarchy sets strict guidelines for the music and musical texts used in local worship. There is no LDS equivalent of the "contemporary Christian music" craze. Murals and mosaics are not allowed, and flowers are the only decoration permitted in the chapel. Lighted candles are forbidden in the ward building. And within the ward the bishop must endorse each guest speaker for any of the auxiliaries.

The most distinctive aspect of the Mormon system, however, is found at the most basic levels. All children are baptized at age eight, and at twelve each boy takes his place of church responsibility and status by joining the "priesthood." The similar Jewish rite of passage, the bar mitzvah, tends to be a graduation from synagogue schooling, but for the Mormon boy it is the beginning of serious church responsibility and involvement. This is a holy moment, since Mormons believe that John the Baptist appeared in upstate New York in 1829 to restore priesthood authority directly through Joseph Smith and his followers.

The universal lay priesthood, including the emphasis on two-year missionary assignments, is no doubt a major reason why LDS children remain loyal and involved through adolescence and young adulthood. Every boy from age twelve is incorporated into the system with special status. And priesthood carries with it eternal consequences. The centrality of the priesthood explains the grievance of the small band of LDS feminists who would like the same status rather than being channeled into female auxiliaries. It also explains why it was a severe deprivation for Mormons of African descent to be denied the priesthood before 1978.

Holders of the priesthood have weekly ward meetings and also form small "quorums" of a dozen or more, each with its own leaders. The priesthood process is accelerated for adult converts, but it works as follows for the typical boy raised in the church.

A boy is ordained into the lower of two priesthood levels, the *Aaronic priesthood,* at age twelve and progresses through three subcategories. As a *deacon,* he distributes the sacrament, collects fast offerings, cares for the building and grounds, and helps out otherwise by assisting the elderly, acting as a messenger, and so forth. The major program for deacons consists of church-sponsored Boy Scout troops. Between the ages of fourteen and sixteen he becomes a *teacher.* He can now perform all deacon functions and ordain deacons, and also prepares the sacrament, ushers, is allowed to speak at church meetings, and participates in "home teaching" (the monthly visit to each ward household for spiritual strengthening). Finally, he becomes a *priest* between the ages of sixteen and eighteen. He can teach and exhort during home teaching sessions, baptize, administer the sacrament, and ordain teachers and deacons to the priesthood.

The higher level, the *Melchizedek priesthood,* also has three categories and is entered at age eighteen or older. As an *elder,* the entry-level member of the Melchizedek priesthood has the power to perform any Aaronic priesthood function. He can also lay on hands to pronounce blessings or pray for healings, and he can confer the Melchizedek or Aaronic priesthood on others. One must be an elder to receive a call as a church missionary or to hold many ward and stake leadership positions. *High priest* is the rank reached by a ward bishop, stake president, or higher church authority. The rank of *Seventy* or *Apostle* is reached by men who hold those respective titles among the General Authorities.

Quinn's meticulous history of the LDS hierarchy shows that during the church's first century family relationships and connections through marriage played a major part in the choice of leaders, making the LDS hierarchy almost "an extended family." For instance, of the 123 men appointed as General Authorities from the church's founding through 1932, half were relatives of one or more of the existing General Authorities, and 47 of them were second cousins or closer. However, the so-called Mormon dynasticism did not limit church control to any one family and did not stand in the way of appointing people without kinship ties.

The church has been led by fifteen presidents over the years, among whom only one was not a native-born American: the third president was the Englishman John Taylor, who died in 1887. All of the last nine presidents since 1918 were born in Utah or Idaho. In the current First Presidency, all three members are Utah natives, as are eight of the Twelve Apostles (and two of the other apostles hail from Idaho). In the Presidency of the Seventy, all seven men are from Utah or Idaho, as are all three members of the Presiding Bishopric. Only at the level of the First Quorum of the Seventy does representation among the General Authorities broaden. Of the forty-three men in this rank, ten are foreign-born (one Asian and the rest from Europe, Canada, and Latin America); among the thirty-three Americans, six were born in states other than Utah and Idaho.

In other words, as the church prepared to enter the twenty-first century and become a worldwide religion, it was led by men from a very narrow geographic and cultural background. It will be intriguing to see whether the Mormon hierarchy is able to broaden itself in the same way that the Italian-dominated College of Cardinals has become a truly international body in recent decades. And if a non-Italian pope, why not a non-American Mormon prophet someday?

CHAPTER 10
FAMILIES FOREVER

TAKE A LOOK AT A SNAPSHOT FROM A MORMON FAMILY ALBUM.

In the photo is a handsome grouping of eight. They are smiling politely for the photographer because these are polite, earnest people. You can tell that just by looking at them. They are the sort of people who might take turns driving a sick neighbor to the clinic, which in fact they do, three times a week.

They are, of course, devout members of the church, which means that Dad serves on several committees in the local ward in addition to his full-time job. Mom is in charge of a committee in the women's Relief Society. They each devote fifteen hours a week to church activities. They are as charitable with treasure as time, giving the church over 10 percent of their gross income. The older family members work on a local Mormon welfare farm or at the local Bishop's Storehouse stacking bags of food. No one in the family smokes or drinks anything stronger than milk. The oldest boy is about to embark on the expected two-year term as a missionary, heading for Taiwan. His two younger brothers are already Eagle Scouts. Everyone in the family is trustworthy, loyal, helpful, friendly, courteous, kind, obedient, cheerful, thrifty, brave, clean, and reverent. They value their family time together and faithfully participate in the weekly Family Home Evening program. They believe deeply in education, and all of them have either been to college or are heading there.

What's wrong with this Hallmark picture? Very little, and that's the point. Though no family is perfect—we'd have to add in the son who dropped out of Brigham Young University to play in a metal band in Fresno, or the daughter who smokes cigarettes, hates religion, and plans to pattern her life after William Burroughs novels—it's remarkable how many Mormon families look at least something like the idealized group. In a way, there's not much more to it. Mormon culture is simple, family- and church-dominated, and intensely practical. Families are at the heart of the system, perhaps even more than the local church. And for believers this is not just a matter of the here and now. Wards may pass away, but families are quite literally eternal, which is doubtless one of the faith's most attractive evangelistic themes. Even God himself is married.

Our picture-book family is a fictional composite; an actual example is the thoroughly middle-class Dickson family of Cedar Park, Texas. They may not be the ideal American Mormon family, but they are close to it. Stewart and Lorraine Dickson, handsome thirtysomethings, live in one of Mormondom's many boom areas. In just six years during the 1990s the regional stake in greater Austin, Texas, split once, and when membership exceeded 10,000, the two stakes were ready to give birth to a third. New meetinghouses are going up. Young missionaries are busily canvassing. LDS charities for tornado and flood victims are active. Though still a tiny minority in a metropolitan area of one million, the LDS flock is an extremely successful, confident organization that is hitting its stride. And the Dicksons are happily part of it.

Just off busy Route 183 is the chapel of the Anderson Mill ward, a typically plain, icon-free building adorned only with the occasional bouquet of ersatz flowers. The walls are largely undecorated, the ceilings high and white, the carpets pristine. It is Sunday morning, and the first of the three hours of combined town-hall meeting, hymn sing, testimony time, and Sunday school that constitute the certified Mormon sabbath. At the plain oaken lectern the Dicksons are addressing their congregation on the subject of—what else?—the family. Their five extremely cute children, ranging from thirteen to three, fidget quietly in the third pew. (The thirteen-year-old, Jeff, has just caused a mild sensation by returning from Scout camp with his hair "buzzed.")

Mom and Dad plow earnestly through their plainspoken peroration. Lorraine speaks of her marriage, which is not just for life on this earth but has been "sealed forever" through secret ritual in a Mormon temple. Preaching the primacy of the family, she quotes liberally from a succession of LDS prophets. From Ezra Taft Benson, for example: "In the home we may experience a taste of heaven." She exhorts the members to strengthen their families, to build tighter bonds. "The currents in the world," she says, "are eating away at our children's sense of values and self-worth."

After she finishes, the worshipers sing, "Time doth softly, sweetly glide when there's love at home."

Next it is Stewart's turn. He continues on in the same vein, then turns to a large stack of recommended materials, a family curriculum of parents' guides, Family Home Evening guidebooks, the *Gospel Principles* manual, a book called *Truth Restored* by the reigning prophet himself, Gordon B. Hinckley, and some spiritual comic books for the kids.

Both of the Dicksons grew up in Idaho. Stewart earned two degrees from the University of Utah; Lorraine attended Utah State, Brigham Young, and the University of Utah but never finished. They moved to Texas in the 1990s to open a Great Harvest Bread Company franchise. Stewart has done very well with the business: he has opened a second office and sold a third in San Antonio to Lorraine's brother, who now runs it. They live in an attractive, new, four-bedroom home and have a shiny new burgundy Chevrolet Suburban parked in the driveway.

The ideal Mormon is deeply committed to work, and Stewart is no exception. He quit his earlier career as the director of human resources at a Utah company and later as a consultant because, he says, all that his kids knew about his work was that "I carried a briefcase." He says he wanted to make it on his own; he also wanted his kids to understand what he did for a living.

"Each of the children has been down to the shop and kneaded bread," he remarks with satisfaction. "Jeff and Paul [age twelve] have worked at the counter. It gives me an opportunity to translate work into sensory experience." Stewart says he runs his business "with integrity," and that extends to strict rules about the sort of language employees may use on the job. Like the good Mormon mom, Lorraine stays home with the kids, but she also pitches in at the bakery shop on holidays, as do the kids.

Leaving the church fastness of Utah was difficult, but Lorraine says she thinks their minority status in Texas has actually been good for the kids. "It has really helped the children cement their testimony and cement their beliefs, and when they have to stand up and be a little bit different, I think that is great," she says. "And they have many friends in different religions."

(Interestingly, a churchgoing Protestant in Salt Lake City, former University of Chicago law professor now at University of Utah, Michael McConnell, one of the nation's leading experts on the First Amendment religion clauses, agrees with the Dickson perspective. He says he is glad to be in a location where "our religious views are in a distinct minority. I think that's all to the good. It would be very difficult to raise children when the culture around you is the same as your faith. It's so hard to distinguish between what you believe and what is just cultural coloration. It would be very hard to grow up Mormon in Utah because so much around you is Mormon that it doesn't force you to think about why you believe what you believe.")

Several years before the Dicksons landed in Texas, in 1986, Bruno and Cari Vassal made the opposite decision, moving with their five school-age children from New Jersey to a sprawling Utah Tudor home within the gated Pepperwood community in Sandy in the Mormon heartland and a half-hour drive from Salt Lake City. Bruno, a bishop in his New Jersey ward, left his career as an Avon executive to run a consulting business from his home in the Northridge ward. They still miss New York sometimes, but in Utah their teenagers did not have to tumble out of bed to attend the daily 6:00 A.M. religion classes (called "seminary") before school. They were able to attend these readily as "released time" during the normal public school day. Cari's aging mother lived with them for five years before she died, and Bruno's mother lives nearby. It became easy for their children to socialize with lots of other Mormon children because the Pepperwood community is 90 percent Mormon.

Both husband and wife are Mormon converts. Cari, who grew up in New Mexico, was a child when she and her mother were baptized; her sisters and father never converted. Bruno, fourteen, was impressed by Mormon missionaries he met on the boat when his family was en route to a new home in Brazil. He and his mother were baptized in São Paulo; his father, a Johnson & Johnson executive, never converted. Later, Bruno served a mission in Italy and Germany, and a quarter-century later his son Bruno IV served his mission in Brazil. Cari and Bruno are both graduates of Brigham Young University, and Cari taught elementary school until the babies began to arrive.

The Vassals' church engagements are similar to those of the Dicksons. They are the sort of true believers who subscribe to the church-owned *Deseret News* and not the Gentile daily, the *Salt Lake Tribune.* They carefully file back issues of *Ensign,* the church's official monthly magazine. They have never even heard of the independent magazine *Sunstone.* Bruno is the ward's Boy Scout leader, an important assignment of trust within a Mormon congregation. With her Relief Society friends, Cari enjoys social activities like progressive dinners and hobbies such as tying quilts for refugees in Bosnia.

Temple work is an important priority. Back in New Jersey, temple duties meant arduous twenty-hour days for the monthly trips down to the Washington, D.C., temple. In Utah there is a temple nearby. Both Bruno and Cari performed vicarious temple baptisms for their non-Mormon fathers after they died, in hopes that they can be united with both parents in eternity. In fact, Cari has done ordinance work for about 165 forebears. Genealogy is theology for Mormons, who operate the largest genealogical archive on earth. The assiduous attention to family trees is part of an elaborate effort to offer the possibility of salvation to past family members by performing such baptisms for the dead.

The Vassals have a special goal lined up for the year 2005. By then they expect their youngest child, now in high school, to be launched in life and their family responsibilities to be largely behind them. Their dream is to sell their large Pepperwood house, buy a condo, and volunteer to serve as adult missionaries together. For now, though, another sort of vocation prevails in their lives. The Maytag is constantly humming, laundering linens for the stream of short-term and long-term visitors who pass the impressively antlered caribou head in the foyer (Bruno enjoys big-game hunting) and climb the circular staircase to one of the seven bedrooms upstairs. One of those visitors who enjoyed the Vassals' warm hospitality was a young man named David Denniston, who came and ended up staying a full year. He arrived a Protestant and left a Mormon.

Back in New Jersey some years earlier, David's musician mother had taught cello to a Vassal daughter. Around the same time David, a French horn player, left the Manhattan School of Music, one course shy of his master's degree, to join the pit orchestra for the touring production of Broadway's *Phantom of the Opera.* After nearly four years on the road, and earning good money, David landed with the troupe at Salt Lake City. The job's glamour had worn thin. He had enjoyed the Presbyterian and Methodist churches of his youth, and his own family is loving and supportive. But years had passed; David was lonely and burned out, and his family was over 2,000 miles away. When the Vassals opened their home to him during *Phantom*'s Salt Lake run of several months, he was happy to accept.

The Vassals "never put a Book of Mormon on my pillow," says David. But over time, watching the family members' interactions with one another, the central role of church and prayer in the home, and the broad church support for a close family lifestyle, he decided he wanted to appropriate all that for himself. So in 1996 David was baptized a Mormon. He worked odd jobs for a time and then went to BYU to begin working all over again on a master's degree in music.

At BYU another Mormon family began. David met nineteen-year-old Tara, another French horn major, and she became his bride in August 1998. Two weeks before the wedding David testified to his newfound faith at a Northridge ward Sunday meeting. He spoke of witnessing to his brother, who had recently visited Utah and "was able to see that I was a happier person and at peace." Sharing the eager anticipation for his approaching wedding day, he testified, "Never before have I had such hope that I could have a strong and happy family. . . . The Book of Mormon has changed my life, has saved my life." All this, he said, was "brought forth by the hand of God."

Twelve days later David and Tara were sealed "for time and eternity" in a temple marriage, then treated to a festive reception prepared by Cari with decorated tables set around the Vassals' backyard trout pond and waterfall, the majestic Wasatch rising behind. David's parents, two brothers, grandparents, some aunts and uncles, all new to Utah, flew in from New England, California, and the South for the wedding.

But none of David's kin could attend the actual wedding. Gentiles are not permitted in temples, not even for the marriages of close relatives or friends. (Also barred are all children and Mormons who lack temple recommends from their bishop.) The awkwardness of this has led many Mormons to hold external ring ceremonies after temple sealings in order to share a nuptial ritual with non-Mormon friends and relatives on the wedding day. Church officialdom opposes this practice. Its 1989 *Handbook of Instructions* stated that couples may arrange with their bishop for a "special meeting" involving those not allowed in the temple. But at such occasions "no ceremony should be performed, and no vows should be exchanged." The 1999 *Handbook* allows rings to be exchanged outside the temple, but warns that this "should not appear to replicate any part of the marriage ceremony, and the couple should not exchange vows."

The eternal significance of the nuclear and extended family is one of the most fundamental and powerful messages in Mormon doctrine. By contrast, classic expressions of traditional Christian orthodoxy give an austere view of heaven. The Westminster (Presbyterian) Shorter Catechism begins with the question, "What is the chief end of man?" Answer: "Man's chief end is to glorify God, and to enjoy him forever." Traditional Christians generally assume that "forever" includes earthly family and friends, but the Bible gives no flat assurances of that. Joseph Smith's latter-day revelations, however, did. The Mormon heaven is a far cozier place.

The Mormon focus is on the human family. Marriages are sealed for time but also exist forever through marriage in the temple. Marriages populate the earth by giving the opportunity of mortal birth to preexistent souls waiting to be born, and children are sealed to their parents for eternity; all this produces family reunions that go on and on, world without end. It is an appealing picture in a contemporary culture of disintegrating human relationships and lonely individuals seeking to connect. Playing to this central concept, Mormons produce a stream of pamphlets, books, and videos with titles such as "Family First," "Together Forever," and "Family Answers," aimed at both members and Gentiles. The illustrations show relentlessly smiling family groups, couples headed hand in hand toward the horizon, the scenes romantically backlit.

In Mormon manuals, art, and articles, traditional gender roles dominate. The Hinckley First Presidency and Twelve Apostles issued a 1995

"Proclamation to the World" on the family specifying that "gender is an essential characteristic of individual pre-mortal, mortal, and eternal identity and purpose." In this life fathers are to "preside over their families in love and righteousness and are to provide the necessities of life and protection for their families. Mothers are primarily responsible for the nurture of their children." However, within marriage men and women are "obligated to help one another as equal partners." The decree reiterates the Mormon doctrine that with the help of sacred temple ordinances family relationships will be "perpetuated beyond the grave" and families will be "united eternally." Marriage, the proclamation continues, is not only ordained of God but "essential to His eternal plan."

Marriage, therefore, is not just the "holy estate" traditional in Christendom; it is a sacred duty in Mormonism. Preparation for it, accompanied by strict chastity standards, is stressed throughout the Aaronic priesthood manuals for boys aged twelve to eighteen as well as in the daily four-year religion classes required of high school teenagers. Junior high boys are taught lessons in "Respect for Mothers and Their Divine Role," "Sexual Purity," "Pure Thoughts and Clean Language," and "The Sacred Power of Procreation." The high school priesthood curriculum includes sessions on "The Eternal Importance of Families," "Understanding Women's Roles," and "Advance Preparation for a Temple Marriage." Lessons for the late teens include classes on "Choosing an Eternal Companion" and "Celestial Marriage—A Preparation for Eternity."

Coed high school seminary classes teach that without temple marriage one cannot achieve the highest status within the "celestial" or highest level of Mormonism's three-tiered heaven. The eternal family, then, is a reward for the spiritual progress that Mormons call "exaltation," which continues throughout eternity. The college-level institute textbook *Achieving a Celestial Marriage* states in the very first paragraph that God is married. "Our Heavenly Father and mother live in an exalted state because they achieved a celestial marriage. As we achieve a like marriage, we shall become as they are and begin the creation of worlds for our own spirit children." Exaltation is available only in family units, and with celestial marriage one can "procreate the family throughout eternity."

One man's family, c. 1901. Joseph F. Smith
(1838–1918), who had six wives and forty-eight
children, was president of the LDS Church from
1901 to 1918 and in 1904 reaffirmed the church's
ban on polygamy. *(Utah State Historical Society)*

Joseph Smith Jr. (1805–44), the first prophet and
president of the Church of Jesus Christ of Latter-
day Saints. *(Courtesy of the Reorganized Church of
Jesus Christ of Latter Day Saints)*

Emma Hale Smith (1804–79), the wife of Joseph
Smith Jr. She never moved with the church to
Utah. *(Courtesy of the Reorganized Church of Jesus
Christ of Latter Day Saints)*

The First Vision by Del Parson shows Joseph Smith Jr. during his First Vision in the Sacred Grove. God the Father and God the Son appear before him. Mormons believe God the Father has a body and was also once a man. (© *1998 by Intellectual Reserve, Inc. Used by permission*)

LEFT: The room in Carthage Jail in Illinois where Joseph Smith Jr. and his brother Hyrum were murdered by a mob on June 27, 1844. Joseph Smith fell from this second-story window. The hole in the door is from the bullet that killed Hyrum. *(Joan K. Ostling)*

RIGHT: This daguerreotype, c. 1846, shows Nauvoo after the city had been largely abandoned. The newly completed temple is on the horizon. *(Courtesy of the Church of Jesus Christ of Latter-day Saints)*

ABOVE: The church's General Authorities and the Mormon Tabernacle Choir at a semiannual General Conference. *(Joan K. Ostling)*

LEFT: Statues of Utah's founder Brigham Young and of the Angel Moroni atop the Salt Lake City Temple stand guard over the city that Young built. *(Joan K. Ostling)*

LEFT: Octogenarian Mormon President Gordon B. Hinckley addresses a General Conference in the Salt Lake Tabernacle. *(Joan K. Ostling)*

RIGHT: The ultramodern Temple of the Reorganized Church of Jesus Christ of Latter Day Saints stands opposite the headquarters of the rival Church of Christ (Temple Lot) in Independence, Missouri. The Utah-based Latter-day Saints have property across the street. *(Joan K. Ostling)*

LEFT: A meeting in Nigeria's Aba stake. Missions in black Africa opened up after 1978, when the priesthood was extended to males of African descent. *(Courtesy of the Church of Jesus Christ of Latter-day Saints)*

Jesus Christ's appearance in the New World, a Book of Mormon scene reenacted
in the annual Hill Cumorah pageant in Palmyra, New York.
(Courtesy of the Church of Jesus Christ of Latter-day Saints)

ABOVE: A Bible lesson during Family Home Evening in Bayonne, New Jersey. *(Joan K. Ostling)*

RIGHT: Paul and Melanie Prestwich and their children in prayer during Family Home Evening. *(Joan K. Ostling)*

The same chapter of Mormon scripture that lays out the now-abandoned polygamy principle promises exaltation and godhood in eternity through marriage sealed in the covenant (D&C 132:19–20). Putting it another way, a woman's spiritual fulfillment and her rewards in the hereafter come through her husband's priesthood. There is no other path to the highest level of exaltation in the celestial kingdom. That is tough news for singles. As a practical matter, Protestant and Catholic churches often have difficulties ministering to singles, too, but no other church relegates never-married singles to a permanently and officially inferior spiritual status. The LDS Church has established some special singles wards to meet the recreational and spiritual needs of never-married young Mormons. There are also student wards.

Church presidents have not been insensitive to the pastoral difficulty the Mormon scriptures present. Spencer W. Kimball once addressed the issue in *Ensign*, writing, "We promise you that insofar as eternity is concerned, no soul will be deprived of rich and high and eternal blessings for anything which that person could not help," and that such a person, if righteous, would "eventually" receive all the blessings to which he or she was "entitled." He went on with paternal advice to the lovelorn, counseling young people to be desirable catches on the marriage market. "We encourage both men and women to keep themselves well-groomed, well-dressed, abreast of the times, attractive."

It can also be difficult for the divorced in this world of happy poster families. Eternally sealed marriages may become a less-than-appealing tenet to Mormons who are caught in unhappy marriages. Utah has always had a high divorce rate overall, but the divorce rate for temple marriages is quite low. The church has never actually forbidden divorce, but with its "families forever" doctrines, divorce carries an eternal significance. Divorced men and women can apply to have sealings broken, but the matter of children's sealings is complex. Legally adopted children are ritually sealed to their adoptive parents. Children born within a sealed union are automatically sealed to their parents, and in the case of divorce, they remain sealed to both parents. The sealings regulations in the church handbook stipulate that children cannot be sealed to one parent only. Sticky cases are appealed all the way to the First Presidency and decided on an individual basis.

Mormons have traditionally had large families, to provide "mortal bodies for the spirit children of God" waiting in a preexistent state and to bestow on themselves eternal increase, exaltation, and big family gatherings in the celestial kingdom. The church maintains an unwavering theological stance against abortion. "The only possible exceptions," according to the 1999 *Handbook,* are cases involving rape, incest, "serious jeopardy" to the life or health of the mother, or a determination by a physician that there are "severe defects that will not allow the baby to survive beyond birth." And even those conditions do not automatically justify abortion. Those who submit to, perform, or facilitate an abortion may be subject to church discipline. Although stillborn children had lives in the Mormon preexistence, temple ordinances are not performed for them because "there is no direct revelation on when the spirit enters the body."

The First Presidency members have stated that they "deplore" surgical sterilization to limit births, and the church "strongly discourages" the practice. But the policy is looser than that of the Roman Catholic Church and allows sterilization to be considered in cases of mental incompetence or serious danger to life or health through childbearing.

On birth control, the church has softened its position. The 1999 *Handbook* says that the number of children a couple has is "extremely intimate and private and should be left between the couple and the Lord." Sex is not merely for procreation but is also "a means of expressing love and strengthening emotional and spiritual bonds between husband and wife." This is a considerable departure from some statements by previous presidents. David O. McKay, president from 1951 to 1970, father of seven, suggested that birth control puts a marriage on a level with "the panderer and the courtesan" when a couple seeks to "befoul the pure fountains of life with the slime of indulgence and sensuality." As recently as 1987 President Ezra Taft Benson directed the Saints, "Do not curtail the number of children for personal or selfish reasons."

The Associated Press writer Vern Anderson, discussing the current *Handbook* wording, credited President Hinckley with the change. In 1983, when then-President Spencer W. Kimball, an outspoken foe of birth control, was largely incapacitated and Hinckley was effectively already running the church, Hinckley told a BYU audience that he was "willing to leave the question of numbers to the man and the woman and the Lord." The 1989 edition of the *Handbook* was ambiguous, and by 1992 the quasi-official *Encyclopedia of Mormonism* entry made the number and spacing of children a private, prayerful decision. Mormons today have fewer children than their parents had, but their families are larger than the non-Mormon American average.

The *Handbook* currently in force covers numerous family-related topics. Church leaders are told to discourage adopted children from seeking to identify their natural parents. "Dating and get-acquainted businesses" are specifically barred from operating on church premises or using church mailing lists—a problem that would not arise in most other denominations. As for agonizing end-of-life decisions, the Saints are not obligated "to extend mortal life by means that are unreasonable" when "dying becomes inevitable." But the religion condemns assisted suicide or deliberately putting to death someone with an incurable condition. Decisions on organ transplants and donations are left up to the individual. Surrogate motherhood, artificial insemination with donor sperm, and in vitro fertilization using donor sperm or eggs are "strongly discouraged" but not flatly prohibited.

Like other religious traditions, Mormonism teaches that God desires abstinence from sexual relations outside marriage and strict fidelity within the married state. Mormon parents are directed to make sure that the public school sex education of their children is "consistent with sound moral and ethical values." In cases of unwed pregnancy, the First Presidency states that every effort should be made "to establish an eternal family relationship," but if a successful marriage seems unlikely for the parents, the church encourages adoption. "Generally, unwed parents are not able to provide the stable, nurturing environment so essential for the baby's well-being."

Family relationships receive regular attention in inspirational homilies from the ward level on up to conference speeches. They absorb much Relief Society attention, cover a lot of space in issues of *Ensign,* and account for the new "School of Family Life" announced in 1998 for BYU, a curriculum without parallel elsewhere in American higher education. Previously the school operated a division of "family sciences" that included an old-fashioned home economics major. The new school is also intended to focus research on marriage, parenting, and related public policy issues.

Politically the LDS Church is willing to join hands with conservative Protestants and Catholics on such family values issues as abortion, euthanasia, and same-sex marriage. The most important and successful such campaign to date in which it has participated was the defeat of the Equal Rights Amendment (ERA) to the U.S. Constitution, which was seen as a threat to the traditional American family.

The ERA was passed by the U.S. House of Representatives in October 1971, and by the U.S. Senate in March 1972. By December 1972 it had already been ratified by twenty-two states. In these early stages the LDS church did not openly oppose the amendment, which was passed in a number of states with significant Mormon populations, including Idaho, Colorado, California, and Hawaii. A survey published by the church-owned *Deseret News* in November 1974 showed that 63 percent of Utahns favored the ERA.

At this point the church big guns swung into action and developed a behind-the-scenes strategy guided largely by future President Gordon B. Hinckley, then a special policy adviser to the First Presidency. But Hinckley's involvement in the headquarters-directed anti-ERA activities receives only a single sentence in Sheri L. Dew's thick 1996 biography of Hinckley, published by the church-owned Deseret Book Company. "Elder Hinckley," she writes, "acted several times as a Church spokesman on the matter."

After Relief Society President Barbara B. Smith delivered a significant anti-ERA speech, the Utah legislature defeated the ERA in February 1975. By 1976, thirty-four states had ratified the ERA, and only four more were needed to make it part of the Constitution. Strategy included some important public addresses by church leaders in states with large Mormon populations. Though Idaho's legislature had passed the amendment with a two-thirds majority, it was rescinded by a simple majority of voters in a referendum that followed a major address by Apostle Boyd K. Packer. Throughout 1977 LDS leaders worked behind the scenes to control state-level International Women's Year conferences. According to D. Michael Quinn, at some of these "there was the now-familiar sight of a Mormon man coordinating women delegates with a walkie-talkie."

The LDS Church was politically ready to join hands with allies such as the conservative Catholic Phyllis Schlafly to achieve its concept of pro-family goals. By 1979, says Quinn, Hinckley had devised a clear set of guidelines for LDS involvement. People should not be "set apart" for political activities; the LDS name should not be used in the title of political organizations; church buildings and church meetings could be used to discuss ERA issues; church funds should not be used; political candidates should not be endorsed, but incumbent voting records should be published. Much of this strategy, of course, is also used by non-Mormon Religious Right groups, including the Christian Coalition.

The *Ensign* frequently published articles on the ERA, including statements by President Spencer W. Kimball. Leaflets were widely distributed discussing the issue and sometimes suggesting how to vote in referendum elections or for state legislators. Anti-ERA speakers were invited to speak in ward chapels; massive letter-writing campaigns were mounted. A *Boston Globe* headline read, "It's Do or Die for the ERA: Mormon Power Is the Key." Nationally the tide was turning. By 1982 the ERA was dead.

The major "family values" public policy issue currently facing religious conservatives in the United States is same-sex marriage. The 1995 family proclamation was emphatic that marriage can exist only between a man and a woman, ordained as such by God and "essential to His eternal plan." About gays and lesbians Hinckley told a 1998 General Conference: "We cannot stand idle if they indulge in immoral activity, if they try to uphold and defend and live in a so-called same-sex marriage situation. To permit such would be to make light of the very serious and sacred foundation of God-sanctioned marriage and its very purpose, the rearing of families."

This became a pressing matter in 1993 when the Hawaii Supreme Court said the state had no constitutional right to bar same-sex marriage licenses. The "full faith and credit" clause of the U.S. Constitution requires all states to honor each other's statutes and legal bonds, and moral traditionalists feared that homosexual marriages would have to be recognized nationwide. The Mormon Church was active with other religious groups in the legal maneuvering, as well as in the 1998 referendum in which Hawaiian voters, by 69 percent, gave the legislature the power to ban same-sex marriages.

The church also played a dramatic role in Alaska, where a superior court judge had ruled in favor of a gay couple's marriage application. The Mormon Church contributed $500,000 to the successful 1998 referendum drive to ban same-sex marriages, quintupling the war chest of the Alaska Family Coalition. It was the largest contribution to a ballot measure campaign in state history.

It remains to be seen how the church's involvement in such U.S. political controversies might affect its image, status, and activities overseas. But however public issues evolve in the United States and elsewhere, the church's twenty-first-century stand on the family is clear. The family, defined in notably old-fashioned and prefeminist terms, is the basic unit of secular society and of the church. The LDS authorities consider it among their most sacred trusts to do everything in their power to protect it.

CHAPTER 11
A PECULIAR PEOPLE

ONE FINE DAY IN 1990 RAY BECKHAM, WORKING IN THE PUBLIC RELATIONS office at Brigham Young University, received a mysterious call from church headquarters. Phone home and tell your wife you will be gone for three days and come right now, as you are, he was told. Beckham's wife was provided with no information about where he was headed or why. He was given blind instructions to drive eighty miles into the desert.

With no knowledge of his destination or of what lay behind the orders, Beckham obediently followed church instructions. At his destination he found 150 or so men, women, and children milling about. It turned out to be a secret mock disaster exercise, one of five such unpublicized projects under Presiding Bishop Victor Brown, carried out to determine survival needs under different conditions.

In this exercise, Beckham, as the top-ranking church officer on the scene, quickly took charge. At the time he was a regional representative responsible for about ten stakes. At the "disaster" site a meeting was held with the "survivors," who were divided into teams to lay out a tent camp and assigned other duties such as cooking. With shortwave radio contact provided, helicopters dropped in equipment: generators, tents, blankets, food and water, a portable camp kitchen.

Sunday was set aside for questioning. A team of twenty interviewers came in to interrogate each participant privately while camp was being torn down. The intent was to try to develop emergency pods for storage in different worldwide locations for use in disasters. These self-sufficient units were to have enough equipment and supplies to last three days, since outside help would probably arrive by then. Different pods were to be developed from exercises carried out to simulate such conditions as severe winter weather, earthquake, and floods.

Beckham does not know what use was made of the information developed from these exercises, but the survivalism behind such projects remains a part of Mormon culture, though muted. It lingers both as an expression of millenarianism, the scriptural belief that turbulent times will precede Christ's return, and in memories of pioneer privation. There is in Mormonism always something of Scarlett O'Hara's famous vow in Tara's radish patch when she railed at the heavens, "As God is my witness . . . I'm going to live through this, and when it's over, I'm never going to be hungry again."

The most obvious at-home expression of this prudent attitude toward providence is the church admonition that every family is to store a year's worth of food supplies. The idea is not to store everything a family might actually eat in a normal year but to store enough dried or preserved commodities to survive a year of privation. Hence the stress on canning, dried milk, and grain storage.

Some Mormons today are embarrassed about the food storage practice, aware that it strikes outsiders as, well, a bit peculiar. But *Ensign* frequently prints advisories on the topic. There are standard church publications to guide storage principles worldwide (*Essentials of Home Production and Storage*, manual, 1978, item no. 32288; and *Providing in the Lord's Way*, manual, 1991, item no. 32296). The faithful are advised that in some parts of the world taro or manioc, for example, can replace cereal grains. In certain areas keeping live animals might be appropriate. Survival list supplies in a Deseret Book catalog include a handcrank radio and flashlight, and such book titles as *Don't Get Caught with Your Pantry Down*, the *Emergency-Disaster Survival Guidebook*, *Food Storage Planner*, and *A Year's Supply*.

A September 1997 *Ensign* piece reprints Ezra Taft Benson's 1974 words reminding the Saints: "For the righteous the gospel provides a warning before a calamity, a program for the crises, a refuge for each disaster." "The Lord has warned us of famines," he continues, "but the righteous will have listened to prophets and stored at least a year's supply of survival food."

Due to Mormons' traditional apocalyptic edginess, Utah has a goodly number of businesses based on survival merchandise. Saints can buy 72-hour emergency survival kits and 3,600-calorie food bars from Deseret Book stores by mail order as well as in person. *This People,* an upscale, glossy, independent, conservative Mormon quarterly, ran a full-page ad in its Fall 1998 issue trumpeting, "What Will You Do When Money Can't Buy Food?" Perma Pak of Salt Lake City promised immediate delivery ("While the supply lasts!") of top-quality low-moisture foods. ("DON'T TAKE CHANCES. Fix the cost of food TODAY!")

With Y2K computer fears mounting in 1999, business was booming for Utah food storage and survival merchandise companies, which are something of an Intermountain West cottage industry. Companies like Perma Pak and Emergency Essentials received a landslide of non-Mormon as well as Mormon orders for such merchandise as fifty-five-gallon water barrels, one-hundred-hour candles, forty-pound bags of grain, and food packed in large rustproof cans.

Mormon children are accustomed to growing up with closet and basement shelves dedicated to survival materials and stored food items, regularly rotated. Young adults get practical advice in the institute manual *Achieving a Celestial Marriage* in a lesson on "Family Preparedness." Reminding Saints of biblical warnings about famines, pestilences, and earthquakes, the manual admonishes that preparedness should include fuel, clothing, and a two-week supply of water as well as food.

How does a young family get started with all this? The manual offers these practical suggestions: buy extra work and cold-weather clothes and bolts of cloth and leather; find someone in your area who sells grain in bulk and buy a ton or so; set aside 25 to 50 percent of your normal Christmas budget to begin your storage program; mend old clothes and furniture and spend the cash saved on storage essentials; forgo a vacation one year and put the money into emergency supplies; buy sugar and salt by the case; save a year's supply of seeds to plant a garden.

The survivalist emphasis is unique to Mormonism, but some other aspects of the demanding lifestyle resemble Protestant Evangelicalism, especially the emphasis on chastity and on abstinence from tobacco and alcohol, as well as drug and substance abuse, as required by the Word of Wisdom, an 1833 revelation given to Joseph Smith and enshrined in D&C 89. (Word of Wisdom observance, along with the tithe, is required for a temple recommend.) Mormons, unlike other religions, have added caffeine to their list of prohibited substances.

It is a healthy lifestyle. Various studies show that, on average, Mormons live eight to eleven years longer than other Americans. A 1997 UCLA study showed their death rates from cancer and cardiovascular diseases to be about half those of the general population. The strong emphasis on chastity also lowers their risk of contracting sexually transmitted diseases. This study, carried out on adult, active priesthood holders in California, shows that these persons experience only 16 percent of the deaths normally expected from smoking-related cancers and only 6 percent of the deaths expected from emphysema, asthma, ulcers, cirrhosis of the liver, homicide, and suicide. Some of the results probably relate to the fact that Mormons have a strong emotional and practical support network in their family and church community. Indeed, studies show similar results for devout members of other churches, such as the health-conscious Seventh-day Adventists, who have accumulated a particularly impressive array of data on themselves.

The Word of Wisdom specifically counsels against "wine or strong drink"; tobacco, as it is "not for the body, neither for the belly," though acceptable as an herb for sick cattle; and hot drinks, later defined as coffee and tea. (Cold caffeinated drinks, such as colas, were added later.) Despite the strict prohibition on alcohol, tobacco, and caffeine, the counsel of verses 12 and 13 in the Word of Wisdom is largely ignored: "Yea, flesh also of beasts and of fowls of the air, I, the Lord, have ordained for the use of man with thanksgiving; nevertheless they are to be used sparingly; And it is pleasing unto me that they should not be used, only in times of winter, or of cold, or famine." Mormons, in contrast to Seventh-day Adventists, have no vegetarian tradition.

That the Word of Wisdom was not consistently applied as church law throughout Mormon history has been a somewhat touchy subject in church headquarters. Just how touchy was discovered by the late Leonard J. Arrington, official church historian from 1972 to 1982. Widely regarded as a distinguished scholar by Mormons and non-Mormons alike after the 1958 Harvard University Press publication of his *Great Basin Kingdom,* Arrington suffered his first snarl the following year on home turf. That year he wrote a piece for *BYU Studies* in which he noted that early Mormons regarded the Word as guidance rather than law.

In that article, Arrington quoted from an 1861 speech by the colorful Brigham Young, who took note that "many of the brethren chew tobacco" and ended with these instructions: "We request all addicted to this prac-tice, to omit it while in this house [the tabernacle]. Elders of Israel, if you must chew tobacco, omit it while in meeting, and when you leave, you can take a double portion, if you wish to." The quote was accurate enough; that was not the problem. The problem, as Arrington observed, was that the "quote was better forgotten. I should have learned a lesson from this." *BYU Studies* learned *its* lesson. Publication was suspended for a year.

A later tangle over the Word of Wisdom history occurred in 1974 with the appearance of *Letters of Brigham Young to His Sons,* edited by Dean Jesse and published by the church's own Deseret Book Company. This was the first completed project of the new church history department as organized under Arrington. The letters, generally appealing expressions of warm fatherly concern, included a letter to Brigham Jr. (later one of the Twelve), suggesting that the son stop using tobacco. Boyd K. Packer, prob-ably the most outspoken and conservative member of the present-day Quorum of the Twelve, objected. Strenuously. It appeared that Packer wanted future history department projects to be run past the church's Correlation Committee before publication (see chapters 14 and 15 for more on this committee).

In real life, history is a bit messy. There is evidence that Joseph Smith himself liked a nip every now and then, especially at weddings. But in 1836 he acceded to the temperance preferences of his colleague Sidney Rigdon and substituted water for wine as the beverage used in the sacrament of communion. (This tradition continued even after pasteurized grape juice was invented and swept much of the Protestant marketplace.) Still, Smith's own Mansion House, which operated a hotel, maintained a fully stocked barroom, and Nauvoo also had a brewery that advertised in the church newspaper, the *Nauvoo Neighbor*. According to the writings of Smith's fellow prisoner John Taylor, later the church's third president, the prophet requested and drank wine at Carthage Jail the night before he was murdered in 1844.

The church's own quasi-official *Encyclopedia of Mormonism*, which appeared in 1992—nearly two decades after *Letters* and other publications outside the church had made these issues more a matter of public domain—now interprets the original revelation as "counsel or advice rather than as a binding commandment." It dates the abstinence requirements for a temple recommend as beginning in 1930. (For more about the church's ideas on how history should be written, see chapter 15.)

The other famous Mormon lifestyle commitment that has also varied throughout church history is the tithe. The tithe, defined as a biblical 10 percent of income, amounts to a compulsory head tax for the faithful member. Failure to tithe does not result in excommunication, but without it a Saint cannot hold major church office or employment and will not receive an annual temple recommend card.

Most devout Mormons define the 10 percent in terms of gross, not net, income, though this is not a matter of church law. Children are taught the tithing principle from an early age. If they receive an allowance of ten quarters, they are taught to set aside one quarter to give to the church. They also learn early of two major responsibilities in addition to the tithe: the fast offering, money given in lieu of two meals the first Sunday of each month, to be used for welfare and humanitarian purposes; and the savings account they are to establish to finance their own missions.

Church authorities from the top down regularly stress tithing in conference and stake talks, and church publications such as *Ensign* print exhortations about the responsibility to tithe as well as inspirational pieces on the blessings of tithing. Sometimes there is unofficial discussion in places like *Sunstone* about sticky issues and special cases. Should a family's support of a missionary count toward tithing? Should noncash job benefits be computed as part of the tithe? Must one estimate the value of noncash gifts as part of his cash tithe? Is it fair for two families of the same income to be required to pay the same tithe if one family also has huge medical expenses? Are pensions or inheritances to be tithed?

An annual tithing "settlement" is held at the end of each year with the bishop, and the entire family is required to attend. Families do not display their 1040s at the annual tithe settlement. At this meeting, members are told privately what they have donated during the year and then asked two questions: whether they wish to submit extra donations, and whether they are full tithe payers. Normally the conversation ends at that point, left to the member's own conscience.

However, that does not mean the church is casual about its tithe-collecting activities, as Steven Epperson discovered when his career as a BYU assistant professor of history was terminated in 1997. There were several issues in the Epperson case, but it appears likely that he was the first publicly known casualty of BYU President Merrill Bateman's 1996 announcement that all church members employed by the university were required to carry the annual ecclesiastical endorsements that certify temple recommends. Bateman maintains that temple worthiness was always the standard for BYU employment, though previously it was not formally codified and strictly enforced. At the time Epperson had been paying fast offerings but not tithes because his wife was starting a nonprofit children's music conservatory and family finances temporarily were unusually tight. In early 1996 his bishop refused to certify his temple recommend. Epperson offered to reestablish his tithe-paying after the music school's summer camp in July, when the family's cash flow would ease, but this did not satisfy his bishop. In October Epperson was notified that his teaching contract would not be extended beyond the current school year.

The tithe and welfare systems amount to a compromise of the church's original ideal: communal equality. In the early Ohio years the "Law of Consecration" was supposed to mean that members deeded their possessions to the church and received their needs in common, holding lands and businesses in stewardship for the church. That didn't work well. In Nauvoo this principle was revised: church members were expected to give one-tenth of all their possessions to the church, then one-tenth of their annual "increase" as well. Persons with no property were expected to tithe their time and work for the church one day in ten. In Nauvoo this work was often devoted to construction on the temple.

In the early Utah decades tithing was often paid "in kind," including produce, grain, and livestock. Cash tithes might be paid in U.S. currency, scrip, or gold dust. Mormon institutions were also expected to pay a 10 percent tithe on their earnings. Complicated in-kind tithes, combined with necessary community and welfare needs, sometimes expressed what was something of a barter economy. A Saint might turn up at the tithing office with a cow in tow and get clothes and scrip in change.

Brigham Young was concerned that in practice tithing "surplus" was often nothing more valuable than animals ready for the glue factory: "Some were disposed to do right with their surplus property, and once in a while you would find a man who had a cow which he considered surplus but generally she was of the class that would kick a person's hat off, or eyes out, or the wolves had eaten off her teats. You would once in a while find a man who had a horse that he considered surplus, but at the same time he had the ring-bone, was broken-winded, spavined in both legs, and had the pole evil at one end of the neck and a fistula at the other, and both knees sprung."

In-kind tithes were not abolished until 1908, by which time Utah's commerce had clearly merged with the nation's and maintained no pretense of being the self-sufficient economy of a theocratic enclave within the United States. Today, of course, tithing continues as a necessary standard for members in good standing.

More intimate and unusual than tithing, one very personal aspect of Mormon life is the wearing of temple garments. Some religious material items in other faiths are meant to be on view to the public as well as to remind the wearer of religious commitment. For centuries Christians have worn crosses of many kinds. One current fad among Evangelical Protestant teenagers is wearing bracelets with the letters WWJD (What Would Jesus Do?), a parallel to the fashion among Mormon youngsters for wearing a ring with CTR (Choose the Right) as a visible reminder of piety. Special religious clothes are found in other religions, of course: Orthodox Jews wear their *yarmulkas* and fringed *tzitzit;* Mennonite women wear their little white prayer caps. Mormons wear sacred underwear.

These temple garments are different from other religious-wear items. The Saint wears them next to the skin, unseen by the outside observer. They are bestowed on the day of one's endowment ceremony at the temple, usually as a young adult, and are to be worn at all times thereafter. Originally they were like coverall union suits; gradually they became skimpier in deference to modern fashion, though the women's version (scoop neck, cap sleeves, bloomer-length panties) requires fairly modest outer clothes. They can be removed as necessary for participation in sports. When they are worn out, the sacred insignias are supposed to be cut off for ritual disposal, and what is left is considered an ordinary rag.

The meaning of the garments varies from wearer to wearer. Some invest the garments with protective power, and there are many folktales in Mormon tradition about their effect as a type of spiritual amulet. Others regard them as a private reminder of their commitment to a holy life. For all Saints the garments are a strong link of loyalty to their believing community.

A Mormon's diet, money, even his clothes, are affected by membership in the church. But most important of all are the church's claims on moral choices and time. The church stands uncompromisingly for chastity and moral responsibility. Mormon young people do not date before age sixteen. Saints are to refrain from acquiring debt and from gambling, including state-run lotteries, to shun pornography, and to be good citizens in the secular community. Social science studies cited by the church show that members reap rewards from these behaviors: they tend to be happier in their family lives and marriages, less likely to indulge in sexually or socially deviant behavior, and far less likely to be involved in any kind of substance abuse than average Americans. By keeping God's covenants, Mormons believe God promises them they will be a "peculiar treasure unto me above all people" (Exodus 19:5). God wants to "purify unto himself a peculiar people, zealous of good works" (Titus 2:14).

The time commitment for a Mormon begins at the local ward. Each Sunday is devoted to a three-hour bloc of sacrament, testimony meetings, and lesson classes for all ages. The sexes are segregated for an hour of this in priesthood and auxiliary meetings. During the week there may be extracurricular activities: a Relief Society meeting with a professional family therapist as speaker, approved by the bishop, or a potluck dinner; a stake choir rehearsal for teenagers. The official ward youth program for Mormon boys is Boy Scouts; legions of Eagle Scouts are turned out each year. Ward, stake, and regional levels encourage a wide variety of social opportunities for believers of all ages, including theatrical projects, youth orchestras, athletic competitions, choirs, mini-trek campouts, square dances, and devotional or cultural "Fireside" evening talks by visiting scholars or General Authorities.

But no church events are scheduled on Monday evenings. That is sacred time. Monday is Family Home Evening. This is a central program in the church design. Going radically against America's culture of latchkeys and serial dinners, Mormons are directed to shut out the world and gather with the nuclear family one night a week for devotionals and instruction, following standard church manuals, as well as for sharing wholesome secular activities. The authorities first directed the observance in 1915 but had to reinforce the idea with follow-up pronouncements in 1946, 1961, and 1964, perhaps an indication that it was something of a hard sell. In 1970 Monday was mandated as the churchwide Family Home Evening; temples were locked and ward activities prohibited.

Family Home Evening with Paul and Melanie Prestwich in their modest apartment in Bayonne, New Jersey, is probably typical for a family with young children. After a dinner of their favorite homemade pizza, three little Prestwich boys—eight-year-old Kieffer, four-year-old Bowen, and two-year-old Sam—sprawl on the floor and sofa while Daddy presents a lesson on Daniel and the lion's den. Kieffer knows most of the answers. Melanie, a convert from Catholicism, holds the long-awaited newborn daughter, Elizabeth, during lesson time.

During prayer time the toddler Sam is coached to pray, his childish soprano following Paul's lead phrase by phrase, "We thank thee—for the prophet—the church leaders—we pray for the Spirit—to help us choose the right."

After lesson time comes fun time. Grandmother Anne Prestwich, visiting from Colorado to help with the new baby, helps the boys decorate lion cookies with icing. They get to eat the cookies, too. And soon, after a little more small-boy romping, it is time for bed.

The church supplies lesson manuals and guidelines, but members are free to vary their lessons and activities—and if necessary, the actual day—to suit the needs and interests of their own families. Wards make an effort to bring together individual members without families nearby to form social and spiritual groups as a kind of substitute relationship network.

As the Prestwich children grow, they will follow the usual steps of church activities, but their four high school years will involve a major commitment of time unique in religious education. Each morning, five days a week for four years, they will rise before dawn to attend intensive catechism classes before their regular school day begins. They will study the Old and New Testaments, the Book of Mormon and other Mormon scriptures, and church doctrine and history. They will be expected to develop a lifelong habit of writing personal journals on their lives and spiritual growth. The boys will be taught to plan and save for a two-year mission commitment, two years given to the church before they finish college.

The children will learn to value the heritage represented by their church's unique history, and they will probably visit sites such as Hill Cumorah and Nauvoo; perhaps they will participate in a short enactment of the trek or devote a family vacation to cast participation in one of the big church pageants. They will be taught to participate as good citizens in the secular world, to work hard in school, in business, and in professional life, and to treat the "setting apart" for any church call as a privilege and command. They will hear exhortations on chastity and advice on the importance of thrift and avoiding debt; they will be expected to keep the Word of Wisdom and not to gamble; they will be taught to respond to the needs of their neighbor as well as those of their church.

It's a tall order, all that. But for the most part, it works.

CHAPTER 12

RITUALS SACRED AND SECRET

LIKE A CHILD'S OVERSIZE ERECTOR SET, IN 1999 THE NEW BOSTON TEMPLE perched on a rock outcropping, looming over the cars whizzing by on Route 2 in suburban Belmont. Mormons like to locate new urban temples near major crossroads. The six spotlighted spires of the mammoth, white Washington, D.C., temple pierce the sky next to the capital city's eight-lane Beltway. The New York City temple, also due for dedication early in the twenty-first century, is just off the intersection of the Hutchinson River Parkway with Interstate 287, the main street of suburban Westchester County. The new St. Louis temple, its golden trumpet–blowing Angel Moroni statue atop a 150-foot spire, is poised over Highway 40 not far from the I-270 beltway.

Neighbors aren't always pleased. The location of the Denver temple, opened in 1986, had to be changed three times to overcome not-in-my-back-yard objections. In Boston construction proceeded while nearby homeowners fought the project, especially its 139-foot spire. Matters were not helped by the annoyance of the extensive blasting made necessary by the site's granite ledge. Meanwhile, in a careful attempt to be a good neigh-

184

bor, the church sent regular teams of window washers to scrub construction dust off the nearby upscale homes. A small dirt mountain was put in place temporarily to help contain construction noise.

The Boston temple will serve a region that currently has about 40,000 Saints. Local Mormons are excited that they will have their very own temple in which to carry out their most sacred rites. They will no longer have to travel to Washington or Toronto twice a year for ordinance work or fly to Utah for a wedding. "It's going to be unbelievably wonderful to have our children married right at home," said devoted laywoman Margaret Wheelwright as she viewed the steel skeleton rising above her ward's meetinghouse.

For the members of the Belmont ward, the new temple and the meetinghouse next to it are particularly poignant symbols of their faith's growth in the region. The church acquired the fifteen-acre property in 1982 and constructed the ward building on part of the site. In 1984 the new meetinghouse was badly damaged just before its dedication by a fire of suspicious origin. Members of other local churches were horrified and fell over each other in the rush to offer facilities for Mormon use. As a result, Mormons held services in St. Joseph's Roman Catholic Church, the First Armenian Church (United Church of Christ), and Plymouth Congregational Church of Belmont before they were at last able to occupy their chapel in 1985.

Steel for the Hub's temple was manufactured in nearby Vermont; the granite to shield the skeleton came from Italy; the art glass for its windows was produced in England. The Moroni statue for the spire was designed by the sculptor Cyrus Dallin, some of whose nonreligious works are on display in Boston's Museum of Fine Arts. The new temple, at 69,000 square feet—about one-third the size of Washington's and similar to the plan for New York—is considered medium-sized and is costing $26 million, not counting the cost of the land and site preparation.

The temple will have facilities similar to those of the temple dedicated in St. Louis in 1997. Outside, the grounds will be landscaped with 22,000 plantings. There will be a picturesque walkway with a fancy bronze railing that, says Lyal Zaugg, will be just the spot for photographers to take their brides for a shot with the temple in the background. Elder Zaugg, a retired civil engineer from Idaho, and his wife Joyce are in Belmont as missionaries to oversee the construction.

The main-floor entrance will have a security area where people will be required to show their wallet-sized temple recommend cards for admission. The ground floor will have administration office spaces and locker rooms where patrons change into all-white temple clothes. Men wear white shirts and pants; women wear simple white long dresses; both wear white slippers. Many worshipers will bring their own temple clothes, but rentals will be also available. The lower floor will have the traditional huge baptistry supported by twelve carved oxen representing the tribes of Israel. It will also have laundry and cafeteria facilities, more locker rooms, and utility areas.

The most sacred rooms are upstairs. As a medium-sized temple, the Boston facility will have four "sealing rooms" where marriages for time and eternity will take place and children will be everlastingly sealed to their parents; four "ordinance rooms" to be used for endowment ceremonies; and one "Celestial Room" symbolizing the highest level of heaven. A temple may have any number of sealing and ordinance rooms, but there is always just one Celestial Room, the holiest space of all, where Saints may meditate and pray before leaving the temple.

"It's been a dream to have a temple here," said the local bishop, Grant Bennett, as he proudly watched the crews at work. "Symbolically, you move through stages of life, and the Celestial Room represents the joy of what you can have if you lead a pure and virtuous life." His fellow Saint Coleen Baird anticipated the joy of doing vicarious ordinances in the temple: "You finish the endowment in the Celestial Room. Everyone is dressed in white, and you are taken out of the world. There is no class distinction, and all is peace and quiet."

A typical temple interior resembles a luxury hotel: perhaps some paintings but no traditional liturgical symbols, domed ceilings, chandeliers, gold leaf, thickly padded upholstery, densely plush carpets. The color scheme becomes lighter and the flow of light turns brighter as one ascends toward the Celestial Room. Mormons like to say their temples are sacred, not secret, and there are no secrets about the physical plant. Before the temple is dedicated, the LDS Church will hold open house for several weeks, during which time any interested person may inspect all the facilities and learn about the rites that will be held there. After that, no non-Mormon will ever again be admitted to the temple's precincts.

Several Boston Saints were bemused at some rumors spread among the Gentiles, such as the notion that Mormons burn all the desecrated carpet just before the dedication and replace it. Mormons, of course, are far too thrifty for such nonsense. However, all those attending the open house will be required to wear plastic slippers over their shoes; like Muslims at mosques, the Mormons do not profane temple carpeting with street shoes.

Nothing expresses the Mormon diaspora more clearly than the worldwide campaign of temple building in the last two decades. The first temple, dedicated in Kirtland, Ohio, in 1836, has long been in the hands of the rival Reorganized Church of Jesus Christ of Latter Day Saints and is always open to the general public. The second, dedicated in Nauvoo, Illinois, in 1846, after the prophet's murder and just before the Utah trek, was destroyed by fire and storm soon thereafter, now to be rebuilt early in the new millennium. Then came four Utah temples, culminating with the great one in Salt Lake City, dedicated after forty years of construction.

In the twentieth century, new temples began to dot the globe, especially over the last decade or so. This escalating pace is revealed in the fact that the St. Louis temple of 1997 was only number fifty among the more than one hundred temples in operation or on the planning board. It took a century and a half for the LDS Church to build twenty-five temples, and only fourteen years to add twenty-five more.

Many of the newer temples, however, are of a smaller design. The baptistry, for example, may be supported by only six oxen, with the additional six suggested through artfully placed mirrors. The smaller temples may lack certain facilities, such as laundries and cafeterias, and operate on limited hours, but all will have the necessary facilities for the full range of sacred ordinances. The goal is to have temples accessible to Saints anywhere in the world and to elevate these Mormon rituals as an essential aspect of ongoing life.

When a Saint entering a temple presents his recommend card, an attendant verifies the date and signature. The bearer must pass annual interviews with his bishop and stake president to hold this card, which, among other things, signifies that he is active in his ward and pays the full 10 percent tithe to the church. In the recommend interview the bishop also inquires whether the member is loyal to church leaders, faithfully upholds church teachings, lives a morally clean life, obeys the Word of Wisdom, and wears the sacred underclothes.

The temple concept is not rooted in New Testament Christianity. Its inspiration reaches back to the Old Testament, especially Solomon's temple and the idea that certain sacred activities can be accomplished only in sacred space. In Joseph Smith's day, Masonic lodges believed that their own key rituals had a direct linkage to those conducted in Solomon's temple. Smith was an active Mason when he introduced the endowment ordinance two years before his death, and many scholars have noted the strong resemblance between the Mormon ordinance and Masonic ritual.

Temple baptism, however, has no parallel in Masonic ceremony. Ordinary living believers, both children raised in the faith and converts, undergo baptism by full immersion in a ward meetinghouse. Baptism in the temple, however, is a vicarious ordinance conducted on behalf of dead persons, sometimes one's own ancestors. White-robed teenage boys and girls can serve as stand-ins during the ceremony, and this is considered an honor, much like altar service for a Catholic boy or girl. Each name presented requires a separate immersion, although the same proxy might perform twelve or fifteen in a row. This baptism does not "save" the deceased person. It provides a choice in the afterlife; using his "free agency," the person may accept or reject the offer of receiving Christ and entering his kingdom.

Mormons use I Corinthians 15:29 as New Testament justification for these proxy baptisms. Paul wrote, "Else what shall they do which are baptized for the dead, if the dead rise not at all? Why are they then baptized for the dead?" The church's *Encyclopedia of Mormonism* explains the verse as "part of Paul's argumentation against those who denied a future resurrection." Non-Mormon writers provide various explanations for this difficult verse. But they point out that Christ never mentioned baptism for the dead, Paul's words do not contain any command or recommendation to carry out the practice, and the rest of the New Testament is silent on the subject, so there is no reason to regard this as a usual or required practice.

The Mormon interpretation is that baptism for the dead was an early Christian practice that was lost with the early apostasy of the church and restored by Joseph Smith.

Saints normally concentrate their proxy activities on their own ancestors, but their activities have reached beyond their own families. Ordinances have been carried out for dead U.S. presidents and signers of the Declaration of Independence, among others. In 1926, however, the First Presidency reaffirmed the church policy that temple ordinances could not be performed "for people who had any Negro blood in their veins." The policy was affirmed again in 1966 with a First Presidency letter. According to D. Michael Quinn, the church's genealogical department flagged the names of "those of known Negro blood" to prevent their use in proxy endowments and sealings, but the General Authorities quietly changed the policy in 1974 after learning of a potential NAACP lawsuit and congressional investigation of racially discriminatory use of census records.

The church's "name extraction" program uses volunteers to take the names of deceased persons from public records and submit them for ordinance work. This program yielded 13 million names between 1985 and 1990 alone. One Catholic journalist, covering the 1998 October LDS General Conference, spent a lunch break visiting the genealogical library and returned to the press gallery visibly shaken and muttering angrily because she had just discovered that her late and very Catholic Irish mother had been vicariously baptized Mormon. Some Catholics have been disturbed to discover that many famous Catholic saints have been given Mormon ordinances posthumously. Officially, the Catholic Church ignores the matter.

The practice is especially offensive to Jews. A highly sensitive vicarious baptism issue erupted publicly in the mid-1990s when baptism for Jewish victims of the Holocaust—some 380,000 of them—created an angry backlash from the American Gathering of Jewish Holocaust Survivors. The names had all been submitted by nine zealous Mormons who had visited concentration camps and Holocaust museums in Europe. The situation surfaced when Ernest Michel, a founding member of the survivors' organization, discovered in the genealogical library that his parents, both of whom died at Auschwitz, had been given Mormon baptisms. In 1995, after a year of negotiations, the church agreed to remove all such names and to refrain from baptizing deceased Jews unless they were ancestors of living LDS Church members or the church had written permission from all living members of the person's family.

Vicarious ordinance activities, not only baptisms but sealings and endowments, account for the Mormons' passionate interest in genealogy. It would be splendid to have all of one's family tree enjoying eternity together so that death does not sever these most sacred relationships. The church, in fact, teaches that Saints have a moral *obligation* to trace their families and perform temple ordinances on their behalf.

The task of baptizing and endowing all the billions upon billions of humans who ever lived is unimaginably vast, and records before A.D. 1600 are scant, so fulfillment awaits the millennial kingdom. But in the meantime, Saints are expected to do what they can to provide spiritual assistance to their forebears. The result is the most astonishing and extensive genealogical library in the world, religious or secular, staffed by 200 paid workers and 400 trained volunteers. The Family History Library based in Salt Lake City has more than 2 billion names on various kinds of records, over 700,000 microfiche files, and nearly 2 million rolls of microfilmed records ranging from Korean clan genealogies to Scottish church records to the American Social Security death index. The microfilmed holdings are equivalent to more than 7 million books of 300 pages apiece.

This collection expands by 5,000 microfilm rolls a month. Eastern Europe is currently the big area of exploration since it has just been opened up to genealogical workers, who photograph everything from church to civil records. The collection has doubled in size just since 1985, when the Temple Square library building was completed. To protect the originals of its genealogical records from nuclear holocaust or other disaster, in 1966 the church opened a massive, humidity-controlled vault 700 feet below the surface of a granite mountain at Little Cottonwood Canyon. Besides the Salt Lake operation, which handles 2,700 visitors a day, the church operates 2,800 branch centers scattered across 64 nations and went on the Internet in 1999 (www.familysearch.org). By mail or computer, the branches have access to all headquarters records. Gentiles and Saints alike have free use of this vast collection, with nominal fees for photocopying or mailing. Never in the history of organized religion has a doctrinal tenet produced such an elaborate and expensive archival effort.

Temple sealings are ceremonies for living Mormons as well as vicarious ordinances for the deceased. Spouses are joined or "sealed" for eternity in a five-minute rite conducted by a "sealer." Rings may be exchanged but are not required, and there is no music. The church has guidelines for wedding gowns, and brides who arrive for the ceremony in insufficiently modest attire are provided with temporary cover-ups to insert in their dresses. Large temples have several rooms that can be used for weddings, scheduled fifteen to twenty minutes apart. The great Salt Lake Temple has fourteen sealing rooms and ten sealers on staff; its all-time wedding record was 167 in one day. Across the street, next to the church office building, is a cement stoop where photographers snap the bridal parties in a continuous parade, posing them in front of a picturesque temple view with fountains, spires, and the gleaming golden Angel Moroni.

For a temple wedding, both parties must be temple-worthy church members. Any future children will be automatically sealed within the covenant. Married converts can have sealing rites performed, binding themselves as a unit for eternity, kneeling with their children around the altar. Mirrors on opposing walls exchange infinite reflections, symbolizing eternity. Proxy sealings performed for deceased persons provide the possibility of uniting for eternity a family that may have been religiously split in life.

A temple bridegroom probably received his endowment before leaving on his two-year mission. The bride typically receives hers a day or so before her wedding. The sacred underclothes are received at the endowment, and a secret name is bestowed as a type of password into the eternal world. The male may know his bride's sacred name; the female does not know the man's. This complex ceremony, which at one time took six to nine hours and is still more than two hours long, is a singular, once-in-a-lifetime ritual. The endowment may also be experienced by unmarried mature adult Mormons, as well as by adult temple-worthy converts. Pious Mormons, officially encouraged to do temple work each month, will repeat the endowment many times as proxies for deceased persons who are candidates for vicarious endowments.

The temple rituals are the most devoutly protected of all the LDS Church's secrets. Sensitive about the secrecy issue, Mormons frequently repeat the "sacred not secret" refrain. But official policy is to guard them as secret, and that policy became a matter of widespread church discipline in 1990 following published reports of changes in the endowment ceremony. Mormons are not supposed to describe the specifics of the actions, recitations, or vows to nonbelievers. Stories about the revised ceremony appeared that year in the *Salt Lake Tribune* (its story originated with Vern Anderson of the Associated Press) and many other newspapers and national magazines. Some of these articles were quite general. Others reported considerable ritual detail, and a number of the pieces compared Mormon and Masonic ritual details.

These stories quoted anti-Mormons and former Mormons, including the well-known Sandra Tanner, as well as current Mormons in good standing. Most of the latter made only general remarks indicating that they liked the changes, statements that would strike non-Mormons as innocuous. But the church made it clear that individual Mormons were not to comment publicly on such matters, even in bland, general terms. All persons known to have done so were questioned by their bishops, stake presidents, or General Authorities. As news of these meetings spread, the church communications department felt it necessary to release a statement defending the interrogations.

Most of these visitations were reportedly low-key, though they undoubtedly served as warnings, but *Sunstone* reported that at least two were not. One Saint, F. Ross Peterson, former editor of *Dialogue,* visited by all three Seventies for his area, was questioned at length about his loyalty to church authorities and shown a thick church file of clippings collected on him since his college days. His temple recommend was removed and "further action was intimated" if he spoke or wrote anything further about the temple. His recommend was restored after he wrote a protest and several members petitioned authorities on his behalf. Keith Norman, who holds a Duke University Ph.D. in religion, had presented a paper on the subject at the 1990 Sunstone Symposium in Washington, D.C. Norman's bishop later said that he had been instructed to deny Norman a temple recommend for one year. When Norman asked his bishop what it was for which he needed to repent, the bishop reportedly responded, "I don't know."

The endowment ceremony was introduced in Nauvoo in 1842. It was a far more complex ceremony than the simple washings and anointings that had been followed in the Kirtland, Ohio, temple, and the general shape of the ritual remains faithful to the Nauvoo version. The 1990 changes softened the symbolic violence of the revenge referred to in penalty oaths; modified some of the resemblance to Masonic rituals; moved somewhat toward more equality of the sexes; and eliminated the drama segment in which the Devil hires a Protestant minister to teach false doctrine.

The endowment ceremony today, as described publicly by the church, has four main segments: a drama, formerly by live actors but since the 1950s presented on film, which presents the story of salvation and redemption as a human journey moving from pre-earthly beginnings, through the Creation and Fall, and Christ's life and death; progression to a brighter room, where believers learn about God's blessings; an exchange of promises with God, then moving through an opening in a curtain or veil to represent the passage from this life into immortality; and entrance into the Celestial Room, representing the highest level of heaven.

The relationship between Masonry and Mormon ritual, especially in the endowment, remains a sensitive matter in the church. Extensive research on this has been done by Mormons using published statements by church leaders and historical documents that the church made available for a time in the 1970s, as well as by non-Mormons using widely published writings by former Mormons. The latter includes books by Jerald and Sandra Tanner, whose polemical tone is resented by loyalist Mormons, though their work is generally acknowledged to be factually accurate and honest. Other writers on the subject who were Mormons at the time of publication included David John Buerger and D. Michael Quinn.

Mormon loyalist Reed C. Durham Jr. was silenced by the church after his 1974 presidential address on the subject to the Mormon History Association (MHA) meeting in Nauvoo. He told the MHA that Joseph Smith received "immediate inspiration from Masonry" in designing the endowment ceremony and that the similarities were too clear to be denied. Durham was then director of the LDS Institute of Religion near the

University of Utah. He issued a public apology after being censured by church education administrators, and his MHA speech was not published, though unofficial versions of the address have been printed. Durham thereafter maintained silence on the subject.

The best study currently available is probably an article by Michael W. Homer in the Fall 1994 issue of the independent LDS intellectual journal *Dialogue.* Masons may believe that Smith "stole" the ritual, and anti-Mormons may accuse him of plagiarism, but Homer maintains that for "those who believe in continuing revelation, the divine origin of the LDS temple endowment does not depend on proving there is no relationship between it and Masonic rites or that Joseph Smith received the endowment before his initiation into Freemasonry."

Early Mormons were fairly open in recognizing the connection between the endowment ritual and Masonry. Apostle and First Counselor Heber C. Kimball wrote that Smith believed in the "similarity of preast Hood in Masonary." Other early church leaders taught that the Masonic ceremony was a corrupted form of temple rituals that had descended directly from the biblical Solomon and were restored to the true, pristine form by the inspired Joseph Smith. Early Mormons believed in the antiquity of the Masonic ritual, at least before Robert Freke Gould's *History of Freemasonry* (1885) and other studies debunking the ancient origins of the ceremonies. Gould did admit that some of the associated symbolism adapted by Masons probably had ancient origins.

Scholars today are generally agreed that Masonic ritual developed largely in the seventeenth century or so as a syncretistic mixture of influences from ancient Egyptian rites, symbols borrowed from alchemy, astrology, the occult, the Bible, Rosicrucianism, and Jewish kabbalistic mysticism. Joseph Smith became a Mason in March 1842, advancing all the way to Master Mason the next day. This was highly unusual since the normal minimum wait between each of the three degrees is thirty days. In the weeks that followed he observed Masonic ritual degree advancements thirteen times before introducing the endowment ceremony on May 4 and 5, 1842.

The essentially British version of Masonry as probably practiced in Nauvoo included such elements as ritual anointing of body parts; a creation drama as a metaphor for a spiritual journey; bestowal of a secret name (as a password into eternity); special garments (in Mormonism, sacred undergarments) when stepping through a veil in a glorified ascent to a Celestial Lodge; secret handshakes and tokens; promises to fulfill moral obligations; penalty oaths to protect secrecy; progression through three degrees toward perfection; the use of special temple robes and aprons; and the word *exalted* to signify becoming kings in connection with the Royal Arch degree. Masons regard the lodge as a temple. All these elements have strong parallels in Smith's endowment ceremony. In addition, Masonic symbols that have been adapted by Mormons on everything from temples to gravestones to logos include: the beehive, the square and compass, two triangles forming a six-pointed star, the all-seeing eye, sun, moon, and stars, and ritualistic hand grips. Traditional Christian liturgical symbols such as the cross, crucifix, Chi-Rho, or ichthys (fish) are absent.

Women were not Masons, but according to Homer, some American and British Masons favored female participation, and in 1774 French Masonry recognized female auxiliary lodges. Smith extended the endowment to women in 1843.

The endowment ceremony was always performed in English until 1945, when a Spanish ritual was introduced; now it is performed in dozens of languages. A filmed version of the drama was first provided in 1953 when a presentation suitable for the new, small Swiss temple was needed, according to David John Buerger. This production included 350 feet from Disney's *Fantasia* to provide lava for the creation episode. Three revised versions followed. Buerger reports, "According to the actor who portrayed the minister in the third filmed version, the role of Satan was to have originally been filled by an African-American, but due to protests by LDS Polynesians, a Caucasian filled the role."

Even more mystery than usual surrounds another of Smith's temple rites known as the "second anointing" or "second blessing" subsequent to the endowment. According to Buerger, these rites were conducted for thousands of Saints early in the twentieth century. But in 1926 President Heber J. Grant (who ruled until 1945) said they could thenceforth be performed only by the president of the church on the recommendation of one of the Twelve Apostles. The restriction to an elite reduced the number of anointings precipitously. According to Apostle George F. Richards, only eight were performed in the years from 1930 to 1942. Buerger says there are only "bits of information" about the practice in recent times, but he assumes that the authorities do not consider such a limited ceremony to be a prerequisite for exaltation in the afterlife.

Whatever his reliance on the Masonic tradition, in developing ceremonies for his Latter-day Saints Smith probably knew little of traditional Christian liturgies as preserved in Eastern Orthodox, Catholic, Episcopal, and Lutheran worship, except as included in modified Methodist forms. His own early background was in Protestant nonliturgical or "low church" worship. This influence has been retained in Mormon congregational worship, with its Evangelical-style songs, testimony talks, and icon-free chapel design.

Sunday may be the high point of the week in a traditional Christian cathedral, but on Sunday all Mormon temples are closed. Important as temple rituals are to Mormons, the local congregation (ward) is central to the worship and community life of the faith. On Sunday the Saints are busy in their local meetinghouse. It is there that babies are presented for blessing several weeks after birth; that tots lisp their first testimonies; that eight-year-olds are baptized and confirmed to receive the gift of the Holy Spirit with the laying on of hands; that parents and friends speak at missionary farewells; and women bring green Jello salad and potato casseroles for the meal that follows a funeral.

In each ward communion is distributed weekly by young priesthood holders, using water instead of grape juice or wine along with the bread. Weekly frequency was a mark of the Protestant "restoration" movement that arose just before Mormonism and gave birth to today's Churches of Christ, "instrumental" Christian churches, and Christian Church— Disciples of Christ.

Mormons call communion "the sacrament," but theologically it is an ordinance of reminder and remembrance, not a rite to bestow spiritual grace as that term is used in mainstream Christian churches. The sacramental prayers enjoin Mormons to "eat in remembrance of the body" and to "do it in remembrance of the blood." The traditional Christian words of institution used by mainstream churches from Luke 22:19, "this is my body" and "this is my blood," are never spoken in the Mormon sacrament. The two prayers recited before distribution of the bread and the water are virtually the only fixed liturgy in Mormon ward worship. The wording was part of the Native Americans' Christianity, as reported in the Book of Mormon (Moroni 4:3 and 5:2). If even one mistake is made in the scriptural recitation, the LDS officiant must repeat the entire prayer.

The sacrament meeting in the Northridge ward of Sandy, Utah, is typical. It is the first Sunday of the month, so the Saints have skipped breakfast and lunch in order to give the equivalent expense as fast offerings for the needy. Three wards use this meetinghouse; a typical block is from 9:00 A.M. to noon or from noon to 3:00 P.M. The required schedule includes an hour each for sacrament meeting, Sunday school for all ages, and priesthood sessions for males with simultaneous auxiliary meetings for females. Families will eat their evening meal together.

Clothes are formal Sunday best; even the littlest boys wear shirts and ties. Since this is the first Sunday of the month, it is also testimony meeting. A red-haired twelve-year-old Scout talks haltingly of having been on a mini-trek, and cutting himself while whittling, and says he is "grateful to be in a neighborhood where so many people go to church." Next comes a five-year-old blonde in a blue dress who adjusts the mike with aplomb and announces: "My name is Amy. I'd like to say I know how to obey the scriptures. I know this church is true. In the name of Jesus Christ, Amen." A stream of young teenagers follows, then the mother of a missionary currently serving in Germany. A pony-tailed seven-year-old gives thanks for her family, ending, like all the others, with the formula, "I know the church is true. In the name of Jesus Christ, Amen."

A well-dressed and attractive mother of eight children comes next to testify with tears, "I want my children to know how grateful I am for them." She reaches into the tissue box judiciously located on the podium and dabs at her eyes before continuing. "I want them to know I have a testimony. I know Joseph Smith was the true prophet. I feel overly blessed."

Another woman in her fifties takes a tissue as she begins talking about family matters, including a recent death, thanking the ward for love and support. "We are not left alone. We are carried by our Father's love. I am grateful for trials that have helped me see the hand of the Father." Another parade of teenagers follows, varying considerably in polish, some indicating awkwardly that their priesthood leaders had done some pump-priming in getting them to speak. They talk about being thankful for believing friends, their families, the gospel, the prophet. They *know* the church is true.

The members carefully use the *thee/thou* second-person pronoun in their prayers, as required by denominational policy. Even on nontestimony Sundays, there is never a prepared sermon delivered by an educated professional, as would be the case in most other churches. Instead, there are brief amateur talks by ordinary local members that provide a mixture of personal testimony and inspirational advice.

The Sunday school lesson comes next, divided by age. The adult class this Sunday covers II Kings 2, taught by Patty Howells, the wife of Utah Jazz basketball manager Tim Howells. She rotates teaching duties with a male teacher. The lesson is interrupted by twenty youngsters coming in to sing lustily for the grown-ups, "Follow the Prophet." After Sunday school the sexes separate into priesthood and auxiliary meetings.

Although Northridge is home to the Mormon upper crust, the expanding church incorporates many kinds of neighborhoods. The mission branch in Bayonne, New Jersey, is in a working-class area with Spanish signs, storefront Pentecostal churches, and neat if aging frame houses. In one of these modest homes the Saints gather for their Sunday morning services, an abbreviated two-hour version of the Sunday bloc. A Spanish congregation of similar size will meet there in the afternoon.

About forty people squeeze into the tiny living room of this rental home occupied by the married missionaries Elder Kent and Sister Loujean Walker. The Walkers left their nine children and twenty-eight grandchildren in the Intermountain West to accept this mission call. Sister Walker has shed a few tears this week: she has missed her family tradition back home of giving the first bath to each new grandbaby. Her oldest daughter will be her stand-in for the newest arrival while she stays at her New Jersey mission post.

For the morning's English service, Paul Prestwich is at the Yamaha keyboard. Hymns include some familiar to Protestant Evangelicals, such as "I Stand All Amazed" and "How Great Thou Art," but others are unique to Mormons, including "Families Can Be Together Forever" and the children's song "I Am a Child of God," with its reference to preexistence in the line "I'll live with him once more." Frankie Salcedo, a thirteen-year-old priesthood holder of Puerto Rican and Dominican background, helps distribute the sacrament. This morning's talks are given by a local member and by a visiting missionary who describes the activities at the nearby genealogical branch center.

Those in attendance include Sonia Molina, a single mother here with her teenage son. She moved from the Bronx to Bayonne a year ago, seeking a safe area for her son. Some time back she had been baptized Mormon in Puerto Rico, then drifted away, but here in Bayonne she was drawn back into the church by a pair of young missionaries. Four young elder missionaries assigned to the area are present.

Most of those attending today's service are wearing Sunday best, the four elder missionaries in their trademark suits and ties, but one man is in a leather jacket, and another is dressed in a windbreaker imprinted with the logo of a neighborhood deli, worn over a plaid flannel shirt. A young black man in a wheelchair is carried up the concrete stairs into the house and back to the street. Worshipers are invited to attend the baptism of a new convert in the baptistry at a Union City meetinghouse later in the day. After a Sunday school lesson on the Holy Spirit, a young Hispanic couple thank people for bringing them meals the preceding several days. It has been quite a week for them: they were baptized just the previous Sunday, and they are here today with their four-day-old newborn in their arms. In several weeks the newborn will be given the traditional infant blessing during a testimony meeting.

Blessings are another important form of ritual for Mormons. In times of stress it is traditional for fathers in the Melchizedek priesthood to lay hands on the heads of their wives or children and pronounce a blessing. But a special and mysterious event, unique to the Mormon religion, is the Patriarchal Blessing, which bears some resemblance to prophecies in Pentecostal religion, just as early Mormons practiced speaking in tongues. The "Patriarch to the Church" once had the power to give blessings for anyone in the entire denomination and was a churchwide General Authority. These patriarchs held office through a hereditary line going back to Joseph Smith's family. But no churchwide patriarch held the chair from 1932 to 1942, and since 1979 the office has fallen into disuse, perhaps never to appear again.

The patriarchs are officers of the regional stake, appointed with the approval of the Quorum of the Twelve. The noted Columbia University historian Richard Bushman has held this post for the New York City area. During the sacred session a patriarch is led to declare a person's literal lineage tracing back to the Twelve Tribes of Israel. As the First Presidency defined the role in 1957, he also provides "an inspired and prophetic statement of the life mission of the recipient, together with such blessings, cautions, and admonitions as the patriarch may be promoted to give." A patriarch bestows the Lord's blessing sensitively within a knowledgeable context of the recipient's personality, abilities, aspirations, and spiritual life.

Cayr Lewis, the oldest daughter of Bruno and Cari Vassal in the Pepperwood community, and her husband had difficulty as they attempted to start a family. As Cayr struggled with becoming pregnant and carrying a child successfully to term, her Patriarchal Blessing predicted she would become the mother of children. Today, as she watches curly-haired Jayd, age two, tear around the house with her four-year-old brother Justin, she remembers how she clung to the comfort of the Patriarchal Blessing during her time of discouragement.

If rituals related to family, from the weekly Family Home Evening all the way to vicarious temple ordinances, are a special mark of Mormonism, perhaps the biggest ritualistic family reunion this side of mortality is the semiannual General Conference in Salt Lake City. It is held for two days each April and October in the century-old Tabernacle in Temple Square. In April 2000 the first conference of the new millennium will be held in the new 21,000-seat assembly building that is being completed across the street for a reported $240 million.

Thousands of people throng into Salt Lake City, the lucky ones with passes for the Tabernacle, others happy to hear the closed-circuit proceedings piped into the Assembly Hall nearby or to sit on blankets spread over the grass in Temple Square. Both the *Deseret News* and *Salt Lake Tribune* run headlines like "Faith, Family Dominate General Conference," or, "Tabernacle Choir Truly Electrifies." Media are advised to dress appropriately for the religious services. They are also advised that landscapers will have thousands of petunias, geraniums, marigolds, datura, begonia, coleus, dahlias, cosmos, heliotrope, crepe myrtle, zinnias, snapdragons, verbena, vinca, nicotiana, and lobelia in bloom on Temple Square and the adjacent plaza of the church office building for the occasion.

Outside, people on the sidewalk waiting for the tabernacle doors to open break spontaneously into song: "How Great Thou Art" and "Count Your Blessings." It is raining outside, but umbrellas are not permitted inside. By the thousands, umbrellas are piled onto folding tables. A dubious reporter is assured that her umbrella will be there after the session. It is.

Inside, President Hinckley, members of the Quorum of the Twelve, and other General Authorities give what Mormons call "talks." Each session is opened and closed with prayer; the talks are separated by prayer, congregational singing, and choir music. The text of each talk is distributed to journalists beforehand; the complete set of talks fill each May and November issue of *Ensign,* and taped sets of talks from previous conferences can be purchased at the nearby ZCMI Center's Deseret Bookstore. Saturday night talks are for male priesthood holders only, so ZCMI keeps the stores open late for special "ladies' night" sales.

Newcomers to the ranks of the General Authorities are always sustained by unanimous vote, a ritual unchanged from the early days of the church. Talks treat such subjects as the importance of tithing, commitment to one's family, and obedience to the standards of chastity. In October 1998 President Hinckley raised the sensitive subject of whether Mormons are Christians: "Are we Christians? Of course we are Christians. We believe in Christ. We worship Christ." Responding to recent reports of polygamous activities by splinter-group Mormons, Hinckley reaffirmed the modern LDS opposition to the practice: "I wish to categorically state that this church has nothing whatever to do with those practicing polygamy," he said. "They are not members of the church. Most of them have never been members."

The "gathering" to Zion used to mean that Saints physically relocated to Utah. Today the church officially encourages believers to stay living in their homelands and to build the kingdom there. But they can be part of the conference by satellite. Over 3,500 LDS stake centers and other church buildings in the United States, Canada, Puerto Rico, Haiti, Jamaica, and the Dominican Republic are equipped with satellite receivers. More than 1,200 cable TV systems and radio stations carry the General Conference sessions on a public service basis. Downlink equipment receives live transmissions in fifteen European nations, and videotapes of conference sessions are distributed through church centers elsewhere in the world. Simultaneous translations of some sessions are transmitted in thirty-five languages as well as in sign language and through closed-caption TV transmissions for the hearing-impaired. All around the world, Mormons gather to watch and listen to the conference proceedings.

To the non-Mormon the inspirational talks are routine, even banal. Nothing ever happens at a Mormon General Conference. No issues are discussed; anything decided in Mormonism is decided in secret, far from the eye of the membership, much less the general public and the press. To the average Mormon believer, none of this matters. The General Conference is an important Mormon ritual, a homecoming and reunion for those in Salt Lake City and a worldwide Mormon family gathering for those who are not.

On Temple Square more than 200 volunteer ushers serve the visitors. An estimated 35,000 pass through the square on conference Sunday. Some anti-Mormon Protestant Fundamentalist young people are picketing on the sidewalk and buttonholing conference-goers. But reverse proselytizing is fair game, and the mood is cheerful, respectful, polite on all sides. After the last session the faithful pour out of the tabernacle and past a beggar seated outside the east Temple Square gate with a big plastic bowl. Begging is hardly the Mormon style, but everyone's mood is happy. The beggar's bowl is full.

CHAPTER 13

TWO BY TWO

THE STREETS ARE MEAN AROUND THE GRAND CONCOURSE. AT NIGHT IT IS not unheard of for a stray bullet to whiz down those cement canyons of the South Bronx. Drug sales are frequently observed in the neighborhood. The brand-new brick-and-cement chapel of the Church of Jesus Christ of Latter-day Saints, built at a cost of $8 million, has a certain fortress feel to it. Located on the corner of Kingsbridge and Valentine, a block off the Grand Concourse and not far from a hulking Veterans Administration hospital, it has no windows anywhere near ground level. Its glass doors are protected at night by a solid steel sliding security door. Neighborhood artists have already added graffiti to help it blend in with the local decor.

Emerging from Kingsbridge Chapel into the sun and the chill, Elders David Freston and Nathan Van Noy are ready to begin yet another day on the street. Both are Eagle Scouts, blond, fit, and twenty years of age. Name tags clipped to their lapels, they carry backpacks stuffed with tracts and paperbound copies of the Book of Mormon. They are clean-shaven, and their hair is trimmed short. They are wearing dark pin-striped suits, sub-dued ties, and neatly pressed shirts in regulation white and are shod in thick, sensible walking shoes, meticulously polished. Each detail of the grooming and attire has been mandated by the manual for missionaries. (For the elders: no sports coats, no light-colored or baggy slacks, no jeans, boots, or loud ties. And for the sisters: no "oversized or peasant-style clothes," no "sporty shoes," no skirts that are floor-length or that ride above midcalf.)

They are typical of the industrious young Mormon missionaries at work across the United States and worldwide, always in pairs. The men serve for two years, while the minority of young women volunteers have eighteen-month terms. There are 60,000 in the field at any one time, double the total as recently as 1985. (The church also assigns some older couples, about 7 percent of missionaries, often serving in specialized, humanitarian, or administrative posts.) This remarkable army, which operates with military discipline and regimentation, constitutes by far the largest force of short-term evangelists on earth. Billy Graham, who worries that U.S. Evangelicals may be losing their international zeal, credits Mormons with "great missionary urgency." The Mormon missionary program fuels the steady increase in converts worldwide and, perhaps just as strategically, plays a powerful part in bonding its young people, especially its men, to their church.

Out on the sidewalk for a day of contacting prospective converts—variously called "finding," "tracting," or "fearlessing"—Freston and Van Noy smile and politely greet strollers. "Hi! How are you doing? I'm from the Church of Jesus Christ of Latter-day Saints. We have a church around the corner. Do you have a minute to talk about something that can bring you happiness?" Responses vary. Some simply shake their heads and walk on. If one is a missionary, one must be well prepared for continual rejection. Two young women pushing a sleeping toddler agree to permit a home visit and provide their address. A young man seems interested in visiting the chapel; he has heard it has a basketball court.

The elders approach an apartment building. The door is locked, but they slip in when a resident returning from an errand unlocks it. Now begins the religious equivalent of the telephone salesman's cold call, knocking on doors uninvited. Door after door yields silence until finally, after a peephole check, a resident opens up despite the taped sign: "Este Hogar es Catolico; No aceptamas propaganda Protestante ni de Otras Sectos: Viva Christo Rey!" ("This House is Catholic. We do not accept propaganda from Protestants or Other Sects: Christ the King lives!")

Resident turnover is high in this neighborhood, so the sign may have been posted by a previous tenant, but in any case it would not have daunted Freston and Van Noy. Neither elder speaks Spanish, but with a few broken sentences the woman agrees to a later visit from a Spanish-speaking team. Van Noy writes down her name and address. A report will be turned in at Kingsbridge Chapel, and Spanish-speaking elders will soon visit. The required filing of elaborate reports on such contacts and on other day-by-day activities—including TPT (Total Proselyting Time)—is a heavy burden on the missionaries.

Among the 240 elders and sisters it has on tap, the New York mission is able to supply missionaries to handle two dozen languages, including American Sign Language. Van Noy is from Twin Falls, Idaho, and Freston is from Sandy, Utah, two traditional Mormon strongholds, but the New York mission also has 25 non-American missionaries from China, Africa, Laos, Mexico, Russia, Bulgaria, Ukraine, Bulgaria, and Poland.

No locked lobby entrance bars admission to the next two apartment buildings, but the knocks yield only three opened doors and no appointments. The occupants say they have no telephones. In this area disconnects for nonpayment are not uncommon. It is time for lunch. The first two elevator buttons are broken, and the next delivers them to the basement rather than the lobby. They walk up to street level and pass a razor discarded on the pavement as they stride briskly to their apartment.

Their place is a walk-up next door to the Revival Christian Church ("Good neighbors," says Elder Freston). The apartment, shared with another missionary pair, in many ways resembles college digs: rugless floor, yellow plastic sofa, odds and ends of secondhand, mismatched furniture, dark blue sheets tacked over barren windows for privacy, small framed personal pictures scattered about. By the door are cartons with tracting supplies, such as paperbound copies of the Book of Mormon and videotapes with titles like "Lamb of God" and "Together Forever." The apartment is spartan, but the plumbing works. What is unusual is the absence of standard college dorm possessions: there is no computer, no television, no sound system, not even a cheap radio. A slightly frayed zone map of the South Bronx dominates the wall behind the sofa because Van Noy and Freston are zone leaders, supervising twenty elder and two sister missionaries.

A missionary companion is a missionary shadow. Two by two, they tract, pray, eat, shop, worship, do laundry, study, relax, sleep on separate beds in the same bedroom, and do everything but shower in tandem. If the apartment door is opened, two come in or two go out. They are always to address each other politely as "Elder ———" or "Sister ———." The pairing is assigned and frequently rotated, but moving is not difficult since during their two years missionaries are strictly limited to two suitcases of belongings.

Newly arrived missionaries are always paired with "senior" missionaries with a year or more in the field. This is essential for foreign-language assignments, since the newcomer may start out relying only on his few weeks of language drill at the Missionary Training Center. It is also critical in helping an Idaho kid fresh off a farm acquire big-city street smarts. The companion system provides instant fellowship, an aid to safety, and, less readily discussed, a check on behavior. Companions are supposed to report problems or infractions to their superiors. Some form lifetime friendships with their partners. For others, the loss of independent privacy and difficulties in the enforced relationship are the toughest aspects of missionary life. As some joke, "Good training for marriage!"

After lunch Van Noy and Freston have an appointment to teach the second lesson prescribed for new members. The convert, baptized a week ago, is a thoughtful young Zimbabwean living with his sister's family. Back in Africa he had been a Methodist. This is typical; most converts come from some kind of Christian background rather than no religious background at all. Very soon this young man will be granted the Aaronic priesthood, and if he remains active, as an adult convert he will be ordained to the Melchizedek priesthood a year or so later. The young man is intelligent and responsive to the lesson. He, too, likes to play basketball. Back on the street again, the two elders cheerfully greet passersby. Attempting to carry out another discussion appointment, they announce their arrival to an apartment voice box, but this time they have been stood up.

They will continue their work, with an hour out for dinner, until 9:30 P.M. Their day began at 6:00 A.M. with prayers and study and will end at 10:30 P.M. after more of the same. Missionaries get one partial "Preparation Day" off each week on which they have until 5:00 P.M. to do their laundry, shopping, and personal chores. They may also use some of these off-duty hours in community service; both of these elders have served in local soup kitchens, and Freston has helped paint a Kingsbridge Chapel member's apartment.

If they have dinner with a local church member, guidelines remind them to keep the visit to one hour. All telephone calls, local or long-distance, must be approved by a district functionary. The New York rule-book forbids missionaries to play football, baseball, hockey, or any team competition, or to go rollerblading. Informal half-court basketball, softball, and soccer, however, are "authorized for exercise purposes." Missionaries may attend two sporting events and two Broadway shows per calendar year, with permission. Approved productions, as of 1998, were *Phantom of the Opera, The King and I, Cats, Show Boat, Beauty and the Beast, My Fair Lady, Carousel,* and *Les Misérables.* Those with tape or CD players are expected to limit themselves to "appropriate classical music," Mormon Tabernacle Choir recordings, and LDS religious songs.

Missionaries are expected to keep regular personal journals and to write home once a week. They are not permitted to communicate with family and friends by fax or e-mail and are allowed only two telephone calls home each year, on Christmas and Mother's Day. Collect. The telephone restriction is observed even in emergencies. When Van Noy's younger sister was critically injured in a traffic accident a few months earlier, all communication was through an intermediary at the New York mission office. The sister recovered, but had she died, Van Noy would have been expected to remain focused on his assignment in New York and not fly home for the funeral. Missionaries are not allowed visits from family or friends during their tours either, though such draconian restrictions are not applied to the older missionaries, who are usually couples. (Individual widows can serve, but widowers are not accepted.)

Missionaries may not date, and all contact with the opposite sex is strictly regulated. The missionary handbook warns them, "Never be alone with or associate inappropriately with anyone of the opposite sex. Flirting or dating is not tolerated. You are not to telephone, write to, or accept calls or letters from anyone of the opposite sex living in or near mission head-quarters." They are advised to visit single members or "investigators" (potential converts) of the opposite sex only with additional adults present, a precaution always to be carefully observed "even if the situation seems harmless."

Freston, with two months in his call remaining, has baptized nine converts; Van Noy, who will be released in seven months, has baptized seven. Freston has siblings who have served missions in Montreal, Finland, and Belgium; Van Noy is the first in his family to receive a call. When released, both have college plans. Their faces glow when they talk about what a privilege it is to watch people's lives change, and how much they love the streets and people of New York.

Supervising the 220 young soul-winners and 10 older missionary couples in the area is 47-year-old Ronald Rasband, who in mid-1999 was completing three years of service as president of the New York mission. Rasband himself served a youthful mission as one of 80 New York proselytizers in 1970–72. Back then the New York LDS membership totaled 3,862; three decades later it topped 20,000. Like his young foot soldiers, Rasband receives no salary as mission president and pays his own expenses. After accepting his New York call, Elder Rasband left his career as president of Huntsman Chemical Corporation.

"The church has taught me a desire to put God first and not the things of the world," says Rasband, "and if some of those things come my way—as I have been blessed to have—to use them for the good of mankind." So in 1996, when a call came, Elder Rasband, a native Utahn and fifth-generation Mormon who traces his family roots to Nauvoo, submitted his leave of absence to the company's Mormon owner Jon Huntsman, uprooted his family from his large stone Pepperwood area mansion perched on a Wasatch hillside in Sandy, Utah, moved east, and enrolled his children in the Scarsdale public schools.

The New York North Mission extends from the tip of Manhattan up the Hudson to Saugerties, west through the Catskill Mountains, and eastward to include a bit of suburban Connecticut. The city was the base for one of Mormonism's first missions, established in 1839 in the state where Mormonism began. Today there are 331 missions worldwide, each governed by a president and two counselors. The New York turf has been subdivided many times. There are four mission districts covering New York

State, overlapping the system of thirteen established stakes that mission congregations join as they become established. Mormons are usually assigned to wards and branches on a strict geographic basis, but New York also has two sign-language branches, a military branch at West Point attended by seventy to eighty cadets, student and singles wards, and congregations in Spanish, Korean, Russian, and Chinese.

The metropolis is expensive, but the church is prepared to invest serious money there. Besides the costly Bronx building, the church in 1999 was building a $7 million chapel on an empty Riverside Drive lot in Upper Manhattan, designed to be shared by four wards, three Spanish and one English. Before returning to Utah, Rasband expected to watch groundbreaking ceremonies for the first New York temple, a 70,000-square-foot structure planned in nearby suburban Harrison, to be the only temple between Washington and the new one in Boston.

Like the salesman he once was, Rasband motivates his young charges to make one more call, knock on one more door. He gave the mission its official slogan, "One More." Like the highly successful executive he also was, he analyzes strategy. Taking a leaf from street-corner soapbox evangelism of yesteryear, and the colorful array of present-day New York sidewalk vendors, under Rasband's direction missionaries have developed alternative methods using street displays with portable tables. They also target strategic spots such as Grand Central Terminal, through which more than half a million commuters flow each weekday.

Rasband is sensitive to missionary morale. It is not easy to be rejected thirty or forty times a day. Safety is also a concern. Approving apartments is his responsibility, and "I look at these apartments and ask myself if I would want my own child there," he says. One of his daughters served a mission in Detroit, where inner-city streets can be as mean as in the South Bronx.

Newly arrived missionaries, some initially terrified at the prospect of urban service, go through training sessions in which they receive practical advice on becoming street-savvy. This includes hints on how to walk in lit and unlit streets (for the latter: don't); car safety; bicycle safety; how to recognize and avoid potentially dangerous groups. There is a telephone call chain each night between 9:30 and 10:30 P.M. to check that all missionaries are safely in their apartments. In his years as mission president,

Rasband has supervised 600 workers, only two of whom cut their service short for nonmedical reasons.

Freston and Van Noy trained at the Missionary Training Center (MTC) in Provo, Utah, the largest of the fourteen such boot camps the church operates. Residency numbers fluctuate at Provo. The maximum capacity at the center is 4,348. During 1998 more than 27,000 missionaries were prepared there. Missionaries called to English-speaking assignments train for four weeks, while those learning one of the forty-seven foreign languages in the curriculum will spend nine weeks there in all. There is also training in English as a second language. The Provo center employs seventy-two full-time paid staffers, shares some services with its giant next-door neighbor, Brigham Young University, and hires more than one thousand part-time paid instructors, most of them returned missionaries studying at BYU or Utah Valley State College nearby. (In the BYU student body, nearly three-fourths of the undergraduate men have served on missions.)

Each missionary goes through careful ecclesiastical screening in his home stake and receives an appointment letter direct from the president of the world church. Male missionaries are eligible for a call at age nineteen, but female missionaries cannot serve until age twenty-one, possibly to allow for prior calls in the direction of marriage while encouraging them to complete their education before babies arrive. The 1999 *General Handbook of Instructions* states that "women should not feel obligated or be urged unduly to serve full-time missions" and that bishops should not recommend women for assignments "if it will interfere with imminent marriage plans." The 1989 *Handbook* was more sweeping, opposing recommendations "if a mission will interfere with marriage." Nonetheless, about 14 percent of the church's young missionaries today are female.

About half of eligible young LDS men in Utah serve missions and about one-third nationwide, a level of devotion that is without parallel in other denominations. Not all missionaries are American; the LDS Church stresses developing indigenous local leadership. Take, for example, the Philippines, with the church's fourth-largest national membership and number one in Asia (more than 400,000). Half of the 2,000 missionaries there are Filipino; 83 percent of the converts are from a Catholic background. The three largest flocks outside the United States are also found in

Catholic nations: Mexico (783,000), Brazil (640,000), and Chile (462,000).

In Nigeria and Ghana, where activities began developing with the 1978 revelation opening the priesthood to blacks, there are 49,000 Mormons and over half of the 1,000 missionaries now active are native Africans. All but twenty or thirty older couples are young proselytizing personnel. "We want the Africans to join because they believe the Book of Mormon is true," says James O. Mason, who is retired from a distinguished career in the U.S. Public Health Service that included appointment as assistant secretary of the U.S. Department of Health and Human Services. Elder Mason is the current president of the Africa Area Presidency and a member of the Second Quorum of the Seventy. Food as needed is distributed through local bishops, as in the United States, but, says Mason, the church "does not want them to join for the wrong reasons." No Rice Mormons.

On the average Wednesday the Provo MTC processes 550 new missionaries, accompanied by 3,500 camera-toting relatives, anxious but proud. The Polynesians are especially noted for bringing large extended family groups, including awed younger brothers and sisters. The arrivals have received their destination assignments just a few weeks earlier. They have been honored individually in their home wards with farewell services during which family and friends traditionally give talks. When they have completed their terms, they must return directly home—no recreational travel is permitted en route—to be formally released from their call and to share their testimony again with their home ward.

With the usual Mormon organizational efficiency, they are divided by alphabet into six groups staggered an hour apart. Yellow-tagged volunteers mark the new arrivals with orange stickers; families spend half an hour at the center, most of it in an orientation meeting. There is a welcoming speech, a spiritual pep talk that stresses journal-keeping and temple attendance, a brief movie showing missionaries two by two working in different spots around the world on foot and bicycle, then prayer. The climax is the singing of the traditional missionary hymn "Called to Serve."

> Called to serve Him, heav'nly King of glory,
> Chosen e'er to witness for his name,

Far and wide we tell the Father's story, . . .
Onward, ever onward, . . . Called to serve our King.

Tears then, as parents hug their sons and daughters good-bye. Visitors and missionaries depart through separate doors. After orientation, the next glimpse that parents get of their children is a half-hour visit allowed at the Salt Lake airport when the missionaries are en route to their assignments.

"They grow up. Today they are boys; they will return as men," says Merrill C. Oaks, observing what is a very familiar scene for him. Seven of his nine children have served missions to Hong Kong, Austria, Paraguay, Chile, Guatemala, Montana, and Texas. Elder Oaks, brother of Apostle Dallin Oaks, former president of BYU and member of the Quorum of the Twelve, is a Provo ophthalmologist who retired early to serve the church unsalaried and full-time. A member of the Second Quorum of the Seventy, he serves in the North America Southwest Area Presidency.

At the MTC contact with the opposite sex is limited to chaste hand-shakes; room visits are beyond the pale. Trainees may not leave the MTC grounds without permission, which is normally granted only for weekly temple visits or medical necessities. Every hour is carefully scheduled and every activity regulated, down to the notations that bathroom urges should be handled during the five-minute break between classes and at dinner only one trip to the dessert line is allowed.

The standard prep courses reinforce commitment to the basic message and quickly teach the routines of the trade (pray continually, be person-able, remember first names, strike up a natural conversation but be confi-dent in your convictions). There is very little education in the culture and history of the host destination.

Most trainees will, in timeworn LDS fashion, go door to door, two by two, hoping to coax people into allowing a series of weekly return visits so the young zealots can present and preach the restored gospel. Where pos-sible, the missionaries attempt to develop personal interaction with poten-tial converts and to involve more than one family member in home visits. The trainees memorize six discussions for prospective converts and prac-tice how to teach six more lessons to new converts. They critique each other's presentations. The foreign-language trainees learn by immersion, working in classes of eight to twelve students in three three-hour blocks of daily language classes, memorizing market talk and the religious discussions in their new language. By their fifth day at the MTC they are to refrain from using English.

Theologically the first several missionary discussions go only slightly further than the bland inspirational talks of the Mormon Tabernacle Choir broadcasts. The first discussion introduces the prophet Joseph Smith and his Book of Mormon as scripture in addition to the Bible. Missionaries are trained to find out in the beginning about the religious background and interests of investigators. By the second discussion they introduce baptism and attempt to have investigators agree to baptism on a certain date. Missionaries are coached to avoid debate and taught to build discussions around beliefs held in common.

Certain unique LDS beliefs are touched on by the fourth discussion: preexistence, the future eternal family, vicarious baptism for the dead. There is no fudging on the lifestyle demands. Investigators are told about the chastity requirements as well as about abstinence from tobacco, liquor, and caffeine. The distinctive Mormon beliefs about God are brushed over lightly. We are "literally children of our Heavenly Father" with whom we lived "before we were born on this earth." Investigators are told that "our spiritual bodies were created in the image of our Heavenly Father," though in some ways human beings are "unlike" God, who "had progressed far beyond us spiritually" so that in premortal existence humans "did not have a physical body, as he does." But God loved us and "wanted us to become like him," so he "prepared a plan that would allow us to come to earth." To support these ideas missionaries cite a mixture of Mormon and Bible scripture, sticking to the King James Version in English. Two such references are Jeremiah 1:5 ("Before I formed thee in the belly I knew thee") and Acts 17:29 ("We are the offspring of God").

The fifth session introduces other lifestyle demands, including fasting and the principle of tithing. By this time the investigator should be attending church services and missionaries are asked to confirm a baptism date if it has not already been set. The sixth discussion, to be held a few days later, provides a doctrinal overview and stresses the principle of salvation and eternal life, here called "progression in exaltation" or "holiness" and sometimes referred to elsewhere in LDS literature (but not in missionary discussions) as "deification."

Perhaps the real genius of the Mormon missionary system is its effect on its own members, especially young people. Nothing like it in scope exists in any other denomination. At an age when the youth of most religions are beginning to avoid church activities, Mormon youngsters are baby-sitting, mowing lawns, and pumping gas after school to save the $375 per month they must someday deposit with the church to cover expenses when they serve a mission.

Anyone who notices the regimentation at the MTC and omits the palpable excitement of the students misses the story. Mission duty taps powerfully into youthful idealism, the desire that adolescents have to be a part of something bigger than they are. For two years they set aside everything in their own lives, their education, their professional goals, their personal relationships, to serve the church wherever the church elects to send them.

Oaks, who served his own youthful mission in Ontario, Canada, says, "They learn how to immerse themselves in serving others." Those returning home can be more nervous than the ones going out due to the shock of adjustment. They have matured and learned a great deal about dealing with people. Their view of life and focus on their own future have changed. And from their ranks will come the future church leadership. As mission president in the Seattle area, Oaks supervised two missionaries from Ukraine who, he said, clearly developed leadership skills that they took back to the small flock in their homeland, where a mission was launched in 1992.

The MTC trainees can hardly wait to undertake their assignments. "I know that there's somebody out there that only I can bring to Christ," says Australia-bound Jeremiah Bigelow of Rigby, Idaho. His classmate Chet Sanders of Kaysville, Utah, has always planned on a mission tour; he spent a year installing windows to pay his way. Winnipeg-bound Emily Banford of Fruits Heights, Utah, says, "I'm really excited because the gospel brings joy and makes people happier. I want people to be happy the way I'm happy."

"We try to make sure every missionary returns home with a great experience," states Earl Tingey, a former corporate attorney with Kennecott Copper and now executive director of the missionary department. Tingey is in the seven-man Presidency of the Seventy, a General Authority rank-ing just below the Quorum of the Twelve. "We want them to say, 'This is the best two years of my life,' and to return each one a convert to the church himself."

The hundreds of classified ads in the *Deseret News* announcing mis-sionary reunions during each semiannual General Conference in Salt Lake City attest that this goal is often reached. A gathering of those who served in Manchester, England, under the mission president Bryan Richards, is typical. A ward chapel is filled with 250 mingling twentysomethings, some beaming with pride over the new babies they have brought to show off. There are a few middle-aged returnees as well, and several Manchester converts visiting along with the missionaries who baptized them. The rec-ollections flow forth amid the chatter. It was "a blessing." "It was a chal-lenge to get along with my companion." "I disliked the administrative work but liked the 'real' work." A quietly self-confident Tryon Gibbons gives a formal talk. "That two-year period builds character more than any other period in your life," says Gibbons, now a college student in Arizona. "I have a focus and get grades that are very different from my life before." The most difficult part of Gibbons's mission experience was staying in England when his younger brother was killed in an accident.

The reunion concludes with hymn singing, prayer, and spiritual pep talks from Richards and his wife Lynn. She reminds the group that "you don't get to the celestial kingdom without a spouse," while her husband tells them that their work was "a continuing strength and foundation from which we build." He urges the former missionaries to remain in contact with their converts because "what you did as missionaries goes on and on; it has a ripple effect, into eternity."

The General Authorities have an important advantage in missionary strategy over Protestants, who operate a huge number of mission agencies that rarely coordinate and sometimes compete with each other. Salt Lake headquarters can decide where promising converts are most likely to be found and directly deploy their forces accordingly. The LDS Church tends to target overseas populations that are already literate, limiting education to catechism training, whereas Protestants and Catholics often operate extensive educational systems at all levels of schooling.

Tingey downplays any tensions over the foreign expansion of a church tightly controlled from the United States. The General Authorities make sure that the program is universal and identical worldwide. Critics often question whether the identification of the church with American culture, especially the capitalistic ethos symbolized even in the business suits that missionaries always wear, makes Mormonism vulnerable to anti-American reaction overseas. Tingey shrugs this off. "We don't push it, but we can't escape it," he says. "Americans are respected worldwide. In many parts of the world being American is a big plus. Americans have a way of getting things done."

One continual hassle faced equally by Protestants and Catholics is how to function in Third World lands while refusing to pay bribes to officials. Another problem, particularly tricky for the Mormons, is handling conversions in polygamous cultures. Bedeviled by its own polygamous history and then strict policy against it, the LDS Church instructs missionaries to inquire discreetly about the marital situation in the first home session. If the home is polygamous, the missionaries are instructed to go no further and not to bring such a convert to baptism. Nor are missionaries in the lax South Sea Islands cultures allowed to instruct or baptize persons who are living together without benefit of marriage.

According to those detailed reports that each missionary files, during 1997 there were 317,798 convert baptisms, compared with 75,214 baptisms of eight-year-old children of members. A complex reality lies behind those totals. Ordination to the Melchizedek priesthood among adult converts provides a better picture of the retention rate. A male growing up in a Mormon family normally reaches that rank at about age nineteen, and an adult convert about a year after joining the church. In 1994 Lawrence A. Young, BYU sociology professor, reported data available from the 1983 church almanac about the percentage of adult male members in various nations holding the Melchizedek priesthood. In Utah, about 70 percent of baptized males reach this level; the overall United States average is 59 percent and Canada, 52 percent. But that figure drops off dramatically overseas, reaching a low of 19 percent in Mexico and 17 percent in Japan.

There would appear to be significant numbers of dropouts after baptism. As with other religions, a segment of those on the rolls are baptized members of record only. Many converts drift away into inactivity or join other churches, yet their names are not removed except in rare instances where they formally request resignation or are excommunicated.

Expansion of the church worldwide may, at some point, pose financial challenges, even to the affluent Mormon Church. Developing indigenous leadership is another major challenge, as is the critical matter of avoiding doctrinal dilution in areas located far from Utah. Most Mormons outside the United States are first-generation believers, and it remains to be seen how effectively the faith will be passed on to succeeding generations.

Cultural problems also pose special difficulties in certain places. The same hymnbook and the same music, for example, are required worldwide, and always with keyboard accompaniment. The vibrant African style of music and drumming heard in many Catholic and Protestant services, for example, is completely absent in LDS chapels. Peggy Fletcher Stack of the *Salt Lake Tribune* described the Guguletu Branch near Cape Town, South Africa, where only three of eighteen baptisms in 1997 were of men age eighteen or older, and only one of the three remained active a year later. With 253 members on the rolls, weekly attendance was about 65. A local leader told Stack that a number of Mormon practices conflict with local tribal culture.

One non-Mormon scholar, the sociologist Rodney Stark, has tracked the exponential growth of the LDS Church over the last two decades and proclaims it an emerging world religion. Stark has a strong personal reason for his admiration of the church. His parents converted to Mormonism late in life, and he observed how the LDS community supported and helped them in their declining years.

What works for the Mormons? An adherent may be born and raised in a particular religious culture or may be drawn in through networking. Cold-call evangelism with isolated individuals, says Stark, is effective in maybe one in a thousand cases. But if a prospect agrees to a missionary chat that includes friends or family, he figures the "take rate" can approach 50 percent. Faith is primarily a matter of belonging, and LDS conversion typically comes in a social context rather than individually. Growth rates function like the principle of compound interest in economics.

Stark maintains that those with frail interpersonal attachments—for instance, newcomers to an area—are most apt to be recruited. Relationships such as kinship, marriage, and friendship play a major part in helping along conversion. Those whose prior religious ties are casual are the most ripe for recruiting, but when people change religion they are most likely to "make small changes related to their own culture." That is, Mormonism succeeds by building on a preexisting Christian culture and by being seen as an add-on, drawing converts through a form of syncretism. Mormonism flourishes best in settings with some prior Christianization.

According to Stark, religious ideology plays "almost no role in the beginnings of the conversion process." New Mormons, he says, learn what they believe perhaps six months *after* they have joined the church. In the meantime, they have been socialized into the church through a broad range of activities and enjoy the support of an emotionally satisfying and highly responsive community while gradually identifying with very demanding lifestyle commitments.

The historian Jan Shipps, another widely recognized expert who is also a Gentile outsider, would disagree. She insists that the faith content is an "extraordinarily important part of why people become Mormon." Moreover, she observes, the statistics of conversion must be tempered with the recognition that "conversion operates like a strainer. Many are converted but only some stay."

Similar cautions come from the Reverend David B. Barrett, a former Church of England missionary to Africa and the leading religious demographer as editor of the *World Christian Encyclopedia* (published by Oxford University Press). Compared with the 60,000 Latter-day Saints, he estimates that the mainstream Protestant, Catholic, and Orthodox churches combined field around 400,000 full-time career missionaries, plus perhaps up to 400,000 other personnel on short-term duty ranging from weeks or months to a year or two. Unlike the LDS workers, the career missionaries are usually experts on their host nations and pursue a wide variety of educational, medical, and humanitarian tasks as well as the proselytism that is the sole task of the LDS youth. As for money, Barrett has not the remotest idea how much the LDS spends on its efforts, nor does anyone else, but "it's huge; it's enormous."

As a statistician, Barrett notes that a recently introduced religion inevitably has a faster growth rate than longer settled groups. Thus, he says, LDS growth rates exceed those of the old-line churches, but not of the newer, expanding Christian movements: for example, the Congo's Kimbanguist church, which is spreading across Africa and into Europe; the El Shaddai movement and Jesus Is Lord Fellowship, which are growing in the Philippines and among ethnic Filipinos overseas; or, inside America, the Willow Creek Association, which has encompassed more than 1,000 congregations in rapid order. On the other hand, for 1998 the Southern Baptists, the Mormons' mission-minded rivals, reported their first membership loss since 1926.

One interesting parallel to the LDS Church is the Assemblies of God, a Missouri-based Pentecostal body that is half as big as the LDS Church in the United States, considerably younger (established in 1914), and has posted a higher U.S. growth rate than the LDS in two of the past four years. More remarkably, membership in the self-governing churches overseas that are affiliated with the Assemblies exceeds 28 million, a 78 percent jump in a decade. "It's a phenomenon probably unparalleled in church history," contends the Reverend Thomas Trask, the Assemblies' general superintendent (chief executive). The Assemblies field 1,775 career missionaries from the United States, aided at any one time by hundreds of short-term volunteers.

Barrett cautions against judging any church from baptized membership alone, since in religion worldwide on average for every ten persons a group baptizes, three eventually defect. Thus, Barrett concludes, the LDS church is not an extraordinary success story overseas "except in certain areas like Fiji and Tonga, where they have latched on when older Protestant groups have lost appeal. They're just one of many religious organizations experiencing remarkable growth" in many nations, he says. Also, LDS folk "work in areas where proselytism is possible and easy, rather than working among non-Christian peoples or tough areas for evangelism."

So the Church of Jesus Christ of Latter-day Saints is not alone in its expansion across the globe. But it is still obvious that the word "remarkable" does fit Mormonism, under anyone's definition, and that the faith's unique system of missionary staffing accounts for a good part of its strength.

CHAPTER 14
SAINTLY
INDOCTRINATION

THE CAMPUS IS A PICTUREBOOK DREAM: PERFECTLY MAINTAINED, MODERN buildings brightened by green lawns (regularly watered—this is, after all, semidesert country), shaded by maples and other deciduous trees (imported—also carefully watered), surrounded by the snow-dusted, spiky peaks of the Wasatch Range. Every twelve hours teams of students scour the grounds and buildings. There's not a gum wrapper in sight. Graffiti artists wouldn't dare.

This is Brigham Young University in Provo, Utah, the crown jewel in Zion, "the Lord's University," as the campus slogan goes. Students here salute the flag each day when it is raised and lowered. Male students are required to be clean-shaven (unlike many past church presidents); earrings are forbidden. No one goes barefoot. Girls are dressed according to the Honor Code printed in the catalog: "modest in fabric, fit, and style," with skirt hemlines at the knees or below. Anything "sleeveless, strapless, or revealing" is unacceptable. In order to maintain the "dignity of representing Brigham Young University and the Church of Jesus Christ of Latter-day Saints," the catalog warns, students should maintain "a clean and well-cared-for appearance," since modesty and cleanliness reflect "personal dignity and integrity." The students, some 30,000 of them, comply.

The students, in fact, comply with a great many restrictions beyond those associated with personal grooming. Other rules, like those on dozens of Evangelical Protestant campuses, forbid visiting the dorm rooms of the opposite sex, drinking, and doing drugs. The BYU administration keeps a wary eye on student publications and campus cultural activities. In 1997 it pulled four nude works from a visiting exhibition of the nineteenth-century French sculptor Auguste Rodin. Campbell Gray, director of the university's art museum, said the figures in *The Kiss, The Prodigal Son, St. John the Baptist Preaching,* and *Monument to Balzac* might offend some viewers. In 1998 the campus movie theater restricted its cinema showings to G-rated films after tangling with several Hollywood producers, such as Steven Spielberg, over permission to edit out scenes deemed unacceptable. As a result, BYU students never saw *Schindler's List* or *Titanic*—at least not on campus.

BYU is far and away the largest religiously sponsored university in the United States and ranks second only to New York University among all private campuses (not counting the huge University of Phoenix with its "distance education" by computer). The church tie is an omnipresent reality, not a vestigial aspect, as it is at Duke or Southern Methodist. For good reason, the Princeton Review in 1997 ranked BYU as the nation's most religious school and number two in its "stone-cold sober" section. BYU says that 73.4 percent of its men and 26.6 percent of the women will have served church missions by the time of graduation. And more than half (53.3 percent) of the students will be married before they leave, an extraordinarily high rate. BYU is a strategic venue for finding LDS marriage partners and starting loyal LDS families.

Behind the polite and pious appearance of these well-groomed students lie 30,000 bright young minds. The average freshman arrives with an ACT score of 27.3 (equivalent to an SAT composite score of about 1230), and an average high school grade point average of 3.74. The student body is about evenly divided between men and women, and 98.6 percent are Mormon. Enrollment is limited in aspects besides religion. Only 0.4 percent of students are black. The typical BYU student comes from the Intermountain

West. Some 94 percent are from the United States or Canada; the remaining 6 percent include a smattering of students from Asia, Latin America, the South Pacific, and Europe.

Education here is a bargain. President Merrill J. Bateman, former professor, dean, and senior vice president of the Mars candy company, declined to divulge a figure, but reportedly about 70 percent of the budget comes from church tithes. With that subsidy, tuition for LDS students was a mere $1,360 a semester for the 1998–99 academic year, a modest $5,400 a semester if one adds in room and board charges, the cost of books, and estimated personal expenses. The extra tax is just $680 more for non-LDS students, but there aren't many. To maintain their access to this good, cheap education, all the LDS students are required to provide the university with an annual recommendation from their ward bishops, a significant control mechanism.

The faculty is homogeneous as well: 97 percent are temple-worthy Mormons, a figure said to be heading toward 98 percent, compared with 93 percent a decade ago. By contrast, the faculty at Graceland College of the Reorganized Church has headed in the opposite direction. Twenty years ago its faculty was only 8 percent non-RLDS, and currently only about half are members of the Missouri-based church, "which is about the right balance," says one RLDS professor.

The BYU mission statement declares that the purpose of the school is to "assist individuals in their quest for perfection and eternal life." Such preparation is supposed to reach beyond the development of the student's own potential to "bring strength to others in the tasks of home and family life, social relationships, civic duty, and service to mankind." Four goals are cited: teaching all students the "truths of the gospel of Jesus Christ"; pursuing "all truth" in a "broad university education"; providing education in "special fields" so that students will be "capable of competing with the best in their fields"; and promoting research, scholarly activity, and education in "selected graduate programs of real consequence."

Students at BYU can receive a solid education in most fields, and learning with distinction in some. Early in the twentieth century church officials debated whether the school should concentrate on practical vocations, but a comprehensive curriculum won out over a narrower program. There are no graduate degrees in religion, only graduate minors in ancient scripture, church history, and doctrine, aimed at training instructors for the Church Educational System (CES).

After years of languishing in the third tier of *U.S. News & World Report's* oft-disputed annual ratings, in 1998 BYU was bumped up to the second group of sixty-seven schools, which were grouped alphabetically without number ranking. (The first tier of fifty schools was listed in numerical order, beginning with Harvard.) BYU's score was a bit lower than that of the Southern Baptist Baylor University, while Catholic Notre Dame and Georgetown were counted in the elite first tier. BYU had complained that its ranking was adversely affected by its relatively low freshman retention rating, the result of the uniquely Mormon custom of male students temporarily withdrawing for two years of mission duty. It was probably good news for BYU that its local competitor, the University of Utah, remained in the third tier. Both schools earned the same score in overall academic reputation.

Most frequently mentioned as matters of BYU pride are the law and graduate business schools. Of about 1,750 graduate students, nearly 500 are in the Marriott School of Management, and almost as many are enrolled in the J. Reuben Clark Law School. In the 1999 ranking of graduate and professional schools by *U.S. News & World Report,* the business school is ranked number forty-nine in a two-way tie. The law school was in a five-way tie for twenty-ninth place.

The 1997 *Gourman Report* from the Princeton Review ranked BYU lower, placing its law school fifty-seventh, ignoring BYU in its list of the top fifty business schools, and leaving it out of its list of the nation's one hundred top undergraduate schools. In its own scorings it rates BYU close to two other Utah universities, giving the University of Utah a 3.80 score, BYU a 3.62, and Utah State a 3.60.

On the other hand, *Public Accounting Report's* 1997 annual survey of undergraduate and graduate programs by professors in the field ranked the BYU accounting program third in the nation. The same year's *Chicago–Kent Law Review* survey, which ranks scholarship production by quantity, counted BYU's law faculty as twenty-eighth. The school ranked twenty-fourth nationally in the number of National Merit Scholars sponsored by corporations or the National Merit Foundation, and eleventh if one added in the Merit Scholars funded by BYU itself.

Brigham Young has the tightest ecclesiastical control of any religious college or university in the United States. The board is led by the three members of the church's First Presidency and includes six of the Twelve Apostles, one of whom is also head of the churchwide parochial education system, and a member of the Presidency of the Seventy. Thus, the General Authorities have ten of thirteen seats. The other members are the presidents of the women's and young women's auxiliaries (both appointed by the top General Authorities) and a secretary. Bateman, former presiding bishop of the church and now a member of the First Quorum of the Seventy, is the first BYU president to serve concurrently as a General Authority. His 1995 appointment was widely interpreted as a move to tighten the church's grip.

The university has ambitions, and money behind the ambitions. Campus buildings like the 22,000-seat Marriott Center testify to major contributions from wealthy Mormon donors. BYU aims to turn out well-educated, loyal, and active Mormons who will form the leadership cadre of lay volunteers who run the clergyless church of the future. It would appear that the church gets what it pays for. Contrary to common wisdom in the relationship between education and religious activity, some surveys show that Mormons increase religious activity as their level of education rises. And the student body, flying in the face of modern trends, has become more traditionalist in the second half of the twentieth century.

A 1935 study of BYU students showed that 88 percent of them believed Joseph Smith was a true prophet; 76 percent believed Mormon authorities receive continuing revelation today; and 81 percent believed the Mormon Church was more divine than others. A similar survey in 1973 showed clear conservative trends: 99 percent believed in Joseph Smith as a prophet, 99 percent in continuing revelation, and 98 percent in the divine nature of the church. Perhaps the most stunning example were the answers to this question: "Do you place obedience to authority above your own personal preferences?" In 1935 the positive response was 41 percent; by 1973 this figure had risen to a resounding 88 percent. The key difference most likely is that the annual bishop recommendations to ensure obedience and orthodoxy were not required in the 1930s.

"The evidence is overwhelming that attending BYU, even for only one semester, produces young adults who are highly active in the church," wrote five of the university's sociologists in an internal study leaked to the Associated Press in 1996. The study covered BYU students from 1971 to 1988 and showed them to be more likely to marry in the temple than Mormons who attended secular colleges (86 percent compared to 77 percent) and more likely to pay full tithes (77 percent compared to 62 percent). BYU Provost Bruce Hafen reportedly ordered that the study be withheld from publication, possibly because of the information about church members' tithing compliance.

The successes of BYU, intellectually and in terms of loyalty to the Restored Church, would have been appreciated by Joseph Smith. "The glory of God is intelligence" is one of his scriptural aphorisms (D&C 93:36) frequently quoted by Mormons. Though Smith had little formal education, he had a curious mind and a love of books and learning that he explored all his life. In Kirtland, Ohio, he studied Hebrew with a tutor. Despite the impoverished background of most Saints, schools popped up on the scene from the earliest days of Mormon gathering. Today Utah ranks close to the top of the U.S. states in the proportion of youth population in school and the median number of school years that citizens complete.

The earliest Mormon-organized effort at education was Kirtland's School of the Prophets. Opened in 1833, the school was originally intended to train missionaries but soon expanded into secular subjects such as grammar, arithmetic, Hebrew, and history. A similar school began meeting in Jackson County, Missouri, and existed until about 1836. With the move to Nauvoo, a system of "common schools" was soon established for elementary instruction. At its height the system had schools in each ward and about eighty teachers on its payroll. Texts were chosen by a twenty-three-man board of regents that was answerable to the municipal council.

In 1841 Nauvoo chartered a municipal university. This was essentially a secondary school with classes in religion, philosophy, science, mathematics, music, foreign languages, and literature. The university's first chancellor was John C. Bennett, also mayor of Nauvoo before he had his falling-out with Joseph Smith in 1842. Bennett was one of the better-educated citizens of Nauvoo. He had become a medical doctor by apprenticeship with his uncle and served as president of an Ohio medical college before moving to Illinois. Mormons in Nauvoo dreamed of having a university campus, but meanwhile classes met in whatever buildings were available, including homes and the local Masonic lodge. The First Presidency's ambitious dream was to make the university "one of the great lights to the world," though acting on that dream had to wait for decades after the trek to Utah.

Early Utah, of course, was as much a theocracy as Nauvoo had been, and the establishment and supervision of common schools fell under bishops' responsibilities. During the trek itself, classes were sometimes held around campfires and in wagons or tents; in the Great Basin they often met in whatever buildings also served as ward meetinghouses. Compulsory public school up to age fourteen came with statehood, but universal public secondary education did not arrive until 1911, so thirty-five stake academies filled the gap for several decades.

In the early twentieth century the church began to divest itself of some of its school facilities and secular educational responsibilities. The state increased its secondary school activities, and by the early 1920s the church had turned over its academies to the states. For about another decade the church operated several two-year teacher training colleges; by 1933 these had been transferred to the state of Utah. What had started as the University of Deseret—chartered in 1850, before Utah was a territory—later became the Salt Lake Academy and eventually, in 1903, the state's University of Utah. Provo's Brigham Young Academy eventually metamorphosed into Brigham Young University.

The church today retains a junior college, Ricks College in Idaho (1997–98 enrollment: 8,551); the LDS Business College in Salt Lake City (877); and a major degree-granting branch of BYU in Hawaii (2,231). Outside the United States, below the college level, the church still operates schools for about 8,700 primary and secondary students.

A possible new direction in Mormon education is on the horizon. An independent college committed to the LDS faith, Southern Virginia College, had 300 students in 1998–99, its third year of operation. The group of Mormon investors who bought a women's seminary to start this college hope to gain regional accreditation by 2001, and they project an eventual enrollment of 1,200. Administrators have received inquiries about starting similar ventures in Texas and California. The church itself, however, has stated that it will not formally support any additional institutions of higher learning.

Instead, the LDS is focusing on expanding and strengthening the Church Educational System (CES). Mormon wards operate weekly Sunday school classes, as most Protestant churches do. But among major U.S. religious denominations there is nothing remotely comparable to the CES system in scope. It operates a worldwide "seminary" program, which does not refer to graduate-level professional theological study but to catechism instruction for high school students, who are expected to attend an hour a day, five days a week, for four years. In the 1998–99 school year there were more than 379,000 seminary students enrolled worldwide, including more than 140,000 outside the United States, with some 15,000 each in Brazil and Mexico alone. The "institute" program offers college-level training for Mormons attending non-LDS campuses, with 117,000 enrolled in the United States for 1998–99 and 149,000 elsewhere. CES classes, all using identical instructional materials translated into many languages, reach into 144 countries. The massive network reports 3,300 full- and part-time paid employees, assisted by 34,000 volunteers and missionaries. A 1998 church study shows that 96 percent of institute graduates receive temple endowments, 96 percent of the men serve missions, and 98 percent of their wedding ceremonies are temple rites.

The seminary program began as a response to public secondary education. It started in 1912 in a church-owned building adjacent to Salt Lake City's public Granite High School so that secular learning could be supplemented by daily religion classes. At first Utah schools granted credit for these courses and permitted students to be taught during the normal school day on a released-time basis. Today many students in western states other than California attend seminary on a released-time basis but do not receive secondary school credit for the courses. Most of the rest attend early morning classes before their regular school day. A small number of students who live in areas with a sparse LDS population, mostly outside the United States, complete the seminary program on a home-study basis, meeting weekly with a teacher. The church estimates that more than two-thirds of eligible teens attend seminary; in some areas with released-time programs the figure rises to 80 or 90 percent. The required course sequence covers the Old and New Testaments, the Mormon scriptures, and church history.

The institute program provides both courses and social interaction for post-secondary school young people. BYU students are required to take fourteen hours of religion courses; these, including classes on the Book of Mormon and Doctrine and Covenants, are part of the CES institute curriculum. The ambitious CES goal is to provide institute courses near every major college or university worldwide with a sufficient concentration of Mormon students. Like the Catholic Newman Centers or the Jewish Hillel, these institutes also provide social gathering places for students of the same faith. The church tries to have an institute building of some kind and a resident missionary couple in every school where there are one hundred or more LDS students. A CES institute is a place where young people can meet fellow Mormons, eat lunch, or play pool as well as take courses.

On the first Sunday evening of the month during the school year the CES usually provides a "Fireside," an inspirational message typically given by a major church authority speaking from BYU. Translated into Spanish, Portuguese, French, and several other languages, the message is transmitted by satellite to stake centers and institute buildings around the United States and abroad. The Fireside begins with a song, a prayer, a welcome from the CES administrator Stanley A. Peterson to young adult listeners "wherever you are," and an introduction of the speaker. The 22,000 seats in BYU's Marriott Center are generally filled to capacity, but the audience may also include fifteen young people sharing refreshments while listening at a stake center in Brazil or Boston, all reminded that they belong to something bigger than they are.

Curriculum materials for this huge enterprise have become more conservative in the late decades of the twentieth century, with all materials standardized and carefully vetted by the officially constituted screening committee. The Mormon sociologist Armand Mauss, a retired professor at Washington State University, says, "An in-depth historical and contemporary study of the Church Educational System would almost certainly demonstrate in great detail the gradual (and probably deliberate) transition from a pedagogical philosophy of intellectual articulation and reconciliation to one of indoctrination."

CES materials in the early decades, according to Leonard Arrington, drew on non-Mormon as well as Mormon scholarship, attempting to relate Mormon doctrine to the wisdom of the world. The idea was to replace a "kindergarten level faith" with a faith that could withstand a "maturing scrutiny," he wrote in a *Dialogue* essay celebrating the founding of the institutes. Students were helped to understand their faith "in terms which are not only intellectually respectable but are in every respect equivalent to the sophisticated terminology and conceptualization of, say, advanced physics and econometrics."

Sometimes the CES sent its most promising young scholars, with church support, to graduate study at the University of Chicago and other elite schools, though as early as the late 1930s this was regarded with some uneasiness on the part of such General Authorities as J. Reuben Clark and Joseph Fielding Smith. Writes Mauss, "A struggle thus ensued within CES between the original philosophy of reconciliation with outside learning and the emergent philosophy of particularistic indoctrination."

Mauss believes the latter philosophy has "gained clear ascendancy," since the new teachers selected by CES are those "much more amenable to the indoctrination philosophy." The remarks of Apostle Mark E. Peterson at a 1962 CES staff summer school made a strong impression on George S. Tanner, longtime director of the institute at the University of Utah. As Tanner recorded the message in his journal, loyalty had priority over learning, and CES teachers were to develop faith and testimony in their students while avoiding intellectualizing. The CES had no room for academic freedom or intellectual inquiry, and teachers who did not like it were to go elsewhere. Since then, writes Mauss, "CES has become increasingly anti-scientific and anti-intellectual, more inward-looking, more intent on stressing the uniqueness and exclusiveness of the Mormon version of the gospel as opposed to all other interpretations, whether religious or scientific."

Institute courses are nonanalytical, avoiding critical or controversial issues. The textbook for Religion 121–122, a survey of the Book of Mormon, provides no critical framework and is a catechism-type explication. The

church history course, Religion 341–343, tends to sidestep sensitive historical matters that might reflect badly on the church or raise delicate questions. The institute's history textbook, for example, devotes four pages to
the Haun's Mill Massacre of 1838 in which seventeen Missouri Mormons
were mercilessly slaughtered, including a young boy. The story legitimately
stresses the persecutions of early Mormons.

By contrast, the Mountain Meadows Massacre of 1857, described in two
pages, is not indexed in the history textbook. Not mentioned is the fact
that, as documented by Mormon historian Juanita Brooks, the ill-fated
emigrants had posted a white flag and laid down their arms, complying
with the instructions of white flag–carrying Mormons. As planned, the
murders were carried out with one Mormon "guard" assigned to each emigrant, Indians following Mormon instructions to kill the women and
older children while the Mormons disposed of the men. Also unmen-
tioned is that John Lee, executed twenty years later for the crime "with the
connivance of the Mormon church," was made the scapegoat, as Jan
Shipps put it in a foreword to a recent edition of Brooks's classic study. As
previously mentioned, Brooks's research did exonerate Brigham Young of
involvement in the massacre, but the textbook tiptoes around the full disclosure of Mormon involvement in the tragedy. Mormons, of course, were
living in a vigilante culture: they were both victims and perpetrators.

Another obvious subject from Mormon history, polygamy, is treated
gingerly. The curriculum avoids the murky complications after the 1890
Manifesto. The actions or decisions of past or present church leaders are
not to be criticized or questioned. Students read nothing about Joseph
Smith's well-documented activities with magic and interest in the occult or
about the influence of Masonry on the temple endowment ceremony. The
textbook for religion stresses the suffering and courage of the Mormons,
the misconduct of anti-Mormons, the drama of the pioneer trek, the
heroic faithfulness of the Saints, and the triumphalistic march of the
church in new times.

Apostle Dallin Oaks in 1985 told a summer convocation of CES teachers at BYU that "some things that are true are not edifying or appropriate
to communicate. Readers of history and biography should ponder that

moral reality as part of their effort to understand the significance of what they read." Official church literature, he maintained, has no more responsibility to present both sides than does anti-Mormon writing. "Criticism is particularly objectionable when it is directed toward Church authorities," said Oaks. "It is one thing to deprecate a person who exercises corporate power or even government power. It is quite another thing to criticize or deprecate a person for the performance of an office to which he or she has been called of God. It does not matter that the criticism is true."

Oaks, who had become a member of the Quorum of the Twelve the previous year, is a true intellectual, a rarity among the Apostles. He had been a law professor at the University of Chicago, executive director of the American Bar Foundation, and a Utah Supreme Court justice. He was also president of BYU from 1971 to 1980. During his years at the helm, BYU busily hired faculty with academic credentials from major universities, scholars with a strong commitment to professional excellence in their own disciplines. This was to yield a positive benefit as Brigham Young emerged on the national scene as a major university. It was also to yield a challenge in the form of significant intellectual ferment boiling toward crises in the 1990s.

Strains between faith commitment, as defined by supporting constituencies and administrative bodies, and academic freedom, as perceived by faculties and sometimes students, are frequent grounds for conflict in religiously oriented institutions of higher learning. The battle between the theologian Charles Curran and the Catholic University of America spread over two decades and Curran was eventually fired. Catholic University was censured in 1990 by the American Association of University Professors (AAUP). Other denominational schools blacklisted by the AAUP have included Yeshiva University (1982), Southwestern Adventist College (1985), Southern Nazarene University (1987), and the Christian and Missionary Alliance's Nyack College in New York (1995). Brigham Young University joined the list in 1998.

As the BYU administration pointed out, twenty of the fifty-five AAUP-censured schools have a religious affiliation. It is a difficult task to balance a faith commitment with academic freedom. The history of religion in

American higher education is largely the history of secularization, as Notre Dame history professor George M. Marsden has shown in his study *The Soul of the American University: From Protestant Establishment to Established Nonbelief* (1994). Catholics are troubled about whether a parallel trend is well under way in Catholic higher education.

BYU's first purge occurred in 1911 when the hot issues were evolution and higher criticism of the Bible. Three or four of its better professors resigned under pressure. The outwardly placid period of Ernest Wilkinson's presidency (1951–71), when BYU's well-groomed undergraduates contrasted so favorably with the disheveled student demonstrators disrupting other campuses, witnessed some of the school's worst assaults on academic freedom. A supporter of the John Birch Society (as was then-Apostle Ezra Taft Benson), Wilkinson organized students into spy rings to report on their professors. One outgrowth of this unsavory chapter— which was eventually publicly acknowledged by Wilkinson—was the establishment of an AAUP chapter on the BYU campus.

Ecclesiastical entanglements affect aspects besides academic freedom. In one lively 1996 incident, a Mormon high schooler who was a hot basketball prospect told the *Deseret News* that Roger Reid, the most successful basketball coach in BYU and conference history, berated him for going to Duke instead of BYU. "He said I was letting nine million people down. He said I was letting down the Prophet and the Authorities." Reid denied that he had invoked the Prophet and Apostles, but the damage was done. For this and other reasons, Reid's midseason resignation soon followed.

Science, business, law, and technical subjects are not likely to seed intellectual unrest on contemporary religious campuses. Trouble typically arises in English departments, philosophy, the social sciences, and on student publications. BYU follows this pattern. Its official student newspaper, *The Daily Universe,* has predictably been reined in; an independent off-campus student publication, *Seventh East Press,* which lasted from 1981 to 1983, died after the BYU administration prohibited on-campus distribution. Especially objectionable to BYU administrators had been an interview in which the University of Utah philosophy professor and Mormon gadfly Sterling McMurrin criticized church officials for limiting access to historical materials and said he did not believe the Book of Mormon to be an ancient text. Surviving is a more recent off-campus student publication, the *Student Review*, which is distributed at off-campus locations frequented by students.

Troublesome faculty at BYU have also tended to come from the predictable disciplines, particularly English and any academic specialty that approaches Mormonism or Mormon studies analytically. These are the areas of scholarship in which ideas may challenge traditional assumptions or cause students to assess their beliefs from a new perspective.

Tenured BYU German professor Scott Abbott, writing in a 1992 issue of *Sunstone,* described some of the pressures on Mormon studies, saying that in many areas scholars can get funding for research, but that "when professors write about sexuality among Mormon adolescents, or query working Mormon women about their opinion of President Ezra Taft Benson's advice that they stay at home, or speak about Mormon women from a feminist perspective, or ask why Mormon chapels are bombed in South America (these are four recent, actual cases), immediate pressure is applied." In a 1997 *Sunstone* article Abbott reported that President Bateman on December 13, 1996, had informed the humanities faculty that about one hundred professors were under investigation with the possibility of termination.

First in a series of highly public faculty firings was that of David P. Wright, an assistant professor of Asian and Near Eastern languages who is now on the faculty of Brandeis University. A highly ranked scholar and teacher approaching his three-year tenure-track review, Wright was terminated in 1988 for his "examination of LDS texts with the scholarly tools of biblical criticism, which examine issues of authorship and influence by contemporary sources," according to a report in the May 1988 issue of *Sunstone.* The article reported a division between the College of Religion, which houses the CES institute instruction on the BYU campus, and the nonreligion faculty. The former "did not want seminary and institute teachers being exposed to his views when they took Hebrew and other biblical classes" in Wright's department, while the nonreligion faculty found it embarrassing for the university to graduate students who were uninformed about methods of contemporary biblical scholarship.

Wright issued a statement acknowledging that his views departed from the LDS belief system. The Book of Mormon, he wrote, "is best explained as a nineteenth-century work of scripture rather than a translation of a document from ancient America around 600 B.C.–400 A.D." He went on to state that "while some Mormon scholars, mainly at BYU, argue for its antiquity, more and more Mormon scholars are recognizing that if the book does not entirely derive from a nineteenth century provenance, it has been largely colored by concerns of that era."

Over the next several years a number of troubling events pointed to disturbing trends. In 1992 the nation's most prestigious academic honors society, Phi Beta Kappa, for the third time rejected BYU's application for a chapter on the grounds that its mission as defined was incompatible with academic freedom. The same year BYU's administration and board of trustees adopted a formal statement on academic freedom written by a faculty committee appointed by the administration. The statement distinguished between protecting the freedom of an institution with a mission to pursue a particular religion, and the academic freedom of individual faculty. The policy regards limitations as reasonable on any activity or expression that "seriously and adversely affects" the mission of BYU or the church. Faculty have complained that the definition is too broad, vague, and nonspecific and that only the administration decides how it is applied; the administration has maintained that it will not be changed.

Ecclesiastical discipline was tightened. Though faculty had traditionally been expected to be temple-worthy, the rule was systematized, with the bishop of each teacher sent a checking-up letter annually. That made all scholarly careers subject to the endorsement of nonacademic, off-campus church officials. In 1993 several faculty members appealed the negative results of their tenure reviews; two, David Knowlton and Cecilia Konchar Farr, went public about their dismissals.

In anthropologist Knowlton's case, Mormon doctrine was not the cause for trouble. Rated highly for his scholarship and teaching, Knowlton came under fire when he criticized certain "problems within the Mormon cultural system." A specialist on Latin America, he studied why missionaries are sometimes targets for terrorism and quoted Latin Americans who linked the church with American imperialism. He was also criticized for publishing in *Dialogue* and *Sunstone*. Farr, a popular English teacher, was fired for her feminism and support of abortion rights, though she maintained that she personally does not favor abortion.

Another highly publicized English department case was that of Brian Evenson, son of a former dean and BYU physics professor, who was hired in 1994 and fired in 1995 over criticism of the violence in his award-winning book of short stories, *Altmann's Tongue,* published by Alfred A. Knopf during his first year at BYU. He did not use the book in his classes, but his job review was sparked by an anonymous letter sent by a student to an LDS church official. When he left BYU for a job at Oklahoma State University, his second book, *Dark Property,* was ready for the press and a third was under way with the help of a grant from the National Endowment for the Arts.

Yet another English department cause célèbre, the 1996 refusal of tenure for Gail Turley Houston, produced the AAUP investigation and censure. Houston, a feminist who had taught at BYU for six years, was refused tenure on the grounds that she advocated praying to Mother in Heaven as well as Father in Heaven. She now teaches at the University of New Mexico. Mormon theology does indeed say that God the Father is married, so there is a mother in Heaven, but Gordon Hinckley, then First Counselor, gave a 1991 speech stating that "I consider it inappropriate for anyone in the church to pray to our Mother in Heaven."

President Hinckley, who is BYU's board chairman, said in his *Time* magazine interview that "anybody who persists in opposing the church, who is in public opposition, speaking out against it, I think may receive some discipline from the church. It's just that simple. But those cases are so very, very, very few." He also observed that "every university in America . . . draws some parameters around what it classifies as academic freedom. They all have some rules. They have to have some rules to live by. They can't just have anarchy." He contended that BYU's policies do not limit "intellectual curiosity."

University President Bateman explains, "Although we want to ensure that every faculty member has the right to discuss and analyze as broadly and widely as possible any topic, including religious topics, including fundamental doctrine of the church, we do not believe they should be able to publicly endorse positions contrary to the doctrine or to attack the doctrine. Secondly, we don't believe they should be able to attack the church deliberately, or its general leaders."

An anonymous BYU insider in a 1996 *Sunstone* essay wrote that problems at BYU run significantly deeper than the few highly publicized firings. The article detailed a bias against women's studies; a pattern of refusing to hire scholars chosen for appointments to the English department, placing that department in "virtual receivership"; the "dismantling of Honors and General Education as the intellectual center of the university"; the harassment of the *Student Review;* and the threat of tenure denial to Larry Young, an assistant professor of sociology whose research suggested that the church's international activity level is considerably lower than convert baptisms suggest. Young's tenure and promotion were granted only when he convinced the church's commissioner of education, Apostle Henry B. Eyring, of his sincere testimony.

The *Sunstone* essay listed a number of discouraged faculty who had departed in recent years. And the Associated Press carried reports that a prestigious business school professor who had been sounded out concerning a possible major appointment had declined because of the church endorsement policy and academic freedom issues in general. Bateman responded in fury, and the professor then said he had made his decision for "private reasons" but declined to specify.

Current BYU professors have of necessity learned to exercise self-censorship. In 1998 the university passed its reaccreditation evaluation with ease, as expected. The evaluators did note, however, that there seemed to be some indication of poor faculty morale and concern about academic freedom. Meanwhile, with as many as half of its professors leaving by attrition or retirement from 1995 to 2000 or so, church officials have ample opportunity to redesign the BYU faculty, assisted by the oversupply of newly minted Ph.D.'s in some fields and the undersupply of academic jobs. The hiring process at BYU is cumbersome, involving a dozen steps in interviews and approvals. Prospective faculty are often asked whether they would be willing, should the brethren ask, to suppress potentially troublesome research. A January 1994 memo sent to deans by Assistant Academic Vice President Alan Wilkins, and obtained by the Associated Press, stressed that "we should not hire people who are a threat to the religious faith of our students or a critic of the Church and its leaders."

The independent *Student Review* has complained that prospective women faculty members are asked about their marital status and family plans, which the publication considered a potential violation of federal rules, but the BYU administration says that such inquiries are legal under Title IX of the 1972 education amendments because of exemptions that apply to religious institutions. Women make up only 15 percent of the faculty at BYU, half the national average, a proportion that seems unlikely to increase significantly.

The hiring decisions currently being made will shape Brigham Young University, and the leadership of the Church of Jesus Christ of Latter-day Saints, well into the twenty-first century. The educational system is successfully feeding into the church the kind of members and leaders it wants: bright, dedicated, disciplined, hardworking, intensely loyal, obedient, fairly homogeneous in outlook, impressively capable of altruism and personal sacrifice, generally highly submissive to ecclesiastical authority, and committed to official orthodoxy as defined by the hierarchy.

CHAPTER 15

FAITHFUL HISTORY

"My third great-grandmother, Catherine Prichard Oaks, lost most of her possessions when a Missouri state militia drove the Mormons out of that state in 1838. Seven years later, when state authorities stood by while a lawless element evicted the Mormons from Illinois, she lost her life from exposure on the plains of Iowa. My wife's second great-grandparents, Cyril and Sally Call, hid in a cornfield as a mob burned their home in Illinois. My great-grandfather, Charles Harris, was sent to prison in the Utah Territory in 1893 for his practice of plural marriage. His eldest daughter, my great-aunt Belle Harris, was the first woman to be imprisoned during federal prosecution of Mormons in the 1880s."

This recital is vintage Mormon remembrance. The speaker is Dallin Oaks, member of the LDS Quorum of the Twelve, former president of Brigham Young University, Utah Supreme Court judge, University of Chicago law school professor, and law clerk to Chief Justice Earl Warren. The occasion is testimony delivered June 22, 1998, before the U.S. Senate Judiciary Committee on behalf of the Religious Liberty Protection Act of 1998.

Mormons remember. Great-grandfather's memoirs are privately published and bound in leather, passed down for succeeding generations to cherish. Great-great-grandmother's diaries describe a time and a life lived and relived by her descendants. Bound blank books are a staple on sale in Deseret Book stores and church distribution outlets. From the time they are young priesthood holders, Mormon youths and their sisters are exhorted to keep journals as part of their religious commitment. Missionaries are reminded by their superiors that these journals represent a part of their sacred duties. They are fulfilling a command that the Lord gave Joseph Smith on April 6, 1830, the day the church was organized in Palmyra, New York.

The Lord said, "Behold, there shall be a record kept among you" (D&C 21:1), and the first historian to keep that record was the newly appointed apostle Oliver Cowdery. John Whitmer was added as Cowdery's assistant in 1831, also by scriptural command of the Lord (D&C 69:3, 8), to "continue in writing and making a history of all the important things which he shall observe and know concerning my church; . . . writing, copying, selecting, and obtaining all things which shall be for the good of the church, and for the rising generations."

The church has had an official church historian continuously from the day it was founded up to the present day. All but one of them, Leonard Arrington from 1972 to 1982, have been General Authorities and, since 1842, apostles. (Therein lies a tale to come.)

So Mormons remember, and they remember in great detail. The remembrances bind them as a people. They tell and retell their stories of pioneer privations and persecutions, of courage and faithfulness. Pioneer Day in Utah is celebrated each year on July 24 as a major holiday with parades, picnics, and reenactments with sunbonnets and covered wagons rumbling through the valley. Each summer stakes, and Mormon Boy Scout troops make mini-treks through a small patch of desert to learn something about dust and ash cakes, and how a handcart is tough to pull.

In 1897, as part of a jubilee celebrating fifty years in Utah, a monument to Brigham Young was unveiled near the temple in Salt Lake City. A few years later, under President Joseph F. Smith, the church began to purchase, rebuild, and restore some of its old sites to enshrine the past for the memories of coming generations. In 1903 the Mormons acquired Carthage Jail in Illinois, the site of the prophet's assassination fifty-nine years before. Shortly after that the Solomon Mack homestead in Vermont was purchased and a granite monument was erected in time to honor the centennial of the prophet's birth, December 23, 1905.

In 1904 the church acquired a site in Independence, Missouri, indicating the Saints' continuing interest in the future Center Place of Zion. Since the tiny Temple Lot splinter church owned the actual temple site marked out by Joseph Smith, the LDS had to content itself with twenty-five acres across the way; it would build a visitors' center there in 1971. In 1905 the church purchased the Smith homestead near Palmyra, New York, including the Sacred Grove in which the prophet had received his First Vision in 1820.

The original generation of those who had known the prophet was gone; to remind the new generation and new converts, history became religious ritual. Visitors' centers, restored houses, historic parks, monuments, and trail markers sprouted everywhere. The "This Is the Place Monument" was dedicated at Emigration Canyon, two and a half miles from Salt Lake City, in 1921. A monument to the Mormon Battalion, the 500 who in 1846 had volunteered for the Mexican War and marched to California, was erected on the state capitol grounds in 1927, a few blocks from Temple Square. Hill Cumorah near Palmyra, New York, the place where the Angel Moroni gave the golden plates to the prophet, was purchased by the church in 1928. In the 1930s and 1940s more than 300 historic markers were placed by the Daughters of Utah Pioneers.

Today Mormon history buffs can follow the trek across Iowa, visiting restored cabins, an old ferry house, and a monument at Winter Quarters (Omaha, Nebraska) that lists the names of the more than 600 men, women, and children who died there. Around Palmyra, besides watching the lavish annual Hill Cumorah pageant each July, they can visit a reconstruction of the Smith family homestead cabin and a restoration of the original family farmhouse, see the homes of Peter Whitmer and Martin Harris, stroll in the Sacred Grove where Joseph Smith received his First Vision, and admire the restoration of the Grandin print shop where the original 5,000 Book of Mormon copies were printed. In Ohio they can visit the original Kirtland Temple (though that is owned by the Reorganized Church). Missouri has Liberty Jail. The Nauvoo restoration in Illinois is divided between the RLDS and LDS Churches. And Salt Lake City has places like the Lion House and Beehive House, where Brigham

Young lived with some of his wives, though guides tiptoe around the polygamy question. Altogether the church maintains forty-four such sites, nineteen with visitors' centers, and provides tours at thirty-three locations of special interest. Staffing is generally by missionary volunteers.

Some of the restorations are more successful than others. Liberty Jail has a certain theme-park flavor, reconstructed with an exploded front and encased in a large climate-controlled visitors' center shell, the jail populated by wax figures. Sister missionaries guiding a tour press buttons to activate recorded readings from the prisoners' letters and diaries. It is hard to feel cold and isolated as the real 1838 prisoners must have felt.

The Nauvoo restoration provides tourist Saints with an idealized "City of Joseph." A film producer used New York State's restored, secular Genesee Country Village as the backdrop for some of the "Nauvoo" scenes in a Mormon documentary being prepared for public television because the real present-day Nauvoo is just a mite too pretty. But then, how many visitors to Williamsburg remember the slave quarters? Even with the neat lawns and the exquisite sculpture gardens, something of the ghosts of the real Nauvoo seems to haunt the old Mississippi River town.

Reenactment is a central ingredient in what Davis Bitton calls "the ritualization of Mormon history." In that ritualization certain stories achieve a status of mythic proportion; they become cherished legends in a somewhat romanticized and simplified communal heritage. It is a process common to secular patriotism, to the shared history of any religious body or American ethnic group, even to any successful family.

The Miracle of the Seagulls is an example of the ritualization process. It is one of the first faith-promoting stories a Mormon child learns, in simplified version, at home or in Sunday school. Later that child may enact the story in a stake drama or pageant. Over the years the same young Mormon will see the story as the subject of paintings and engravings, curriculum, and magazine graphics. It has become a deeply emotional symbol of pioneer faith, struggle, and triumph. Visitors to Temple Square can view the 1913 Seagull monument; honored visitors may be given a miniature replica. The seagull story became an episode in "Promised Valley," the huge outdoor musical pageant first presented in 1947 centennial celebrations and then decades afterward for tourists in Manti, Utah.

The actual event, seagulls appearing to devour a cricket invasion that threatened to destroy the first pioneer summer crop, did not seem so miraculous at the time, according to the research of William G. Hartley. Diaries of 1848 Great Basin pioneers generally talk about the crickets but ignore the gulls. A letter to Brigham Young did express the belief that "the hand of the Lord" brought the gulls. But the 1848 harvest, because of the crickets, frost, and insufficient irrigation, was marginal. Hartley writes that the official 1848 First Presidency report rated the gulls as "helpers but certainly not as rescuers." The harvest would have been worse without the birds. The gulls did not suddenly appear in Utah in 1848; they had been mentioned in explorers' memoirs decades earlier, and their cricket-eating habits have been observed by ornithologists in major cricket wars elsewhere in the nation as recently as 1952. "Miracle" status apparently has grown since an 1853 General Conference mention by Apostle Orson Hyde, amplified and reinforced over the years by stories in Mormon publications and official church histories.

The Temple Square movie for tourists, *Legacy*, is an example of ritualized history, effectively idealized and simplified. The movie dramatizes the early Mormon story from Palmyra to Salt Lake City through a composite fictional female character based on real pioneer journals and letters. It provides little clue as to why midwestern Mormons were persecuted other than that they were misunderstood and opposed slavery. There is no hint of polygamy or millennial land claims or any other distinctive Mormon doctrine, just the idea that a prophet named Joseph Smith came up with a new sacred book asking people to lead holy lives. Missouri Governor Boggs's famous "extermination" order is quoted, ignoring the fact that Smith's counselor Sidney Rigdon had actually introduced the word, throwing down the gauntlet in a published sermon delivered the previous July 4. Smith dies off-camera with someone crying, "They've killed him! They've murdered Joseph Smith at the Carthage Jail!" There is no scene that shows the smashing of the *Expositor* press or gives a real clue to the issues raised by the newspaper. The drama and scenery of the trek are so beautifully photographed that many Mormons see the movie over and over, every time they visit Temple Square.

"Any people in a new land may be pardoned for being solicitous about their history: they create it, in a sense, by remembering it," writes Wallace Stegner. "But the tradition of the pioneer that is strong all through the West is a cult in Utah."

As a popular expression of ritualized history, Mormons have developed something of an annual outdoor pageant circuit, presented to tourists but faith-affirming to participants and most of the audience. The first of the great pageants was "The Message of the Ages," presented April 6, 1930—during the centennial celebration of the church's founding—in Salt Lake City's Tabernacle, with a cast of 1,500. The first pageant at Hill Cumorah near Palmyra, "Footprints in the Sands of Time," was presented on July 24 of the same summer. The Hill Cumorah pageant, now "America's Witness for Christ," has been presented annually in July since 1937. Regular large-scale pageants are presented in eight U.S. locations, from Hill Cumorah to Nauvoo ("The City of Joseph") to Independence, Missouri ("A Frontier Story"), to Manti, Utah ("Mormon Miracle Pageant"), to Oakland, California (the triennial "And It Came to Pass").

But the Hill Cumorah pageant is something special, because this is where it all began. When lightning strikes, volcanoes belch, and the sky is swept by a powerful beam so bright that it requires FAA clearance, the citizens of Palmyra know it is pageant time again. Years ago the locals resented the annual LDS influx; now a typical hand-lettered sign in a pizza shop window across from the Grandin print shop reads, "Welcome LDS Members." In 1991 the LDS suggested that local civic groups should handle a food concession tent on the pageant grounds. Smart move, and everyone's happy. Now four local clubs share these responsibilities, each organization clearing $8,000–10,000 in profits for scholarships and local civic projects. It's "our" Palmyra pageant. Since 1937 more than two million visitors have seen it.

Troupe members—630 actors and more than 150 on the support staff—are volunteers who pay for the privilege, treating it as a short-term mission, the cast giving 17 days of vacation time, the crew longer. In a typical year the administration receives 1,800 applicants; about 30 percent of the cast are repeaters, and many families participate together. One recent year Donny Osmond played Samuel the Lamanite, and a young son of his was also in the cast; the previous year the Osmond clan had watched the show, sitting somewhere in the ocean of 8,000 folding chairs. Each year the personnel arrive in vans and station wagons, many with campers and tents to set up in the nearby "Zion's Camp" campground, while others check in at the dormitory of a nearby college.

Each incoming participant receives a folder carefully outlining elaborate rules and directions. Cast members are admonished not to chew gum when in costume, nor to risk stains by sitting on the grass. Wigs and costumes each year must be refitted and refurbished, replaced by set rotation. At cast meetings boys aged twelve to fourteen are warned not to continue the war backstage; banner carriers are cautioned not to let the flags drag in the mud because "these props belong to God." Cast members have only slightly more than a week before things must fall together for the first performance, but the daily schedule includes devotions in the morning and evening and a brief prayer meeting session before bedtime. Cast members are supposed to read through the Book of Mormon in the weeks before arriving, and again during their days in residence.

To many it is a deep family as well as religious experience. For Dan Kimbler, a Saint from nearby Holly, New York, 1998 was his fourth year in the cast along with his four sons ranging from ages eighteen to six. His wife had died of cancer five years earlier, so Kimbler takes vacation time for this each year as a "good experience for the whole family."

Another repeater in 1998 was Bill Matthews, a Chicago-area FBI agent who played Abinidi the prophet; his wife and six children were all in the cast. "It's a wonderful experience to share with your family," says Matthews, "but that's a side benefit, though important. The central message is to be a witness to Jesus Christ."

Bruce Marshall, a career army major from Huntsville, Alabama, has been a cast member twice with his wife and six children, but 1998 was a year just to come and soak it in. "It's a real testimony builder," says Marshall. "You can see the change in kids backstage, kids crowded together reading the Book of Mormon." This year his kids had the choice of visiting Disney World or the pageant for vacation. They chose the pageant.

The 1998 pageant was typical with its cast blending blue-collar workers with professionals; this year included a newlywed couple from Utah using their honeymoon to participate; one Air Force full colonel; a California college student who had saved for months to come and had dreamed for years of being in the cast; a woman who had returned for twenty-two years, whose husband converted through pageant involvement, and whose three married children now return each year with spouses and children.

After a day of rain 150 LDS youths visiting from Kentucky wiped down the folding chairs with mildew preventive, preparing for the public dress rehearsal. Before the performance, Artistic Director Rodger Sorensen reminded his cast, "How close are we to being God? The performance is nothing without your testimonies." Cast members got drenched in a downpour, but the show went on, and most of the audience remained, cheerfully loyal and huddling under plastic ponchos. Only lightning or dangerous high winds cause cancellation, and since 1937 that has happened only two or three times.

A good percentage of the crowd each year is probably Mormon, but there are visiting Gentiles as well, drawn by the (free) spectacle of special effects, elaborately dashing cape and feather costumes, dramatic lighting, waterfalls, smoke, and swords. Staging is on a seven-level hillside venue under a monument to the Angel Moroni. Sound is high-tech, with the voices of the Mormon Tabernacle Choir, a children's chorus, and the Utah Symphony. The actors lip-synch their parts. In a typical year 80,000 attend the seven performances, leaving 1,500 inquiry cards with the missionaries in costume who circulate to work the crowds before the pageant begins each night. But the most important result of each year's pageant is in the lives of the Saints who participate and attend, an experience confirming them in their shared history and faith.

History, for the Church of Jesus Christ of Latter-day Saints, is more than pageants, parades, trail markers, monuments, and restored homesteads. There is a very real sense in which the church's history is its theology, and that not merely the supernatural events surrounding the church's beginnings with the Angel Moroni and the golden plates at Hill Cumorah. In a body that believes itself the recipient and expression of continuing revelation, it is everything that has happened to the church ever since. And just as creedal churches have official statements of faith, the Mormon Church tends to have official versions of sacred history.

With the zeal for record-keeping in the church, which goes all the way back to 1830, quorums and auxiliaries have kept minutes of meetings and other relevant documents; church newspapers and periodicals have published accounts of events; members have written their own diaries and journals. This has reaped an enormous harvest of primary-source and contemporary secondary-source materials. Much of this archival resource, a sort of mammoth ecclesiastical history scrapbook, was uncataloged until the 1970s.

The church has owned printing presses almost from the beginning, and they have kept very busy producing newspapers, from the *Times and Seasons* in Nauvoo to the *Millennial Star* in England and *Deseret News* in Utah, to magazines for the whole church and individual auxiliaries, books, and pamphlets. Joseph Smith began his own history of the church. After his death Willard Richards compiled much of the prophet's history, including items published in *Times and Seasons,* minutes, records of ordinances, sermons and speeches, and the prophet's diaries and letters. This work was continued later by church historians whose labors included compiling all the Brigham Young documents. In the 1970s historians went through some papers still boxed in the original containers used for hiding items from the feds in the 1858 Utah War.

From 1854 to 1886 a semimonthly periodical, the *Journal of Discourses,* printed the sermons and speeches of important church authorities. Wilford Woodruff, before he became church president, worked for twenty-seven years as assistant church historian publishing biographies of church leaders and editing Joseph Smith's sermons for the *History of the Church.* B. H. Roberts and Joseph Fielding Smith wrote officially sanctioned histories, and Roberts edited a seven-volume version of the original prophet's *History of the Church,* published by the denomination in 1932.

A newly established tradition tends to reinterpret the past through its own eyes. Thus, Christians view the Old Testament from a different perspective than do Jews. Similarly, Mormons view Christian history through eyes that are different from those of traditional Christians. In the process of doing so, they are shaping their own tradition and interpretation of the past.

Jan Shipps, a non-Mormon scholar, believes that during the years of the "gathering" Mormons were conscious of living through their own sacred history in a new age. They were also, in a sense, recapitulating the sacred history of scripture through their own experiences. When Brigham Young led his people to the Great Basin, he led them "backward into a primordial sacred time." The Saints were in a holy time and a holy space where they would build God's kingdom, a new Israel on earth.

When the Book of Mormon and the Smith canon broke into history in 1830, it introduced a startling gap in Christian history. According to it, after Christ's resurrection the church fell almost immediately into what Mormons call the "Great Apostasy." Truth was hidden until discovered by Joseph Smith. For Catholics, Christian history is continuous from the early church to the present day. Protestants vary in their degree of historical amnesia, but most recognize that their own history borrows from Catholic continuity. Mormons are different. For them, Christian history after the period of the primitive church is what Shipps calls a lacuna, a complete void of 1,400 to 1,800 years before Joseph Smith's restoration. Mormonism had to shape for itself a new and usable past.

For Mormonism more than other religions, history evolves as part of the church's canon. High school and college students in their seminaries and institutes take required church history courses; in addition, the required Doctrine and Covenants study is largely history as well, with a great deal of governance and lifestyle matters embedded in the context of revelation. The D&C doctrinal teaching involves surprisingly little of what traditional Christian catechism would call "pure theology." In the famous George Orwell quote, "he who controls the past controls the future and he who controls the present controls the past." The LDS Church even has a body with the Orwellian-sounding name of "Correlation Committee" charged with the responsibility of ensuring that all church publications, from periodicals to curriculum materials, follow official policy and express official interpretations.

This means that sensitive historical issues frequently are downplayed, avoided, or denied. As Martin Marty observes, Mormon beginnings are so recent that there really is "no place to hide. What can be sequestered in Mormon archives and put beyond the range of historians can often be approached by sources outside them. . . . There is little protection for Mormon sacredness."

Much of the church's own shaping of its past is to be expected, but the results occasionally can be unintentionally comical. The church's biennial almanac, for example, carries brief biographies of all the church presidents. It lists Emma Smith as Joseph's wife, and the wives of all the presidents from George Albert Smith to the present day. The almanac's silence on the marital history of Brigham Young, John Taylor, Wilford Woodruff, Lorenzo Snow, Joseph Fielding Smith, and Heber J. Grant would seem to imply that these polygamists represent an unbroken string of celibate bachelors.

Never mind Brigham Young's twenty or more wives and fifty-seven children. The 1997 manual published in twenty-two languages for required study worldwide by the Relief Society and all Melchizedek priesthood holders, *Teachings of Presidents of the Church: Brigham Young*, presents Young as a monogamist. A "Historical Summary" outlining Young's life with dates mentions his first marriage, the date of that wife's death (1832), and the date of his second (legal) marriage (1834). Mention of any other marital history is completely missing. Also noticeably absent are Young's controversial ideas that are no longer propounded by the church: blood atonement, for example, and the idea that Adam was God the Father and Eve was one of God's wives. The quotes representing his ideas are chosen to avoid offense on gender, race, and nationality. Mormonism's most flamboyant leader has been rendered acceptable for the twenty-first century—and almost carefully colorless.

Even the scriptures have been rewritten to fit current doctrine, in line with the idea of continuity and progressive revelation. But once a new version is published, historians are not supposed to notice the change, nor can they write about variations in previous editions. The church regards such reminders as unacceptably embarrassing. The result has been something of an underground traffic in early church documents and editions.

The Mormon historian D. Michael Quinn notes, perhaps with chagrin, that the noted career apostates, onetime Mormons Jerald and Sandra Tanner, have published the only "extensive comparison" of changes in Joseph Smith's *History of the Church* in its various published versions. Compilers of that work "deleted evidence, introduced anachronisms, even reversed meanings in manuscript minutes and other documents which were detailed and explicit in their original form." Furthermore, Quinn writes, "in 1835 the Doctrine and Covenants began a policy of retroactive editing by reversing previous meanings, adding concepts and whole paragraphs to the texts of previously published revelations. The official alteration of pre-1835 revelations is the more fundamental context for the later pattern of editing in the *History of the Church*."

The result of this is that for Mormons history—and truth, which is supposedly embedded in history—is dynamic and fluid. There is nothing quite like what the poet T. S. Eliot called "the still point of the turning world." As Mark P. Leone writes in *Roots of Modern Mormonism*, in Mormonism truth is not absolute or fixed; it is changeable, flexible, and additive. According to Leone, "it is no wonder that the church has discouraged any intellectual tradition that would interfere with disguising historical factors or with maintaining much of the social reality through the uncritical way lay history is done."

Mormon teachers are required to present the currently acceptable, faith-promoting, official view of history, Apostle Boyd Packer said in a famous speech to the annual Church Educational System Religious Educators' Symposium in 1981. Packer, giving marching orders to CES seminary and institute teachers, gave four "cautions": (1) "There is no such thing as an accurate, objective history of the Church without consideration of the spiritual powers that attend this work"; (2) "There is a temptation . . . to want to tell everything, whether it is worthy or faith-promoting or not. Some things that are true are not very useful"; (3) "In an effort to be objective, impartial, and scholarly, a writer or a teacher may unwittingly be giving equal time to the adversary. . . . In the Church we are not neutral. We are one-sided. There is a war going on, and we are engaged in it"; (4) The fact that something is already in print or available from another source is no excuse for using potentially damaging materials in writing, speaking, or teaching: "Do not spread disease germs!"

Packer quoted President Ezra Taft Benson warning CES teachers not to purchase books or subscribe to periodicals that publish writings of church critics, particularly "known apostates," for either seminary or personal bookshelves. Benson had told the seminary and institute teachers, "We are entrusting you to represent the Lord and the First Presidency to your students, not the views of the detractors of the Church."

This stance has led to open warfare in history scholarship. On the one side are the proponents of "faithful history," scholars such as Louis Midgley and David Earl Bohn—not historians but professors of political science at Brigham Young University. These men write essays for independent journals such as *Sunstone* as well as church-sanctioned publications, defending the idea that "objective" or neutral history scholarship is an illusion. If one's research into history proceeds from naturalistic presuppositions, it will inevitably do violence to faith claims. Only history that proceeds within the language of faith can do justice to an understanding of the sacred. This is the approach of "traditional" or "faithful" history. Its opposite is presented as a form of positivist deconstruction, history corroded by the caustic acids of criticism. Such history obscures God's role in history. And such history is capable of undermining faith—hence Packer's warnings to teachers in the Church Educational System.

Somewhere on the other side are scholars of "new Mormon history," such as the aforementioned Leonard Arrington, the late church historian who eventually ran afoul of Apostle Packer (which is easy to do). Another is D. Michael Quinn, whose research into post-Manifesto polygamy and other sensitive areas of LDS history led to his eventual resignation from a tenured professorship at Brigham Young University, loss of his temple recommend, and finally his church membership.

The church has always tried to retain a proprietary hold over the telling of its own history. The earliest clear example of this is the checkered history of mother Lucy Mack Smith's *Biographical Sketches of Joseph Smith, the Prophet, and His Progenitors for Many Generations,* first published by Apostle Orson Pratt in Liverpool in 1853. Brigham Young was unhappy with the book and ordered the printing destroyed.

The traditional explanation for the suppression of Lucy's book is that Young had various disagreements with Pratt and was unhappy with the book's favorable presentation of the prophet's brother William. Jan Shipps, studying the evidence, believes the real reason Young quashed the book was that the prophet's mother had emphasized the Smith family rather than simply Joseph Jr. alone, thus implying the legitimacy of a concept of Smith lineage in church leadership. This would become the teaching of Utah's rival, the midwestern-based RLDS, of which Joseph III eventually assumed the leadership. Brigham Young recalled the book, therefore, because "buried in its pages could be found an implicit challenge to [his] legitimate right to lead the Mormon Church."

The most serious problems occur when the church suppresses evidence that is contrary to official interpretation. "Faithful history" tends to be apologetic and celebratory, to downplay or avoid sensitive aspects of Mormon history. It is not, for example, politically correct to suggest that Mormons, while victims, were not always innocent victims, or that though holiness may be an affront to the observer, ordinary Saintly holiness was not usually the cause of Mormon persecutions.

There is, Quinn writes, such a thing as simple honesty among scholars. If "omission of relevant evidence is inadvertent, the author is careless. If the omission is an intentional effort to conceal or avoid presenting the reader with evidence that contradicts the preferred view of the writer, that is fraud." He contends, "Traditional Mormon apologists discuss such 'sensitive evidence' only when this evidence is so well known that ignoring it is almost impossible."

The second half of the twentieth century saw an outpouring of history by Mormon as well as non-Mormon scholars. The Mormon History Association was founded in 1965, and soon thereafter many history articles were published by the *MHA Journal,* the independent *Dialogue: A Journal of Mormon Thought,* the RLDS John Whitmer Historical Association and its journal. More interest in history developed in *BYU Studies* and there appeared other forums for presenting papers, such as the B. H. Roberts Society.

If the scholar was Mormon and the church did not like the message, it attacked the messenger. Mormon studies became an increasingly dangerous area for Mormon scholars, especially if they were members of the Brigham Young University faculty. In 1981 the head of the BYU history department, Eugene Campbell, told a session of the American Historical Association that authorities had warned him to discourage faculty scholarship relating to polygamy or blacks and the priesthood.

The first of the censured Mormon historians was probably Fawn Brodie, excommunicated for her caustic 1945 biography of the first prophet. First Counselor J. Reuben Clark Jr. had the *Deseret News* publish his critique of the book, though he had refrained from reading it. Next came Juanita Brooks with her 1950 book *Mountain Meadows Massacre*. She averted excommunication by local church officials but received an ecclesiastical blacklisting. The First Presidency learned about Warner Brothers movie studio plans to produce a major film based on Brooks's book about the massacre on November 5, 1951, and in seven days managed successfully to pressure the studio to kill the project.

The 1984 biography *Mormon Enigma: Emma Hale Smith* by Linda King Newell and Valeen Tippetts Avery presents a sympathetic portrait of a complex woman, as well as the deceit of Smith toward her over his practice of polygamy. The Utah church has traditionally been critical of Emma because she remained in the Midwest and eventually lent support to the RLDS. Also, she had bitter disagreements with Brigham Young over the distribution of her husband's estate. Smith's financial affairs had been hopelessly entangled with the church. For a year after the book's publication, church authorities banned Newell and Avery from speaking publicly in church meetings.

The sensational 1985 Mark Hofmann murder and forgery case could only have happened in connection with the curious mixture of paranoia and obsessiveness with which Mormons approach church history. In the early 1980s there was a sudden boomlet in valuable documents relating to early Mormon history. This was exciting to some private collectors, and it was of more than passing interest to the church. Some of the documents seemed to verify traditional views of church history; some threatened to embarrass the church. The dealer and discoverer of the documents was a young former pre-med student, Mark Hofmann, a returned Mormon missionary, husband, father, and, like many other Saints, church history buff.

Private collectors began to vie for the privilege of buying exciting Hofmann discoveries. Through collector donations and outright purchases, the church began to acquire documents from Hofmann. The church publicized some of the acquisitions; it orchestrated public relations for some that were known to be sensitive; others it acquired secretly and suppressed. Gordon B. Hinckley, then second counselor in the First

Presidency, largely handled policy in these matters and directed the public relations responses of the church.

For a time Hofmann made a handsome profit in one of the most brilliant forgery projects of the century. In 1983 Hinckley paid $15,000 for a letter from Joseph Smith to Josiah Stowell that showed Smith to be experienced at money-digging treasure hunting, raising the delicate matter of Smith's occult and folk magic activities in the 1820s. Another purchase was a Lucy Mack Smith letter, price estimated at $30,000. The so-called salamander letter, which the church acquired indirectly through the collector Steven Christensen, later one of Hofmann's murder victims, cost $40,000. According to this letter, a magic white salamander appeared to Joseph Smith, not the Angel Moroni, in the prophet's First Vision. In the end the church acquired forty-eight documents from Hofmann directly, plus the salamander letter.

Eventually Hofmann's fraud began to catch up with him. To create a decoy, Hofmann killed Christensen and one other innocent person and injured himself with pipe bombs in three separate Salt Lake City incidents in October 1985.

The forgeries had fooled a number of document experts. Not only the church but a number of distinguished historians had also been deceived, and some scholars had to adjust their research to account for the fraudulent documents. During Hofmann's murder trial the forensic document examiner George J. Throckmorton developed new ink and paper tests that proved the forgeries. For Hofmann forgery had been a profitable and interesting game, as well as financially rewarding. But another motivation that propelled the forger was the desire to embarrass the church by undermining traditional church history. Hofmann, it turned out, was a closet apostate. He is currently in prison serving life without parole.

The church, in the aftermath, attempted to do everything possible to correct the record. *Ensign* published a list of Hofmann forgeries it had used over the years. The LDS Church had received a genuine original Smith Book of Commandments (precursor to the D&C) from the RLDS in exchange for a Hofmann document purporting to be the Joseph Jr. blessing of his son Joseph III. The blessing would tend to affirm the patrilineal succession used by the RLDS Church. After the forgery was exposed the LDS Church voluntarily returned the Book of Commandments to the RLDS.

The public relations damage as well as the forgery losses meant the church was also a Hofmann victim. Policy today is to strongly encourage donation rather than purchase of historical materials, and the church history department readily submits documents to the most sophisticated forensic analysis as needed.

The most poignant episodes of the church history department relate to its most distinguished historian, the late Leonard J. Arrington. A true-blue believer, lover of life and good stories, Arrington was solidly in the front rank of scholars with the achievement of *Great Basin Kingdom* and other publications. His first brush with running afoul of official history, as previously mentioned, had been his essay on the history of Word of Wisdom observance in the first issue of *BYU Studies* in 1959. Apostle Mark Petersen had taken exception to Arrington's exposing the fact that nineteenth-century pioneers regarded the Word as advice rather than as prohibition. The journal had been suspended for a year.

Arrington described the *BYU Studies* episode in his 1998 memoir, *Adventures of a Church Historian.* A historical footnote was added in 1999. *BYU Studies* published a fortieth anniversary issue with a brief essay of reminiscence by each of its former editors. The founding editor, Clinton F. Larson, wrote, "Nephi does not prescribe limitations for writers who are pure at heart." There is no mention of the 1959 suspension. The journal's second editor, Charles D. Tate Jr., wrote in the anniversary issue, "The Brethren never did exercise any control over *BYU Studies* while I was the editor. I can only assume it was the same with those editors before and after me."

Arrington's teaching career included a year as a Fulbright professor at the University of Genoa in Italy; a visiting professorship at the University of California at Los Angeles; and a professorship at Utah State University. He had been founding president of the Mormon History Association, an organization that includes RLDS scholars, non-Mormons, and interested persons who are not professional historians. His strong commitment to church service included a stake presidency position.

Through the 1960s Joseph Fielding Smith had recognized the need to organize and catalog the church's vast library and archives along professional lines. In 1970 Smith appointed Apostle (later President) Howard Hunter to follow him as church historian; Hunter similarly recognized the need to professionalize the church's vast archives. In 1972 the First Presidency and the Twelve decided to establish a professional history division, headed by a professionally trained church historian. Notifying Arrington of his appointment, Apostle Hunter assured him that the church was "mature enough that our history should be honest." The position included a half-time professorship at BYU. On April 6, 1972, at the spring General Conference, Arrington was sustained as church historian; James B. Allen and Davis Bitton, two old friends who were also professional historians, were sustained as his assistants.

Arrington discovered that the copy of *Great Basin Kingdom* in the church historian's office had been cataloged with a little letter "a" on the index card to signify "anti." The book apparently had not provided enough supernatural explanations, so a librarian decided "if it wasn't pro-Mormon it must be anti." The index card was a harbinger of things to come.

At first the church historian's office was exhilarated by the expanding opportunities that lay just ahead. A number of researchers and support personnel were added to the staff. Ambitious projects were planned: inauguration of an oral history program; a series of articles for church magazines; a sixteen-volume sesquicentennial history for publication by the anniversary year of 1980; two one-volume church histories, one for a Mormon audience to be published by Deseret and the other aimed at non-Mormons to be published by Alfred A. Knopf; several biographies of church leaders; editions of autobiographies and letters; training fellowships and development of support organizations.

James Allen and Glen Leonard wrote the Deseret one-volume history, *The Story of the Latter-day Saints;* Arrington and Bitton produced the history for Knopf, *The Mormon Experience;* contracts were signed with various scholars for the anniversary history; several shorter projects got under way.

But trouble was also soon under way. Apostle Boyd K. Packer was unhappy with *Letters of Brigham Young to His Sons,* edited by Dean Jessee. Apostle Hunter thought the letters were "warm and wonderful," but Packer wrote a four-page missive to the First Presidency objecting to the new history department's "orientation toward scholarly work" and the book's mention, for instance, of such negative details as family litigation against Young's estate.

The Allen-Leonard volume would strike any knowledgeable non-Mormon reader as circumspect, but some members of the Quorum of the Twelve disliked "the absence of inspiration," for example, the lack of emphasis in the seagull story on God's miraculous intervention. Ezra Taft Benson and Mark Petersen were especially negative in their reactions. Benson spoke out publicly against "historical realism" and those who "inordinately humanize the prophets of God." Benson disliked the term "communitarian" used in connection with nineteenth-century cooperative economics, possibly because it was too close to "communism." (Benson had been a John Birch Society supporter.) However, these objections were not generally brought directly to the church historian, who said he sometimes felt "like a mouse crossing the floor where elephants are dancing."

The Allen-Leonard book sold out quickly but was not permitted to be reprinted until 1986. By 1977 the history department had a new "managing director," G. Homer Durham, and Arrington was informed that a subcommittee consisting of Apostles Hinckley, Petersen, and Packer was going to investigate all publications flowing from the church historian's office.

Arrington notes in his memoir a catalog of observations he had listed in his July 1977 diary, detailing the troubling anti-intellectualism of church leaders:

Eugene England and Lowell Bennion were not permitted to publish with Deseret Book or Bookcraft by direct intervention of two members of the Twelve. Carol Lynn Pearson was blacklisted from church publications until she was able "through prayers and tears" to get one of the Twelve to reverse the decision. Jim Allen was viewed with suspicion because of the *Story of the Latter-day Saints.* The *Church News* could not review *Building the City of God* or any other book by our History Division employees without specific clearance from the Twelve. Claudia Bushman and Scott Kenney could not be published or mentioned because of their connection with *Exponent II* and *Sunstone.* Several Mormon intellectuals were publishing under pseudonyms.

The bright hopes of the church history department had dimmed. By 1978 the ambitious anniversary history was shelved; the church bought out the contracts, and eight of the projected sixteen volumes were later published independently. Of the department's remaining work, Durham examined "every article, manuscript of a talk, and preliminary book manuscript" like a "professor [going] over term papers, theses, and dissertations." More was to come. "Most damaging to our work were the steps he took to remove all the scholars from the department," writes Arrington. Some got transfers; others found replacement jobs; one went to law school.

In 1979, Arrington writes, the chairman of the church's Strengthening Church Members Committee arranged with two BYU students to spy on Arrington's teaching activities and report back weekly. After two weeks one of the pair confessed the arrangement to Arrington. The following year the history division was officially moved to BYU as the Joseph Fielding Smith Institute for Church History, thereby severing its direct connection to the church archives in Salt Lake City. The church history department was restructured by Hinckley and Durham.

In 1982 the First Presidency sent a personal letter to Arrington informing him that he had been released from his call as church historian and director of the history department. The release was not publicly announced in General Conference.

As the 1980s progressed, the church historian's office in Salt Lake City instituted restrictions limiting access to church archives and asking researchers to sign releases giving the church permission to exercise prepublication censorship. Access to many materials, including the papers of deceased General Authorities, formerly available to non-Mormon researchers as well as to loyal Mormons, was restricted or denied. D. Michael Quinn, in a lengthy footnote to his 1998 revised and enlarged edition of *Early Mormonism and the Magic World View,* details the gamesmanship between researchers and archive policies. Some families have acquired photocopies of the General Authority ancestors' diaries that they had donated to the church; they donate their photocopies in turn to other libraries so that researchers can have open access to church-restricted sources. Some researchers have donated their transcripts of now-restricted documents to other libraries. Quinn lists the sources and the libraries.

Arrington continued to be well loved in the community of history scholars and beyond. President Hinckley attended his February 1999 funeral. But the final ecclesiastical footnote to his career is a certain absence in the hall near his onetime office as church historian. In the 1983 words of Davis Bitton, Arrington's former assistant:

If you visit the East Wing of the Church Office Building you will find in the hallway a gallery of portraits. These are the Church Historians, from Oliver Cowdery to G. Homer Durham. But where is Leonard Arrington? Nowhere to be seen. The official explanation is that to be a Church Historian one has to be a General Authority. A brief period of our history, awkwardly embarrassing to someone, is thus erased. Orwell's Truthspeak did not have to wait for 1984.

CHAPTER 16

THE GOLD BIBLE

"WERE THERE REALLY GOLD PLATES AND MINISTERING ANGELS, OR WAS there just Joseph Smith seated at a table with his face in a hat dictating to a scribe a fictional account of the ancient inhabitants of the Americas?"

Resolving that problem haunts loyal Mormons. The blunt questioner quoted is Brigham D. Madsen, a liberal Mormon and onetime history teacher at Brigham Young University who left for a distinguished academic career at the University of Utah. Madsen loves the Book of Mormon. He thinks the Saints should treasure it for its lessons and let its history go.

Book of Mormon apologists have a much tougher job than apologists for the Bible. Not a single person, place, or event unique to Joseph Smith's "gold Bible" has ever been proven to exist. Biblical apologists considering the difficulties in the Old Testament accounts of Jericho may have to explain problems in dating or chronology—but at least there indisputably is a very real Jericho, and it is very old.

(Though Mormon writers consider the term "apologist" to be pejorative, this book uses it in its dictionary sense—as one who provides a case for the defense: for example, Plato's *Apology* or Newman's *Apologia Pro Vita Sua.* Many orthodox Christian seminaries offer courses, often required, in philosophical and practical Christian apologetics. The word does not mean that the faith has anything for which it should "apologize.")

Mormon apologists build what they call "plausibilities" as explanations to satisfy the faithful. At bottom, commitment is a matter of faith, not a matter of rational propositions. John L. Sorenson has written that he does not "undertake to 'test' the Book of Mormon for its truthfulness" because, despite interesting parallels shown through Mesoamerican archaeology, "no number of them would unequivocally establish the book as an authentic pre-Columbian document, nor would failure to find parallels disprove it. Conclusive results can never be obtained by that procedure."

For years the Smithsonian Institution in Washington has received occasional queries about using the Book of Mormon as a guide to archaeological expeditions. Since 1951 the institution's response has been a slightly testy form letter saying there is "no connection" between the archaeology of the New World and the Book of Mormon; the Smithsonian has never used the book as a scientific guide.

That letter was a sore point for Mormons. In 1993 Sorenson, a retired BYU anthropology professor and one of the church's leading apologists for ancient scripture, wrote a point-by-point response to the Smithsonian for the Foundation for Ancient Research and Mormon Studies (FARMS), an apologetic organization for the church now housed at BYU. He drafted a proposed statement for the Smithsonian, carefully separating the Book of Mormon from the current assumptions of most secular Mesoamerican archaeology, and suggesting that, "since the book is primarily religious in nature, concern with it does not normally or appropriately fall within the Institution's mission, any more than the Bible or the Koran."

The Smithsonian did not quite bite. But the Smithsonian is, after all, dependent on Congress for funds, and there are now eleven LDS congressmen and five LDS senators. FARMS people met with a Smithsonian representative, and as of March 1998 this circumspect statement became the Institution's brief answer to Book of Mormon archaeological questions:

> Your recent inquiry concerning the Smithsonian Institution's alleged use of the Book of Mormon as a scientific guide has been received in the Office of Communications. The Book of Mormon is a religious

document and not a scientific guide. The Smithsonian Institution has never used it in archaeological research and any information that you have received to the contrary is incorrect.

"Ancient scripture" in Mormon usage includes the Book of Mormon, the Pearl of Great Price, and Joseph Smith's own Bible translation, as well as the Old and New Testaments. The Pearl of Great Price is a selection of materials accorded scriptural status by the LDS Church (but not the Reorganized Church) that were largely produced by Joseph Smith during his Kirtland period and first published as a unit in 1851, seven years after his death.

The Book of Mormon was controversial from the outset. The contemporary Protestant leader Alexander Campbell, in an oft-quoted phrase of 1831, characterized it as gathering "every error and almost every truth discussed in New York for the last ten years." From the beginning to this day, the reaction of Book of Mormon readers has been divided between those committed to it as ancient literature and those who consider it a product of the nineteenth century.

The older polemical traditions split on two sides of a simple prophet/fraud dichotomy: either Joseph Smith was everything he claimed to be, a true prophet entrusted with a new scripture from authentic ancient golden plates, or he was a charismatic fraud. Some participants in current discussion, however, would like to carve a middle path. These include respectful and sympathetic non-Mormons who recognize the moral and spiritual values in the Book of Mormon as well as liberal Mormons who value their heritage, with its disciplined lifestyle and communal bonding. The former group includes such scholars as the brilliant literary critic Harold Bloom; the sociologist of religion whose projected growth figures understandably delight the LDS, Rodney Stark; and the scholars of the history of religion Martin Marty and Jan Shipps. The latter group also includes many excommunicated Mormons who still identify as Mormon, as well as some thoughtful Saints who are carefully circumspect in what they say and write but regard the Book of Mormon as most likely of nineteenth-century origin.

Some friendly non-Mormons celebrate Joseph Smith as a highly creative religious original. Bloom, for example, loathes C. S. Lewis, the twentieth century's most influential traditional Christian apologist. Bloom rates Lewis's *Mere Christianity* as "one of my least favorite books" precisely because Lewis "shrewdly associates the Christian surrender of the self with *not* seeking literary originality." On the other hand, Bloom admires Smith because he was "an extraordinary religious genius" in his creative imagination, the "greatest and most authentic of American prophets, seers, and revelators."

Marty, rejecting the prophet/fraud dichotomy, thinks the important thing is to "seek to understand" Smith's message rather than to debate its literal historicity. He advocates an approach that would move "from primitive to secondary naiveté or from belief before criticism to belief through criticism and interpretation." Shipps is interested not in whether the Book of Mormon is literal history but in how Smith, Brigham Young, and the Mormon people have developed for themselves a usable, sacred myth, and how that myth functions to bind the Mormon communal memory.

Stark, speaking to the 1998 Mormon History Association convention, likened Smith's inspirational originality to the musical genius of Mozart and Gershwin, both of whom said they simply wrote down the music they heard coming to them. Stark also compared Smith and his Book to Muhammad and the revelation of the Quran. Both seemed to be relaying scriptural dictations. Both had strong family support, resulting in a sort of holy family that was central to the movement.

Stark thinks Mormonism may be the first important new world religion to arise since Islam appeared in the seventh century A.D., providing interesting phenomena for sociologists to observe. Islamic and Mormon beginnings shared three characteristics in common, according to Stark: (1) a general culture of revelations in the surrounding culture so that the recipient of the new movement's revelation must have had previous intense contact with another person or persons who also received visions or revelations; (2) the new movement leader had the support of an intense primary group, typically the family; (3) the founding network was intense but open to building contacts with others.

For Stark the divine acts through history with human agents, and application of a social science model does not necessarily imply hostility to the supernatural. Stark thinks that ideology plays almost no role in the beginnings of conversion, which occurs almost entirely through human networking. As he sees it, questions of literal historicity are not central to the Mormon religion.

The RLDS leadership is open to a flexible account of the Book of Mormon, though the opinions of the rank-and-file membership vary across the spectrum. "I believe this subject must be approached with intellectual honesty," wrote William D. Russell in a 1982 *Sunstone* article when he was president of the Mormon History Association.

Russell's article analyzes the problems of historical and literary anachronism in the Book of Mormon; it does not deal with archaeological difficulties. Russell, the social science division chairperson of the RLDS Church's Graceland College, concludes, "Perhaps what Stanley Kimball calls 'an exciting, readable adventure story' can come much more alive for us if we read it as a writing of Joseph Smith, from which we can grow spiritually." As some suggest, "the objective of the Christian faith is not assent to propositions but Christian discipleship. If that be the case, then the Book of Mormon is important for us not in giving us events to affirm as historically accurate but rather in helping us become better disciples of the One for whom the book claims to be a 'second witness.'"

LDS Church authorities do not consider this revisionist solution acceptable. And it has not escaped their notice that the LDS Church is growing rapidly while the RLDS Church is faltering. For ordinary Mormons, strong belief demands are a positive aspect of the church. As President Gordon B. Hinckley has observed, people like a church that stands for something, a church that knows what it believes.

From its beginnings, the church has declared it essential that the Book of Mormon be accepted as it presents itself, as historical fact, not inspired fiction. Apostle Orson Pratt, in his 1851 *Works,* wrote, "The Book of Mormon claims to be a divinely inspired record. . . . This book must be either *true* or *false.* . . . If false, it is one of the most cunning, wicked, bold, deep-laid impositions ever palmed upon the world, calculated to deceive and ruin millions who will sincerely receive it as the word of God. . . . If true, no one can possibly be saved and reject it; if false, no one can possibly be saved and receive it."

Current loyalist scholars express the same idea. BYU Professor Louis Midgley maintains, "To reduce the Book of Mormon to mere myth weakens, if not destroys, the possibility of it witnessing to the truth about divine things. A fictional Book of Mormon fabricated by Joseph Smith, even when his inventiveness, genius, or 'inspiration' is celebrated, does not witness to Jesus Christ but to human folly. A true Book of Mormon is a powerful witness; a fictional one is hardly worth reading and pondering."

Within the loyal Mormon community, there is a moderate intellectual group that believes the Book of Mormon does have ancient roots but, as part of the process of revelation properly understood, is expressed through nineteenth-century thought processes. Blake Ostler develops this view in a 1987 *Dialogue* essay presented in 1995 at Brigham Young University and widely discussed among BYU religion faculty and seminary and institute personnel. Applying source, motif, and form critical analysis—some of the standard tools of "higher criticism" in biblical studies—Ostler sees the "Book of Mormon as an ancient text mediated through the mind of Joseph Smith. . . . The prophet is an active participant in revelation, conceptualizing and verbalizing God's message in a framework of thought meaningful to the people." Smith's "revelatory experiences naturally assumed the world view arising from his culture." At the same time, Ostler believes the book has ancient elements that cannot be explained by the nineteenth century.

The foundational truths of the Mormon Church begin with the validity of Smith's visions. Possible explanations include the hoax theory frequently adopted by anti-Mormon opponents, as well as by some en route to becoming ex-Mormon, such as Fawn Brodie in *No Man Knows My History.* In the twentieth century some scholars introduced the notion of abnormal psychology. Lawrence Foster is one historian who suggests this interpretation. In this view, Smith really believed his visions from the outset, or came to believe them in the process of delivering the Book of Mormon. Other writers, not wanting to call Smith's mind diseased, call him a mystic. Visions, after all, are a subjective experience. With this perspective, the question of truth content is sidestepped.

Perhaps the most delicate matter, to faithful Mormons, is interpreting Smith's activities in magic and the occult during the 1820s. Quinn's *Early Mormonism and the Magic World View,* published in 1987 while he was still a BYU professor and holder of a temple recommend, created a stir. Here was an emerging prophet deeply involved with mystic amulets, divining rods, incantations, magic seer stones, and related rituals. The research was not sensationalized, nor was it lurid; it was, moreover, painstakingly documented. Quinn attempted to place his research in a sympathetic context: folk religion, practiced outside the "establishment" culture, was widespread at the time.

On the other hand, though the Smith family's activities were not unusual for people living on the margins of society, Emma's father had opposed their marriage because he regarded Joseph's money-digging as a disreputable way of avoiding doing real work for a living. It was also the cause of Joseph's being hauled into the Bainbridge court in 1826. Magic, mysticism, the occult, widespread vision experiences, revelations, and other manifestations of religious excitement raise uncomfortable questions about the context from which the Book of Mormon arose.

Quinn himself, in spite of his 1993 excommunication, has continued to maintain that he believes in the ancient golden plates and the First Vision. But his thorough research, republished in an expanded version in 1998, details an immersion in folk magic and occult beliefs that inevitably casts a long shadow over how Mormons understand the context of their church's beginnings, as well as the development of its sacred temple rituals.

Apologists from the earliest times to the present day have stressed Smith's lack of education as proof that he was not the author of the Book of Mormon. How could a simple farm boy have written such a complex literary work as the Book of Mormon, and so quickly, dictating while he looked into his hat? Lucy Mack Smith laid the groundwork for this defense in her 1853 family biography, saying that he was thoughtful but less bookish than her other children; Emma Hale Smith at the end of her life reminisced that Joseph was not capable of writing a literate letter, let alone composing so complex a work as the Book of Mormon.

A current expression of the same idea comes from Richard Bushman, a Columbia University history professor and a devout Mormon: "How did these 584 pages of text come to issue from the mind of an untaught, indolent ignoramus, notable only for his money-digging episodes?" Yet some of Smith's contemporaries believed he had a startlingly unique knowledge of divine things. Pious Islamic tradition similarly maintains that Muhammad was not literate, and the Quran is also highly complex, though Mormons do not recognize it as scripture.

Joseph Smith's limited formal education must be understood in the context of his place and time and of what is known of his personality and abilities. His father had been a schoolteacher. Quinn documents the extensive number of books and periodicals available at the time in the libraries and bookshops of Palmyra and nearby towns. Lucy Mack Smith, in her family biography, details Joseph's extensive boyish knowledge and interest in Indian lore. The language he used in his account of the First Vision was the expression of a youth deeply immersed in biblical vernacular. His later activities revealed a lively intellectual curiosity as well as a documented use of books and a profound interest in learning. Still, whether divine inspiration or the product of rare human creativity, there remains something of mystery in the genesis of a work such as the Book of Mormon.

Every copy of the Book of Mormon is printed with the Testimony of the Three Witnesses and of the Eight Witnesses. Like everything else in early Mormonism, the witnesses are controversial. What is not ambiguous is that, to the end of their lives, none of them disavowed their written testimonies even though most broke with Smith's church. That very apostasy has been used as a debating point in favor of their witness by the Book's defenders. Three of them—David Whitmer, Oliver Cowdery, and Martin Harris—were the primary witnesses to whom Smith's angel appeared. Jan Shipps interprets the written testimonial as a spiritual formula, given to Joseph Smith by revelation.

Each of the Three Witnesses later left the church. At the time of their testimony, Smith had promised the men that with prayer and faith they would see the plates. They strolled in the woods together and prayed a long time. Nothing happened. Disturbed by his failure to receive a vision, Harris asked to withdraw and pray alone. With Smith present, Cowdery and Whitmer then received their visions. Smith went after Harris, the two men prayed together, and Harris was rewarded with his vision too. All three signed a testimonial that had been written by Smith.

Harris's testimony is the most problematic. He was a somewhat unstable person, prone to visions and mystical experiences. He once reportedly saw Jesus Christ in the form of a deer as he walked alongside and conversed with him for two or three miles. In a number of later statements, Harris explained that he saw the plates with his "spiritual eye" or "eye of faith" rather than his naked eyes. Conflicting reports assert that he and the other witnesses never saw the bare engraved plates, only something covered with a cloth.

Witnesses to the same statement sometimes reported it differently. An 1838 letter written by Stephen Burnett to Lyman E. Johnson reported that Harris said publicly that none of the witnesses had literally seen the plates with their physical eyes. A letter written by Warren Parrish supports Burnett's interpretation. But one written by George A. Smith describing the same speech emphasized only that Harris witnessed to the truth of the Book of Mormon.

Not many statements exist on the Eight Witnesses. Two were Smith family members; two died fairly early; the other four apostasized. Some of the apostate witnesses were rebaptized later.

Anachronisms, both literary and archaeological, raise questions about Book of Mormon authenticity to even the most casual reader. Christ coming to minister in the New World is a matter of faith; there seems little prospect that the claim could be flatly proven or disproven. More jarring is the Christian testimony of Old Testament characters such as Adam, Abraham, Noah, Enoch, and others.

Another area of difficulty is the relation of the Book of Mormon to the Bible. Nearly one-third of Isaiah is quoted in the Book of Mormon, with some changes unique to the Mormon scripture and the 1769 edition of the King James Bible that Joseph Smith used. Initially Mormons hoped the Dead Sea Scroll translations would support the biblical text as it appears in the Book of Mormon. That did not happen. The differences are unique to the Book of Mormon, while the translations of the Dead Sea Scrolls have shown that the Old Testament we have today is surprisingly faithful to manuscripts that are some 2,200 years old.

The Beatitudes and the Sermon on the Mount turn up among the Nephites. Twentieth-century scholarship has revealed errors appearing in the Book of Mormon that are unique to the Bible version that Joseph Smith used. In 1986 Stan Larson, then working in the LDS Church's translation department, and holder of a Ph.D. in New Testament studies from the University of Birmingham, England, collated the best texts he could find for the Sermon on the Mount and compared them with III Nephi. He criticized Smith's usage of the text, concluding that the errors unique to the 1769 King James Bible proved the text was not a genuine translation from golden plates but a paraphrase produced in the nineteenth century. Larson was forced to resign.

Non-Mormon scholars point to historical anachronisms in ancient culture as depicted in the Book of Mormon. Some critics say the stress on individual moral responsibility and conversion in mass revivalist meetings conducted by Nephi and other Book of Mormon prophets bears a suspicious resemblance to the exhortations to repentance by evangelists at camp meetings in nineteenth-century upstate New York. Others see a relationship between nineteenth-century market capitalism and Smith's Book of Mormon characters who "were exceedingly industrious, and they did buy and sell and traffic one with another, that they might get gain" (Ether 10:22). Some of the development, according to these critics, sounds much like nineteenth-century urbanization: "And it came to pass that there were many cities built anew, and there were many old cities repaired. And there were many highways cast up, and many roads made, which led from city to city, and from land to land, and from place to place" (III Nephi 6:7–8).

Mormons are sensitive about the fact that virtually no significant non-Mormon scholars take the Book of Mormon seriously as ancient literature. Despite the fact that millions have read and been influenced by it, "literary scholars studiously ignore" the Book of Mormon, even as a classic of popular American literature, laments Eugene England, founding editor of *Dialogue* and a retired BYU English professor. Few non-Mormon scholars other than historians have actually read it.

Because of this, and because very few Mormons are fully credentialed in scriptural studies, ancient languages, and related critical studies, Mormon thinking in these areas takes place almost entirely within its own enclosed world. When Mormons step outside that enclosure, they tread on thin ice. The Hebraicist David Wright applied the principles of higher criticism he learned during his doctoral work at U.C. Berkeley to Book of Mormon studies and believes that BYU students and Church Educational System teachers should at least be aware of those tools. He is still a productive scholar—but from Brandeis, not BYU, from which he was dismissed. As a result of those tools, Wright concluded that the Book of Mormon is a nineteenth-century work, and BYU correctly interpreted that as opposition to the doctrinal stand of the LDS Church.

During much of the twentieth century more apologetic energy was focused on archaeology than on any other area of Book of Mormon studies. Much of this has been aimed at attempting to locate a plausible geography for the Book of Mormon stories. At first, Joseph Smith and the nineteenth-century Saints generally assumed that the sacred history had taken place in upstate New York, around the vicinity of Hill Cumorah where Smith found the plates.

The Saints' interest in Mesoamerica as a possible setting was first tickled by Jon Lloyd Stephens's 1841 best-seller *Incidents of Travel in Central America, Chiapas, and Yucatan,* with its awe-inspiring descriptions of ancient Mayan ruins. Passages were excerpted in Nauvoo's *Times and Seasons* in 1842 with an unsigned editorial wondering whether some of the ruins could have been the Mormon scriptural Zarahemla. It is not clear whether Smith was the editorialist.

Mayan cultural characteristics have obvious attractions for Mormon interests. The Mayans were literate and sophisticated; they built great cities; they even built pyramids that seem at a glance to resemble the pyramids of Egypt. One key problem for all Mormons attempting to relate Mayan cities and culture to the Nephites, however, is that Mayan civilization is dated 200 or more years after the destruction of the Nephites.

The Book of Mormon describes the Hebraic migration to the Americas by the Jaredites at the time of Babel, perhaps around 2250 B.C., and by the Nephites, around 600 B.C. A great civilization arose, and crafts and cities developed. They were a Semitic people, but their written language was something the prophet called "reformed Egyptian." Then around A.D. 400 at Hill Cumorah came the great final battle between the Nephites and the Lamanites, resulting in the death of perhaps 230,000 Nephites and the end of Nephite civilization. The Lamanites remained. Most Mormons believe the American Indians are Lamanite descendants. The introduction to the current edition of the Book of Mormon declares the Lamanites "are the principal ancestors of the American Indians."

Mormon interest in Mesoamerica increased in the twentieth century. The first scholarly work tying that area to the Book of Mormon was the work of an RLDS researcher, Louis E. Hills. The Yale anthropologist Michael D. Coe credits Hills, in books published in 1917 and 1919, with labeling the "narrow neck of land" in the Book of Mormon geography as the Isthmus of Tehuantepec in southern Mexico, placing Zarahemla (present-day Guatemala and Belize) to the east and Bountiful to the west. If so, then there must have been two Hill Cumorahs: one in Mesoamerica, where the great battle took place; another thousands of miles away in upstate New York, where the exiled Moroni buried the golden plates he eventually gave to Joseph Smith. The theorists offer no explanation of how or why the sacred metal tablets would have been transported from Mexico to the Palmyra area.

The most common Mesoamerican setting is the one proposed by Sorenson, using the Isthmus of Tehuantepec, a strip of land 500 or 600 miles long. Such a site is large enough to have supported a population of several million by A.D. 400, and possibly a highly developed culture, agriculture, and commerce. Its geography could coincide with a number of Book of Mormon descriptions. One key problem is its directionality. To account for the Book of Mormon locale, one must tilt the map sixty degrees. Otherwise, the land northward is westward and the land southward is eastward. Most ancient peoples had a clear concept of north and accounted for direction by the rising and setting of the sun.

The LDS Church has wisely refrained from officially committing itself to a specific Book of Mormon geographic location in spite of its insistence that the book describes literal historic events. According to Joseph Fielding Smith, a major LDS doctrinal authority and later president of the church: "It is the personal opinion of the writer that the Lord does not intend that the Book of Mormon, at least at the present time, shall be proved true by any archaeological findings. The day may come when such will be the case, but not now. The Book of Mormon is itself a *witness* of the truth, and the promise has been given most solemnly that any person who will read it with a prayerful heart may receive the abiding testimony of its truth."

But when a church is founded on events that took place in real history and claims its sacred book records that history, the quest for supportive evidence remains. FARMS publications concentrate on Mesoamerica research, and travel agencies in Salt Lake City have brochures for tours to Book of Mormon lands, that is, to southern Mexico and northern Central America. Michael D. Coe, now retired from Yale and possibly the country's most distinguished specialist in Mesoamerican anthropology, has observed that "in hundreds of motels scattered across the western United States the Gentile archaeologist can find a paperback Book of Mormon lavishly illustrated with the paintings of Arnold Friberg depicting such scenes as Samuel the Lamanite prophesying on top of what looks like the Temple of the Tigers in Chichen Itza, Yucatan."

Meanwhile, many rank-and-file Mormons still believe that the great battle of Hill Cumorah was fought near Palmyra, just as Joseph Smith thought. "The first time you walk on the grounds you know something big happened here," says the career army major Bruce Marshall, who visited the 1998 Hill Cumorah pageant with his family. "You can feel it, like visiting Gettysburg. The Book of Mormon had to be sealed. It had to be sealed by blood. I believe the battle did take place here. It's just something I feel."

Marshall and others like him have had support in high places. The late Apostle Bruce R. McConkie (with typical Mormon interconnectedness, Joseph Fielding Smith's son-in-law) was a firm believer in one Cumorah, the hill in upstate New York. In his *Mormon Doctrine,* a widely used reference work since its first appearance more than forty years ago, McConkie writes: "Both the Nephite and Jaredite civilizations fought their final great wars of extinction at and near the *Hill Cumorah* (or *Ramah* as the Jaredites termed it), which hill is located between Palmyra and Manchester in the western part of the state of New York." Influential Apostles James Talmage and LeGrand Richards were also supporters of the traditional New York Cumorah.

In spite of the more scholarly FARMS industry, new books continue to be written building the case for the traditional upstate New York location for the Jaredite and Nephite epic. The most recent is the 1998 *Return to Cumorah,* written in the tradition of amateur Mormon lay scholarship by Duane R. Aston, a retired California physics professor. His narrow neck of land is at Niagara Falls. Aston's analysis is geographic; he explains the thin archaeological evidence by writing that it is the way of the Lord "that our testimony of the Book of Mormon remain a matter of faith, and not based upon external proofs found from archaeology."

The father of LDS Mesoamerican research was another Mormon amateur, Thomas Stuart Ferguson, a California lawyer who in 1946 "rolled up his sleeves, threw a shovel over his shoulder, and marched into the remote jungles of southern Mexico" to "shut the mouths of the critics" who said evidence to prove the Book of Mormon did not exist. Ferguson was tireless; over the years he made twenty-four trips to Central America, raised money, and helped establish the New World Archaeological Foundation, which brought in non-Mormon experts as well as Mormons. The young John Sorenson turned his first shovel on a Ferguson expedition.

Ferguson published frequently over the years; his first book, *Cumorah—Where?* (1947), was initially banned from Deseret stores because he proposed a Mexican hill as the site of the great Nephite battle rather than Smith's hill in upstate New York. His last book was *The Messiah in Ancient America* (1987, coauthored with Bruce W. Warren). Publicly the book printed a testimonial to Ferguson's faith in the Book of Mormon. Privately, although Ferguson continued to attend ward meetings and to socialize as a Mormon, after a lifetime committed to proving the historicity of the Mormon scripture he had concluded that the book was a piece of fiction. The ex-Mormon polemicists Jerald and Sandra Tanner received seven letters from Ferguson expressing his disillusionment with the Book of Mormon. For Ferguson the final straw was insurmountable difficulties in Smith's later translation of another Mormon scripture, the Book of Abraham.

Since 1979 much Book of Mormon research has been funneled through FARMS, formerly independent and now incorporated into BYU. FARMS publishes two semiannual journals, the *Journal of the Book of Mormon Studies* and the *FARMS Review of Books,* as well as books, occasional papers, and reprints. FARMS research includes history, language, and various aspects of ancient culture as well as archaeology and literary analysis of scriptures.

Archaeology, and not only matters of geography, remains an interest. The Book of Mormon presents major historical anachronisms, that is, cultural and physical evidence dropped into the wrong period of history. Though Joseph Smith would not have known it, these historical details do not appear to fit into the ancient Jaredite-Nephite time frame. Utilitarian use of the wheel, for example, was unknown in pre-Columbian America. The horse came to the New World with the Spanish conquest, as did most domesticated animals. There is no archaeological evidence for plants such as wheat or for metallurgy involving the smelting and casting of the type of steel swords used in Book of Mormon warfare. Sorenson attempts to explain some of these anachronisms as arising from the difficulties any translator has in finding word equivalents. Some of the explanations might be reasonable: silk, for example, could be a silk-like fabric other than actual silk. Other explanations stretch thin: for example, explaining the horse as some kind of a deer.

Stephen Williams, a Harvard anthropology professor, treats the Book of Mormon dismissively in a chapter of his 1991 book *Fantastic Archaeology: The Wild Side of North American Prehistory.* He claims to analyze the nineteenth-century "nonsense" in his field. Coe is a rare secular scholar in being well acquainted with the Book of Mormon as well as with Mormon history and scholarship. Writing in a 1973 *Dialogue* article, he said, "The bare facts of the matter are that nothing, absolutely nothing, has ever shown up in any New World excavation which would suggest to a dispassionate observer that the Book of Mormon, as claimed by Joseph Smith, is a historical document relating to the history of early migrants to our hemisphere."

The anti-Mormon writer Bill McKeever checked up on Coe in 1993 to see whether two decades of archaeological research had changed the Yale scholar's mind. McKeever printed Coe's response in his newsletter: "I haven't changed my views about the Book of Mormon since my 1973 article. I have seen no archaeological evidence before or since that date which would convince me that it is anything but a fanciful creation by an unusually gifted individual living in upstate New York in the early nineteenth century."

One key missing link is any evidence that Hebrews ever migrated to pre-Columbian America. So far DNA evidence supports the orthodox connection of Native Americans with Asia but has not provided any link with the ancient Near East. The usual explanation by anthropologists is that Asian peoples probably migrated over the Bering Strait many thousands of years ago. Recent archaeological digs have revealed evidence of much earlier migrations, possibly from Europe and Asia, and by sea. Nothing, at least so far, links these finds to the Hebrews or to migrations within the Book of Mormon time frame.

A stone with a supposedly ancient Hebrew inscription discovered in Bat Creek, Tennessee, in 1889 is sometimes cited as support of pre-Columbian cultural contact with the ancient Near East. Originally the inscription was thought to have been Cherokee, but in 1970 the Brandeis Semitic language scholar Cyrus Gordon identified the letters as a paleo-Hebrew inscription of the first or second century A.D.

An amateur Mormon Hebraicist, J. Huston McCulloch (an economics professor at Ohio State University), has energetically pursued the Bat Creek case. But on technical grounds, Gordon's findings have been disputed by two scholars in Near Eastern studies, Frank M. Cross of Harvard (retired) and P. Kyle McCarter Jr. of Johns Hopkins. McCarter also suggests that there is evidence of fraudulent contamination of the find by the original discoverer in 1889. A McCulloch-McCarter exchange was published by the *Biblical Archaeology Review* in 1993 and reprinted by FARMS with a carefully neutral introduction by the FARMS writer Stephen D. Ricks.

In recent years literary analysis of the Book of Mormon has been edging toward center stage, both as general study of the sacred book and for apologetic purposes. In a 1997 FARMS title, *Book of Mormon Authorship Revisited: The Evidence for Ancient Origins,* only three of the sixteen essays deal with archaeology and geography. This book, written for a faithful Mormon audience, recognizes the arguments advanced by liberal critics, including ex-Mormons such as David P. Wright and others who wrote for the 1993 Signature book edited by Brent Lee Metcalfe, *New Approaches to the Book of Mormon: Explorations in Critical Methodology.*

Emphasis is currently being placed on studies that attempt to show that the Book of Mormon had many writers rather than just one (that is, Joseph Smith). The work includes wordprint analysis, which aims to show that different patterns of word usage prove different authors. Another approach is the study of chiasmus by John W. Welch, a BYU law professor who is on the board of FARMS and is editor-in-chief of *BYU Studies*. Chiasmus is the use of parallel phrases repeated with some reversals, seen frequently in the Bible. Welch argues that these complexities imply ancient authorship. The extensive scholarship of BYU's Hugh Nibley over the years has emphasized parallels between the Book of Mormon and ancient Near Eastern culture and language. The aim of Nibley's work is to provide evidence for Book of Mormon cultural materials that were not known in Joseph Smith's time. His extensive scholarship has included study of the Book of Mormon in relation to ancient names, geographic detail, and military, social, and political institutions.

One of the most delicate situations that FARMS and Book of Mormon defenders ever faced was the 1985 publication of B. H. Roberts's *Studies of the Book of Mormon* by the University of Illinois Press. Roberts, a General Authority who died in 1933, has been a legendary figure in the church; a bright gadfly intellectual and individualist in a church that values conformity; and one of the church's most valiant writers and speakers in defense of the Book of Mormon.

In the early 1920s, at the request of the First Presidency, Roberts undertook a study of the Book of Mormon with the intention of developing a well-reasoned apologetic to explain difficulties in the book. Among the problems he pondered were the important linguistic difficulties ("no vestige of either Hebrew or Egyptian appears in the language of the American Indians") and the historical anachronisms (the horse, wheat, steel swords, and so forth).

Then Roberts also undertook a study comparing the Book of Mormon with Ethan Smith's *View of the Hebrews,* a work by a clergyman in Poultney, Vermont, on the Israelite origin of the Indians, published in 1823 and 1825. The book was successful, as multiple early editions attest. It drew on some ideas that were commonplace at the time. Oliver Cowdery, Smith's scribe and one of the Three Witnesses for the Book of Mormon, had lived in Poultney until 1825; his stepmother and three half-sisters had been members of Ethan Smith's church. It is probably safe to assume that Joseph Smith was familiar with the book.

Roberts's study had included an eighteen-page typescript showing parallels between *View of the Hebrews* and the structure and content of the

Nephite story in the Book of Mormon. Some copies of the parallel list circulated privately after Roberts's death, but Roberts himself had withheld some of his materials from the General Authorities. Publication came decades later after his family donated Roberts's manuscripts to the University of Utah. Sterling McMurrin, a philosophy scholar at the University of Utah who had written a biographical chapter for the study, later charged that there was an unsuccessful effort to have the University of Illinois Press suppress publication of the study.

Regarding the historicity of the Book of Mormon, Roberts had written:

In the light of this evidence, there can be no doubt as to the possession of a vividly strong, creative imagination by Joseph Smith, the Prophet, an imagination, it could with reason be urged, which, given the suggestions that are to be found in the "common knowledge" of accepted American antiquities of the times, supplemented by such a work as Ethan Smith's *View of the Hebrews,* would make it possible for him to create a book such as the Book of Mormon is.

Roberts could not be dismissed as an outsider or an anti-Mormon, so FARMS went into high gear: Roberts must have been playing devil's advocate; he had continued to testify to the truth of the Book of Mormon right up to his death; McMurrin and Brigham Madsen (who edited the volume) had misrepresented Roberts's final views about the historicity of Mormon scriptures. *BYU Studies* and FARMS churned out responses. McMurrin and Madsen suggested a public panel discussion with their critics, who declined to appear. In 1996, many years after it had been available through Jerald and Sandra Tanner, and more than a decade after the University of Illinois published Roberts's study, Ethan Smith's *View of the Hebrews* was published in a BYU edition.

Most Mormons are either unaware of these scholarly finds or unperturbed by them. To them the final decision is one of faith, of accepting the church's authority, of committing one's life to a book one chooses to accept as sacred scripture. As the FARMS review editor Daniel C. Peterson has written, in words substantially repeated by every Mormon child in his first ward testimony and by every General Authority at the end of each General Conference talk: "Most importantly, the evidence of the Spirit is available to those who seek it. I, for one, have received the witness of the Spirit, and I bear testimony that the Book of Mormon is what it claims to be, and that the gospel is true."

CHAPTER 17

DISCOVERING "PLAIN AND PRECIOUS THINGS"

WAGONS BEARING MEDICINE SHOWS AND CARNIVALS CREAKED ALONG THE dusty roads of frontier towns in the early nineteenth century, bearing entertainment and curiosities to feed the imaginations of village citizens. In 1835 an Irish immigrant named Michael H. Chandler worked his way to Kirtland, Ohio, with a wagon holding Egyptian mummies and some ancient papyri for sale. Originally there had been eleven mummies; Chandler had sold seven to museums, including two in Philadelphia. The mummies had attracted considerable attention in Cleveland. Along the way Chandler heard that Joseph Smith Jr. was able to translate "reformed Egyptian." He had four mummies and some papyri left by the time he reached Kirtland. Would the Mormons be interested?

They were. And despite the financial desperation of the Kirtland church, they anted up the then-enormous sum of $2,400 to buy the lot. The mummies—which, like the papyri, were documented and authentic pieces of Egyptian antiquity—became a popular exhibit in Kirtland, and later in Nauvoo, a museum curiosity for tourists to admire. But what really mattered for the newborn faith was the papyri.

Joseph was excited. Soon after the purchase he wrote, "With W. W. Phelps and Oliver Cowdery as scribes, I commenced the translation of some of the characters or hieroglyphics, and much to our joy found that one of the rolls contained the writings of Abraham, another the writings of Joseph of Egypt, etc.,—a more full account of which will appear in its place, as I proceed to examine or unfold them. Truly we can say, the Lord is beginning to reveal the abundance of peace and truth."

This was a period of eager interest in such antiquities. The Rosetta Stone had been discovered in 1799; its trilingual inscription was translated in 1822 by the Frenchman Jean François Champollion, but the unlocking of the mysterious Egyptian hieroglyphics was not published in Europe until 1841, and not until even later in the United States. Such scholarship was unknown to Chandler, to the academics Chandler consulted, and to Joseph Smith.

Smith went to work on the papyri and, with the help of his scribes, developed a working list of characters, his *Egyptian Alphabet and Grammar,* which is in the Utah church's possession, as are four manuscript copies of the Book of Abraham. No mention is made of the work from 1836 until 1842, when it was published in three installments in the church's paper *Times and Seasons.*

Abraham was, and still is, published with three facsimiles of the papyri used in the book's translation. The book claims to be Abraham's own story, transmitted in his own hand, and provides materials on Abraham's life that are not present in the biblical Genesis account. It introduces doctrines distinctive to Mormonism, especially the plurality of gods, the preexistence of human souls, polygamy, and the doctrine that the gods' creation was organization rather than the traditional notion of divine creation *ex nihilo*—out of nothing.

After publication, the Abraham story—five short chapters with three facsimiles and explanations—was on its way to becoming Mormon scripture. As part of the Pearl of Great Price, it was published in Liverpool in 1851. The Abraham headnote written by Smith describes the papyri as "writings of Abraham, while he was in Egypt, . . . written by his own hand, upon papyrus." The Pearl also includes selections from the Book of Moses, a selection of the Gospel of Matthew as retranslated by Smith, a brief biographical statement including the canonized version of his First Vision, and a list of the thirteen Articles of Faith. This collection was made part of the "Standard Works" of scripture by the Utah church in 1880.

Mormons believe in an open canon and the principle of continuing revelation. They are promised that more scriptures will be discovered; more revelations could be canonized by the current seer, revelator, and prophet. The Bible, though officially a "standard work" in Mormonism as well and cited by its missionaries, is read through the lens of this open canon and the interpretation of Mormon prophets, especially Joseph Smith. The Book of Mormon teaches that, due to the Great Apostasy of "the great and abominable church, . . . there are many plain and precious things taken away from the book, which is the book of the Lamb of God" (I Nephi 24:28).

Of the many "plain and precious things" restored to the Latter-day Saints by the prophet Joseph Smith, these few pieces of ancient Egyptian papyri and the Book of Abraham are, to non-Mormons, among the strangest. For Mormons the Book of Abraham presents one of the church's most difficult apologetic challenges.

Gentiles were dubious about Abraham's authenticity early on. In 1837 the Ohio non-Mormon William S. West wrote, "Is it possible that a record written by Abraham . . . containing the most important revelations that God ever gave to man, should be entirely lost by the tenacious Israelites, and preserved by the unbelieving Egyptians, and by them embalmed and deposited in the catacombs with an Egyptian priest? . . . I venture to say no, it is not possible. It is more likely that the records are Egyptian."

The first professional Egyptologist to translate the Mormon papyri was the French scholar Théodule Devéria, who came upon a Liverpool Pearl pamphlet in the late 1850s and recognized the facsimiles as common Egyptian funerary papyri. Devéria's work, "Fragments of Egyptian Funerary Mss. Considered by the Mormons to be Autograph Memoirs of Abraham," appeared in French in 1860 and was published in London in English the following year.

The next critic was T. B. H. Stenhouse, who republished Devéria's scholarship in several New York and London editions over the closing decades of the nineteenth century. In 1912 an Episcopal bishop from Utah,

Franklin S. Spaulding, sent the Abraham facsimiles to eight Egyptologists as far afield as New York, Chicago, Munich, and London, all of whom returned verdicts as negative as Devéria's a half-century earlier. They all reported that the prophet's interpretations were fraudulent nonsense. The LDS Church then had no scholars qualified to respond.

The papyri themselves had disappeared. Along with the mummies, they had reportedly ended up in a Chicago museum and had been destroyed in the city's great fire of 1871. To everyone's surprise, some of them surfaced in 1966 at New York's Metropolitan Museum of Art when the University of Utah professor Aziz S. Atiya, a Coptic Christian and scholar, was search-ing through papyrus manuscripts for Coptic materials. The first of the eleven fragments that Atiya saw was a fragment he recognized from fac-simile No. 1 of the Book of Abraham. The file also contained a bill of sale from Emma Smith Bidamon, the prophet's widow (she married Lewis C. Bidamon after Smith's death). After the find was authenticated, Atiya arranged for the materials to be donated to the LDS Church.

The discovery created a stir. So did a publication of Jerald and Sandra Tanner, Salt Lake's most prominent ex-Mormons. In 1966 they somehow managed to obtain a microfilm copy of Smith's *Egyptian Alphabet and Grammar,* a restricted item in the church historian's office, and published a photomechanical reproduction of it.

Hugh Nibley, a BYU scholar in ancient Near Eastern studies but not an Egyptologist, began an explanatory series in the church magazine, *Improvement Era,* the precursor to *Ensign. Improvement Era* published sepia-toned photographs of the papyri. In 1967 Thomas Stuart Ferguson, well-known amateur LDS archaeologist, provided photographs of the Smith papyri to Henry L. F. Lutz and Leonard H. Lesko, both Egyptologists with the University of California at Berkeley. Both quickly identified the fragments as from an Egyptian *Book of the Dead.* At this time there were as yet no qualified Mormon Egyptologists. *Dialogue* devoted much of 1968 to studies on the subject, turning to qualified non-Mormon Egyptologists to translate and analyze the newfound papyri.

The 1968 articles by Egyptologists such as John A. Wilson and Klaus Baer at University of Chicago's Oriental Institute, and Richard A. Parker of Brown University, agreed with all the earlier scholars' findings: the

English content of the Book of Abraham was unrelated to the content of either the three facsimiles printed with it or to the papyri Joseph Smith had used. The facsimiles and the papyri were Egyptian funerary documents of a fairly common type, and the papyri could be dated from about 100 B.C., some 2,000 years after the time of Abraham. Facsimile No. 1 was based on fragment No. 1 and fragment No. XI, which had originally been joined. Missing parts in the figures of fragments Nos. 1 and XI had been incorrectly restored to produce the Abraham facsimile No. 1.

In addition, it was clear that the *Egyptian Alphabet and Grammar* had been the Smith working documents for producing Abraham. Columns of characters taken from the papyri appeared with English text used in Abraham, content that had nothing to do with the Egyptian original. I. E. S. Edwards, an Egyptologist at the British Museum, wrote that Smith's *Egyptian Alphabet and Grammar* "reminds me of the writings of psychic practitioners which are sometimes sent to me."

In time the LDS Church produced several fully credentialed Egyptologists of its own. The most accomplished is Stephen E. Thompson of Brown University, the only one to establish a full-time career in his specialty outside of the church and its institutions. Thompson's conclusions resemble those of the other scholars. Comparing the facsimiles against the text of the Book of Abraham, Thompson described the text, in *Dialogue* in 1995, as "not in agreement with the meanings which these figures had in their original, funerary, context." He also finds that the text of Abraham presents some historical problems with its use of several anachronistic names such as the title "Pharaoh," which is not attested until 1504 B.C., centuries after Abraham. In addition, Thompson considers the "account of the attempted sacrifice of Abraham extremely implausible" and concludes, "I see no evidence that Joseph Smith had a correct conception of 'Egyptian religious practices' or that a knowledge of such was essential to the production of the Book of Abraham."

The LDS response has largely been twofold: much of the papyri Smith used in producing the Book of Abraham is still missing; or else translation for the prophet did not mean finding linguistic equivalents from one language to another—the papyri served as a sort of mnemonic device or catalyst to inspire him toward revelatory work. In other words, the papyri should be severed from any direct relationship to the content of the Book of Abraham in spite of the three facsimiles always published with it in the LDS scriptures. The known existence of Smith's *Egyptian Alphabet and Grammar* and Smith's extensive journal entries about his own translation work make the catalyst theory particularly difficult to sustain.

"No one ever suggested explanations like that—the idea that the papyri was a catalyst for inspiration or a mnemonic device—before November 1967," comments Stan Larson, late of the church translation staff and now a University of Utah librarian. "They had to find new explanations to account for the Book of Abraham, after-the-fact explanations."

The Columbia University historian Richard Bushman, a loyal Mormon, is willing to accept Abraham on faith, by moving to a revisionist position about its translation. He thinks Smith's discovery of the Egyptian writings "was an occasion for inspiration in a broader sense than word-for-word translation. So far there's nothing to support it as a literal translation." Bushman thinks the work does have an "Israelitish ring."

Mormon defenders of Abraham speak of the book's literary beauty, its doctrinal importance, and its apparent fidelity to ancient Near Eastern, especially Hebrew, culture. Non-Mormon critics find it baffling to conceive of the Hebrew God using pagan papyri as a source for Judeo-Christian inspired scripture.

Klaus Hansen, an LDS history professor at Queen's University, Ontario, mused about the effect of the Abraham problems in a 1970 *Dialogue* piece:

> Mormons, of all people, ought to remind themselves that religion is not based primarily on reason or logic. To a professional historian, for example, the recent translation of the Joseph Smith papyri may well represent the potentially most damaging case against Mormonism since its foundation. Yet the "Powers That Be" at the Church Historian's Office should take comfort in the fact that the almost total lack of response to this translation is uncanny proof of Frank Kermode's observation that even the most devastating act of disconfirmation will have no effect whatever on true believers. Perhaps an even more telling response is that of the "liberals," or cultural

Mormons. After the Joseph Smith papyri affair, one might well have expected a mass exodus of these people from the Church. Yet none has occurred. Why? Because cultural Mormons, of course, do not believe in the historical authenticity of the Mormon scriptures in the first place. So there is nothing to disconfirm.

Hansen appears to be correct in his opinion that the average Mormon is untouched by the controversy. A 1995 book by H. Donl Peterson of the Church Educational System, *The Story of the Book of Abraham,* goes on for 302 pages about mummies and Egyptian digs, who Chandler was and how he acquired the items, the way the ancient corpses were saved from thieves in Kirtland and displayed in Nauvoo, and the details about Atiya's discovery. It briefly speculates about missing papyri, then disposes of the findings of Egyptologists with one sentence: "Several of Joseph Smith's explanations are similar to interpretations of some Egyptologists, but some are not." Without further elaboration, Peterson reminds his readers that "Egyptology is not an exact science." He cautions, "Our understanding will be faulty until we have the entire text with which Joseph Smith was working."

Though the Book of Abraham presents several distinctive doctrines that are important to Mormonism, it is Doctrine and Covenants that is central to the everyday life and organization of the church. Students undergo required D&C coursework in high school seminary and college-level institute classes. The present-day LDS Doctrine and Covenants is a compilation of 138 revelation chapters and two special declarations. The vast majority—133—came from Joseph Smith. Others came from Oliver Cowdery (chapters 102 and 134), Brigham Young (136), John Taylor (135), and Joseph F. Smith (138). The compilation is not strictly chronological and reflects some editing changes over the years. The two declarations are the 1890 Manifesto on polygamy issued by Wilford Woodruff and the 1978 statement ending racial discrimination in the priesthood, issued under Spencer W. Kimball.

The revelations embody the church's principle of continuing revelation: the First Presidency and the Quorum of the Twelve affirm a new revelation, which is presented to the membership at General Conference to be unanimously "sustained." Three revelations have been added in the twentieth century: D&C 137—an 1836 Joseph Jr. vision of the Celestial Kingdom; D&C 138—a 1918 vision of the redemption of the dead by President Joseph F. Smith a few weeks before his own death; and the 1978 priesthood declaration. The two visions were canonized into the Pearl of Great Price in 1976 and moved into the D&C five years later.

Concerns in the early years reflect church organizational matters and Smith's need to establish his unique prophetic authority. It was a period when many claimed revelations and visions, and Smith hastened to assert that he alone held the keys. Unlike the Book of Mormon, in these revelations Smith is the Lord's mouthpiece, delivering the commands in the first-person voice.

"I, the Lord, am God, and have given these things unto you, my servant, Joseph Smith, Jun., . . . And you have a gift to translate these plates; . . . I have entrusted unto you, my servant Joseph, for a wise purpose in me, and it shall be made known unto future generations; . . . And to none else will I grant his power, to receive this same testimony among this generation," proclaimed a March 1829 revelation (D&C 5:2, 4, 9, 14). This concept would be repeated from time to time: "But, behold, verily, verily, I say unto thee, no one shall be appointed to receive commandments and revelations in this church excepting my servant Joseph Smith, Jun., for he receiveth them even as Moses" (D&C 28:2; September 1830); there is "none other appointed" to receive revelations that speak for the church (D&C 43:1–6; February 1831).

Early revelations included the testimony of the Three and Eight Witnesses to the Book of Mormon (5 and 32); concern about missions because the "field is white already to harvest; therefore, whoso desireth to reap, let him thrust in his sickle with his might, and reap while the day lasts" (D&C 6:3; April 1829); establishment of the Aaronic priesthood (section 28); and incorporation and administrative organization of the church itself (section 20; April 1830).

As time passed, the revelations ranged from missionary assignments (the first mission to the Lamanites, American Indian tribes, is assigned in section 32; October 1830) to the practical advice for missionaries to go about two by two (section 52; 1831). Mundane matters included caring for widows and orphans (179), administering the Bishop's Storehouse (78), and organizing economic affairs (104).

The Lord stressed the importance of keeping careful written church records (102 and 127). The concern for written records included appointing a church historian (21, 47, and 69) as well as a command to collect and keep careful track of anti-Mormon literature ("all that are in the magazines, and in the encyclopedias, and all the libelous histories that are published, and are writing, and by whom, and present the whole concatenation of diabolical rascality and nefarious and murderous impositions that have been practised upon this people"; D&C 123:5), an order Mormons continue to take seriously.

Some of the revelations are simply announcements of appointments to office. Others cover issues of governance such as tithing, church conferences, information about the priesthood, missionary callings, duties of bishops, organization of the First Presidency, and commands to build temples. American geography enters scripture through these revelations: Smith located the Garden of Eden in Jackson County, Missouri, and prophesied that Adam would return there in the end times (116); Independence, Missouri, was singled out as the "Center Place of Zion," the spot where the Lord will return one day (57). There is a time frame too: the temporal existence of the earth is given as 7,000 years (D&C 77:6). Meanwhile, the Saints are to obey civil law (58) and regard the American Constitution as divinely inspired (101).

A study of the Doctrine and Covenants is a walk through early Mormon church history: the temporary abode in Ohio; the persecutions in Missouri; the Zion's Camp expedition; the desire to seek redress of grievances; the trek to Utah. Practical concerns inspired revelations. Woven throughout are many words of spiritual guidance, pithy aphorisms of religious advice: "Seek not for riches but for wisdom" (D&C 11:7); "Without faith you can do nothing" (8:10); "Search diligently, pray always, and be believing, and all things shall work together for your good" (90:24); "He that trembleth under my power shall be made strong, and shall bring forth fruits of praise and wisdom" (52:17).

The millennial heritage of the church expresses itself in a dozen revelations. The elect are to be gathered because "the hour is nigh" (D&C

29:10); there will be plagues and desolations before the Second Coming of Christ; the elect are to be gathered to Zion; after the resurrection there will be judgment. These themes are repeated a number of times: in the end times there will be wars and rumors of wars; the righteous are to gather to Zion, and to prepare, and for the faithful there will then be nothing to fear.

Future predictions are usually left vague, with one significant exception: D&C 87, Smith's famous prophecy about the Civil War. Both the LDS high school seminary and college institute D&C course textbooks use this revelation as evidence that Smith was a prophet who spoke by divine inspiration. In this prophecy, issued December 25, 1832, Smith predicted that war would soon come, beginning in South Carolina, with slaves rising up against their masters, dividing North and South, and spreading into a world war.

However, Civil War fears and South Carolina's rebellion were much in the news in 1832, and "soon" was a matter of a twenty-eight-year wait. Four days before Smith's Christmas revelation, Eber D. Howe's *Painesville Telegraph,* published just twelve miles from Kirtland, had editorialized that "civil war" was at hand and that it was possible "our national existence is at an end." There were, of course, wars elsewhere in the world in the 1860s, but the American Civil War did not evolve into a world war. This prediction was not published until 1851, when it appeared in the Pearl of Great Price, then noncanonical. It was not canonized until 1876 when the LDS church added it to the D&C.

Embedded in the D&C are many revelations containing doctrines central to the Mormon faith. The theology of God is discussed in section 20 and further explored in depth in sections 91, 130, and 132. Celestial marriage and polygamy are discussed in sections 131 and 132 (with the Lord admonishing Emma to obey and accept it). Other topics include baptism for the dead, exaltation (progression toward holiness in the afterlife), angelology, the nature of heaven, and proclamations that the restored church is the one true church.

How "open" is the canon of revelation? One early dissident was David Whitmer, one of the original Three Witnesses, who began to have severe doctrinal disagreements with Smith around 1835 and was excommunicated in 1838. Whitmer tried to establish a church under his own leadership and always maintained his Book of Mormon testimony. But he objected to the changes and additions to D&C, and in a late-in-life statement charged that "the meaning is entirely changed on some very important matters; as if the Lord had changed his mind a few years after he gave the revelations." In the twentieth century, however, changes were infrequent.

The open-canon principle, and Smith's translation work mentioned frequently in Doctrine and Covenants, point to the final book in the Latter-day Standard Works: the Bible. Missionary talks and proselytizing activities emphasize that Mormons share belief in the Bible with other Christians. For English-speaking Saints, the required Bible is that familiar old standard, the King James Version (KJV). The Bible is taught in Sunday school and studied in required seminary and institute courses. But the status of the Bible in Mormon usage can be understood only within the framework of Joseph Smith's concept of revelation.

For Smith, writes LDS scholar Philip L. Barlow, the Bible "was not the static, final, untouchable, once-and-for-all Word of God that it was for many antebellum Christians." Smith was profoundly affected by it, but for him it was "provisional, progressive, relivable, subject to refinement and addition, spoken as well as written, varied in its inspiration, and subordinate to direct experience with God."

The Mormon prophet himself had appeared by name in the Book of Mormon, the Lord declaring to the biblical Joseph in Egypt, "A seer shall the Lord my God raise up. . . . And I will make him great in mine eyes; for he shall do my work . . . bringing . . . the knowledge of their fathers in the latter days, and also to the knowledge of my covenants," and then the scriptural Joseph prophesied, "And his name shall be called after me; and it shall be after the name of his father" (II Nephi 3:6–8, 15).

For Joseph Smith, the Bible was not sufficient revelation; it was subject to his prophetic interpretations, changes, and additions. Because the Bible was not sufficient, and because Smith as prophet had direct access to divine inspiration, he produced further scripture to serve the needs of the latter days and restore the "plain and precious things" lost in the Great Apostasy of the early church.

The Book of Mormon, besides echoing King James diction, uses large sections of biblical materials, especially from Isaiah, Matthew, and

Hebrews, sometimes reworking the material and adding to it. Isaiah in the Book of Mormon has 433 verses, of which 199 are directly from the King James Version and 234 appear with changes. The D&C also draws heavily from biblical materials in individual verses and phrases.

The word "plagiarism" as sometimes used by critics seems inappropriate. When the "William Tell Overture" appears in Shostakovich's Symphony No. 15, for example, it is a musical quotation, not plagiarism: Shostakovich expected that sophisticated listeners would recognize Rossini. Similarly, the culture of Smith's day was immersed in biblical literacy in a manner hard to conceive of today, and the only English translation people used was the KJV. It was natural for the Book of Mormon, the D&C revelations, and other Smith writings to reflect that diction.

As the body of D&C revelations began to emerge, Smith felt the need to harmonize the Bible with his doctrinal developments, so he began work on his own "translation" of the Bible. "There are many things in the Bible which do not, as they now stand, accord with the revelations of the Holy Ghost to me," Smith wrote in 1843. A body of his Genesis additions, the Book of Moses (now part of the Pearl of Great Price canon), was written around the summer of 1830. With the help of scribes, Smith worked his way through the Bible from 1830 to 1833. His most extensive changes—both corrections and additions—were in Genesis, Exodus, Isaiah, Psalms, Matthew, Luke, Romans, 1 Corinthians, Galatians, Hebrews, James, II Peter, and Revelation. Smith rejected Song of Solomon as inspired scripture, though the church includes it in the LDS edition of the King James Version along with a footnote giving Smith's judgment of the book.

Smith had no knowledge of biblical languages, so "translation" of these materials was clearly approached as revelatory inspiration. The full collection of his biblical writings is known as the "Inspired Version" or the Joseph Smith Translation (JST). By the time Smith produced the Book of Abraham, he had begun to take some Hebrew lessons. He was intrigued by his discovery that the one Hebrew designation for God, *Elohim,* is a plural noun.

Smith's *Elohim* usage turns up in the Book of Abraham as a plurality of gods directing the creation of the world. Instead of the biblical "God created the heavens and the earth," Smith wrote (Abraham 4:1) that "the Gods organized and formed the heavens and the earth." His idiosyncratic use of *Elohim* in Abraham, and later in the "King Follett Discourse" of 1844, had no foundation in the text of his tutor, Rabbi Joshua Seixas. Seixas's *Grammar*, in an 1834 edition, defines *Elohim* in the standard Hebrew manner as "a singular noun with a plural form," normally interpreted in Judaism and in Christianity after it as an intensifier to stress magnitude, not as plurality of number.

Some of the themes that receive special emphasis in the Smith version include extensive materials related to the Melchizedek priesthood, the Christian understanding of prophets in pre-Christian times, and Christ's Second Coming. The LDS scholar Robert J. Matthews lists twenty-three D&C revelations that contain doctrinal material directly related to changes that Smith made in his translation. In at least four D&C revelations, entire sections are directly from Smith changes in the Bible. Matthews emphasizes the importance of the JST for Mormon doctrines. The "pre-earth life, the degrees of glory in the resurrection, much information concerning Adam, Enoch, and the ancient patriarchs, of Cain, of the work of Satan, views of the Church respecting the Apocrypha, an explanation of the Revelation of John, the age of accountability, and probably also the doctrine of the eternal marriage covenant are associated directly with the translation of the Bible." The books of Abraham and Moses in the Pearl of Great Price bring additions to Genesis materials.

Some seemingly minor changes have larger implications. In Genesis 2:11–13, for example, Abraham tries to protect his comely wife Sarah from the Egyptian by instructing her to lie about their marital status. In the parallel account of the Book of Abraham (2:23–25), it is God who is the author of deception, telling Abraham to lie.

The JST was not published in Smith's lifetime. The manuscript remained with the prophet's widow Emma and was first published in 1867 by the Reorganized Church. For more than a century it was the official RLDS Bible, though in recent years the RLDS has backed away from exclusive endorsement of the JST. On the other hand, the Utah church has been moving closer to canonizing the JST. In 1968 the Reorganized Church gave Matthews access to the original manuscript of the Smith translation.

This was a critical juncture in LDS scriptural scholarship because the church was about to embark on a major project correlating all its standard works in an edition of the King James Bible that is now always printed with a complete interpretative apparatus that Mormonizes the Bible. Barlow in his study *Mormons and the Bible* credits Apostles Boyd Packer and Bruce McConkie with largely shaping the project, which "will continue to guide the Mormon mind for the indefinite future."

McConkie's *Mormon Doctrine* remains an all-time LDS best-seller. He did not know any of the ancient biblical languages. The cross-reference to the topic "Higher Criticism" in McConkie's *Mormon Doctrine* reads, "see Apostasy." Most Mormons remain aloof from such questions as the philosophy of interpretation or the principles of hermeneutics. Biblical materials are subject to Smith's revelatory changes, but miracles are interpreted literally. The Mormon approach to the Bible is an idiosyncratic blend of linguistic liberalism in defining inspiration combined with a strict literalism in matters pertaining to history, narrative, miracles, and the supernatural.

The new LDS edition of the Bible includes interpretative chapter headnotes written by McConkie; a Bible dictionary that Barlow calls "not really a Bible dictionary but a dictionary of LDS theology, conservatively construed, using biblical terms"; an LDS topical index; cross-references incorporating all the Mormon Standard Works; excerpts and footnotes incorporating all doctrinally important differences with JST material; and a gazetteer and maps.

An example of a "Mormonizing" McConkie headnote cited by Barlow is the summary sentence introducing Romans 4: "Man is justified by faith, righteous works, and grace." Writes Barlow, "Now, it is true that the Apostle Paul did have more to say about the importance of 'works' than is sometimes acknowledged by those in the Augustinian tradition, but this does not occur in the fourth chapter of the Epistle to the Romans."

After seven years' work this edition of the King James Bible was published in 1979. The King James Version is the required official LDS Bible; although this edition has not been "sustained" in the permanent canon, in practice it is regarded as the normative edition for use by the Saints. The church's 1979 edition of the KJV, with its notes and other apparatus, incorporated all the doctrinally important, distinctive changes that the prophet made in the Joseph Smith Translation.

The KJV will probably remain the official English biblical text for Mormons into the indefinite future. It is practical for missionaries, wrote Joseph Fielding Smith in the 1950s. Later the church's tenth president, he viewed the KJV as providing "a common ground for proselytizing purposes." Matthews echoed that sentiment in a 1995 Brigham Young University symposium, "As Translated Correctly": "As a missionary tool, for public relations reasons, a Bible that the world at least tentatively accepts such as the King James Version has advantages."

Unlike modern translations and editions by traditional Christians, this current Mormon edition was published without reference to scholarly considerations of the best available ancient manuscripts, the scholarly enterprise called "lower criticism." The Bible is actually the best-attested body of literature from the ancient world. The Codex Sinaiticus and the Codex Vaticanus (the latter lacking the last books of the New Testament) are full biblical manuscripts dating from circa A.D. 350. But there are thousands of other ancient New Testament texts or fragments and sixty other codices (complete books). The oldest are extensive portions dating from circa A.D. 200 and a fragment of John dated at A.D. 110 to 125. Some would date the Chester Beatty Papyrus II containing all of Paul's epistles except the three Pastorals as early as the late first century. The major Hebrew Old Testament "Masoretic" Texts include Codex Leningrad B, dated A.D. 1009. But the Dead Sea Scrolls, one thousand years earlier, preserve parts of all the Hebrew books except Esther, and all sixty-six chapters of Isaiah. There are other ancient texts in Greek, Syriac, and Aramaic.

All these ancient texts indicate that the text of the Bible we have has substantially been transmitted through the ages with surprising accuracy. Some of the New Testament fragments represent a shorter time span back to the biblical author than the time span from our day to Joseph Smith. As evidence for translation, all the ancient texts share in common support for the traditional Bible text; none support any changes introduced by Joseph Smith.

From the Mormon perspective, however, all of this, the entire scholarly enterprise of textual criticism, is irrelevant. In a canonized article of faith in the Pearl of Great Price, Smith wrote, "We believe the Bible to be the word of God as far as it is translated correctly." The standard of judgment applied to the Bible for "correct translation" is the revelations of the prophet Smith. "I believe the Bible as it read when it came from the pen of the original writers. Ignorant translators, careless transcribers, or designing and corrupt priests have committed many errors," Smith wrote.

"It is not scribal error that we are talking about, nor is it faulty translation," said Joseph Fielding McConkie, speaking at a 1995 symposium. In the view of McConkie, a BYU professor of ancient scripture, and the son of Bruce R. McConkie, parts of the original Bible are missing thanks to the "great and abominable church," which removed those parts as "deliberate, premeditated mischief." What is the evidence for this? McConkie said, "The restoration of the gospel is the most perfect evidence." In other words, the revelations received by Joseph Smith correct the traditional, faulty Bible, and the Smith revelations themselves are all the evidence the believer needs to prove this.

As would be expected with this perspective, Mormon scriptural scholarship functions almost entirely within an enclosed, intramural world. According to Barlow, there are no full-length Mormon commentaries on the Bible. Despite regular rotations of Sunday school study, he finds that, except for "brief proof-texts and favorite poetic passages," most modern Mormons "are not deeply familiar with the Old Testament once they pass Genesis and the first twenty chapters of Exodus, nor with the New Testament after the Gospel of John."

Mormon Bible scholars face serious problems. Stepping outside the enclosure is risky, as excommunicated scholars such as Stan Larson and David Wright discovered. Barlow observes, "Sensitive areas are studiously avoided by many scholars. And, unlike historians, Mormon biblical students have relatively few employment opportunities outside Church-owned facilities."

For the believer, it is a faith choice. In the words of the FARMS writer Kevin Christensen, it is a choice "between competing world views. Which community, if any, has authority? Should prophets take their license for seeing from the community of secular scholars? Must we have secular academia's permission to believe? Is personal spiritual experience valid?

Can we ignore scholarly and scientific opinion and survive as a faith? . . . What kind of faith should we have? . . . What, if anything, in this life deserves our commitment?"

These kinds of questions shape the life choices of the Saints, as they shape the life choices for all believers.

CHAPTER 18

"HOW GOD CAME TO BE GOD"

THE MOST RADICAL CHASM BETWEEN MORMON BELIEF AND THE ORTHO-dox Judeo-Christian tradition centers on the doctrine of God. This is the great divide.

"I am going to tell you how God came to be God," declared Joseph Smith in his "King Follett Discourse" of 1844, the theological culmination of his career. "God himself was once as we are now, and is an exalted Man. . . . If you were to see him to-day, you would see him like a man in form—like yourselves, in all the person, image, and very form as a man. . . . We have imagined and supposed that God was God from all eternity. I will refute that idea, and will take away and do away the vail, so that you may see. . . . The mind or the intelligence which man possesses is coequal with God himself. . . . Intelligence is eternal and exists upon a self-existent principle."

Joseph Smith's theology of God is summed up in an oft-quoted couplet by the fifth president of the LDS Church, Lorenzo Snow: "As man is, God once was. As God is, man may become."

This is "quite bizarre," was the reaction of Reverend Thomas Hopko, dean of St. Vladimir's Orthodox Theological Seminary, upon first reading the Follett sermon. In Hopko's view, the doctrines are not rendered less bizarre by the attempts of the LDS scholars Philip Barlow and David L. Paulsen to locate support for them in the writings of early church fathers. According to this Orthodox academic, writers like Barlow and Paulsen "just didn't understand" the patristic writers and the theological context of the early Christian church.

Educated Mormons are well aware that their doctrine concerning God the Father, particularly the idea that he was once a mortal man and has a literal body, is offensive to traditional Judeo-Christian believers. President Gordon B. Hinckley sidestepped the question in two 1997 interviews. Queried on that point by the *San Francisco Chronicle* religion writer Don Lattin—"Don't Mormons believe that God was once a man?"—Hinckley responded, "I wouldn't say that. . . . That gets into some pretty deep theology that we don't know very much about."

Hinckley's response was almost identical when the same question was posed by Richard Ostling (this book's coauthor) during an interview for the PBS *NewsHour with Jim Lehrer* and for *Time* magazine. Was God the Father once a man as we are? "I don't know that we teach it. I don't know that we emphasize it. I haven't heard it discussed for a long time in public discourse. I don't know all the circumstances under which that statement was made. I understand the philosophical background behind it, but I don't know a lot about it, and I don't think others know a lot about it."

On the other hand, addressing an in-house, all-Mormon audience shortly afterward at General Conference, Hinckley talked about media depictions of the church and, in an apparently pointed reference to those interviews, assured his listeners, "None of you need worry because you read something that was incompletely reported. You need not worry that I do not understand some matters of doctrine." He added, "I think I understand them thoroughly." His understanding audience laughed.

Mormons fear, with some justification, that their theology might be trivialized. When they pray, most typical Mormons probably do not consider themselves to be praying to a limited, contingent deity. And the church's "plurality of gods" doctrine does not translate into prayers addressed to any god other than God the Father (as some feminists have discovered, to their dismay, when they sought to invoke the Mormon mother in Heaven). The doctrine of exaltation—progression toward deification—is a doctrine of eventual human potential, not a declaration of arrival anytime in this life.

Paulsen, a philosophy professor at Brigham Young University, has written that there is no "comprehensive or systematic statement of authoritative Mormon theology," but the best approximation is the work of B. H. Roberts. He also says that Sterling McMurrin, the University of Utah philosophy professor, helped explain LDS beliefs in terms of traditional theological categories.

Roberts, in a famous 1901 exchange with the Jesuit priest C. Van Der Donckt, listed three "complaints" that traditional Christians have against the Mormon doctrine of God. These points still divide Mormons from the Judeo-Christian tradition:

First, we believe that God is a being with a body in form like man's; that he possesses body, parts and passions; that in a word, God is an exalted, perfected man.

Second, we believe in a plurality of Gods.

Third, we believe that somewhere and some time in the ages to come, through development, through enlargement, through purification until perfection is attained, man at last may become like God—a God.

Mormon religion generally is uncomfortable with paradox, and it is not grounded in a culture of professional-level theology, philosophy, or training in biblical languages. From its founding, the church has made a point of forbidding the development of any professional clergy "class." The church leaders responsible for declaring and interpreting doctrine, right up to the First Presidency, are prayerful, practical men with no professional training in religion studies. Although Brigham Young University does have some scholars trained in ancient biblical languages, philosophy, and religion studies, the General Authorities who define doctrine—even the most influential ones such as Roberts, James Talmage, Joseph Fielding Smith, and Bruce McConkie—are not professionally trained in these disciplines.

This lack of professional or scholarly training reaches back to the origins of the church. "The revelation of the Book of Mormon is not a glimpse of higher and incomprehensible truths but reveals God's words to men with a democratic comprehensibility," writes Thomas O'Dea in *The Mormons.* "'Plainness' of doctrine—straightforwardness and an absence of subtle casuistries—was for its rural audience a mark of its genuineness."

One: God as an Exalted Man

Mormon tradition, from Joseph Smith on, has tended to interpret literally the Bible's miracles and anthropomorphic descriptions of God. Roberts writes, "The Bible emphasizes the doctrine of anthropomorphism by declaring in its very first chapter that man was created in the image of God: 'So God created man in his own image, in the image of God created he him.'" Similarly, Mormons believe that the biblical passages where God speaks to his people "face to face" must mean that God has a literal image or face. The Mormon God is tangible and comprehensible. The Mormon scriptures say, "The Father has a body of flesh and bones as tangible as man's; the Son also; but the Holy Ghost has not a body of flesh and bones, but is a personage of Spirit. Were it not so, the Holy Ghost could not dwell in us" (D&C 130:22).

If a believer's understanding is uncorrupted by philosophy, according to Roberts, then the idea of man created in the image and likeness of God naturally tells us that man is the "counterpart of God in form." This leads to the God of flesh and bones described by Smith in his Follett sermon and in the Doctrine and Covenants, since the Son is "in the express image of [the father's] person," as in Hebrews 1:3. We know Jesus had a body, Roberts reasons; this verse tells us that God the Father must have had one too.

It follows that in Mormonism the incarnation of Jesus is not, in principle, a unique event. Roberts writes: "I think the main difference between the Latter-day Saints and 'Christians' on the subject of the incarnation, is that the Latter-day Saints believe that incarnation does not stop with the Lord Jesus Christ. Our sacred books teach that not only was Jesus Christ in the beginning with God, but that the spirits of all men were also with him in the beginning, and that these sons of God, as well as the Lord Jesus Christ, became incarnated in bodies of flesh and bone (D&C 93)."

Mormons believe that spirit is matter, and that those biblical passages implying that God is immaterial must be a mistranslation. Smith freely rewrote biblical passages that conflicted with his own concepts. Exodus 33:20 states, "And he said, Thou canst not see my face: for there shall no man see me and live." The Joseph Smith Translation changed that to: "And he said unto Moses, Thou canst not see my face at this time, lest mine anger be kindled against thee also, and I destroy thee, and thy people; for there shall no man among them see me at this time, and live, for they are exceeding sinful. And no sinful man hath at any time, neither shall there be any sinful man at any time, that shall see my face and live."

John 4:24 in the King James Version reads, "God is Spirit: and they that worship him must worship him in spirit and in truth." In the JST version this becomes, "For unto such hath God promised his Spirit. And they who worship him, must worship in spirit and in truth." The KJV of I John 4:12 reads, "No man hath seen God at any time." In Smith: "No man hath seen God at any time, except them who believe."

The Mormon God exists within time; in traditional Christian theology, God is outside time. Mormonism conceives of time as a line indefinitely extending back into the past and ahead into the future; in Mormon usage such terms as "infinite," "eternal," and "everlasting" are redefined and limited by being embedded within the context of this line. In traditional Christianity "eternity" and "infinity" are another realm, outside of this time line, and God's time is this other realm, beyond human time. He does not participate in sequential time, as we do. This leads some Mormon writers to describe the traditional Christian God as "static," a term perhaps more appropriately reserved for some conceptions of Buddha.

For Mormons, everything is matter and the elements are eternal. God, existing within the eternal of the Mormon time frame, organized the world out of chaos; the term "creation" in Mormon thought does not mean *ex nihilo,* out of nothing. Rather, God organized already existing matter.

Intelligence is also eternal in the Mormon understanding, and the intelligent spirit of man—in principle the same race of being as God—is on that same eternal line as God's. God has progressed to his present exalted state, passing through mortality in former times until his immortal body is incorruptible. We are God's spirit children. Our intelligence is coeternal with God's in our premortal existence. When we are born, we progress through the next stage, our mortal existence. In the next life we have the potential of progressing into immortality and becoming like God.

At a theological level, this belief results in a finite, limited deity. A God who progresses is a God who changes, and a God who progresses must be more powerful today than he was yesterday. Apostle John A. Widtsoe wrote in 1915: "God must have been engaged from the beginning, and must now be engaged in progressive development, and infinite as God is, he must have been less powerful in the past than he is today. . . . We may be certain that, through self-effort, the inherent and innate powers of God have been developed to a God-like degree. Thus he has become God."

The semi-official *Encyclopedia of Mormonism* continues in the same vein. God "the Father became the Father at some time before 'the beginning' as humans know it, by experiencing a mortality similar to that experienced on earth." The central point of this doctrine, according to the *Encyclopedia,* is that "Gods and humans are the same species of being, but at different stages of development in a divine continuum, and that the heavenly Father and Mother are the heavenly pattern, model, and example of what mortals can become through obedience to the gospel. . . . Knowing that they are the literal offspring of Heavenly Parents and that they can become like those parents through the gospel of Jesus Christ is a wellspring of religious motivation."

The most sophisticated explanation of the Mormon deity is in the writings of McMurrin, who delivered his ideas in "The Philosophical Foundations of Mormon Theology," an address given at BYU and four other campuses in 1957–58. McMurrin believed that Mormon theology, having "developed for the most part within concrete historical contexts" rather than from abstract metaphysics, dealt creatively with the most profound human questions. He also thought that Mormon beliefs present a more reasonable approach to the problem of evil than does traditional Christian doctrine.

In traditional Judeo-Christian doctrine, God creates the world and its laws. The universe and its creatures are contingent on him. God is "necessary being" in orthodox theology, and "only God has the ground of his being within himself," while in Mormonism "God is not the ultimate ground of all being" and "the human spirit has the foundation of its existence within itself."

The absolute power of the sovereign orthodox Christian God raises the moral problem of accounting for those elements in his creation that are, as McMurrin puts it, "not compatible with his goodness." Traditional theologians have to struggle with theodicy, the "great paradox" of Christian theology: how can a perfectly good, all-powerful, all-knowing God create an imperfect universe in which pain and evil exist?

In orthodox theology, according to McMurrin, "what is meant by eternal is not that God has an endless existence but rather that his being is timeless in that he is not involved in the temporal sequence of past, present, and future." For this kind of God, "all things happen simultaneously." So, in addition to raising problems of moral theology, this conception of eternity has an obvious effect on questions of history and human freedom. With this kind of God, where is free agency?

In Mormon theology, says McMurrin, "God is an embodied being with a spatially configured form." Mormonism affirms "the intrinsic worth of material things, including the human body," as well as "the ultimate value of temporal human enterprise." The future is not predetermined by God's present, as in traditional theology, and the responsibility for moral evil can be assigned to freedom of the will.

McMurrin also poses an interesting definition of "supernatural." The usual Christian definition of it is "that in miracle the supernatural intrudes upon the natural in such a way as to set aside the ordinary processes that are described by natural law." For Mormons, he says, "an event is miraculous only in the sense that the causal laws describing it are unknown." (James Talmage, the early-twentieth-century apostle-theologian, said substantially the same thing.)

Traditional Christian philosophy, writes McMurrin, stresses absolutes, following the influence of Greek philosophy. It provides a theology of God *being*. Mormon theology has more in common with "process theology": it is a theology of *becoming*. One difficulty is in satisfactorily tying a theology of *becoming* to an ethic of moral absolutes. Here McMurrin sees

Mormonism as pragmatic but leaning toward value absolutes. His lecture does not resolve the problem of how a philosophy of *becoming* can posit a moral philosophy of absolutes or normative ethics.

Mormon thinkers believe the LDS tradition is better equipped than traditional Christian theology to resolve the problem of evil since it does not posit the orthodox sovereign God. The usual question of how an all-powerful and loving God can allow the existence of evil does not exist, in the same way, with a limited deity. Eugene England, founding editor of *Dialogue,* likes McMurrin's description of Mormonism as a combination of liberal theology with a conservative personal ethic. For Blake Ostler, "rejection of absolute omniscience is consistent with Mormonism's commitment to the inherent freedom of uncreated selves, the temporal progression of deity, the moral responsibility of humans, and consequential denial of salvation by arbitrary grace alone." Traditional Mormonism denies the doctrine of original sin and stresses human free agency. Ostler writes, "God makes all things possible, but he can make all things actual only by working in conjunction with free individuals and actual entities."

On the other hand, if a finite God—a God with limits who did not create the world out of nothing—is off the hook on the question of being responsible for the existence of pain and evil, this leaves open another question: from where do we derive the principle of moral good? It is a difficult question if, as McMurrin seems to indicate, Mormonism favors the principle of an absolutist or normative ethic rather than a relativist or situational ethic. With a finite God, and a philosophy of progressive becoming, how does one introduce the idea of universals? How does one define moral goodness without the moral sovereignty of God?

Kim McCall examined the question of moral obligation in a Sunstone Symposium paper, contending that "morality, in Mormonism, is independent of the will and dictates of God." McCall holds the traditional Mormon belief that "God and man are the same type of being." He regards moral commandments as "revelations in which God enlightens us concerning truths independent of himself." He finds that what matters is "not the action," but "the reason it is being performed." In a sense, we make our own moral laws, test and revise them in practice, and through this "self-realization and moral development" we, like God, progress "in developing our moral intuitions and capacities."

A. Bruce Lindgren, now RLDS church world secretary, objected that McCall's analysis results in an antinomian, relativistic ethic. "If right and wrong do not carry moral obligation with them, then they are meaningless terms. . . . God is not the source of moral obligation. . . . In what sense, then, is God really God?" he asks. That kind of God "has become nothing more than Superman." Identifying himself as a conventional theist, Lindgren writes that he "cannot worship a God who is simply a reflection of the limitations found in human experience. Right and wrong have their ground in God."

The "omni" issue is a difficult one for Mormon theology. The Mormon God is a God who in some sense is finite and changes. Joseph Smith, in the famous "King Follett Discourse," said that God became God. Roberts writes, "God cannot be considered as absolutely infinite, because we are taught by the facts of revelation that absolute infinity cannot hold as to God; as a person, God has limitations, and that which has limitations is not absolutely infinite."

As O'Dea puts it: "Mormonism has developed the notion of a self-made deity, who through activism and effort has achieved a relative mastery over the world . . . a God whose transcendence is merely relative to human perception and whose relatively transcendent position with regard to man and other uncreated elements of the universe is the result of a conquest. God is God because he has risen to 'Godhood' by his own labor."

How does one describe the characteristics of such a God? Currently popular writings by such BYU scholars as Robert Millet, dean of religious education, and Stephen Robinson, professor of ancient scripture, borrow a conventional vocabulary to describe a God who sounds very traditional: omniscient (all-knowing) and omnipotent (all-powerful), with the physically omnipresent element provided by the Holy Spirit.

But their BYU colleague Paulsen expresses it differently in his Ph.D. dissertation in philosophy, contending that LDS "eternalism," the self-subsistent and uncreated quality of all matter, plainly entails the "finitism" of God, even though God is not explicitly characterized in this way. He relies on the thought of Roberts and others to deny that in the Mormon conception God is omnipotent, omniscient, immutable, omnipresent, or eternal, as those terms are defined in conventional discourse. God, writes Paulsen, "once dwelled on an earth and earned the honorific title 'God' through a process of growth and development." As he notes, this is "radically heretical" from the standpoint of Christian orthodoxy.

One obvious difficulty is how to balance absolutist descriptions against the Mormon theology of God as a being who is progressing. England, now a BYU English professor emeritus, always found "the doctrine of eternal profession in knowledge" to be "one of the reasons our ideal of becoming like God is so attractive . . . to experience the joy of learning forever."

England believes that Brigham Young and B. H. Roberts developed a concept capable of resolving the "apparent contradiction." In this explanation, "God is perfect in relation to our mortal sphere, has all knowledge regarding it, but is learning and progressing in spheres beyond ours that have nothing to do with ours—thus not endangering in any way his perfect redemptive plan and power in our sphere." With this, the believer can "talk of God as perfect and unchanging when praising him in regard to us and our sphere" and speak "of him as developing and enjoying new ideas and experiences when imagining the adventure of Godhood in spheres beyond ours," all the while remaining "right and orthodox" in LDS theology.

Writers such as England, Philip Barlow, and Blake Ostler believe that Mormonism should celebrate its own theological traditions as distinct from the absolutist God of the orthodox Judeo-Christian tradition. England fears that the absolutist vocabulary and ideas expressed by writers such as Robinson may be "part of [Mormonism's] accommodation to American ways which is influencing our theology rather than the other way around."

Ostler writes: "The classical idea of absolute omniscience reduces faith and hope in God to absurdity. For if God infallibly foreknows the future then prayer could not possibly influence him." Ostler believes that "the point is not his [God's] unlimited power and knowledge, but his purpose and love. . . . The classical definitions of timeless omniscience and unlimited power are quite irrelevant to one aspiring to understand his relationship to deity. Religious faith is more a function of intimacy than of ultimacy, more a product of relationships than of logical necessities."

In his view, the believer and God are "truly co-laborers." Mormon Christianity, he believes, celebrates a "personal and therefore finite God who makes a difference in human experience."

Two: The Plurality of Gods

The second "complaint" that B. H. Roberts addressed in his exchange with Van Der Donckt was the Mormon "plurality of gods" doctrine. This doctrine relates to Mormon beliefs about the godhead as well as the belief that men can become gods. Joseph Smith clearly introduced this idea when he declared that the biblical Genesis should be rewritten. In a revelation written from the jail in Liberty, Missouri (D&C 121:32), Smith spoke of the "Council of the Eternal God of all the other gods before this world was." In the Book of Abraham (4:1), the Genesis account becomes: "and then the Lord said: Let us go down. And they went down at the beginning, and they, that is the Gods, organized and formed the heavens and the earth." As previously mentioned, Smith's idiosyncratic understanding of the Hebrew plural *Elohim,* usually regarded as an intensifier to stress the magnitude of God, interpreted the term as indicating plural number.

In Mormon theology, the Father, Son, and Holy Spirit are tritheistic, three separate gods or personages, united in purpose. In the classical Christian Trinity, the three persons are united not only in purpose but in substance, as truly one monotheistic God. Mormons dislike the term "polytheism," generally regarded by non-Mormons as pejorative and pagan; some like to use the term "henotheism," meaning one head God who is worshiped as supreme while allowing for the existence of other gods.

Non-Mormons and many Mormons regard Smith's doctrine as having developed over time, with the Book of Mormon theology showing resemblances to Protestant thought in the late 1820s and early 1830s. In the view of these writers, the distinctives of Mormon theology largely stem from the Nauvoo period and continued development in Utah.

The deity as defined in 1830 (D&C 20:17) was "God in heaven, who is infinite and eternal, from everlasting to everlasting the same unchangeable God." The account of the First Vision that is canonized for today's Mormons was written by Smith in 1838: in it the Father and the Son appear as two distinct personages. However, the earliest written account of the First Vision, penned in 1832, mentions the appearance of only one personage, without the "explicit separation of God and Christ," as pointed out by BYU Professor Thomas G. Alexander, who believes early Mormon theism resembled the Protestantism of that time.

The original version of the Book of Mormon called Mary "the mother of God, after the manner of the flesh." In 1837 this was altered to stress that Jesus was a separate, subordinate personage. The verse (I Nephi 11:18 in the current edition) was changed to read, "mother of the Son of God." Three other changes in the 1837 edition (I Nephi 13:40, I Nephi 11:21, 32) also tended to stress that Jesus is a separate personage from the Father.

According to Alexander, the Book of Mormon "tended to define God as an absolute personage of spirit who, clothed in flesh, revealed himself in Jesus Christ"; he cites Abinidi's sermon to King Noah (Mosiah 13–14) as an example. Much of D&C 20, dating from 1830, resembles traditional Christian creedal formulations, and D&C 20:28 seems to be a ringing endorsement of standard monotheistic trinitarianism: "Which Father, Son, and Holy Ghost are one God, infinite and eternal, without end."

Smith's "Lectures on Faith," delivered in 1834 and 1835, are another matter. Included in the scriptural canon from 1835 but removed in 1921, they appear to be ditheistic. In them Smith taught that there are "two personages who constitute the great, matchless, governing, and supreme power over all things— . . . They are the Father and the Son: The Father being a personage of spirit, glory and power: possessing all perfection and fullness: The Son, who was in the bosom of the Father, a personage of tabernacle, made, or fashioned like unto man." The Son is described as "possessing the same mind with the Father, which mind is the Holy Spirit, and these three are one." The Holy Spirit, in other words, appears to be an aspect of the Father, not a separate person or god.

Smith proceeded from this to the Book of Abraham, in which the plurality of gods is clear. The creation/organization of our world is carried out by "the Gods." The Trinity, as defined by the First Presidency in 1916, is now understood as three distinctly separate personages who share a common purpose, two with corporeal tabernacles.

Some Mormons, such as BYU's Robert Millet, deny that the original Book of Mormon taught traditional Christian theism. In Millet's view, the passages that speak of "oneness" in the godhood "need not imply trinitarianism." Millet argues that the New Testament was not clear about trinitarian formulations; they were imposed on the church by borrowings from Greek philosophy. In discussing the corporeality of God the Father, Millet notes that Smith rewrote John 4:24 (the "God is a Spirit" verse previously analyzed in chapter 17) by revelation in 1832.

Millet cites the second of Smith's "Lectures on Faith" as evidence that the prophet taught progressive exaltation early. In the human family "the extent of their knowledge . . . will depend upon their diligence and faithfulness in seeking after him until, . . . they shall obtain faith in God, and power with him to behold him face to face." This God, writes Millet, is clearly "one who desires to glorify his children and make them even as he is."

Three: Men Becoming Gods

This brings us to the third "complaint" that Roberts sought to address: that, through development, progression, and purification, man may become a God. In early Mormonism, this may have resembled the Methodist and Arminian view of sanctification, a doctrine of man's potential perfectibility through free choice with the help of God's grace. But Methodist sanctification was thoroughly trinitarian and retained a distinction between the creature and the creator. In Mormonism man has the potential for actual godhood through the doctrine of eternal progression, sometimes called exaltation or deification.

In recent years several Mormon scholars have sought validation for their belief in deification by citing evidence in C. S. Lewis, Eastern Orthodoxy, and the writings of the early church fathers. The Mormon scholar Philip Barlow calls Lewis possibly "the most interesting modern adherent of the possibility of human exaltation." Barlow finds the concept of deification "utterly ubiquitous" in Lewis's writings.

Lewis, the twentieth century's best-loved and most influential apologist for traditional Christianity, is quoted so often that he is practically an honorary Mormon. Those who cite him include the late President Ezra Taft

Benson, current Apostles Dallin Oaks and Neal Maxwell, and BYU Professors Hugh Nibley, Robert Millet, and Stephen Robinson. A number of Lewis titles are stocked in Deseret Book stores. The book *Mormons on the Internet* lists a C. S. Lewis home page with the description: "Yeah, yeah, so he wasn't technically LDS. But his personal theology continues to speak to LDS beliefs to such a degree that he certainly deserves the status of honorary member."

Typical Lewis citations chosen to support deification include this one, from *Mere Christianity*, tucked by Robinson into an *Encyclopedia of Mormonism* entry: "He [God] said (in the Bible) that we were 'gods,' and He is going to make good His words. If we let Him—for we can prevent Him, if we choose—He will make the feeblest and filthiest of us into a god or goddess, dazzling, radiant, immortal creature, pulsating all through with such energy and joy, and wisdom and love as we cannot now imagine."

Another frequently encountered Lewis citation is this one from *The Weight of Glory:* "The following Him is, of course, the essential point. . . . It may be possible for each to think too much of his own potential glory hereafter; it is hardly possible for him to think too often or too deeply about that of his neighbour. . . . It is a serious thing to live in a society of possible gods and goddesses, to remember that the dullest and most uninteresting person you talk to may one day be a creature which, if you saw it now, you would be strongly tempted to worship. . . . There are no *ordinary* people. You have never talked to a mere mortal."

Referring to these quotes as expressing Lewis's belief in the Mormon deification doctrine, Robert Millet in *The Mormon Faith: A New Look at Christianity* asserts that Lewis "taught this notion."

Did he? The real C. S. Lewis was aware of the Book of Mormon and assumed that Joseph Smith wrote it. Evan Stephenson, concerned that some Mormon scholars had made Lewis into a crypto-Mormon to the detriment of strengths in LDS distinctives, and had failed to understand the context within which Lewis actually wrote, contributed a corrective essay in a 1997 issue of *Dialogue.* The list of theological differences is long, and "one would sooner fit a camel through the eye of a needle than pour C. S. Lewis's wine into Joseph Smith's bottles," says Stephenson.

Lewis did write a number of passages that do appear to express deification, but all of them are within a context of maintaining the unbridgeable gap between creature and creator, who are "different instruments." Man has no luminosity of his own; he is only capable, through grace, of functioning as a clean mirror to reflect the brightness of God. Lewis developed his moral theology from the classical concepts of natural law and grounded his concept of good in God. Building on traditional orthodox Christian theology, Lewis believed that good is absolute and uncreated, and that evil is not the opposite of good; he believed that evil is the perversion of good.

In contrast to Mormon theology, Lewis's God transcends time and is the immaterial being of orthodox theism. The British don frequently and vigorously disputed the idea of a God defined with literal anthropomorphic characteristics. Such a God is one for "simple-minded" people who are "savages" rather than believers in an "adult religion." "In C. S. Lewis, Latter-day Saints do not find a unique figure who mirrors their own theology," Stephenson writes.

In "Christian Apologetics," Lewis, an Anglican who believed in the theology of the *Book of Common Prayer,* including its thirty-nine Articles of Religion, proclaimed his own faith to be "the faith preached by the Apostles, attested by the Martyrs, embodied in the Creeds, expounded by the Fathers," that is, the conventional, historic faith of traditional Christianity. That was in 1945, in a paper delivered at a conference for Anglican priests and youth leaders. He described God the same way in *Letters to Malcolm: Chiefly on Prayer* (1963), his last major religious work. Lewis's definition shows the clear difference between classical Judeo-Christian theism and the God of Smith's "King Follett Discourse."

God, Lewis writes, is "the Unimaginably and Insupportably Other." In contrast to the progression in Mormon doctrine, Lewis believes that "in Him there is no becoming." The difference between God and his creatures is a difference of kind, not a difference of degree: "All creatures, from the angel to the atom, are other than God; with an otherness to which there is no parallel: incommensurable. The very words 'to be' cannot be applied to Him and to them in exactly the same sense."

Mormon writers, including such leading current scholars as Millet, Robinson, Paulsen, and Ostler, generally criticize this definition of God as one corrupted by Greek philosophy during the "Great Apostasy" in the early centuries of the Christian church as it strayed from the primitive truths of New Testament days. In this, Mormon theology resembles the intellectual critique made by some liberal non-Mormons and taught in many university graduate schools of religion.

Traditionalist scholars disagree with this interpretation. The early church fathers did not import Greek categories wholesale, they maintain; the patristic writers picked and chose carefully, baptizing and transforming what was necessary to develop the church's theology within the bounds of the New Testament. "The idea was cut to fit the Christian faith," writes the English patristics scholar G. L. Prestige, "not the faith trimmed to square with the imported conception. Conceptions of pagan philosophy were radically altered in their Christian context, and not seldom utterly discarded after trial."

Similarly, according to patristics scholar John Meyendorff, a professor at St. Vladimir's Seminary (Orthodox) and at Fordham University (Catholic), adapting Greek words and concepts to the needs of Christian experience was "not simply a verbal adjustment but a radical change and transformation of the hellenic mind. . . . The confrontation between the Academy and the Gospel ended with the reality of Christian Hellenism, not hellenized Christianity."

The New Testament LDS proof text used in support for deification is Matthew 5:48: "Be ye therefore perfect, even as your Father which is in heaven is perfect." Mormons interpret this as New Testament foundation for exaltation in eternal progression. Their writers, such as the BYU professors Daniel C. Peterson and Stephen D. Ricks in a 1988 issue of *Ensign*, often express a kinship to Eastern Orthodoxy in that branch of Christendom's use of the term "deification." Peterson and Ricks trace deification to such early church fathers as Irenaeus (second century A.D.) and to the notion of *theosis*, which is "very much alive" in the Greek and Russian Orthodox Churches.

The embrace, however, is one way. The Eastern Orthodox tradition is also firmly rooted in a distinction of kind, rather than of degree, between man and God. "The idea of deification must always be understood in the light of the distinction between God's essence and His energies. Union with God means union with the divine energies, not the divine essence," writes Timothy Ware (Bishop Ware), Spalding Lecturer in Orthodox Studies at Oxford University, in *The Orthodox Church*. "The human being does not become God *by nature,* but is merely a 'created god,' a god *by grace* or *by status.*"

Bishop Ware has elaborated on Orthodoxy and deification in response to a query:

> It is clear to me that C. S. Lewis understands the doctrine of *theosis* in essentially the same way as the Orthodox Church does; indeed, he probably derived his viewpoint from reading such Greek Fathers as Athanasius. On the other hand, the Mormon view is altogether different from what Lewis and the Orthodox Church believe.
>
> Orthodox theology emphasizes that there is a clear distinction— in the current phraseology "an ontological gap"—between God the Creator and the creation which He has made. This "gap" is bridged by divine love, supremely through the Incarnation, but it is not abolished. The distinction between the Uncreated and the created still remains. The Incarnation is a unique event.
>
> "Deification," on the Orthodox understanding, is to be interpreted in terms of the distinction between the divine essence and the divine energies. Human beings share by God's mercy in His energies but not in His essence, either in the present age or in the age to come. That is to say, in *theosis* the saints participate in the grace, power, and glory of God, but they never become God by essence.

Citing the early church fathers in support of the Mormon deification/exaltation doctrine has become a frequent theme among Mormon apologists toward the end of the twentieth century. Barlow writes that Irenaeus and Clement seem to provide "the earliest lucid and indisputable formulations of the divinization (*theosis*) view of salvation which have been preserved to us." He cautions that some of the allusions he uses may have "only verbal similarities to Mormon understandings of exaltation," but he goes on to affirm the "affinities" as "striking."

Robert Millet, speaking at a 1998 Church Educational System Fireside, said, "A study of Christian history reveals that the doctrine of the deification of man was taught at least into the fifth century by such notables as Irenaeus, Clement of Alexandria, Justin Martyr, Athanasius, and Augustine." Stephen Robinson in his books *Are Mormons Christians?* and *How Wide the Divide?* cites such patristic authors as Irenaeus ("'Ye are gods; and all of you are sons of the Most High.' . . . For it was necessary at first that nature be exhibited, then after that what was mortal would be conquered and swallowed up in immortality") and Athanasius ("'The Word was made flesh in order that we might be enabled to be made gods . . .' ").

But non-Mormon scholars specializing in the patritistic era say the basic theological assumptions that lie behind those quotes—the assumptions of the patristics and of Mormon theology—are radically and fundamentally different. Millet's Fireside address, for example, expressed standard Mormon orthodoxy when he said, "God is not of another species." Traditional Christian scholars say the God of the early church fathers is monotheistic, always the self-existent creator of another species.

A non-Mormon contrast: "The gulf is never bridged between Creator and creature," writes patristics scholar G. L. Prestige. "Eternal life is the life of God. Man may come to share its manifestations and activities, but only by grace, never of right. Man remains a created being: God alone is *agenetos* [uncreated]."

Queried about whether the early church fathers support the Mormon doctrine of deification, Yale professor emeritus Jaroslav Pelikan pointed to his discussion and definition of *theosis* in his Gifford Lectures (1992–1993). In this, according to Pelikan, "It was as essential for *theosis* as it was for the incarnation itself not to be viewed as analogous to Classical Greek theories about the promotion of human beings to divine rank, and in that sense not to be defined by natural theology at all; on such errors they pronounced their 'Anathema!'" In defining *theosis* Pelikan cites John Meyendorff and Georges Florovsky.

That man remains a created being, while God alone is uncreated, is a point Pelikan emphasizes in a discussion of Athanasius (fourth century A.D.): "Athanasius was the spokesman for the Eastern tradition that God the Logos had become man in order that men might become God; but if this was to be the gift of his incarnation and if man was to be rescued from the corruption that so easily beset him, it was indispensable that 'the Logos not belong to things that had an origin, but be their framer himself.'"

Man, according to Athanasius in *Ad Afros,* "cannot become like God in essence. . . . But a mutable thing cannot be like God who is truly unchangeable, any more than what is created can be like its creator." For Athanasius, man is a contingent creature and remains such. In *De Decretis* he writes: "Yet does God create as men do? Or is His being as man's being? Perish the thought. . . ."

Irenaeus (second century A.D.) also writes that God is uniquely self-existent, the one who created *ex nihilo.* "The rule of truth which we hold," he writes, "is, that there is one God Almighty, who made all things by His Word, and fashioned and formed, out of that which had no existence, all things which exist." God "commands all things into existence."

Irenaeus teaches that "God is always the same and unbegotten." He stresses that "in all things God has the preeminence, who alone is uncreated, the first of all things, and the primary cause of the existence of all, . . . being in subjection to God is continuance in immortality, and immortality is the glory of the uncreated One." The Uncreated One is perfect; man makes progress "approximating" to God. But man remains a contingent creature; he does not in essence become God, and God in the patristics writings has never been man.

Humans participate "in the divine activities by faith, through grace," says St. Vladimir's dean Thomas Hopko. The idea that "God himself was human" is not "classical Christian belief." Hopko says that for the ancient Greek fathers, deification clearly meant only that humans "can have divine qualities" or share in "divine life. Other terms for this are participation, resemblance, communion, imitation—becoming imitators of God." He regards the writings of Mormons such as Barlow and Paulsen as a search for patristic proof-texts. "They were trying desperately to find justification for their idiosyncratic teaching in the fathers."

It seems clear that support for the Mormon doctrines of a corporeal and limited God, eternal progress, and deification cannot be found in Eastern Orthodoxy, the early church fathers, or the twentieth-century writings of C. S. Lewis. On the other hand, the idea of eternal progression, which has some parallels with nineteenth-century liberal Christian thought and twentieth-century process theology, is deeply embedded in Mormon doctrine. Behind that lies a philosophical potential of genuine creative subtlety that Mormon thinkers, drawing on their own doctrinal history, are developing into a theological heritage of considerable depth and complexity.

CHAPTER 19

ARE MORMONS CHRISTIANS? ARE *NON*-MORMONS CHRISTIANS?

"THE GOOD NEWS IS THAT MORMONS AND EVANGELICAL CHRISTIANS aren't as far apart in their theology as some of us had supposed. The bad news is that Mormons and Evangelical Christians aren't as far apart in their theology as some of us had supposed."

The wry words are from Eugene England, founding editor of *Dialogue* and a retired BYU professor. He is evaluating *How Wide the Divide?*, and he is ambivalent. *How Wide the Divide?*, published in 1997 by the Evangelical InterVarsity Press, is a dialogue between Craig L. Blomberg of Denver Seminary (Conservative Baptist) and Stephen Robinson of BYU, who first met at an annual meeting of the Society of Biblical Literature, the professional association of Bible scholars. England appreciates the "gracious spirit" of the conversation as a model for interfaith discussion between two old warring religious camps. But he is wary. Blomberg clearly remains an Evangelical, and England thinks Robinson may have given away too much.

Behind the polite dialogue lies an old and impolite question. Conventional Christians ask, "Are Mormons Christian?" and in asking think they already know the answer. And Mormons think they have a better, if unspoken answer. They are not only Christians, they are the *only* true Christians, and their church is the *only* true church of Jesus Christ.

"It is time for some folks on both sides to lower the rhetorical level, even if doing so entails risk. This book makes a strong move in that direction," says Richard J. Mouw, reviewing the same work for *Books and Culture.* "As Robinson would have it, Mormons certainly do believe more than the New Testament's presentation of the gospel, but they do not believe less. . . . I need more convincing." Mouw is president of Fuller Theological Seminary, the nation's largest interdenominational Evangelical seminary. He concludes, "This book should be carefully studied by anyone who is convinced that such a dialogue is a good and important thing to pursue."

But Mouw, too, is wary, especially of Robinson's Evangelical-sounding rhetoric, because of the "larger set of beliefs and practices in which [his] confession is nested." He warns, "Confusion about who God is and who we are before the face of that God is a very serious business."

How Wide the Divide? is a debate on four topics: scripture; the nature of God and the deification of believers; the deity of Christ and the Trinity; and salvation and the eternal state. Each author writes separately about each topic, and there is a joint conclusion about areas of agreement and disagreement. The book has sold well through the Deseret Book chain and Evangelical outlets.

Both authors acknowledge the mutual distrust in their respective histories. Blomberg, for example, remembers that when the Denver LDS temple opened near his home in 1986, some Protestant Fundamentalists picketed, shouted taunts, even threw stones. On the other hand, he notes, more recently some Mormons have slipped into the library at his seminary and stolen or damaged books considered to be anti-Mormon.

Reviewers on both sides have expressed ambivalence: pleased at the civilized discourse, they are nevertheless uneasy about the content of the presentation.

England, for example, is worried that Robinson tilts too much toward the Evangelical side in his handling of grace, works, and the atonement. Salvation, he writes, is "not a quid-pro-quo reward (or punishment) by God but a state of being (or lack thereof), of spiritual growth toward

Godhood achieved through whatever combination of grace and choice and effort best works for each of us." He dislikes Robinson's "scriptural literalism," finding that "he seems to want to define the resources for our theology much too narrowly."

Mouw reacts most strongly against Robinson's charge that traditional Christians have imposed Greek philosophical categories on the pure biblical understanding of the early Christian church. Any perspective can be analyzed in terms of its cultural context. The Book of Mormon, he points out, can be critiqued against the "striking affinities" with nineteenth-century Protestant liberalism in its "finite God, a perfectible humanity, and an emphasis on works righteousness."

The Greek formulations, according to Mouw, were "not impositions of alien philosophical categories but the result of a necessary search for words that would capture the sense of Scripture to guard against dangerous misreadings of the biblical text." He recommends John Courtney Murray's *The Problem of God* (1964) and argues, "If LDS thinkers want to claim biblical fidelity, they must argue, not that they alone come to the Bible unencumbered by philosophical commitments, but rather that their peculiar metaphysical constructs are more adequate explications of the biblical message than those of historic Christianity."

Other Evangelical reviewers were also cautious. One criticism, for example, is that Robinson claimed to believe every verse of the King James Bible while fudging the fact that Mormons interpret the "insofar as it is correctly translated" rule to make the Bible subject to the higher standard of Smith's scriptural writings. Francis J. Beckwith, a Trinity International University professor reviewing the book for the Evangelical *Christianity Today,* is dubious about the absolutes in Robinson's discussion of God. Those concepts do not correlate with the "finite, changeable, contingent God" of Smith's "King Follett Discourse," writes Beckwith.

Mouw's review is titled "Can a *Real* Mormon Believe in Jesus?" The very question touches a very sensitive raw nerve in Mormonism. Mormons obsess about the question "Are Mormons Christian?" A Mormon guiding a friend through the Salt Lake City visitors' center in Temple Square asked, with tears in her eyes, "Why do so many people say we are not Christians? How can they, when the Savior is central to our faith?" The friend paused and then responded, "But do you truly regard non-Mormon believers as fully Christian?" The Mormon, seemingly unaware of the quid pro quo in her answer, exclaimed, "But that's because we have the priesthood!"

Are Mormons Christian? "What could prompt such a question?" asked the Mormon scholar Philip Barlow of Hanover College, speaking at the 1998 Sunstone Symposium. "It's a bit like asking if African Americans are human." Barlow does not shy away from recognizing Mormonism as distinct, though Christian in intent at its core, but he thinks that Mormons should not minimize the difference for public relations and evangelistic reasons. After all, Joseph Smith called other churches apostate, and they have responded in kind. (Speaking on a later Sunstone panel, Barlow asked local Baptist pastor Mike Gray whether Baptists are Christian. In good Baptist fashion, Gray answered, "Not necessarily.")

Robinson wrote a full-length book aimed at an LDS audience asking the question *Are Mormons Christians?* to fortify the Saints with an answer. His BYU colleagues Robert Millet and Noel B. Reynolds put together a proselytizing booklet aimed at non-Mormons, *Latter-Day Christianity: 10 Basic Issues,* and the first section was titled "Are Latter-day Saints Christian?"

The big guns came out before the Southern Baptists arrived in Salt Lake City for their 1998 convention. Apostle Boyd K. Packer and Millet, the dean of religious education, gave February addresses at BYU to brace the students for the Baptist onslaught. Packer pointed to the Christian content of some Latter-day Saint hymns, the reference to Jesus Christ in the name of the church, and the testimony of every prayer and sacrament invoking the name of Christ. Christ, he pointed out, dominates the Book of Mormon, which has lately been subtitled Another Testament of Jesus Christ.

"One need not have answers to all [doctrinal] questions to receive the witness of the Spirit, join the Church, and remain faithful therein," Packer told the students. "Do not be ill at ease or uncomfortable because you can give little more than your conviction. . . . Be assured that, if you will explain what you know and testify of what you feel, you may plant a seed that will grow and blossom into a testimony of the gospel of Jesus Christ."

Millet's devotional address focused on questions the students might face: How does the LDS Church justify its additions to the canon of Christian scripture? What do the Saints believe about God and deification? What do the Saints believe about works and grace? And are the Latter-day Saints Christian?

Along the way Millet quoted from C. S. Lewis, a *Christianity Today* piece admiringly listing five reasons why the LDS is successful, and the British Evangelical scholar-pastor John R. W. Stott. Millet advised the students to avoid disputation, to know that adversaries may not really understand LDS teachings, and to remember that "the Bible is not the source of our doctrine or authority. . . . Ours is an independent revelation. . . . Some of our greatest difficulties in handling questions about our faith come when we try to establish specific doctrines of the Restoration from the Bible alone."

The Presbyterian Church (U.S.A.) is one of the few major denominations in recent times to study officially the question of whether Mormons are Christians. The project began with a national Presbyterian convention in Salt Lake City in 1990, with a follow-up study released in 1995. Presbyterian guidelines state that the LDS church "expresses allegiance to Jesus Christ in terms used within the Christian tradition" but nonetheless is not regarded as "within the historic apostolic tradition of the Christian Church."

Presbyterians are advised to treat Mormons as adherents of another religion, putting relations under the "interfaith" rubric. For instance, according to the guidelines, converts from Mormonism need to be rebaptized; Mormons should not receive Presbyterian Communion; and weddings and funerals involving mixed families are handled as "interreligious" rather than intra-Christian rites. A more sharply edged Utah Presbyterian report said that "it would be accurate to classify Mormon theology as polytheistic rather than monotheistic." It also said, "The only conclusion which can be reached is that the new and distinct religious tradition brought forth by the Mormon Church must be regarded as heretical."

The Saints universally resent it when outsiders consign them to non-Christian or semi-Christian status. They consider the very "Are Mormons Christian?" question an insult. At the same time, however, their own scriptures virtually forbid Saints to recognize that the great churches of

Christianity—Catholic, Orthodox, or Protestant—have any authentic claim to be Christian. Robinson, for example, has written that non-Mormons may have "opportunities to accept the gospel in the postmortal life," but that "the historical church no longer possessed the gospel" after the Great Apostasy.

Asked by an active Mormon whether he considered Mormonism to be "Christian," the ex-Mormon author Charles Larson responded, "I felt the proportion of orthodox Christians who considered Mormonism to be Christian was probably about the same as that of Latter-day Saints who considered orthodox Christianity acceptable in God's sight."

According to Joseph Smith's scriptural account of his 1820 First Vision, he asked God and Jesus which of the competing "sects" was correct. "I was answered that I must join none of them, for they were all wrong; and the Personage who addressed me said that all their creeds were an abomination in his sight; that those professors were all corrupt; that 'they draw near to me with their lips, but their hearts are far from me, they teach for doctrines the commandments of men, having a form of godliness, but they deny the power thereof.'"

In the Mormon understanding of history, the church literally disappeared shortly after Jesus' apostles died, although apostate human organizations perpetuated the false claim to be Christian. The same process of apostasy was repeated among the believers in the New World who were visited by the Mormon Jesus. There was no church on earth during a hiatus of some 1,700 years until God intervened to restore apostolic governance through the prophet Joseph Smith and his successors. Traditional Christians maintain that the Mormon historical lacuna is contrary to Jesus' New Testament promise that the Spirit would guide ("The gates of hell shall not prevail against [my church]"—Matthew 16:18) and that he would always be with the church ("Lo, I am with you alway"—Matthew 28:20).

Hugh Nibley, the emeritus BYU professor, is among those who have spelled out the LDS concept that the church existed for only a short time and dissolved into a severely corrupted form of belief, the Great Apostasy. Nibley contends that Jesus and the apostles expected this rapid end of the pure, primitive Christian church to occur. One indication, as Nibley reads the New Testament, was that the apostles showed "complete indifference . . . to the great business of converting the world" and failed "to leave behind them written instructions for the future guidance of the church"— a "colossal oversight" if they saw any future for the organization. He further contends that Christians in the ancient world rewrote church history by flagrantly fabricating, destroying, and altering the documentary evidence. Conventional historians, of course, present a radically different reading of the evidence, according to which the apostolic church was highly conversion-oriented and established the rudiments of organization that was to develop. Also, they do not find evidence of such flagrant documentary deceit.

The belief that all other purportedly Christian churches have fallen into error is the negative side of the Mormon equation. The positive side is the message that the one true church exists once again in these latter days. In an 1831 revelation to an Ohio elders' conference, now contained in the Doctrine and Covenants, Smith stated that those who received the Book of Mormon had "power to lay the foundation of this church, and to bring it forth out of obscurity and out of darkness, the only true and living church upon the face of the whole earth, with which I, the Lord, am well pleased."

Besides the Ohio revelation, the LDS scriptures are filled with other passages defining the Utah-based denomination as God's only church and the literal kingdom of God on earth. The scriptures cite specific criteria. For one thing, the true church must have "Christ" in its official name. For another, it must baptize youths by immersion at the age of responsibility (eight in Mormonism). Smith's scriptures are particularly insistent that infant baptism is a "mockery before God" and that those who believe in it are "in the bonds of iniquity" and "in danger of death, hell and an endless torment" (Moroni 8:9, 14, 21). That, of course, includes the vast majority of the world's Christians. In Mormonism the true church is believed to have unique power to exercise "the keys" of authority through the two priesthoods, which were restored through personal visitations in New York State by John the Baptist and then by the New Testament apostles Peter, James, and John.

Somewhat similar exclusivist claims used to be found in Roman Catholicism, but the Second Vatican Council clarified matters. The "unity of the one and only Church . . . subsists in the Catholic Church," the council said, but "significant elements" that give life to the church can exist outside the Catholic institution. Non-Catholics, in "certain, though imperfect, communion with the Catholic Church," are regarded as "Christians" and "brothers." Most orthodox Christians regard a baptism carried out with water in the name of the Trinity to be valid across denominational lines. Mormons regard only LDS baptism as valid, so that, for example, they would rebaptize a Presbyterian convert just as the Presbyterians rebaptize the Mormon convert. Each treats the other church as another faith.

On the negative side, the Mormon scriptures contain more than twenty passages denouncing the rest of Christendom as apostate. A typical passage, I Nephi 13, predicts the following course of Christian history. Gentiles form a "great and abominable church" whose founder is the devil himself. The false church takes away "many plain and precious things" from the scriptures and from the gospel. With Christ's true teaching no longer present, "an exceedingly great many do stumble, yea, insomuch that Satan hath great power over them." But in America, "the land which is choice above all other lands," God will again restore his message. In the following chapter, an angel summarizes the point: "Behold there are save two churches only; the one is the church of the Lamb of God, and the other is the church of the devil, . . . the whore of all the earth."

In the very influential, though nonofficial, tome *Mormon Doctrine,* the late Apostle Bruce R. McConkie gives a hard-edged interpretation of this teaching. He explains that there is a "simple test" to determine the authentic church: it will be named after Christ; display the Aaronic and Melchizedek priesthoods and the offices of apostle, prophet, and Seventy; practice such ordinances as baptism for the dead; and teach the latter-day restoration.

The universality of "apostasy" apart from Mormonism, McConkie writes, is seen in the fact that all other churches "believed falsely that God was a mystical spirit essence that filled the immensity of space and was everywhere and nowhere in particular present," rather than Mormonism's flesh-and-bones God. McConkie sets the "priesthood" of the true church over against "priestcraft," which is "of the devil." Except for its ethical teachings, "so-called Christianity does not come much nearer the truth in many respects" than Greek, Roman, or Norse mythology, says McConkie. "Believers in the doctrines of modern Christendom will reap damnation to their souls." Even the Reorganized Church, he teaches, is a mere "apostate faction."

Asked in an interview whether the LDS Church still believes what Smith stated about other churches in his First Vision, President Hinckley put the best face on matters: "We accept that as a statement which came to him, which is printed, of course, and published in his history as a statement. But we go forward with a friendly relationship, with a respect for people everywhere and with an effort to accept them as we meet them and, where opportunity exists, to talk with them and explain to them what we believe. . . . We don't criticize them for what they believe. We accept the good that comes of that understanding which they have, but we feel we have something to offer beyond what they have."

Well, then, could the LDS Church ever join Christian ecumenical organizations, or recognize the baptism of other churches as valid rather than rebaptizing all converts? Said Hinckley, "Anyone who wants to join this church must be baptized into this church. That's the rite of passage into this church. But that doesn't stop us from working with others. We work with other churches on social issues, on moral issues, on humanitarian issues."

Liberal Mormons like to point out the beliefs and spiritual insights they hold in common with non-Mormons, though the LDS Church cannot simply blend into the ecumenical landscape and, presumably, never will. For practical reasons, Saints do cooperate in some interfaith or ministerial organizations on the local level, but the denominational leadership has not pursued membership in world, national, or state councils of churches, nor is it clear that such councils would ever approve LDS membership, since Mormon teaching violates the basis of ecumenical fellowship. The LDS scriptures simply do not allow Mormons to view the others as legitimate churches. Separation, then, makes theological sense on both sides. As Hinckley indicates, that does not bar the Mormons from occasionally channeling humanitarian money through, say, Catholic Relief Services, or allying tactically with conservative Protestants and Catholics in specific political causes of mutual interest.

Proselytizing is, of course, a mutual stress point. The desire of each group to attract the other's sheep feeds an underlying edginess that is probably inevitable and permanent despite polite interfaith dialogue. The Southern Baptists in particular are uncomfortably aware that the greatest recent LDS growth in the United States has come on their own home turf. Mormons number nearly 700,000 now in the Southeast.

Within Mormonism today there appear to be important competing strands relating to such core doctrines as sin, grace, and the atonement, and how to express them. O. Kendall White Jr., a Washington and Lee University scholar, calls one such strand "Mormon neo-orthodoxy" in a book examining his own religious heritage. In this view, the cultural crises since World War II have produced, inside Mormonism as well as among non-Mormon Christian theologians, a perspective of pessimism. As a result, a more negative view of human nature has arisen, along with an increased emphasis on the aspect of sin in human nature. Related to this is more of an emphasis on the sovereignty of God and the contingency of man dependent on God.

In White's view, this change in cultural perspective has affected Mormon theology, which has moved away from its traditional optimism about the nature of man and the use of human agency in progressing toward perfectibility. The Mormons now speak more often in absolutist language and talk more of grace. White is concerned that "a quest for respectability, the pursuit of converts, and expansion of Mormonism throughout the world tempt contemporary Mormons, especially officials, to present Mormonism as mainline Christianity."

LDS apologists at FARMS hated White's book. The reviewer Louis Midgley called it a "fine example" of a book that fails to take the Book of Mormon seriously. White's "underlying assumption" is that faith "is challenged by modernity" and that "believers ought to reach an accommodation with modernity by adopting its assumptions and reflecting its values." Midgley criticized White for ignoring "notions of sin and dependence upon deity that are found in the Book of Mormon and in the early revelations to Joseph Smith." Midgley also criticized the research of the BYU history professor Thomas G. Alexander, who has shown changes in Smith's emphases in theology after 1835 and claims that the later Smith moved toward a more optimistic view of human potential.

Both camps claim to be speaking for "traditional" Mormonism, quoting proof-text support from LDS scriptures, the King Follett Discourse, and later prophets and apostles. Currently popular and influential within Mormonism, Millet and Robinson might be exponents of White's "Mormon neo-orthodoxy," though their writings became popular after the appearance of White's book. The vocabulary they employ when writing about sin, grace, and the atonement, and the *omni* words they use to describe God, sound very similar to the language of Protestant Evangelicals and other traditional Christians. Millet even uses the term "substitutionary" in discussing the atonement. Others, such as Paulsen, England, Ostler, and Alexander, stress the advantages in the concept of a limited deity that flow from the Follett sermon and other early Mormon writings. For instance, such a concept presents an optimistic emphasis and avoids traditional theology's aforementioned problem of theodicy, that is, how a sovereign God can be seen as loving when evil and suffering exist. It also stresses human free will.

Embedded in any Mormon discussion of grace and the atonement is an assumption that "men will be punished for their own sins, and not for Adam's transgression," one of Smith's Articles of Faith. All Mormon factions agree that LDS theology rejects the orthodox Christian doctrine of original sin, though Mormons do believe that all people sin on their own and need redemption through Jesus Christ.

A related theological issue is Christology—how one understands the person of Jesus Christ, the Redeemer. Mormonism clearly rejects the Christ of Christian orthodoxy, who is coeternal and coequal with God the Father and the Holy Spirit in the triune godhead. The Mormon Jesus is subordinate to the Father. Moreover, as the LDS adult Sunday school manual *Gospel Principles* teaches, Jesus is "literally our elder brother," since we are all "begotten and born of heavenly parents," though Jesus had the distinction of being God's firstborn. As McConkie's *Mormon Doctrine* explains it, "By obedience and devotion to the truth he [Jesus] attained that pinnacle of intelligence which ranked him as a God" even in his preexistent state. The divine Son became the creator (that is, organizer) of the earth and was chosen to work out the atonement, and is now "infinite in all his attributes and powers." But in Mormonism, unlike the whole of orthodox Christian theology, the Incarnation is not, in principle, a unique event.

All Mormons also unite in the belief that every human is a child of God by nature. Traditional Christianity teaches that humans are God's children by adoption, through grace, not by nature. In Mormonism humans are God's literal spirit children born in a premortal existence that is forgotten when they are reborn on earth. The *Encyclopedia of Mormonism* says that in the premortal life "individuals existed as men and women in a spirit state and thus coexisted with both the Father and the Son." Mormons believe "the intelligence dwelling in each person is coeternal with God. It always existed and never was created or made" (D&C 93:29). This is regarded as a "central doctrine of the church."

In Mormon theology, humans are given mortal existence and bodies in a state of probation. Marriage and procreation are central to exaltation. "We were placed here on earth to progress toward our destiny of eternal life," Apostle Dallin Oaks told a 1993 General Conference. "To the first man and woman on earth, the Lord said, 'Be fruitful and multiply.' . . . This commandment was first in sequence and first in importance. It was essential that God's spirit children have mortal birth and an opportunity to progress toward eternal life."

In Mormonism God is married. Like God, humans can progress to godhood, continuing their progression and procreation in the afterlife. The Mormon heaven is a very domestic concept, and celestial marriage is essential to exaltation. Humans are born into mortal life without sin but have free agency, and with this free agency they can exercise free will in making moral choices. Through these choices they can sin against moral law, but they can also choose obedience, celestial marriage with a family sealed for eternity, and progress toward godhood.

Mormons believe that Adam's fall was a good thing, not the tragic event of traditional Christian understanding. As Oaks put it, Adam and Eve "could not fulfill the Father's first commandment without transgressing the barrier between the bliss of the Garden of Eden and the terrible trials and wonderful opportunities of mortal life. . . . This transition, or "fall," could not happen without a transgression—an exercise of moral agency amounting to a willful breaking of a law . . . a planned offense, a formality to serve an eternal purpose."

Mormons distinguish between "transgression" and "sin." Adam's transgression was not sin.

The Mormon Articles of Faith state, "We believe that through the Atonement of Christ, all mankind may be saved, by obedience to the laws and ordinances of the Gospel." Mormons use the conventional rhetoric of the atonement and grace, but a genuine understanding of their atonement doctrine must flow logically from the implications of the unique LDS beliefs about the nature of humans as children of God and from their rejection of original sin. That is, if man is not sinful by nature, why is the atonement needed, and what is meant by grace? In traditional Christianity the atonement is necessary to counteract the consequences of original sin, the fall of Adam.

The First Presidency issued a formal statement on its theology of God in 1916; it never issued a formal statement of its theology of man. The lack of systematic theology affects other doctrinal areas as well. Though it is "bound to touch sensitive nerves," writes Keith E. Norman, there is not yet a "definitive doctrine of the Atonement in Mormonism." Mormon writing about the Atonement is "for the most part derivative from traditional Christianity." Norman, a Mormon with a doctorate in early Christian studies from Duke, writes that the Book of Mormon prophet Enos "prays for the redemption of others" and is "told that they must earn it on their own merits" (Enos 9–10).

In Mormonism, when sinners approach Christ "innocently suffering for *our* wickedness, our hearts are softened and we resolve to change our ways." Rather than the traditional absolutist deity, as Norman explains it, this "Mormon God is not the stern judge demanding payment. . . . We cannot become like God by letting someone else take responsibility for our actions. . . . Personal actions have personal consequences. Christ's role is not to let us off the hook, but to show us that it is possible to achieve holiness, to become perfect as God is perfect, to demonstrate how to do it, and to motivate us to follow his example."

Christ's suffering and atonement, then, were his expression of a powerful empathy for his brother, mortal humankind on earth. Men and
women are saved because his example moves their hearts to respond; this
grace, through the atonement, guides their lives and the moral choices
they make, through their free agency and in faith. God gives a sense of
justice and knowledge that enables us to choose the good, and salvation is
a process of becoming more like God. This view of sin and the atonement is very similar to that of liberal Protestant theology. (Mormons
believe in the literal bodily resurrection of Christ, however, and liberal
Protestants typically do not.)

For Mormons, Gethsemane is more central to the atonement than is
the cross. "Gethsemane was the scene of Jesus' greatest agony, even surpassing that which he suffered on the cross," says the *Encyclopedia of
Mormonism,* which considers Gethsemane to be Jesus' "most challenging
experience." According to the late church President Ezra Taft Benson, "It
was in Gethsemane that Jesus took on Himself the sins of the world."
The caption opening the "Atonement" chapter in *Gospel Principles* reads,
"In the Garden of Gethsemane, Christ took upon himself the sins of all
mankind." The lesson teaches: "The Savior atoned for our sins by suffering in Gethsemane and by giving his life on the cross." Mormons take literally the description of Christ's agony drawing sweat as blood in
Gethsemane.

Christ's suffering in Gethsemane was similarly explained by the BYU
philosophy professor emeritus Truman Madsen in an interview with
Newsweek's Kenneth L. Woodward. Mormons, Madsen said, stress the
cross less than "what happened in Gethsemane. You won't find a cross in
any Mormon chapel. That doesn't mean we don't believe he was crucified;
he was. But crucifixion has been suffered by other men. It's a terrible way
to die but it's not unique. What was unique in Jesus' suffering was that he
knelt in Gethsemane. . . . He so identified with the totality of man's sins
and setbacks that it was as if he were guilty of all of them, and he sweat
blood just as Luke says. . . . He experienced such a compassion for
mankind that there is not one condition that you can get in terms of sin,
badness, setback, tragedy, or pain, not one condition in which you can say,

'You don't know what I've been through.' Because he can always say, 'Oh, yes I do. I've been there.' So he suffered that his bowels might be filled with compassion."

Woodward, a Notre Dame–educated Catholic, told *Sunstone* shortly after his *Newsweek* article appeared, "Compassion is an important and admirable virtue, but it's not the same thing as atoning for sins, in the usual sense of that term." Similar to what has sometimes been called the "martyr" or "good example" theory of atonement, the LDS belief functions within a theology that denies original sin and is fundamentally different from the mainstream definitions of orthodox Christian doctrine.

The above explanation of Christ's atoning grace is consistent with the Mormon understanding of God and man, and the operative role of obedience in exaltation. Any discussion about the relation of works and grace, of course, treads on centuries of thin ice. It is easy to trivialize the doctrine of an opponent. Martin Luther disparaged the New Testament book of James because of its stress on works, but Lutherans really do regard James as part of the New Testament canon. Not many LDS General Conference talks cite Romans in explications of Pauline grace, but Mormons really do recognize that Romans is part of the King James Bible. Evangelicals may preach that individuals are saved by grace alone, but even the most extreme among them really do think that God demands continuing works of obedience along with repentance. And the most extreme Mormons and Catholics really do think that what one believes matters, alongside what one does.

As it happens, significant convergence has developed between Protestants and Catholics on the "faith versus works" issue that sparked the Reformation break with Rome. In 1999 the Vatican and the Lutheran World Federation issued a joint accord on that historic sixteenth-century dispute: "Together we confess: By grace alone, in faith in Christ's saving work and not because of any merit on our part, we are accepted by God and receive the Holy Spirit, who renews our hearts while equipping and calling us to good works. . . . We confess together that persons are justified by faith in the gospel 'apart from works prescribed by the law' (Romans 3:28). Christ has fulfilled the law and by his death and resurrection has overcome it as a way to salvation. We also confess that God's commandments retain their validity for the justified. . . . We confess together that good works—a Christian life lived in faith, hope and love—follow justification and are its fruits."

On the faith-works scale, Mormons clearly tilt toward the works side. A typical Mormon proof-text is II Nephi 25:23: "We know that it is by grace that we are saved, after all we can do." This contrasts with the Protestant proof-text in Ephesians 2:8–9: "For by grace are ye saved through faith; and that not of yourselves: it is the gift of God: Not of works, lest any man should boast." Justification by belief alone, minus works, is "a most pernicious doctrine," the LDS Apostle James Talmage writes, while Apostle Bruce McConkie says that it is hard to imagine how pure doctrine "could be more completely garbled and perverted" than the way the Church of England's Articles of Religion treat this point.

"Salvation is attainable only through compliance with the laws and ordinances of the Gospel; and all who are thus saved become sons and daughters unto God in a distinctive sense," according to a 1916 doctrinal exposition by the First Presidency and the Quorum of the Twelve.

The *Encyclopedia of Mormonism* lists five essential steps to salvation: faith that Christ can save from sin; repentance for one's sin; immersion baptism when one is old enough to be accountable; the gift of the Holy Ghost through the laying on of hands by the Melchizedek priesthood (performed immediately after baptism); and "enduring to the end." Using the terms of the LDS Articles of Faith, practicing the church's "ordinances," and giving lifelong obedience to its "laws" are required along with belief.

As the *Encyclopedia* explains, the believer must "remain faithful to all covenants, continue in righteousness, and endure faithfully to the end of mortal life" to receive fully the grace that Christ's work made possible. Or again, as taught by the LDS scriptures, "if you keep my commandments and endure to the end you shall have eternal life, which gift is the greatest of all the gifts of God" (D&C 14:7).

Adam is also an important character in the Mormon view of redemption. The role of Adam in Mormon theology is unique. He is a hero, a prince, and he is also identified as the Archangel Michael. (Other identifications unique to Mormonism: Jesus is the Old Testament Jehovah and Noah is the Angel Gabriel who appeared to Mary to announce the impending birth of Jesus.) In Mormonism, angels are human beings at another level of exaltation, serving as messengers sent from God, while conventional Christianity believes angels are another order of being, separate from humans. According to the *Encyclopedia of Mormonism,* "Noah stands next in authority to Adam in the Priesthood" (Joseph Smith: History of the Church 3:386) and ranks third in position from the Lord.

"For Latter-day Saints, Adam stands as one of the noblest and greatest of all men," according to the *Encyclopedia of Mormonism.* He helped Elohim and Jehovah (i.e., Jesus) in the creation—that is, organization—of the earth. (Mormonism teaches that matter is eternal.) The *Encyclopedia* says that Adam had a "position of authority next to Jesus Christ." In their premortal state, Adam and Eve could not procreate, so their fall was deliberate; they ate of the Tree of Knowledge of Good and Evil and were given bodies and the ability to carry out God's commandment to have children. God also rewarded them by sharing his plan of salvation.

In LDS scripture Adam said, "Blessed be the name of God, for because of my transgression my eyes are opened, and in this life I shall have joy, and again in the flesh I shall see God." And Eve, his wife, heard all these things and was glad, saying: "Were it not for our transgression we never should have had seed, and never should have known good and evil, and the joy of our redemption, and the eternal life which God giveth unto all the obedient" (Moses 5:10, 11).

Adam, (as) Michael, "seems the logical one to give aid and comfort to his Lord on such a solemn occasion [in Gethsemane]," writes Apostle McConkie. "Adam fell, and Christ redeemed men from the fall; theirs was a joint enterprise, both parts of which were essential for the salvation of the Father's children."

B. H. Roberts was in line with this tradition calling Adam "our Father Adam, the 'Grand Patriarch' of our race—the 'Ancient of Days.'" But elaborating on the idiosyncratic position of Adam in LDS thinking, Brigham Young had gone further and identified him with God the Father in his Adam-God doctrine later repudiated by the church. He famously declared in an 1852 sermon that Adam "is our Father and our God, and the only God with whom we have to do." He later preached, "I tell you, when you see your Father in the Heavens, you will see Adam; when you see your

Mother that bear your spirit, you will see Mother Eve." On February 20, 1912, a First Presidency letter issued under Joseph F. Smith's administration denied the essentials of his predecessor prophet's Adam-God teachings, focusing only on the 1852 sermon while ignoring Adam-God teachings through the remaining twenty-five years of Young's life. This Adam-God theology is a dead issue today, although the high status of Adam remains unique to the LDS church.

"Blood atonement" is the other controversial Brigham Young teaching from which the church has backed away. This is the teaching that some sins, such as murder, are so serious that the atonement of Christ does not, by itself, provide sufficient grace for forgiveness. Only the spilling of blood as a form of capital punishment can redeem the offender. The *Encyclopedia* claims that the teaching "is not a doctrine of the Church and has never been practiced by the Church at any time."

Heaven, in Mormonism, exists in three tiers: the celestial kingdom, with the highest degree of exaltation, available to the Saints who have undergone the appropriate ordinances and progressed in obedience to such a state; the terrestrial kingdom; and the telestial kingdom. Progression in degrees of glory is possible in the afterlife, and good people who have not in this life received the "fullness of the gospel" may progress as far as the middle (terrestrial) kingdom. The highest level, the celestial kingdom, is a homey destination in which all the exalted can live with their eternal families and continue to procreate. It is this familial goal of exalted togetherness in the afterlife that is the greatest focus of Mormon theology and expectation.

Some scholars believe that Joseph Smith was a universalist, that is, an adherent of the belief that all will be saved. That belief was a common ingredient in nineteenth-century liberal thinking. The Mormon hell is small; only a relatively few "sons of perdition" will be permanently consigned there. The *Encyclopedia* says that Christ "grants to all the desires of their hearts, allowing them to choose their eternal reward, according to the law they are willing and able to abide."

So are Mormons Christians? The historian Jan Shipps, one of the shrewdest outside observers, redirects the question in *Mormonism*. Clearly, she says, the radical theology of Mormonism, though drawing on the Christian imagination, is not a part of *traditional* Christianity. Its own claims prohibit one from considering it one "slightly idiosyncratic" form of Christianity, since "the Saints think of themselves as Christians and think of their church as the only legitimate Church of Jesus Christ." In reality, she concludes, Mormonism differs from traditional Christianity in much the same way that traditional Christianity came to differ from Judaism. Shipps writes:

> Although the [LDS] gospel is available to all, the "unit of exaltation" is the family rather than the individual. Consequently, the ultimate goal of the Latter-day Saints is not eternity somehow spent in the presence of the Lord Jesus Christ in heaven. Mormonism holds up a different goal: "eternal progression" toward godhood. When this theological conception is added to the peculiar understanding that Saints have of themselves and their Hebraic-Christianness, which grew out of their past as peculiar people, it becomes as clear as can be that, nomenclature notwithstanding, Mormonism is a new religious tradition.

But perhaps for Mormons themselves the best answer to that frequently repeated question is the one President Gordon B. Hinckley gave his flock in a 1998 General Conference talk: "There are some of other faiths who do not regard us as Christians. That is not important. How we regard ourselves is what is important."

CHAPTER 20

RIVALS AND ANTAGONISTS

IN 1999, AT THE TRUMAN PRESIDENTIAL LIBRARY IN INDEPENDENCE, Missouri, the Czech Republic, Hungary, and Poland joined NATO, ceremonially bridging the Cold War divide. Just a few blocks from the library is a location that symbolizes the ongoing divisions among the spiritual heirs of Joseph Smith, the remarkable intersection of River and Walnut streets. Dominating this ecclesiastical crossroad is the Temple, world headquarters of the Reorganized Church of Jesus Christ of Latter Day Saints (RLDS), its 195-foot corkscrew spire thrusting heavenward. The ultramodern $60 million edifice, dedicated debt-free in 1994, is the work of Gyo Obata, the architect who designed the National Air and Space Museum in Washington, D.C., and the renovated Union Station in St. Louis. Catercorner across the way stands the venue for RLDS world conferences, the domed, 5,800-seat Auditorium, opened in 1926. Juxtaposed on the third corner is the large but nondescript visitors' center maintained by the Utah-based Church of Jesus Christ of Latter-day Saints (LDS).

The fourth corner is claimed by a rival denomination with headquarters in a far more humble white clapboard building that replaced the original after it was destroyed by an arsonist. This third group is the Church of Christ (Temple Lot), a.k.a. "the Hedrickites." The little denomination may have a mere 2,300 members in 27 branches (including 400 Maya Indians in Mexico), but it claims to preserve Joseph Smith's original faith. And it proudly commands the precious "lot which is not far from the courthouse" that the prophet Joseph revealed in August 1831 will be the site for the temple where Jesus Christ is to reign in person upon his Second Coming. The location remains infallible teaching in the Utah church's scriptures (D&C 57:3).

Granville Hedrick's Temple Lotters recorded deeds to the land between 1869 and 1877, lost rights to this property in a bitter federal court feud with the RLDS, but won it back on appeal in 1895 after a deed cited by the RLDS was judged fraudulent. The U.S. Supreme Court declined to review the Temple Lotters' victory. The church discovered what it identifies as Smith's original stone marker of the spot in 1929 during an aborted effort to build a temple, and it is now on display in the basement. On weekdays, kindly old Apostle William A. Sheldon beckons any visitors who amble in to sit on metal folding chairs while he holds forth on his church's claims.

These three denominations provide a Darwinian chart of spiritual evolution. The Church of Christ (Temple Lot) sought to preserve the early Smith movement, with its Book of Mormon and reasonably conventional God. Holding that the prophet somehow went astray, it rejected the revelations he rewrote or added after issuing his original Book of Commandments in 1833. The RLDS Church more or less perpetuated the next phase, the Ohio-Missouri religion of the 1830s, including Smith's "Inspired" translation of the Bible and many of the later revelations in the Doctrine and Covenants. But it spurned the innovations of the Illinois years: secret temple endowments, baptism for the dead, theocracy, radical reconceptions of God, and especially polygamy. The Utah LDS Church developed the full-orbed Nauvoo Mormonism that Smith left to members of his inner circle upon his death.

For Latter-day Saints, Independence is the scriptural "Center Place," the location of the Garden of Eden in the biblical past and of Christ's New Jerusalem in the millennial future. But whose Jerusalem is it to be? Relative to size, no American denominational family, not even the

Baptists, has given rise to so many schisms and churchlets as the followers of Smith. Today the RLDS, with some 250,000 members worldwide, is the only sizable rival to the Utah church. Utah's *Encyclopedia of Mormonism* says there have been about 130 splinters, of which few lasted more than a decade. However, the Temple Lot church figures that more than 200 factions exist today. Whatever the total, it has been growing recently, thanks to eruptions in the RLDS.

The 1996 edition of J. Gordon Melton's authoritative *Encyclopedia of American Religions* catalogs sixty-five Smith-related denominations, of which Melton found current addresses for twenty-nine. Melton divides them into four categories: the polygamous Mormon Fundamentalist groups that broke from the Utah LDS; the nonpolygamous Utah splinters; the Missouri wing, including the RLDS and Temple Lot churches; and "other Mormons," mostly groups dating from the chaos after Smith's assassination in 1844, such as the Bickertonites, Cutlerites, and Strangites. What follows is a simplified taxonomy of some of the latter-day fiefdoms, many of which provide information on the Restoration.org web site.

Smith's Saints were fractious from the start. The first schism, the "Pure Church of Christ," erupted only a year after the church was established. The 1837 "Church of Christ" split was led by an embezzler, Warren Parish, but he managed to take three of Smith's Twelve Apostles with him. The prophet expelled man after man from church leadership, culminating in the 1844 schism with William Law over theocracy, polygamy, and theology. Things became even more complex when Smith was suddenly assassinated, owing not only to his own tenets (latter-day revelation, secrecy in rituals and church administration) but to his unfortunate failure to specify a succession procedure or a successor even though his life was in continual danger.

Actually, the problem was not that Smith left no successor but that he left an unlucky thirteen of them. D. Michael Quinn writes that Smith specifically designated at least six:

1. Oliver Cowdery, a Book of Mormon witness, was the first to receive the LDS priesthood along with Smith in 1829 and became assistant president, but was then excommunicated in 1838.

2. David Whitmer, another Book of Mormon witness, was likewise excommunicated in 1838.

3. Joseph's brother Hyrum Smith could claim succession rights as Patriarch to the Church but was assassinated with Joseph.

4. Joseph's brother Samuel Smith would have succeeded Hyrum as Patriarch, and thus had a claim, but died just weeks after Joseph and Hyrum, amid rumors he had been poisoned.

5. The patrilineal claim of succession of Joseph's eldest son, Joseph Smith III, became the foundation of the "Josephite" RLDS.

6. David Hyrum Smith (not yet born when Joseph died) was the prophet's only publicly acknowledged son after Joseph's marriage to Emma was sealed for time and eternity.

In addition, Quinn writes, Joseph Smith provided grounds for these other claimants:

1. Sidney Rigdon had a strong case as the only First Presidency member upon the prophet's death (William Law having been newly excommunicated). He had broken with Smith over polygamy and Smith's polygamous proposal to his daughter Nancy. Nonetheless, Smith had healed the breach by early 1844 and had chosen Rigdon as his running mate for vice president of the United States.

2. Apostle William Smith, the prophet's unstable brother, was next in line to be patriarch and thus had an apparent right to succeed to the church presidency once Hyrum and Samuel were dead.

3. William Marks, president of the High Council, administered the church in Nauvoo.

4. Lyman Wight was the highest-ranking apostle in the secret government body, the Council of Fifty.

5. Alpheus Cutler, a Council of Fifty member, claimed to have been privately ordained by the prophet.

6. James J. Strang, a recent convert, also claimed to have been privately ordained.

7. Collective leadership by the Quorum of the Twelve Apostles, of which Brigham Young had been the leader since 1840, was also a possibility.

Young's obvious leadership abilities swayed popular sentiment in that difficult summer of 1844, and he readily bested Rigdon, his chief rival, in an August 8 membership vote at a Nauvoo church conference (a rare and important instance of LDS democracy). But the outcome of that vote was merely to put the Twelve Apostles in charge. Young was not himself proclaimed the new president of the church until December of 1847, and Smith's other titles as "Prophet, Seer, and Revelator" did not come his way until 1872.

Sidney Rigdon put himself forward to be the "guardian" of the church. Weeks after he lost in the August 8 showdown, the Young forces excommunicated the fiery Rigdon, who organized the short-lived "Church of Christ" back in Pennsylvania and then delivered revelations through the semisecret "Children of Zion" movement. William Bickerton, one of Rigdon's disciples, had in the meantime created the "Church of Jesus Christ" (Bickertonite), a group of turbulent history currently based in the Pittsburgh area.

David Whitmer, Rigdon's fellow LDS pioneer, founded his own "Church of Christ" in 1847, but it did not last long, despite backing from all the surviving Book of Mormon witnesses. He later gave it another try, but most of his followers ended up joining the Temple Lot church.

Oliver Cowdery, who had gone Methodist, wrote his fellow witness Whitmer that they jointly retained LDS authority by right. But he never formally joined Whitmer's group and was rebaptized into the Young wing in 1848 after renouncing his own succession claim but not his monogamist conviction.

James Strang made up for his shaky claim with ample charisma and for one shining moment represented a threat to Young. He lured to his camp Joseph Smith's surviving brother William, two of his sisters, his widowed mother Lucy Mack Smith, the witness Martin Harris, the Nauvoo leader

William Marks, and Apostle John Page. Strang displayed a succession letter from Smith (later deemed to be a forgery) and claimed direct angelic
ordination as well. Like Smith, he said he had found buried metallic plates
in Voree (Burlington), Wisconsin, that were seen by Eleven Witnesses and
became scripture. Disaffection grew when Strang embraced polygamy and
proclaimed the "gathering" of the Saints at Beaver Island, Michigan, where
Strang had George Adams from Smith's Council of Fifty crown him as
king in 1850. Strang was murdered in 1856, but the movement lingers on to
this day in the tiny "Church of Jesus Christ of Latter Day Saints," located
on Mormon Road in Burlington. The Strangite web site adds "The
Original" to the denominational name and proclaims that the "Brigham-
ites" were "apostates."

William Marks had good prospects, since he administered the church at
Nauvoo and the newly widowed Emma Smith, his ally in opposing church
polygamy, claimed he was Joseph's choice to be the successor. But Marks
never pushed himself and instead backed Rigdon's claim, joined the
Rigdonite schism, then the Strangites, then another splinter called
Jehovah's Presbytery of Zion, and finally emerged as a high leader of the
RLDS Church.

Alpheus Cutler at first favored Marks, then staked his own claim and
created the "Church of Jesus Christ," which still survives in Independence,
though most of the Cutlerite flock went RLDS long ago.

Lyman Wight had been dispatched by Smith to launch a Texas colony,
where he defied Young's orders to close up shop and was excommunicated.
He thought William Smith should lead until Joseph III was of age.
Eventually many in his group likewise joined the RLDS.

William Smith, Joseph's brother, got his hereditary post as Patriarch to
the Church under Young but was soon demoted and then excommunicated in 1845. He joined the Strangites, then Wight, organized the "Bride
and Lamb's Life" with the witness Martin Harris, and finally embraced his
nephew's RLDS Church in 1878.

Young David Smith joined brother Joseph III in the RLDS sooner than
his uncle William, spurning Young's offer to preside over the Utah church
if he would only be rebaptized and endorse polygamy. Instead, he briefly
became an RLDS missionary to Utah, then a member of the Josephites'

First Presidency, but he had to be committed to the Illinois Hospital for the Insane from 1877 until his death in 1904.

Though many others were grasping for kingdom power, Joseph Smith III was a rather reluctant prophet. His father had ordained him as his successor when he was six in a private rite, designated him in subsequent public sermons, and had him secretly ordained again in the presence of Council of Fifty members in 1844. (In 1981 Mark Hofmann "discovered" Joseph's written blessing of Joseph III as his successor, which was treated as scripture by the RLDS until Hofmann was convicted of murder and admitted it was a forgery.) Young always understood the Smith boy's right of lineal succession, but only on condition that he accept the practices of the "Brighamite" church. Joseph III was only eleven when his father was slain, so his succession would have required some sort of regency. But as a practical matter, the total hostility of his mother Emma to polygamy, and to Young, made any such arrangement an impossibility.

As a young adult, Joseph III dabbled in Methodism, phrenology, astrology, and spiritualism, tried his hand at farming and shopkeeping, studied a bit of law, and rebuffed a stream of appeals that he assume command of this or that religious faction. Young's Utah church sent emissaries on a final, fruitless visit in 1856. Joseph III got interested in politics, joined the abolitionist movement and the newborn Republican Party, served as Nauvoo's justice of the peace, and ran for mayor, all the while restudying his Mormon roots. Meanwhile, the beginnings of the "Reorganization" had occurred at an 1852 conference at which scattered midwestern Saints denounced the "pretensions" of Young, Strang, and others. The delegates further declared that the rightful successor "must of necessity be the seed of Joseph Smith, Jun., in fulfillment of the law and promises of God."

When Joseph III finally accepted his destiny as prophet and president at the Reorganized Church's conference in April of 1860, he brought with him Emma and many members of the Smith family and took much of the steam out of the other rival branches. The new leader's inaugural address denounced not only polygamy but the idea that his father had ever countenanced the odious practice. In an 1879 interview for the RLDS paper, conducted by Joseph III, Emma unflinchingly reaffirmed her long-running denial of her husband's polygamy.

Joseph III ruled to his death in 1914 and built the increasingly prosperous Reorganized Church on two central principles: presidential succession in the Smith family lineage with continuing revelation powers, and steadfast denial of polygamy and of Joseph Jr.'s polygamous involvements. Meanwhile, the RLDS allowed considerable theological flexibility in interpreting the latter-day religion to ameliorate internal disagreements. The church's crisis of identity in the present generation, however, is all the more acute for its having never elevated a binding creed.

One turning point occurred in 1986 when the RLDS educators' Temple School published a paper by the official church historian, Richard P. Howard. He grudgingly writes that Joseph Jr. had an "accidental" involvement in polygamy but tried to halt the practice when damage to the church became evident. "However, by that time things had gone too far." Given the undeniable facts concerning Joseph Jr.'s "indirect responsibility" for Nauvoo polygamy, Howard says, the century-long RLDS campaign to clear the prophet's name had been "unnecessary." However cautious, this was the first official RLDS acknowledgment of what most everyone else had known all along. Howard's successor, Mark A. Scherer, says that "many today within the Reorganization still believe that the seer [Joseph Jr.] stood against polygamy, even though the historical facts suggest otherwise. Some feel it important to honor memories rather than acknowledge the historical circumstances. Frankly, I must defer to the latter."

In America evangelists tend to pass their organizations on to their sons, and sons occasionally follow fathers in the same pulpit. But the only denominational parallel to the RLDS leadership by family lineage has been found in Hasidic Jewish dynasties. Joseph Jr. was succeeded by Joseph III, who designated his son Frederick as his successor. Frederick Smith was followed in turn by his brothers Israel Smith and W. Wallace Smith. In 1978 the RLDS presidency finally reached the second generation as W. Wallace became "president emeritus" and passed the prophet's mantle on to his son, ophthalmologist Wallace B. Smith. (Utah LDS presidents, by contrast, always serve until death.)

Wallace B. declared by revelation in 1995 that his successor would be W. Grant McMurray, a member of the First Presidency and formerly the church's world secretary. McMurray became president when Wallace B.

Smith retired the following year. This was a major change in the heritage of the RLDS Church. McMurray is not a Smith, not even a Smith in-law. Wallace B. Smith maintained that "the rule of primogeniture operates if applicable," but that it wasn't applicable any longer. Wallace B. had no sons, and he bypassed his daughters, his cousins, and direct descendants of Joseph by matrilineal descent. RLDS lineage has now become strictly spiritual, not genetic.

(In 1958 W. Wallace had broken lineage in the formerly hereditary RLDS office of Presiding Patriarch, bypassing the son of an incumbent who descended from David Hyrum and Joseph Jr. The Utah LDS also filled its Patriarch's office with Smith descendants but has left the post vacant since 1979, presumably never to be restored.)

McMurray, an engaging and straightforward leader, is candid about working other changes. Although he maintains that the unpaid, "self-sustaining lay ministry is still the backbone of our movement," he wants to continue professionalizing the RLDS and promote theological training and full-time career paths for leaders of larger congregations. McMurray himself is the first head of any Smithite branch to hold a divinity degree. His is from St. Paul School of Theology, a United Methodist Church school in nearby Kansas City, and he is continuing the church's longtime drift toward the moderately liberal style of "mainline" Protestantism. Like the Methodists, Presbyterians, and Episcopalians, McMurray's RLDS is now beginning open discussions on the role of homosexuals in the church. (In the resolutely conservative Utah church, there's nothing to discuss.) There is also talk of changing the denomination's ten-word name someday. Yet the RLDS may never completely blend into American Protestantism, due to its exotic background.

Besides those alterations, modernist views of the Bible and the Book of Mormon have been emanating from RLDS headquarters presses and the denomination's Graceland College in Iowa since the early 1960s. Resistance got organized in 1966 with the establishment of the Foundation for Research on Ancient America (FRAA) to promote literalist belief in the Book of Mormon. By 1974, Richard Price, a Bendix Corporation employee in Kansas City and active RLDS layman, produced his self-published book *The Saints at the Crossroads*, the first thoroughgoing critique of the new theology. In 1978 Price launched *Restoration Voice* (later *Vision*) magazine and organized a short-lived annual Restoration Festival at Graceland College. In 1985 Price was stripped of his priesthood license after declaring that all RLDS presidents since Israel Smith were apostate, and was finally expelled from church membership in 1987.

Meanwhile, FRAA maintains headquarters and the Tree of Life Bookstore in Independence. The annual FRAA meetings in the RLDS Auditorium became the rallying point for the old guard. But in 1991 the First Presidency banished FRAA from the Auditorium because meeting there carried "implied authorization" of its conservative views and the group was in violation of several of the hierarchy's policies. The next year a member of the First Presidency wrote in the denominational magazine that "there is no archaeological support for the Book of Mormon" and that its style and concepts are "consistent with a 19th century hypothesis of authorship."

The RLDS was traditionally unique in regarding the Joseph Smith Translation as its Bible, while the LDS used only the regular King James Version. Today, says McMurray, Smith's rewrite retains some sort of official status but the leadership recognizes that it was not a pure translation and considers it to be almost a "theological commentary" on the Bible. As for the authenticity of Smith's Book of Mormon, "it depends on whom you ask. . . . We are comfortable with a range" of opinions. The Utah Mormons "have not proven the historicity of the Book of Mormon by their archaeology," he says, but on the other hand, he sees no credible explanation of how the book came forth other than what the prophet reported.

McMurray says that believers should now view themselves as "a prophetic people" rather than a people with a prophet. The RLDS presidents have traditionally been much more active than the LDS presidents as prophets, continually adding new revelations to the Doctrine and Covenants. But McMurray has dropped the practice of including routine administrative appointments in the RLDS scriptures. He assured the anxious membership that he still expects to receive revelations, but he wants to restrict the scriptures to "words of counsel that may have a more enduring purpose." In modern times the RLDS emphasis has shifted subtly from the establishment of the millennial Missouri Zion to a more general-ized spread of "zionic" justice in society. The RLDS temple talk is less about Christ's imminent Second Coming to reign there than about efforts toward world peace.

The most disruptive RLDS innovation was Wallace B. Smith's revela-tion in 1984 by which the priesthood was opened to women, culminating in 1998 when two women on the denominational staff were elevated to the Council of the Twelve Apostles. The 1984 shift drove some traditionalists into schism, and they have formed various "Independent Restoration" branches. Many more simply became inactive members while remaining on the rolls. The RLDS historian Roger D. Launius reported that the North American membership list went from 171,000 in 1985 to 156,000 in 1995. RLDS finances have always been open, so the financial impact is evi-dent to all: from 1984 to 1994 the number of contributing members dropped by 40 percent. In inflation-free terms, contributions for church programs have dropped by roughly half since 1978. The projected budget for 2000 was $27.75 million, a 48 percent increase from 1998. Nonetheless, Launius contends that his church faces a severe identity crisis and "is on course for extinction."

Besides the opening of the priesthood to women, the RLDS record on race is remarkably different from that of the LDS church. On May 4, 1865, just after the Civil War ended, Joseph Smith III gave his young church the third of his fifteen revelations, declaring in God's voice that "it is expedient in me that you ordain priests unto me, of every race who receive the teachings of my law, and become heirs according to the promise." Reflecting the caution of the day, the revelation added, "Be not hasty in ordaining men of the Negro race," and stated that they were to be "ministers to their own race," although RLDS segregation has long since disappeared. It was 113 years before the Utah church received the revelation that God wished to open its priesthood to blacks. Another difference regards tithing. The Missouri church emphasizes that the principle is only part of a broader concept of stewardship of resources, and it traditionally teaches that the tithe is 10 percent of one's "increase," defined as income minus basic living expenses.

Those who stroll from McMurray's office over to Apostle Sheldon's Temple Lot basement will be handed a leaflet that compares the three denominations that share the holy intersection. The LDS, RLDS, and Temple Lot Churches all believe in latter-day prophets, accept the Book of Mormon, practice the same type of baptism, and believe that some sort of temple should arise in Independence. The groups accept three different lists of Smith revelations, and the RLDS and LDS have added to the scriptures since his death. The Temple Lot Church is led only by apostles with no prophet-president at the top, while the LDS and RLDS Churches maintain the far more complex hierarchy of the later Smith. The Utah LDS alone—and alone among all groups under the banner of Christianity—practices baptism for the dead and spiritual genealogy, celestial marriage, temple secrecy, the revelation of plural marriage (now inoperative), and such Smith theological innovations as the plurality of gods, man's prospect of becoming a god, and God the Father as a being of flesh and bones who was once a mortal man.

Besides these three groups, a miscellany of small modern splinters have built on such Smith-like claims and themes as direct visitations from Elijah or the Angel Moroni, investiture of a new latter-day prophet, heavenly ordination to restore the Aaronic or Melchizedek priesthood, revival of the communal United Order of Enoch economic revelation, or preservation of the previous LDS teachings in favor of polygamy and against blacks in the priesthood.

The Utah church also has to contend with a different network of antagonists who are staunchly opposed to all of the latter-day distinctives and stand totally outside the Smith denominational family. These are what the Utah church refers to as the "anti-Mormons" (suggesting a parallel to anti-Semitism) and one FARMS polemicist labels the "antimormonoids." In a symbiosis of mutual hostility, the antis in turn label the LDS Church a "cult." These ministries vigorously oppose LDS teachings and try to convert Saints to conventional Christianity. It's impossible to gauge their level of success, though back-door LDS defections appear considerably smaller than the number of LDS converts pouring in the front door. Often the most ardent of these outsiders are onetime Mormons who became disillusioned and left the church.

The "anti-Mormon" literary movement has long antecedents, dating back to 1834 when phosphorescent materials about the origins of the latter-day faith were collected and published in Painesville, Ohio, by the journalist E. D. Howe. The title:

> *Mormonism Unvailed: or, A Faithful Account of that Singular Imposition and DELUSION, from its Rise to the Present Time. With Sketches of the Characters of its Propagators, and a Full Detail of the Manner in Which the Famous GOLDEN BIBLE was Brought Before the World. To Which are Added, Enquiries into the Probability that the Historical Part of the Said Bible was Written by one SOLOMON SPALDING, More than Twenty Years Ago, and by Him Intended to Have Been Published as a Romance.*

The affidavits that Howe published were a collection from the Mormon dropout D. P. Hurlbut and included statements from people in Palmyra and Manchester who had known the Smith family. That included the one from Isaac Hale, Emma's father, stating his denial to Joseph of permission to marry his daughter because of his disreputable money-digging profession. Some other affidavits referred to Smith's 1826 Bainbridge trial for vagrancy or disorderly conduct, related to his treasure-digging.

In that spirit, today's flamboyant "anti-Mormons" also issue books, with titles ranging from the neighborly *(Questions to Ask Your Mormon Friend)* to the angry *(The Counterfeit Gospel of Mormonism, How to Rescue Your Loved Ones from Mormonism)*. They also churn out videos, and tracts, and Internet materials of widely varying quality. Their World Wide Web pages are potentially an important means of breaking the hierarchy's hold and disseminating information, as is the case with other religious and political ideologies. Almost without exception, they are Evangelical and Fundamentalist Protestants, who simultaneously view Mormons as moral soulmates and major religious rivals. The U.S. Catholic Church expends little effort on the LDS issue, perhaps because it's too big to bother and it has not yet reacted significantly to competition in Latin America. The mainline and liberal Protestant denominations generally lack the evangelistic and theological energy. The conservative Southern Baptist Convention, America's biggest Protestant body, seems to be the only denomination that invests much sustained effort in the Mormon wars, through its Interfaith Witness division in Atlanta.

Most of the combatants are independent "para-church" organizations that together constitute a cottage industry. The 1996 *Directory of Cult Research Organizations* lists 752 anti-cult agencies and individuals, of which 561 are motivated by Evangelical religion and 102 focus on Mormonism. Some of the Evangelical groups work against a whole range of so-called cults, for instance, the Christian Research Institute of Rancho Santa Margarita, California, and the Watchman Fellowship of Arlington, Texas. James R. White's Phoenix-based Alpha and Omega Ministries takes on everyone from Catholics to Jehovah's Witnesses, but his first love is targeting Mormonism. His volunteers are often seen disseminating tracts during LDS conference time in Salt Lake.

Writing for FARMS, the LDS stalwart Louis Midgley rates five organizations in the first tier of "anti-Mormon" ministries: the Southern Baptists; the Utah Lighthouse Ministry (discussed later in this chapter); Bill McKeever's Mormonism Research Ministry of El Cajon, California; Luke Wilson and Joel Groat's Gospel Truths Ministry (also known as Religious Research Institute) of Grand Rapids, Michigan; and Ed Decker's Saints Alive in Jesus of Issaquah, Washington. The *Directory* lists four others in the front rank: Dick Baer's Ex-Mormons and Christians Alliance of Orangevale, California; Chuck Sackett's Sword of the Shepherd Ministries of Westlake, California; Thelma "Granny" Geer's To Mormons With Love of Safford, Arizona; and John L. Smith's Utah Missions Inc. of Marlow, Oklahoma.

In addition, there's the enormous exmormon.org web site run by the anonymous Recovery from Mormonism (eleven links on temple endowments, thirteen on blood atonement, and links to other ex-Mormon web pages). This site makes religious, secular, and feminist attacks on the LDS system and includes 104 anonymous personal stories in the "Why We Left" section. There is also an e-mail news group and a nationwide list of ex-Mormon contacts. The site claimed to receive 1.85 million hits in a year's time.

Decker's outfit, known for its "God Makers" books and videos, is harshest in the attacks. It has been condemned by the liberal Mormon Alliance and accused of "religious bigotry" by the National Conference of Christians and Jews. But Decker's most damaging critics are Jerald and Sandra Tanner of the Utah Lighthouse Ministry, fellow Evangelicals and fellow ex-Mormons, and the only important Mormon foes based in Salt Lake City. Their newsletter, the *Salt Lake City Messenger,* ran a sharp critique of Decker's latest video. Decker responded with a vigorous protest in his own newsletter ("either the Tanners are the greatest dupes in the business or bald-faced liars"). Next, Decker's attorney sent a letter implying that a lawsuit was in the offing. Unfazed, the Tanners turned around and issued a ninety-four-page booklet, *Problems in "The God Makers II."* The Tanners' newsletter then printed the results of detective work defending LDS President Gordon B. Hinckley against morals charges in the Decker video.

The Tanners, self-taught historical researchers, had previously gained credibility in 1984 by early proclaiming Mark Hofmann's Martin Harris "salamander letter" to be a phony. The salamander letter seemed to provide juicy propaganda for attackers of the Book of Mormon such as the Tanners. But Jerald astutely spotted the fraud even as the LDS Church's experts were judging the document to be genuine. The Tanners were bold and honest enough to expose Hofmann's forgery immediately. The Tanners then used the incident to needle LDS headquarters thirteen blocks to the north: "Since the Mormon leaders claim that they have prophetic powers, many members of the church cannot understand how they could have been fooled."

The Tanners operate out of humble quarters on South West Temple, where they host a monthly support group "for those leaving or questioning Mormonism." While other anti-Mormon evangelists write trade books for Evangelical houses, the Tanners issue their own self-published books and booklets and reproductions of inaccessible or forgotten documents. Their specialty is showing changes and alleging contradictions in what holds itself to be God's one true faith—for example, their *3,913 Changes in the Book of Mormon* and publication of Smith's original Book of Commandments before he re-edited his revelations. A recent catalog lists ninety-four such items on sale, thirty-six of them written by the Tanners. Utah Lighthouse publications are typographically amateurish, hyped with capital letters and underlining, and stiffly written. The Tanners are handicapped by their lack of college education. But the data often make up for the aesthetics, and the Tanners are dedicated, meticulous, and rarely inaccurate, albeit slanted in their interpretations. Their findings underlie the propaganda of many other Evangelical critics.

In the historian Lawrence Foster's apt phrase, the Tanners are "career apostates" who have been involved in the business since 1959 and have scraped out a full-time living from it since 1964, when Jerald quit his job as a machinist. Sandra is a great-great-granddaughter of Brigham Young (along with thousands of others), and Jerald is a descendant of the early Mormon pioneer John Tanner. Both were raised in the faith as active, believing members. Jerald's first doubts came from reading an anti-LDS pamphlet by the Book of Mormon witness David Whitmer. He says he learned good morals as a Mormon but came to believe that "I was a sinner in need of a Savior."

Around that time his future wife Sandra was shaken by a careful reading of the sermons of her great-great-grandfather Brigham. She began attending Jerald's study group for Mormons, trying to figure out whether the church was true. "It didn't take very long for me to see there were major problems in Mormonism," she says. "This set the stage for the rest of my life." The couple married and eventually joined the Christian and Missionary Alliance, a small but expanding Evangelical denomination. They began issuing pamphlets as a hobby, mostly to explain their apostasy to relatives and friends. In 1964 the couple issued the first of many editions of their magnum opus, *Mormonism—Shadow or Reality?*, laboring around the clock on the mimeograph stencils. The Tanners have been surprisingly unharassed over the decades since then, though for years their youngest child's best friend was forbidden to enter their house.

Anonymous sources with good contacts have slipped the Tanners damaging inside documents over the years. In one typical incident, they obtained the text of a 1954 speech to church educators by Apostle Mark E. Petersen. It was delivered at a closed-door meeting on the BYU campus weeks after the U.S. Supreme Court had outlawed school segregation. Petersen insisted that God himself was the author of racial segregation, "and He certainly segregated the descendants of Cain when He cursed the Negro as to the priesthood and drew an absolute line." Petersen also opposed intermarriage of whites with blacks, Asians, and Hawaiians. On another occasion the Tanners acquired and published extracts from a Mormon diary that had been compiled privately by the student Andrew Ehat. Ehat hauled the Tanners into court for misappropriating the material and won a federal court ruling, but in 1986 the Tanners prevailed in an appeal to the U.S. circuit court in Denver. Despite threats, this was the only time they were actually sued.

Though the Tanners invoked threats to freedom of the press, Foster says the Ehat caper violated "standards of ethical scholarship," and he also considers their "unauthorized publication of Mormon archival materials" to be problematic. Foster thinks the Tanners might have played a constructive role in the 1960s, when access to important texts was highly restricted, but says their work later provided the Mormon Right with a pretext "to justify closing off access to vital Mormon records once again." Thus, he says, their documentary muckraking has done more to damage than to help historical scholarship. In his autobiography, the former LDS church historian Leonard Arrington agrees: "Fearful of impious and damaging research, Mormon conservatives used the work of the Tanners as a reason to restrict access to vital Mormon records, leaving responsible historians with limited access."

Given all that history, it was remarkable that in 1998 an objective Associated Press article on the Tanners' work was published by the church-owned *Deseret News*.

Sandra Tanner, the spokesperson for the couple, pleasantly shrugs off these attacks. "I believe we have helped force the church to be more honest in its history" and helped LDS scholars "to justify doing critical studies." There may have been strong antagonism from "the Arrington crowd," she maintains, but "we became the excuse for them doing real history."

CHAPTER 21

DISSENTERS AND EXILES

SHE SEEMED TO BE AN IDEAL CHURCHWOMAN, BORN-AND-BRED LDS, daughter of a bishop, Brigham Young University alumna, and youthful missionary volunteer. As an adult, she spent eight years on the church headquarters staff as an associate editor of the official *Ensign* magazine. In Salt Lake City's Whittier ward she devoted herself to a variety of the assignments that are open to the ladies, such as Primary teacher and Cub Scout den mother. Lately she had served as the pianist and a home visiting teacher for the Relief Society and as a name extractor with the genealogical program.

She was married for time and eternity in the temple. At home, her family held daily devotions and sang hymns together each night after supper. Her husband was the group leader for high priests in the ward; their teenage son was the president of his Aaronic priesthood quorum. Obeying an admonition from the late church president Ezra Taft Benson, each year she read the Book of Mormon through from cover to cover. Spurning the skeptics, she believes that the Book is "an ancient document" and says, "I hear the voice of God speaking to me through it. . . . I consider myself to be orthodox in my beliefs. I strongly believe that Joseph Smith was a prophet, and that Gordon B. Hinckley is an inspired prophet. I believe the teachings of the Mormon Church."

Not good enough.

On September 23, 1993, Lavina Fielding Anderson was excommunicated and has lived ever since in Mormon limbo. By order of her stake president and his advisers, she is no longer a church member and is forbidden to enter the temple, to fill any ward post, to receive the sacrament, or to speak or offer prayers during worship. Her eternal temple "sealings" to her husband and her son have been suspended. It is unclear whether and on what terms she will ever be able to undergo rebaptism and resume her place in the LDS Church. Despite this exile status, she still faithfully—if silently—attends weekly worship and goes to the Sunday school and Relief Society meetings. "I'm in the same place I've been in every Sunday morning since I was a baby."

Anderson is an extremely potent symbol of church discipline because she is involved with several important latter-day institutions that persist in examining religious questions apart from hierarchical control. Such groups are something new in Mormonism.

Around midcentury the LDS subculture began slowly producing a critical mass of self-conscious and outspoken intellectuals, usually with graduate degrees from secular universities. "The church has often swatted down intellectuals individually," Anderson remarks, but until the 1960s they were few in number and had no platforms for independent thinking. The members of this movement regard themselves as faithful and loyal Mormons rather than as dissidents. And by and large they have pursued their endeavors without becoming entangled in controversies over apostasy or excommunication. Most intellectuals have learned to exercise a certain discretion, but eventually some participants in these autonomous organizations were swept into the most systematic clampdown since the internal strife of the nineteenth century.

Anderson has a Ph.D. in English and operates a freelance editing business, so she provides useful skills for Mormonism's small but significant independent sector. She edits the semiannual journal of the Mormon History Association, which publishes some troublesome scholarship from LDS, Reorganized Church, and non-LDS participants. She has been an associate editor of the scholarly quarterly *Dialogue: A Journal of Mormon Thought* (founded in 1966). She has written for the feisty *Sunstone* magazine (1975) and spoken at its Sunstone Symposium in Salt Lake City (held annually since 1979). She is a longtime member of the editors' board for George D. Smith's Signature Books (1981), which continually publishes quality liberal thinking on controversial LDS topics. She edits the quarterly of the Mormon Women's Forum (1988), whose annual Counterpoint conference provides a feminist alternative to official views. And she is a trustee of the Mormon Alliance (1992), which fights what it regards as arbitrary use of church power and sponsors meetings that critique each General Conference the day after it closes.

Anderson also coedits *Case Reports of the Mormon Alliance.* This annual publication documents instances of alleged "ecclesiastical abuse," not only excommunications but such uncomfortable themes as the grievances of homosexual Mormons and the church's handling and mishandling of sexual abuse cases. Interviewed about the latter problem for a 1999 *Houston Chronicle* investigation, a church defense lawyer said in the previous decade a maximum of thirty lawsuits had alleged sexual abuse by LDS officials, of which a third were dismissed without damages, and another twelve to fifteen were settled for less than it would have cost to go to trial. The attorney said most problems predated 1995, when the church instituted a telephone hotline and training to help bishops deal with abuse complaints. But Anderson told the paper there are many other cases where suits were not filed and said some Mormons were excommunicated for reporting abuse to bishops. BYU refused to let women professors issue a study of seventy-one LDS women who had suffered childhood abuse; two of the professors quit and published the research in 1999.

Anderson first raised a dissenter's profile while working at *Ensign* in June of 1981. The magazine had just gone to press with a toned-down version of a conference talk by a General Authority about the sins of the end times (homosexuality, abortion, birth control, and so on). *Sunstone* planned to run a comparison between the published version and the actual talk as captured on videotape. Anderson offered to provide *Sunstone* with the text as the Authority prepared it, prior to the *Ensign* revisions, and sent a copy to a *Sunstone* volunteer in the interoffice mail. A supervisor opened the mailing, and Anderson was sacked on the spot for revealing "confidential" information.

Anderson was never informed exactly what her 1993 "apostasy" consisted of. But everyone knows that she is being punished for a delivering a paper at the 1992 Sunstone Symposium, and publishing a version of it in *Dialogue* in 1993 that compiled data on more than one hundred examples of church repression against intellectuals. After the article came out, church members sent her information on another hundred cases. Rather than being removed for heresy, in other words, Anderson is suffering church discipline because she conveyed information on church discipline. Her most incendiary accusation was that headquarters operates a systematic clipping service to monitor individual Saints, carefully filing their letters to the editor, other writings, quotes in the media, and public activities. "We must protest, expose, and work against an internal espionage system that creates and maintains secret files on members of the church," she has declared.

The First Presidency later admitted that it had established the Strengthening Church Members Committee, led by two apostles, which "serves as a resource to priesthood leaders throughout the world." The Presidency cited precedent in Joseph Smith's 1839 scriptural command that Saints document "abuses" against them and collect the "libelous publications that are afloat" (D&C 123). A spokesman said that Salt Lake officialdom merely supplies the data and that local church officials are responsible for any resulting actions taken against members.

No other sizable religion in America monitors its own followers in this way. The files are only one aspect of a meticulous system of internal discipline through which contemporary Mormonism operates more like a small cult than a major denomination. Ecclesiastical censure as such is nothing unusual. Most religions have some form of discipline on the books, usually to deal with moral misconduct. Most religions with creeds act against dissidents from time to time. In recent times there have been some noteworthy theological prosecutions in such U.S. denominations as the Roman Catholic Church, the Southern Baptist Convention, the United Methodist Church, and Lutheran Church—Missouri Synod (and some noteworthy acquittals in the liberal Episcopal Church). But other denominations usually remove those who are found guilty from their jobs without expelling them from the church altogether. The LDS Church, however, is unusual in penalizing members for merely criticizing officialdom or for publishing truthful—if uncomfortable—information. Also, mainstream churches openly state the charges that are at issue (and Protestants often conduct public tribunals), while Mormon officials shroud their procedures with secrecy. The Mormon Church prosecutes many more of its members than do these other religious groups, which tend to focus discipline on clergy in important positions such as theology professorships. Such discipline of rank-and-file members in other churches is virtually unknown.

The system works, achieving its intended goals of defining policy and fostering obedience and caution among the membership. Few Saints have joined Lavina Anderson in raising their voices against the ecclesiastical judiciary, and few are likely to do so in the future now that she has been expelled from Eden. The events of the 1990s have signaled that the Church of Jesus Christ of Latter-day Saints will tolerate no deviations from stated policy and no public questioning of the General Authorities. For those cast into exile this is usually a life-changing event more significant than, say, a Baptist joining his wife's Lutheran church, or even a divorced Catholic joining the Episcopalians. An exiled Saint is in danger of weakening or severing family ties, long-cherished friendships, perhaps even employment. The Mormon communal bond is so unique that exile puts a person's very identity at stake.

The most noticed of the Mormon defendants were the so-called "September Six." Anderson and these five other Saints were convicted by local church courts during the same month in 1993:

- Avraham Gileadi, an independent scriptural scholar, was excommunicated two years after the publication of his technical tome on the Second Coming, *The Last Days: Types and Shadows from the Bible and the Book of Mormon.* Oddly, Gileadi is a conservative; his book avoids the kookiness associated with some Protestant millennialists; and it was vetted and issued by the church's own Deseret Book Company. Moreover, he had complied when directed to stop promoting his views. The church has never clarified which of Gileadi's opinions might be heretical. Perhaps the church simply wanted to downplay millennial speculation in general. (After all, President Hinckley has ordered temples to be erected in historic

Palmyra and Nauvoo, but not in Independence, the future venue of Christ's Second Coming.) Gileadi managed to gain rebaptism and full membership in 1996.

- Maxine Hanks is a writer and frequent speaker on feminist topics who was excommunicated for urging that the LDS priesthood be opened to women. Another presumed provocation was her editing of a 1992 Signature Books anthology, *Women and Authority: Re-emerging Mormon Feminism,* in which contributors discuss female priesthood and another of the hierarchy's least favorite topics, adoration of Mormonism's Mother in Heaven.

  (The latter issue is a revealing example of the church's ad hoc approach to orthodoxy and the way a statement from a single General Authority can become infallible. In a 1991 speech Hinckley said he could accept the traditional LDS concept that there is a Mother in Heaven as well as a Father. But warning of "small beginnings of apostasy" in the church, he declared that it was "inappropriate for anyone in the Church to pray to our Mother in Heaven," and he urged priesthood holders to correct those who differed. His venue added to the significance: the annual seminar for regional representatives prior to the April General Conference. But Hinckley was merely a first counselor at the time; the doctrine was not formally proclaimed by the church's president or First Presidency, and in the past other Mormons had expressed such views without being penalized.)

- Lynne Kanavel Whitesides, then president of the Mormon Women's Forum, was similarly chastised for her public discussions about women's priesthood and the Mother in Heaven. She was the only one of the Six to be "disfellowshiped" rather than fully excommunicated.

- Paul Toscano, a Salt Lake City attorney, was a founder of the Mormon Alliance and longtime critic of the church leadership. His excommunication trial dealt largely with his observations about the General Authorities in a Sunstone Symposium address titled "All Is Not Well in Zion: False Teachings of the True Church."

• D. Michael Quinn, the most important scholar among the Six and a resigned Brigham Young University historian, wrote a 1985 *Dialogue* article on church leaders' secret involvement in polygamy after the 1890 Manifesto, and the 1987 Signature book *Early Mormonism and the Magic World View,* which raised questions about the spiritual roots of Joseph Smith's religion. Many ins and outs with the hierarchy ensued. But officially his 1993 excommunication stemmed from an article in Hanks's anthology claiming that Joseph Smith effectively gave women the priesthood, and a 1992 *Sunstone* essay on church repression, "150 Years of Truth and Consequences About Mormon History."

When the Six faced tribunals, there were several modest public demonstrations. A few Mormons quit the church in protest, among them Scott Kenney, the founding editor of *Sunstone,* and Steve Benson, the Pulitzer Prize–winning editorial cartoonist with the *Arizona Republic* and grandson of the reigning LDS president.

The September Six cases were only part of a broader cleanup. Former Phoenix journalist Deborah Laake was excommunicated prior to the September Six over publication of her memoir *Secret Ceremonies: A Mormon Woman's Intimate Diary of Marriage and Beyond.* The book recounted Laake's three divorces and bouts with mental illness, devoting only seventeen pages to LDS temple rites. Besides violating the sanctity of the temple, she condemned Mormon patriarchy and exposed the faith to what the ecclesiastical court termed "open shame and public ridicule." The book was panned by non-LDS historian Jan Shipps and Irene Bates of the Mormon Women's Forum, but it landed on the *New York Times* bestseller list for fifteen weeks.

Months before, church tribunals had also looked to the right, pursuing a campaign against numerous extremists who preached conspiracy and end times ruination in the wake of Mormon James "Bo" Gritz's America First presidential campaign. (Gritz drew half his 99,000 votes in the Mormon heartland states of Utah, Idaho, Arizona, and Nevada.)

Three months before the Six were convicted, Brigham Young University had ended the faculty careers of Cecilia Konchar Farr, who publicly favored open abortion laws, and David Knowlton, who gave a

Sunstone Symposium speech analyzing the factors behind terrorism against LDS missions in Latin America. Martha Sonntag Bradley, the coeditor of *Dialogue,* resigned from the history faculty rather than face what she believed would be certain dismissal when she came up for tenure. Following the September Six trial, BYU removed Brian Evenson for his fictional musings and Gail Houston for her Mother-God invocations. And under the new crackdown on faculty members without temple recommends, Steven Epperson was fired for failing to meet demands on church attendance and tithe-paying. Scott Abbott, the faculty's most outspoken champion of academic freedom, had tenure and would have been difficult to dislodge. Instead, the administration refused to promote him from associate to full professor—not for academic reasons, it pointedly explained, but because of his inadequate "loyalty and citizenship" and his "zeal to change policy at BYU."

During the two years following the September Six eruption, controversy continued in the church courts with the excommunications of four more notable dissenters:

- David P. Wright is the Hebrew scripture specialist who had been fired by BYU in 1988 for believing the Book of Mormon was a nineteenth-century writing of Joseph Smith. Now teaching at Brandeis University, he was excommunicated for expressing that view in a 1992 *Sunstone* article and the 1993 Signature Books anthology *New Approaches to the Book of Mormon.* This was one instance of the church excommunicating an intellectual in order to uphold a central and well-defined doctrinal principle.

- Brent Metcalfe, an independent researcher, was expelled for editing the *New Approaches* anthology. Unlike Wright and the others, Metcalfe had not been an active member or believer for years.

- Michael Barrett, a lawyer for the Central Intelligence Agency in Washington, was convicted of apostasy for refusing to obey church orders and stop sending controversial letters to the editors of newspapers. Barrett's letters contained facts about Mormonism's differences with mainstream Christian doctrine and such embarrassing topics as the black priesthood ban, polygamy, and Adam-as-God.

- Janice Allred, a freelance writer and feminist, was convicted over a 1992 Sunstone Symposium paper, "Toward a Mormon Theology of God the Mother," which was later published in *Dialogue*. She exacerbated matters by arguing during a 1994 symposium appearance that LDS tradition provides no basis for the infallibility of church authorities. Allred is also the coeditor, along with Lavina Anderson, of *Case Reports of the Mormon Alliance.*

The Mormon Alliance types draw their principles from secular law and complain that the closed-door ecclesiastical courts do not give defendants clear charges to answer; provide no means for an adequate defense; mingle the roles of prosecutor, judge, and juror; violate due process of law; and are otherwise confusing, arbitrary, and unfair.

Mormonism, however, follows its own ecclesiastical law, the *General Handbook of Instructions* (which most members never see). Eighteen pages are devoted to disciplinary matters and outline five steps of increasing severity that ward or stake leaders can take against members:

1. "Private counsel and caution": This step is taken for minor transgressions by a member who is genuinely repentant.

2. "Informal probation": Various limitations on the defendant's church participation are quietly applied, depending on the seriousness of the infraction.

3. "Formal probation": A church disciplinary council officially restricts one or more forms of church participation by the defendant.

4. "Disfellowshipment": The defendant remains a member of the church, but not in good standing until conditions for restitution are met. A disfellowshiped member cannot enter the temple, hold any church position, receive the sacrament, speak in worship, or (if a man) exercise priesthood functions. This level of punishment is "adequate for all but the most serious transgressions."

5. "Excommunication": Church membership is ended altogether, and the terms of disfellowshipment are made permanent. An excommunicated Saint is also forbidden to wear the temple undergarments or

to pay tithes. Excommunication is prescribed for the disfellow-shiped Saint who fails to repent, who commits "serious transgressions," whose conduct makes him or her "a serious threat to others," or who "significantly impairs the good name or moral influence of the Church." Excommunication is mandatory for murder and almost always for incest.

The *Handbook* requires that a disciplinary council be held when there is evidence of "apostasy," defined as persistently teaching incorrect doctrine, following teachings by apostate sects (especially polygamous ones), or "repeatedly act[ing] in clear, open, and deliberate public opposition to the Church or its leaders." That last catchall clause is the basis for the recent celebrated cases. Interestingly, "Jack Mormons"—those who are on the membership rolls but are no longer involved in church activities—and Mormons who have left to join other denominations are not automatically classed as apostates.

Despite the church's turbulent past, disciplinary cases were becoming rare by the mid-twentieth century. For instance, as church president starting in 1951, David O. McKay backed his friend Sterling M. McMurrin of the University of Utah against disciplinary grumblings from apostles who despised his views on such matters as human evolution. McMurrin, later the university provost and U.S. commissioner of education under President Kennedy, never faced an ecclesiastical court even though his heresies overshadowed those of the 1990s defendants.

The independent sector's most important scholarly periodical is *Dialogue.* The quarterly originated with a handful of Saints in the Stanford University ward attended by the first managing editors, history professor G. Wesley Johnson and an English doctoral student, Eugene England. Both Johnson and England later ended up teaching at BYU. The Palo Alto group enlisted a board of like-minded colleagues across the country (among them Dallin H. Oaks, later an apostle and no ally of the liberals). The slightly older Mormon History Association, led at the time by Leonard Arrington, fostered the fledgling quarterly and provided papers for an annual history issue in the early years.

"We never thought of *Dialogue* as a dissident journal," says England, though others have so defined it. The inaugural issue stated that since the

1950s Saints had been talking about the need for an independent journal and for "open discussion." The editorial said Mormons in the new generation "share the faith of their elders but also possess a restrained skepticism born of the university, the office, and the laboratory."

For conservatives, however, "restrained" was hardly the word for *Dialogue*. From the start it explored fundamental problems in LDS history and theology. In its second year the journal ran a letter from a prominent Mormon, U.S. Secretary of the Interior Stewart Udall, assailing the ban on blacks in the priesthood: "My fear is that the very character of Mormonism is being distorted and crippled by adherence to a belief that denies the oneness of mankind. We violate the rights and dignity of our Negro brothers, and for this we bear a measure of guilt; but surely we harm ourselves even more." Anderson says that during this era perhaps half a dozen Mormons were excommunicated for criticizing the LDS racial doctrine.

In 1973 *Dialogue* ran an article that was as much a landmark as Anderson's 1993 blockbuster on repression. In it the physician Lester E. Bush Jr. explored the historical basis of the black priesthood prohibition. The staff decided to publish despite a last-minute telephone plea from the academic vice president of BYU to kill the piece because "the Brethren" (top General Authorities) were upset. A decade later headquarters prodded local church leaders to bring in for questioning church members who were writing for independent publications, Bush among them. His stake president, the hotel magnate Bill Marriott, told Bush that Apostle Mark Petersen had phoned him personally to complain about the article on blacks.

In 1975, when Scott Kenney was putting the first issue of *Sunstone* to bed, Apostle Boyd Packer told him he hoped the new magazine would not be like *Dialogue* and cited *Dialogue*'s decision to publish the Bush article in defiance of General Authority counsel. (That counsel, of course, did not come from the General Authorities but only secondhand. In fact, Bush had discussed the article in person with Packer, and the apostle never raised with him the idea of killing the article, then or later.) As Packer may have feared, *Sunstone* has turned out to be even more free-spirited than *Dialogue*, perhaps because it worried less about academic etiquette. And the magazine added a dash of humor, a rare Mormon commodity.

Kenney's original prospectus said the magazine would be "independent of official Church direction, but not of Church teachings." It would "not be used as a vehicle for dissidents," nor would it show favor to "any ideological faction or special interest."

The LDS establishment may feel that those promises have not been kept. Both *Sunstone* and *Dialogue* seek to air conservative as well as liberal ideas, but as a practical matter find the task difficult. "We don't want to be perceived as representing only one side," says *Dialogue*'s coeditor Neal Chandler, an English professor at Cleveland State University. "We are open to any contribution. We give all voices a forum." But, he adds, "this kind of discussion is very, very difficult." For one thing, the independents naturally want to publish material that will not find expression in official outlets. For another, conservative loyalists can be wary of appearing in "liberal" publications. Despite those obstacles, and shoestring financing, *Dialogue* and *Sunstone* have become essential reading for today's well-informed Mormon, left or right, as much so as the official and more cautious *Ensign* magazine and the weekly *Church News* supplement in the *Deseret News*.

Sunstone is more of a lightning rod than *Dialogue* because it sponsors the liveliest forum on contemporary Mormon issues, the annual Sunstone Symposium. This Salt Lake City talk-fest was started in 1979 by then-editor Peggy Fletcher Stack (now a religion reporter for the *Salt Lake Tribune*) in order to cover a broader range of topics than was possible at the Mormon History Association meetings. In recent years the magazine has also held several regional sessions each year in places like Washington, Boston, Chicago, Seattle, San Francisco, and Los Angeles.

"There was nothing quite like it previously in LDS circles," says Elbert Eugene Peck, *Sunstone*'s longtime editor. The 1998 symposium, for instance, offered a forty-eight-page program stuffed with intriguing topics unlikely to be aired at official church gatherings, such as BYU faculty hiring practices, the Mormons' missionary competitors in Mexico, the chances that more Saints will become Democrats, the spiritual relevance of the Catholic monk Thomas Merton, Evangelical panelists discussing the question "Are Mormons Christian?", LDS efforts to stem dropout rates, trends in Mormon consumerism, Mormon divorce, and those old standbys, God the Mother, black priesthood, and polygamy.

Peck says the media pay attention to the symposium and naturally "cover the controversial sessions. There are a lot of faith-affirming things too, but they don't get the stories." After the 1991 Sunstone gathering, the First Presidency and the Quorum of the Twelve Apostles issued an attack on unnamed "recent symposia" organized and attended by Mormons. Apparently hackles were raised by David Knowlton's Latin America talk (seen as endangering missionaries), a speech on temple garments by the Gentile scholar Colleen McDannell, and the usual flurry of hierarchy-bashing.

The "symposia" statement said that some matters are "more appropriate for private conferring and correction than for public debate." Though Saints might want to attend in order to defend the church's position, the authorities said, sometimes it is better if loyal Mormons do not "promote a program that contains some (though admittedly not all) presentations that result in ridiculing sacred things or injuring The Church of Jesus Christ, detracting from its mission, or jeopardizing the well-being of its members." A church member who wrote to the *Salt Lake Tribune* complaining about that statement was advised that he could be disfellowshiped.

At the next General Conference Apostle Boyd K. Packer warned believers against "symposia which concentrate on doctrine and ordinances and measure them by the intellect alone." He said, "There is safety in learning doctrines in gatherings which are sponsored by proper authorities."

The decree did not reduce media attention or symposium registration, which still runs around 1,500. But the church leaders did succeed in altering the dynamics. Peck says that "before, there was a large contingent of BYU faculty, maybe seventy, on the program. Now it's five, if we're lucky. The attendance hasn't dropped, but fewer moderate, mainstream Mormons now attend than in the past." Some ward leaders phone to say they can't participate as long as they are holding office. "So people take sabbaticals from Sunstone." (Peck himself had been stripped of his temple recommend prior to the "symposia" attack because *Sunstone* ran a piece repeating what other publications had said regarding changes in temple rituals and reporting on church disciplinary action on the issue. Publisher Daniel Rector lost his temple recommend at the same time.)

The *General Handbook of Instructions* put into effect in 1999 added a new clause that makes the "recent symposia" statement part of canon law and a potential basis for church discipline. It reads: "The Church warns its members against symposia and other similar gatherings that include presentations that (1) disparage, ridicule, make light of, or are otherwise inappropriate in their treatment of sacred matters or (2) could injure the Church, detract from its mission, or jeopardize its members' well-being. Members should not allow their position or standing in the Church to be used to promote or imply endorsement of such gatherings."

Packer, who is the hierarchy's chief theological watchdog, made a highly significant observation in a May 1993 address to a council of top church staff members. He warned that three "dangers," of an "intensity and seriousness that we have not faced before," had made "major invasions into the membership of the church." These were the gay and lesbian movement, the feminist movement, and "the ever-present challenge from the so-called scholars or intellectuals." So feminism had emerged as a vexation equal to independent intellectualism, a trend underscored by the church's actions against the likes of Allred, Anderson, Bradley, Hanks, Houston, Laake, Whitesides, and such male sympathizers as Quinn.

President Hinckley admits that in theory, prayer to the Mother in Heaven or women in the priesthood could be allowed some day through a direct revelation, but he doesn't expect that to happen. He considers aggrieved feminists to be a minor factor, and as a mathematical matter, he's right: "I think you'll find our women are very happy now. We have a dissident now and again, somebody who speaks out very sharply, very strongly. But that's very unusual. Statistically it's such a very small item that you'd hardly reckon with it. . . . They're outspoken. They speak up. They feel strongly about it. That's their prerogative. They talk about it a good deal, and we've heard what they've had to say. We've heard it again and again. We feel they're not right. We let them go forward with what they're doing. If they speak out against the church in a strong, vigorous way, then possibly some action will be taken."

Action was indeed taken early on against a feminist pioneer, Sonia Johnson. Like Lavina Anderson, Johnson had a conventional upbringing, in her case as the daughter of a teacher in the church's high school seminary system. While a wife and mother living in the northern Virginia suburbs of Washington, D.C., Johnson joined a loose band of Mormon women who favored passage of the Equal Rights Amendment at a time when the LDS leadership had mobilized against it, with Hinckley playing a central role. The group formed the small "Mormons for ERA" in early 1978, and Johnson was picked as president because she was teaching only part-time and had some free hours. The group marched under a Mormon banner in an ERA parade, and Johnson testified before a U.S. Senate subcommittee, tangling with LDS stalwart Orrin Hatch. Soon she was traveling here and there as a prized advocate of the ERA.

Things started plummeting downhill when a newspaper reported that Johnson told one audience not to let Mormon missionaries into their homes, though her allies had a videotape to disprove that quotation. Then the church's own *Deseret News* said that Johnson had denounced "the savage misogyny in the Mormon Church," whereas she had used that phrase to indict society in general. Late in 1979 Johnson was summoned before a church court on short notice without any charges being specified. She was excommunicated, and the formal notification cited the two disputed quotes. Technically she was not convicted over her ERA stand but for undermining the authorities and programs of the LDS church.

That was a transitional era for Mormon women in other ways. In 1970 the First Presidency issued a directive that ended the financial independence of the Relief Society, the denominational women's auxiliary. Too much energy was going into fund-raising projects, said the Presidency, so the male priesthood would henceforth take over all money matters, "leaving the sisters free to perform their specially assigned tasks." The Relief Society was to remain a useful vehicle for humanitarian service, training, and wholesome fellowship. But the women no longer raised their own money, no longer paid dues, and no longer decided to join the organization—all LDS women were enrolled automatically. All Relief Society financial assets were turned over to priesthood quorums. In the final indignity, the Relief Society was told to stop publishing its own magazine; there would be one magazine for adult Mormons of both sexes. The ubiquitous Correlation Committee also took charge of the women's educational materials and made the women's separate midweek sessions less important.

Unlike in other denominations, Mormon men control leadership appointments in the women's auxiliary. In the regional stakes the male priesthood picks the Relief Society president and has the right to approve her choice of counselors. The same system of priesthood control operates in the local wards. And the women's national officers serve at the pleasure of male hierarchs. Anderson complains that important decisions by the Relief Society president must get approval up the chain of command to her assigned adviser on the First Quorum of the Seventy, the Presidency of the Seventy, the executive committee of the Twelve, the full Twelve, and then the First Presidency. Though it is not a matter of church law, the authorities discourage women from serving in local Sunday school presidencies, restricting their officeholding to the Relief Society, Primary, and Young Women's auxiliaries. Since 1963 women have not been allowed to be ward clerks (secretaries), and the church also prefers that assistant clerks be men.

In earlier times Mormon women were allowed to impart blessings to the sick. But in 1946 the president of the Twelve, Joseph Fielding Smith, wrote the Relief Society that women should anoint only other women, "with the approval of the priesthood," and, he said, it would be "far better for us to follow the plan the Lord has given us and send for the Elders of the Church to come and administer to the sick and afflicted." From that point, the formal practice of women blessing other women and children died out. On the other hand, in 1978 the First Presidency and the Twelve ruled that it is permissible for women to pray audibly during Sunday sacrament meetings, and an *Ensign* article said Relief Society visiting teachers are allowed to offer prayers in private homes. LDS feminists have chafed perhaps most of all over the emphasis on homemaking and mothering at Young Women's and Relief Society meetings, as opposed to career options, and over the General Authorities' continual suggestion that a good Mormon woman's place is in the home, although that message has been moderated lately—perhaps because surveys show that many Mormon mothers now work outside the home.

In 1974 a group of restive Mormon women in the Boston area began publishing a newspaper titled *Exponent II,* named after a nineteenth-century independent suffragette publication that evolved into the Relief Society's now-defunct magazine. In *Exponent II*'s first issue, its editor,

Claudia L. Bushman, said the purpose was "to encourage and develop the talents of Mormon women." The paper, now using the more militant slogan "in celebration of the strength and diversity of women," remains one of the few outlets for LDS feminist expression. Its current editor, Jenny Atkinson, says, "The church is trying to put in place ways for women to be heard. But in an organization that's set up hierarchically, that's hard to [make] happen, especially when men's and women's roles are set and ordained by God. Even within the parameters of what Mormons can do, I think there would have to be huge structural changes in order to have true equality in terms of gender."

Though no explanations were given, some faculty members assumed that *Exponent II* was the reason that Brigham Young University authorities in 1993 tried to disinvite Bushman as a campus speaker and vetoed an appearance by another *Exponent II* founder, the historian Laurel Thatcher Ulrich. Ulrich, who was supposed to address the annual campus women's conference, is the only LDS woman to have received a MacArthur "genius" grant or the Pulitzer Prize. That same year the BYU board fired Carol Lee Hawkins, who had run the women's conference for six years. Those incidents were included in a 1996 indictment of the school's treatment of women, issued by the local chapter of the American Association of University Professors. Other grievances included the veto of a third woman speaker; rejection of five female faculty candidates who had been endorsed by academic administrators; press reports that Professor Marie Cornwall was criticized for including critical as well as laudatory voices in an academic conference on the Relief Society; and refusal to let the two female professors publish their study on Mormon survivors of childhood sexual abuse. The AAUP concluded that BYU "has a history of suppressing scholarship and artistic expressions representing the experience of women."

In 1996 *Exponent II* opened a new front in the culture wars, running sympathetic articles on homosexuality and listing resources. Not surprisingly, the issue did not recommend the recent Deseret Book title *Born That Way?: A True Story of Overcoming Same-Sex Attraction*. (Years before, Sonia Johnson had turned to lesbianism after her husband left her for another woman.) Although Boyd Packer's triple-threat speech ranked homosexual liberationists alongside intellectualism and feminism, in fact that movement's presence in Mormonism is minuscule. The only noticeable organization is Affirmation, a "support group for Mormon gay, lesbian, bisexual and dual/transgendered persons" formed in 1979. The organization, with a few hundred members and several local chapters, publishes brochures, manages a web site, and holds annual meetings.

One Affirmation member, a father of four, made a typical but unusually articulate plea to a church disciplinary council that excommunicated him in April of 1999. He stated that he met his same-sex partner of eleven years after his wife had decided to end their marriage. "I cannot comprehend our Father in Heaven endowing certain of his children with the unique characteristics of a gay person, then rejecting them," he declared. "There are things about which I do feel guilt, but I feel no guilt for being a gay man. I feel no guilt for sharing my life with my partner." He predicted that the church would change its policy, just as it had on plural marriage, blacks in the priesthood, and birth control.

The leadership of the Church of Jesus Christ of Latter-day Saints makes no apologies for clamping down on some Saints, though sometimes it apologizes for individual statements. One oft-quoted slogan appeared in a 1945 message to ward teachers in the denominational magazine *Improvement Era:* "When our leaders speak, the thinking has been done." When a Unitarian clergyman complained, President George A. Smith replied that the statement embarrassed the General Authorities. But that retraction went to one outsider while the magazine's instruction to the mass of Mormons was left uncorrected. And in 1979 First Counselor N. Eldon Tanner took to the pages of the denominational magazine to endorse the statement of the Young Women's president that "when the prophet speaks, the debate is over." A year later Apostle Ezra Taft Benson presented lavish assertions about the authority of the church president and said the "Living Prophet" is more vital to believers than "dead prophets," the Mormon scriptures, or the Bible. A heading in the 1982 manual for LDS college students proclaimed, "The Lord Will Never Permit the Living Prophet to Lead the Church Astray." In 1994 Apostle M. Russell Ballard told BYU students, "We will not lead you astray. We cannot."

Those are not chance comments, but expressions of a well-defined theology on authority and dissent. Apostle Packer explained the latter-day concept in his important Church Educational System address of 1981. Church history, "if not properly written or properly taught, . . . may be a faith destroyer," he said. "The writer or teacher who has an exaggerated loyalty to the theory that everything must be told is laying a foundation for his own judgment. . . . The Lord made it very clear that some things are to be taught selectively and some things are to be given only to those who are worthy." With an apparent reference to the solemn oaths of loyalty to church leaders that church members take during the temple endowment, he declared, "There is a limit to the patience of the Lord with respect to those who are under covenant to bless and protect His Church and kingdom upon the earth but do not do it. . . . We are at war with the adversary. We are not obliged as a church, nor are we as members obliged, to accommodate the enemy in this battle." Teachers paid by the church have a special responsibility to build faith, he said. "If you do not do that, but in fact accommodate the enemy, who is the destroyer of faith, you become in that sense a traitor to the cause you have made covenants to protect." Similar admonitions came at the 1985 CES symposium from Apostle Oaks. "Satan can even use truth to promote his purposes. Facts, severed from their context, can convey an erroneous impression," he said.

At the General Conference just after the 1993 September Six crackdown, Apostle James E. Faust, an attorney, stated that there is no concept of a "loyal opposition" to be found in the church. Each decision by a presiding quorum is unanimous, following private discussion. Similarly, among the membership at large there will be honest differences of opinion, but any questions are to be raised privately with priesthood overseers. "Those men and women who persist in publicly challenging basic doctrines, practices, and establishment of the Church sever themselves from the Spirit of the Lord and forfeit their right to place and influence in the Church. . . . There is a certain arrogance in thinking that any of us may be more spiritually intelligent, more learned, or more righteous than the Councils called to preside over us."

That November the First Presidency and the Twelve gave an official interpretation of church discipline in light of the September Six debate. "We have the responsibility to preserve the doctrinal purity of the Church. We are united in this objective." The Brethren quoted the *Handbook* on apostasy and, like Faust, distinguished it from mere difference of opinion. "The general and local officers of the Church will continue to do their duty and faithful members will understand."

The hierarchy's top fifteen quoted Joseph Smith: "That man who rises up to condemn others, finding fault with the Church, saying that they are out of the way, while he himself is righteous, then know assuredly, that that man is in the high road to apostasy." They also cited a saying of Jesus during his Book of Mormon ministry among Israelite Native Americans in the New World: "But if he repent not he shall not be numbered among my people, that he may not destroy my people," referring to III Nephi 18:31, Mosiah 26:36, and Alma 5:59. Joseph Smith's revelations provide today's leaders with all the scriptural warrant they need for taking action against troublemakers. Smith and his successor Brigham Young sent numerous close colleagues into exile for their disobedience. From July to November of 1831 alone, Smith uttered four denunciations of the rebellious in the name of God that are part of the LDS scriptures (D&C 1:3, 56:1, 63:2, 64:35).

Yet Joseph Smith Jr. was nothing if not a dissenter in his own time. And dissent has its uses, four of which are listed by Roger D. Launius and Linda Thatcher in their anthology on Mormon dissidents, *Differing Visions: Dissenters in Mormon History.* Dissent helps distinguish between normative and illegitimate positions, generates solidarity among believers as they rally to punish or save malcontents, lets members "blow off steam," and provides a useful "warning sign to church leaders that real concerns need to be reconciled."

BYU's David J. Cherrington says much the same in an *Encyclopedia of Mormonism* article that scans the Mormon History Association, *Exponent, Dialogue, Sunstone,* Affirmation, the Women's Forum, and the rest. "Unofficial organizations and their publications may serve at least six important functions for Church members and/or the Church," he writes. They let Mormons exchange ideas with people from different religions.

They provide social support for their members. They add to the body of Mormon literature. They give the "opportunity to learn and distribute new insights." They allow people with unorthodox beliefs to share questions "in an open forum where they feel adequate acceptance." And they provide a platform for advocacy among "members who feel a need to promote change." Leonard Arrington observed another sort of benefit: he said the appearance of *Dialogue* "reinvigorated" its more official and orthodox rival, *BYU Studies.*

And, it might be added, Mormon dissenters have sometimes been proven right.

But at the end of the twentieth century there is palpable worry and alienation among some of Mormondom's best and brightest who remain loyal church members in good standing. Reflect on the devastating words of one of *Dialogue's* founders, Eugene England, speaking with the *Student Review* (yet another independent publication) at the close of his career at BYU: "I'm pretty pessimistic because it seems like things are just getting narrower and narrower. It's beginning to affect the students." He observes "pressures on the faculty for orthodoxy to the point that they're really afraid to explore questions," and students who distrust their own teachers and are afraid to read anything that is "culturally incorrect."

Or hear the poignant pain coming from Armand L. Mauss, a retired professor of sociology at Washington State University: "I have come to feel increasingly marginal to the Mormon community during my adult life, at least in a social and intellectual sense, despite my continuing and conscientious participation in church activity (including leadership) and despite my own deep personal faith in the religion itself."

For those in charge of any human institution, open debate can be irksome. In a religious institution, especially, uncertainty about belief can bring serious spiritual consequences. But there is always a high price to be paid when certain questions are not to be asked, when certain questioners are not to be welcomed, and when certain leaders are not to be questioned.

CHAPTER 22

MORMONISM IN THE TWENTY-FIRST CENTURY

DESPITE HIS SECULAR SUCCESS, WILLIAM SHEFFIELD, A STATE SUPERIOR court judge in Orange County, California, was unsettled. "The question whether there was a God gnawed at me, and I needed to resolve it." A nominal Episcopalian back then in 1984, Sheffield decided to enter the Yale Divinity School and explore things. In New Haven his wife, a "Jack Mormon" who hadn't been to church in years, began attending LDS services with the kids, so he tagged along, unenthusiastically. When he heard the bishop deliver the standard testimony about Joseph's First Vision and the golden tablets, "I said, personally, I'm not related to Disney or Spielberg." But the bishop coaxed Sheffield into reading the Book of Mormon, and when a Yale Bible professor told him the Book contained some sophisticated theology, he began taking it more seriously. Eventually he decided that "it must be a great lie, or a great truth. It's one or the other," and further study at Brigham Young University convinced him that an ill-educated farm boy like Joseph Smith couldn't simply have made it up. He received LDS baptism in 1985 and resumed his legal career as an arbitrator in California.

Jana Riess, a devout Presbyterian attending Wellesley College, befriended Mormon classmates and "wondered how such intelligent women could be involved in such a wacky religious group." The summer before entering Princeton Theological Seminary to train for the ministry, she visited Joseph Smith's Vermont birthplace and accepted a missionary guide's challenge to read Smith's scriptures for herself. "I really fell in love with the Book of Mormon," she says, and began migrating toward some aspects of LDS doctrine. "Mormons don't really believe Jesus was God, and I don't either." She was baptized LDS in 1993, months before graduating from seminary. Her husband, who remained Methodist, "took it wonderfully." Forsaking a clergy career, she became a doctoral student in American history at Columbia University and the religion book review editor of *Publishers Weekly.*

But adjustments remained to be made, and they may say something about twenty-first-century Mormonism, since the bulk of converts, like Riess, come from conventional Christian backgrounds, and more and more of them are well educated. She said Smith's doctrine that God the Father has a physical body was "a challenge for me, because I was trained as a theologian." No Mormon prophets or apostles have ever had the equivalent of her own Princeton training. As for governance from top to bottom by an all-male priesthood, this self-avowed feminist admitted, "I can't say I have come to terms with it." Further, "it's hard to relate to the cultural baggage, certainly of gender roles, but also the deification of the General Authorities." More offputting yet was the church's campaign against free-spirited intellectuals such as the September Six. "I find this McCarthyite 'guilt by association' stuff very frightening. If they win the victory in those terms, they will lose the war." But at the grassroots level "the church creates a community like none I've seen in other religious groups" or anywhere else in our unstable culture. "I'm much happier as a Mormon than I was as a Protestant."

The sociologist Thomas O'Dea might not have imagined the likes of Sheffield or Riess converting to the church when he wrote his classic 1957 study *The Mormons.* The faith was then disseminated largely on the basis of clan and county and just beginning its nationwide diaspora. To some the future seemed problematic. O'Dea reported that critics (unnamed) thought Mormonism would enter "a long twilight" leading toward "obsolescence," if not "extinction." Once the western wilderness and Gentile prejudice had been conquered, so the thinking went, the church's tightly organized "posture of combat" was ill fitted to cope with American normalcy. O'Dea didn't buy that prophecy of doom, but he did forecast future problems. The budding movement for women's equality would cause no disruptions within the fold, he figured, and the black priesthood issue was so unimportant that he did not even mention it. But O'Dea warned that the church lacked the contemplative and philosophical resources it needed for long-term strength now that the older emergencies were behind it. He saw related difficulties: Mormonism's awkward "encounter with modern secular thought" and the "unhappy intellectual group" that was emerging within the church.

Correct description, wrong prescription. The church has prospered handsomely while doing little to accommodate the philosophical cast of mind, secular thinking, or the Mormons' own intellectual class. Theological confusions and historical anomalies, the sorts of things that bother scholars, have mattered little. Ours is a relational era, not a conceptual one. Members are more likely to be attracted by networking and community than by truth claims. The adherents appear to be contented, or docile in their discontent, except for some thousands of intellectuals.

Reactions to the 1990s purges barely registered on the Richter scale. The LDS church is one of the few large American denominations without a significant feminist wing. The Saints do not seek a voice even on mundane matters. Sure, one of the nation's best-known Mormons can say, "I think people who pay the tithe should be allowed to know how the money is spent." But he's Jack Anderson, an investigative reporter. Some might wonder how an authoritarian and secretive church could maintain appeal within an open democratic culture like that of the United States. However, the Mormon administrative style is inspired by corporate America, not democratic America. The future of Mormonism will be shaped by former businessmen and Church Educational System teachers, not by theologians and social analysts.

Twenty-seven years after O'Dea, another sociologist, Rodney Stark, presented a different sort of forecast. He projected that by A.D. 2080 the

Saints would increase to 63 million, by a conservative reckoning, and to 265 million if they kept up their postwar pace. Mormonism would be the first new world faith since Islam. Updating "the Mormon 'miracle' of rapid growth," Stark's 1998 update has the Saints ahead of schedule, with the membership increase running about 10 percent above his higher projection. The worldwide flock now exceeds 10 million, and counting. In the United States the LDS Church is poised to surpass the Church of God in Christ and the Evangelical Lutheran Church in America and become the fifth-largest denomination (behind the Roman Catholics, Southern Baptists, United Methodists, and National Baptists).

Asked why he thinks converts are flocking in, President Gordon B. Hinckley said, "They find sociability. They find friends. We're a very friendly church. We're a happy, go-ahead people, and others like it." In addition, "they see in this church an anchor in a world of shifting values. The family is falling apart in America and across the world. We're putting strong emphasis on the family. It's appealing to people. They like it. They welcome it. They need help, and we offer that help. Furthermore, it gives purpose to life. We give a point of view. We answer the old questions of where did I come from, why am I here, where am I going? These great religious questions have been asked by men throughout the ages. We give them an assurance of who they are, sons and daughters of God. People find comfort, they find peace, they find strength in that."

To promote that upbeat message and pronounce Mormonism's entry into the American mainstream, the publicist-president booked media appearances with the likes of Mike Wallace and Larry King. An equally telling cultural moment, though not one that the Saints celebrated, had occurred a few years earlier when the playwright Tony Kushner won lavish media attention, and Pulitzer and Tony Awards, for his play *Angels in America.* Kushner mingled fashionable themes of political liberalism, AIDS, and gay pride with a most unexpected element: Mormonism. His treatment of the Saints was "a tourist's invention, rather quaint and smart-alecky," says Michael Evenden of Emory University. Broadway's toleration was carefully limited: Mormons were acceptable so long as they ceased being Mormon. The decade's pop Buddhists received far fonder treatment from the avatars of entertainment. But at least the Saints were important enough to be noticed and commented on. A similar instance of cultural arrival was the snide short story of ex-Mormon Walter Kirn about an LDS teen tour, published by Tina Brown's *New Yorker* in 1997 just before *Time* gave the church more respectful cover treatment.

Such is the give-and-take of a free society. And as Jan Shipps observes, a church that has millions of adherents loses "the protection of minority religious status." As with any large American institution, "what goes on within Mormonism is no longer simply an internal issue." But the thin-skinned and image-conscious Mormons can still display some immature, isolationist, and defensive reactions to outsiders, perhaps because there is no substantive debate and no "loyal opposition" within their kingdom. With some it almost seems that the wilderness is yet to be tamed, the federal "polyg" police are on the prowl, and the Illinois lynch mob is oiling the muskets and preparing to raid Carthage Jail. The FARMS team is particularly shrill in its rhetoric, an odd pose for an organization that seeks to win intellectual respectability for the church. All too often Saints use the label "anti-Mormon" as a tactic to forestall serious discussion.

Nor are the Mormons alone in facing cultural despisers. Catholics put up with continual insults without complaint (except from the Catholic League). And the Protestant Evangelicals, who are not organized enough to create their own antidefamation league, have had to endure the Scopes trial and H. L. Mencken, *Inherit the Wind,* Sinclair Lewis's *Elmer Gantry,* and the stereotypes of the latest made-for-TV movie or comedy routine.

Secular scoffing has done absolutely nothing to deter Mormon advance or to discourage Hinckley in his activist presidency. "The time has come for us to stand a little taller, to lift our eyes and stretch our minds to a greater comprehension and understanding of this, the Church of Jesus Christ of Latter-day Saints," he told his first General Conference as Smith's fourteenth successor. "It is a time to move forward without hesitation." Hinckley unhesitatingly carried the charisma of his prophethood to all corners of the globe and hugely increased the worldwide construction of temples. Meetinghouses also multiplied at a rapid clip.

The campaign is reminiscent of the chapel-building binge that nearly bankrupted the church a generation earlier. But Hinckley's church does not seem short of cash, and his team has devised many of the newer projects as economical micro-temples to serve the increasingly far-flung membership. A larger long-term question looms, however. To what extent are American tithe-payers subsidizing the church in less affluent countries, and how long can they do so if pell-mell growth persists? Given the LDS penchant for secrecy, only a handful of men among the 10 million know the answer.

But chances are that the new temples and meetinghouses are prudently budgeted out of current income since the church dislikes indebtedness. If a crunch occurs, the church has substantial cash reserves and investment resources on hand to supplement current income. In addition, the new temples can be seen as investments in that the announcement of a new temple appears to increase regional members' desire to fulfill the tithing regulation and obtain temple access. Meetinghouses may similarly foster offerings. As for deficit financing overseas, officialdom is thought to be well aware of this problem, rather conservative in the spending of assets, and, due to centralized control and flexibility of the system, readily able to balance expenses and available funding.

The Hinckley era's most ambitious building project is the 21,000-seat, three-tiered assembly building just north of Temple Square, scheduled to open for the church conference in April of 2000 (despite grumbling about the supplanting of the grand old Tabernacle, which will continue in use for the choir programs). The church plans to remake one block of adjacent Main Street. It paid the city $8.1 million to buy that property to turn the block between the temple and church office buildings into a park. Beyond all this comes the 2002 Winter Olympics, bringing glamour and global attention to Salt Lake City after the preliminary headaches and scandals.

The statistical reports that flow across Hinckley's desk enhance the sense of well-being. But the *World Christian Encyclopedia*'s David Barrett provides a useful reminder that other churches are doing as well, or better. The Seventh-day Adventists, for instance, brag with Mormon-style number-crunching fervor that they gain converts at a global rate of one per forty-four seconds and on average establish a new congregation every four hours or so. And LDS scholars have taken a bit of the shine off their church's glowing numbers. As with other denominations, the totals on baptized members do not consider how many have drifted into inactivity or unbelief while remaining on the rolls. Back-door losses, for instance, are the reason Jehovah's Witnesses do not grow faster, despite door-to-door evangelistic efforts far surpassing even those of the Mormons.

The LDS Church's own research unit may know about retention problems, but it releases few of its findings. However, there are shards of information available. Take Brazil, which ranks second to the United States in Mormon population. One student of Brazilian Mormonism estimated in 1988 that among those on the official membership rolls only 15 to 20 percent were very active, another 30 to 40 percent were nominally active, and some 40 to 55 percent had little or no contact with the church. A sour ex-Mormon who had done a mission in Rio de Janeiro claims that most of the converts were children and uneducated adults who yielded to authoritative argumentation and evangelistic pressure for baptism but then quickly abandoned the church.

In South Africa the leader of the black branch near Capetown who told journalist Peggy Fletcher Stack that the members' weekly attendance rate was around 25 percent also said missionaries probably rush prospects into baptism without adequate preparation. In the United States a report found that the attrition rate among African American converts was 60 to 90 percent in Columbia, South Carolina, and Greensboro, North Carolina. If those two towns are at all typical, there is a major, if unacknowledged, problem. It is unclear whether blacks defect as they learn about the Mormon prophets' previous racial theology.

The BYU sociologist Tim B. Heaton reported in 1992 that Mormons' weekly attendance rate in Asia and Latin America was only about 25 percent, so nominal membership is a factor on two continents that encompass one-third of the worldwide membership. (Healthier rates of 40 to 50 percent were reported for the United States, Canada, Africa, and the South Pacific.) In the United States a survey cited by Heaton showed that 33 percent of Mormons were "disengaged," with 19 percent believing but no longer attending and 14 percent neither believing nor attending. (Heaton estimated that excommunication and formal resignation affected less than 1 percent of the membership, though those figures are not made public.)

Lawrence A. Young, the BYU professor who has studied Melchizedek priesthood figures as a clue to retention rates, theorizes that "part of the

failure in some countries is due to Mormonism's inability to find indigenous expressions of its community that allow new members to accommodate to both the church and the host society." In other words, with 70
percent rate of ordination to the Melchizedek priesthood in Utah, the
faith had the closest cultural "fit" there, and did pretty well elsewhere in
North America, but seemed quite alien in a nation like Mexico, where the
retention rate plummeted to 19 percent. Another way to put it is that for
members in Utah, Mormonism is not just a shared creed but an ethnic
identity and a family heritage, with a good dose of frontier nostalgia
mixed in. The same is true, less intensely, in other parts of the United
States. But in most spots overseas, Mormonism is a system of belief seeking to create a community. Perhaps because the statistics are less tri-
umphal than baptismal figures, the church no longer publishes
Melchizedek priesthood figures in its almanac.

Compared with other world missionary faiths, the LDS Church bears
heavy nationalistic baggage. It proclaims that God commissioned a
prophet in the United States uniquely to restore the scriptures and priesthood, that Jesus Christ will return to Missouri and establish the future
millennial kingdom when the earth is 7,000 years old, and that the
American constitutional system is uniquely the product of divine inspiration. When the Mormon folk selected their own special holy day, it was
not the anniversary of their prophet's birth, the coming forth of the Book
of Mormon, the establishment of the priesthood or of the church, but
rather Pioneer Day, celebrating Brigham Young's 1847 arrival at the Salt
Lake Basin. Moreover, Mormons believe that God has granted total control of his one and only church to fifteen men in Salt Lake City, almost all
of whom have been Americans.

Martin E. Marty, the retired University of Chicago historian, says,
"This is the only religion with scripture set partly in America. It's an
American book, ready to go. They know their slot, and it's a huge market:
the Norman Rockwell, Lawrence Welk, flag, Boy Scout, anti-gay, anti-
ERA world. They are so American—after being so hated."

Hinckley plays down the Americanness. "Our message is universal. It
isn't an American message." He also insists that "our leadership is universal," referring to the ward and stake leaders overseas rather than to the

Yankees who retain nearly all the real power at the top. The few foreigners chosen for ascent are quite likely to be those who are the most Americanized and the most obedient to the American hierarchy.

But sometimes the way they get things done raises further issues. Why do missionaries wear the required LDS uniform of white shirts and dark suits when that marks them as outsiders? Should the thinly prepared young missionary volunteers be supplemented by Catholic- and Protestant-style career missionaries who are deeply immersed in the foreign cultures? Why impose generic architectural plans from Salt Lake on meetinghouses in far-off places? Why must each and every women's auxiliary lesson be the same for every nation, written and vetted in Salt Lake? Why celebrate Pioneer Day in Bolivia? Why must African wards sing American hymns to the accompaniment of pianos while drums and dancing are forbidden? BYU interviewing for a nationwide study of American black converts found considerable longing for the gospel music they had left behind in Baptist churches. And will the Americans atop the LDS power pyramid ever agree that the foreigners, now that they constitute a majority of the baptized membership, should be the majority among the apostles?

Young notes that a different strategy would "allow indigenous expression to emerge," which is the reason the Mormons' Evangelical Protestant rivals, with their missiological think tanks, succeed so well in Latin America. The same could be said of the "inculturation" of Catholic worship in Africa. In one listing, twenty-three scholarly studies between 1976 and 1992 demonstrated "ludicrous" consequences when "correlation" policies from Utah headquarters were forced on non-American congregations.

But these are the sorts of questions raised by the intellectual strategists, with whom the hierarchy has a wary if not antagonistic relationship.

One crucial factor for the twenty-first century will be the identity of Hinckley's successors. An LDS president serves for life and is then succeeded automatically by the person with the longest tenure as an apostle. So the next president would very likely be Thomas S. Monson, who has been a member of the three-man First Presidency since 1985. Born in 1927 in Salt Lake and seventeen years Hinckley's junior, Monson was nearly foreordained for the top job in 1963 when President David O. McKay's administration tapped him as an apostle when he was only thirty-six, the youngest appointee in a half-century. But then, Monson had made bishop at age twenty-two. He was the first World War II veteran to become an apostle, and the first with a master's degree in business administration (from BYU, where he also earned a bachelor's in business). At the time of his selection Monson was general manager of the church-owned Deseret Press, a major commercial printing firm, after having served as the sales manager and an advertising executive with the *Deseret News*. While an apostle, he also served as president and board chairman of the Deseret News publishing company. Monson, the father of three, is regarded as an avuncular, middle-roading administrator who has the public relations instincts of Hinckley but not the high-level skills.

It is a far different story with the man next in line. Boyd K. Packer cuts a higher profile than Monson and puts more stock in bluntness than in PR. Though a bit older than Monson, having been born in 1924 in Brigham City, Utah, Packer is thought to be in robust health, so it is quite possible he would live to succeed Monson or Hinckley. Packer, a B-24 bomber pilot in the Pacific during World War II, earned an education degree at Utah State University, taught high school seminary, and did advanced study in education at BYU. The church almanac has for years claimed he has a Ph.D.; his doctorate is actually the less academically rigorous Ed.D. He served as assistant administrator of the seminary and institute program, as an assistant to the Twelve Apostles, and as president of the New England mission before becoming an apostle at age forty-five. He is the father of ten.

A Packer presidency could be a crossroads, since he is quite possibly the most doctrinaire of today's apostles and the most likely to enforce an even harder party line and to let the chips fall. Mormon liberals assume that Packer more than anyone else orchestrated the 1990s crackdown on intellectuals and feminists. Ezra Taft Benson was expected to be that sort of president too, but he was eighty-six and in failing health when he took charge in 1985 and was more amenable to his colleagues than Packer might be.

D. Michael Quinn, the historian of the hierarchy, is more willing than most to speak freely about Packer's method and manner, particularly now that he has been excommunicated: "Packer is combative and willing to go to the mat with the apostles on any issue. They simply acquiesce. If not, every weekly Temple meeting of the First Presidency and the Quorum would be an argument. Howard Hunter [then an apostle and later the church president] told me himself in 1983, 'I don't want to turn every Temple meeting into a fight so I don't say anything,' referring to apostles he called zealots. Leaders like Hinckley are in a quandary because the smooth operation of the church is impeded if every agenda item becomes a knock-down battle, so they have to pick and choose where to oppose him."

Asked about the prospect of a Packer presidency, a well-informed, lib-erally inclined Mormon gave a succinct assessment: "Scary." (For other apostles who might succeed to the presidency, see the Endnotes for this chapter.)

Many leading analysts of the LDS Church agree that the hierarchical defensiveness, disciplining, and "correlation" are natural responses to exponential growth. The leaders fear that things could spin out of control, and they are more detached from the membership. Moreover, the old familial and friendship bonds count for less in a large, bureaucratized sys-tem. A sophisticated analysis of Mormonism's recent "retrenchment" is provided in *The Angel and the Beehive* (1994) by the LDS sociologist Armand L. Mauss.

Earlier in the twentieth century, according to Mauss's account, the General Authorities played down older distinctives, educators made use of outside thinkers, and Mormons generally assimilated with American cul-ture, a process that reached its apex in the 1960s. Certain lifestyle traits (for instance, teetotaling and marrying within the faith) remained. And LDS doctrines were regarded as heresies by traditional Christians, to be sure, but America was indifferent to theology and less interested in God's reve-lations than in personal fulfillment. Mormons had become so successful in living down their nineteenth-century disrepute that they now faced "the predicament of respectability" and felt the need to reinforce their identity and the boundaries of their subculture.

That predicament has conditioned the leadership's policies ever since: centralized control, continuing secrecy, regimentation, "correlation," obe-dience, suspicion toward intellectuals, suppression of open discussion, file-keeping on members for disciplinary use, sporadic purges of malcontents,

church education as indoctrination, the proselytizing push, and reempha-
sis on religious uniqueness (the centrality of temples and related genealogical work, continuous revelation through modern prophets, understanding
the Bible in the light of Smith's special revelations). Mormonism still
desires mainstream status, but largely in order to foster good public relations and proselytism, and in certain cases, alliance with other conservative
religious groups to achieve political influence in selected issues.

In the process of retrenchment, some of the church's best and brightest
have become alienated. Quinn, a brilliant analyst now on the sidelines,
observes that suggestions and complaints from the *Sunstone* and *Dialogue*
set "will have no effect, because the leadership of the church basically
writes off the North American liberals as disloyal. . . . I see Mormonism in
for a long Dark Ages." But he thinks that will change as educated leaders
from other nations arise to "create a climate internationally that demands
a free marketplace of ideas. That may be slow in coming, but I think it's
going to happen." He does not look for alterations in doctrine (such as
women in the priesthood) but believes there may be "fundamental changes
in policy otherwise."

What such liberal interpretations ignore is that Mormonism may
appeal precisely because of its authoritarianism. Evangelical propagandists
keep trying to score points by demonstrating that the Mormon prophets
have changed their teachings. But what matters most to Mormons, perhaps, is not the content of the creed but the confidence with which it is
affirmed and reaffirmed. This is, after all, a church that believes in latter-
day revelation. As Ezra Taft Benson proclaimed, a living prophet trumps
dead prophets. And if Joseph Smith in 1830 could upend several millennia
of Judeo-Christian tradition, why could not the Smith of 1844 repeal the
revelations of 1830? An evangelistic booklet from BYU says proudly, "Some
may see change in the teachings and practices as an inconsistency or weak-
ness, but to Latter-day Saints change is a sign of the very foundation of
strength," namely, that God continues to reveal his will through his
church.

What has remained consistent from 1830 through to the twenty-first
century is the conviction that God has a latter-day prophet and priesthood through which he uniquely works his will upon the earth. If so,

unquestioning obedience is a logical response. And in an age of moral turmoil and 500-channel spiritual choices, many people desire just such
decisive leadership.

The Mormon hierarchs can hardly be inspired to loosen the reins if they
look over the fence at the experience of other denominations.
Conservative Protestant groups that began floating leftward, such as the
Southern Baptist Convention and the Lutheran Church—Missouri
Synod, went through virtual civil war when they decided things had gone
too far and moved forcibly back to the right. The pope and his American
allies have faced great difficulty in their attempts to restore an older era's
form of discipline and to keep Catholic theologians and colleges in line.
Protestant denominations that embraced a liberal policy of theological
pluralism—for example, United Methodist, Presbyterian (U.S.A.),
Episcopal, United Church of Christ, and Disciples of Christ—have suffered drift and decline. The liberalization and resulting confusion in the
Reorganized Church is perhaps most unnerving of all.

In conveying a sense of religious authority, the LDS Church is not alone
in the marketplace. While some look to Temple Square, myriad Catholics
follow the pope, and the most successful variants of Protestantism preach
an infallible and trustworthy Bible with answers to the human plight that
can clearly be understood by all. The Saints' wholesome moral living pays
off in health and contented lives, but such is the case with other faiths as
well. Like the Mormons, the Evangelicals uphold traditional morals and
encourage personalized testimonials. And on certain aspects of religion the
Saints fall short compared with other groups. They lack the meditative
techniques that are so appealing today. Even a mediocre Protestant
preacher is bound to present better Sunday sermons than the ward talks
from Mormonism's lay amateurs. The Saints lack the immense intellectual
resources found in mainstream Judaism and Christianity and, except perhaps for temple rites, the liturgical and aesthetic richness of Catholicism,
Orthodoxy, Lutheranism, and Episcopalianism.

But those religious competitors can learn much from the Mormons.
The Saints outshine most in devotion to what they believe. Generous with
their time, they also put their money where their mouth is, faithfully
tithing for the church and fasting for the needy, even as American society

promotes selfishness. While other Americans yield to the demands of youth, adult Mormons impose high demands on their next generation, requiring them to ingest church teaching an hour a day through high school and expecting the boys to save up their own money and spend two years in hard-core mission work. The system produces young adults with pride and commitment.

"This is a story of success," says Gordon Bitner Hinckley, the Prophet, Seer, and Revelator. "From that pioneer beginning in this desert valley, where a plow had never before broken the soil, to what you see today of this work here and across the world, you can't reach any other conclusion." This success is far more than new buildings or convert tallies arising. The Mormon people encircle each other in a loving community, seeking to make sure that everyone has a divinely appointed task and that no one's needs are overlooked. In modern, fractionated American society, those are accomplishments as impressive as building a city-state on the Mississippi, hauling handcarts across the prairies, or making the arid Salt Lake Basin bloom.

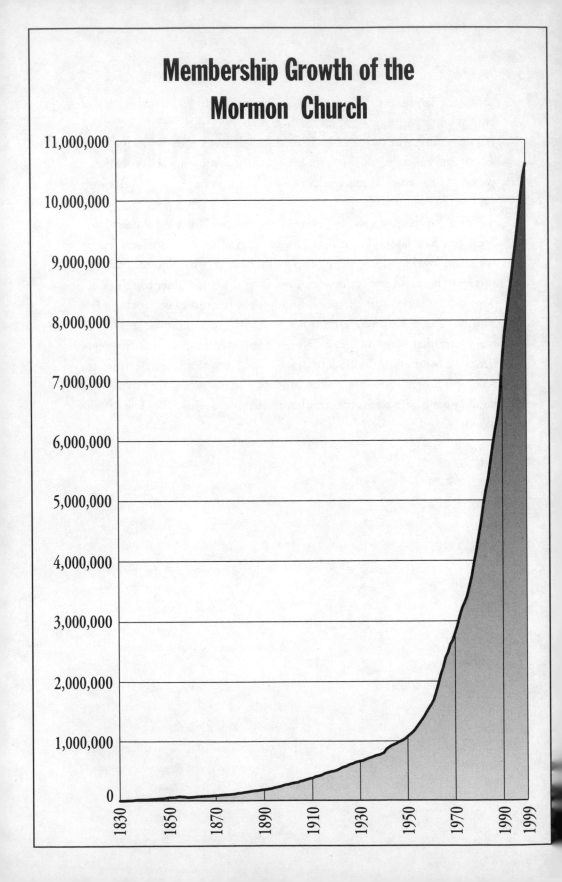

JOSEPH SMITH'S KING FOLLETT DISCOURSE

THIS SERMON, DELIVERED ON APRIL 7, 1844, BY THE PROPHET JOSEPH Smith Jr., is a central source for the Latter-day Saints' unusual beliefs on the nature of God, man, and the created universe. It has a high doctrinal status a bit below that of the Mormon scriptures, which also contain many of these concepts. A eulogy for a well-known Saint named King Follett, it was Smith's last address to a church General Conference; he was martyred only weeks later. Donald Q. Cannon of Brigham Young University says it "may be one of the Prophet's greatest sermons because of its comprehensive doctrinal teachings," while his BYU colleague Robert Millet calls it "one of his most profound and searching sermons," as well as one of the most controversial.

The prophet taught that man has the capacity to become a god, along with related beliefs in the plurality of gods (the church dislikes the synonym "polytheism"), and that God was not always God but had a prior existence as a mortal man. Smith also rejected the orthodox doctrine that God created the material universe "out of nothing" (*ex nihilo*), insisting that matter and human intelligences are eternal along with God, having no beginning or end. The "King Follett Discourse" represents a clear and formal expression of his mature thinking on these crucial theological innovations.

Church sources have continually cited and reprinted the Discourse. The prophet obviously considered it a highly important statement, since four scribes took down his words. There were trivial variations among those transcriptions, and modern LDS scholars have edited a conflated text. The following excerpts come from the version printed in the *Journal of Discourses,* a nineteenth-century British LDS periodical of church leaders' teachings, available on the *New Mormon Studies* CD-ROM.

. . . I will prove that the world is wrong, by showing what God is. I am going to inquire after God; for I want you all to know him and to be familiar with him; and if I can bring you to a knowledge of him, all persecutions against me ought to cease. You will then know that I am his servant; for I speak as one having authority.

I will go back to the beginning, before the [world] was, to show what kind of a being God is. What sort of a being was God in the beginning? Open your ears and hear, all ye ends of the earth; for I am going to prove it to you by the Bible, and to tell you the designs of God in relation to the human race, and why he interferes with the affairs of man.

God himself was once as we are now, and is an exalted Man, and sits enthroned in yonder heavens. That is the great secret. If the vail was rent to-day, and the great God who holds this world in its orbit, and who upholds all worlds and all things by his power, was to make himself visible,—I say, if you were to see him to-day, you would see him like a man in form—like yourselves, in all the person, image, and very form as a man; for Adam was created in the very fashion, image, and likeness of God, and received instruction from, and walked, talked, and conversed with him, as one man talks and communes with another.

In order to understand the subject of the dead, for the consolation of those who mourn for the loss of their friends, it is necessary that we should understand the character and being of God, and how he came to be so; for I am going to tell you how God came to be God.

We have imagined and supposed that God was God from all eternity. I will refute that idea, and will take away and do away the vail, so that you may see.

These are incomprehensible ideas to some; but they are simple. It is the first principle of the Gospel to know for a certainty the character of God and to know that we may converse with him as one man converses with another, and that he was once a man like us; yea, that God himself the Father of us all, dwelt on an earth the same as Jesus Christ himself did; and I will show it from the Bible. I wish I was in a suitable place to tell it, and that I had the trump of an archangel, so that I could tell the story in such a manner that persecution would cease for ever. What did Jesus say? (Mark it, Elder Rigdon.) The Scriptures inform us that Jesus said, "As the Father hath power in himself, even so hath the Son power"—to do what? Why, what the Father did. The answer is obvious—in a manner, to lay down his body and take it up again. Jesus, what are you [going] to do? To lay down my life, as my Father did, and take it up again. Do you believe it? If you do not believe it, you do not believe the Bible. The Scriptures say it, and I defy all the learning and wisdom and all the combined powers of earth and hell together to refute it.

Here, then, is eternal life—to know the only wise and true God; and you have got to learn how to be Gods yourselves, and to be kings and priests to God, the same as all Gods have done before you— namely, by going from one small degree to another, and from a small capacity to a great one—from grace to grace, from exaltation to exaltation, until you attain to the resurrection of the dead and are able to dwell in everlasting burnings and to sit in glory, as do those who sit enthroned in everlasting power. And I want you to know that God, in the last days, while certain individuals are proclaiming his name, is not trifling with you or me.

These are the first principles of consolation. How consoling to the mourners, when they are called to part with a husband, wife, father, mother, child, or dear relative, to know that, although the earthly tabernacle is laid down and dissolved, they shall rise again, to dwell in everlasting burnings in immortal glory, not to sorrow, suffer, or die any more; but they shall be heirs of God and joint heirs with Jesus Christ. What is it? To inherit the same power, the same glory, and the same exaltation, until you arrive at the station of a God and ascend the throne of eternal power, the same as those who have gone before. What did Jesus do? Why, I do the things I saw my Father do when worlds come rolling into existence. My Father worked out his kingdom with fear and trembling, and I must do the same; and when I get my kingdom, I shall present it to my Father, so that he may obtain kingdom upon kingdom, and it will exalt him in glory. He will then take a higher exaltation, and I will take his place, and thereby become exalted myself. So that Jesus treads in the track of his Father, and inherits what God did before; and God is thus glorified and exalted in the salvation and exaltation of all his children. It is plain beyond disputation; and you thus learn some of the first principles of the Gospel, about which so much hath been said.

When you climb a ladder, you must begin at the bottom, and ascend step by step until you arrive at the top; and so it is with the principles of the Gospel: you must begin with the first, and go on until you learn all the principles of exaltation. But it will be a great while after you have passed through the vail before you will have learned them. It is not all to be comprehended in this world: it will be a great work to learn our salvation and exaltation even beyond the grave. I suppose I am not allowed to go into an investigation of anything that is not contained in the Bible. If I did, I think there are so many overwise men here, that they would cry "treason" and put me to death. So I will go to the old Bible and turn commentator today.

I shall comment on the very first Hebrew word in the Bible. I will make a comment on the very first sentence of the history of creation in the Bible—*Berosheit*. I want to analyze the word. *Baith*—in, by, through, and everything else. *Rosh*—the head. *Sheit*—grammatical termination. When the inspired man wrote it, he did not put the *Baith* there. An old Jew, without any authority, added the word. He thought it too bad to begin to talk about the head! It read first, "The head one of the Gods brought forth the Gods." That is the true meaning of the words. *Baurau* signifies to bring forth. If you do not believe it, you do not believe the learned man of God. Learned men can teach you no more than what I have told you. Thus, the head God brought forth the Gods in the grand council.

I will transpose and simplify it in the English language. Oh, ye lawyers, ye doctors, and ye priests, who have persecuted me, I want to let you know that the Holy Ghost knows something as well as you do. The head God called together the Gods and sat in grand council to bring forth the world. The grand counsellors sat at the head in yonder heavens, and contemplated the creation of the worlds which were created at that time. . . .

In the beginning, the head of the Gods called a council of the Gods; and they came together and concocted a plan to create the world and people it. When we begin to learn in this way, we begin to learn the only true God and what kind of a being we have got to worship. Having a knowledge of God, we begin to know how to approach him and how to ask so as to receive an answer.

When we understand the character of God and know how to come to him, he begins to unfold the heavens to us and to tell us all about it. When we are ready to come to him, he is ready to come to us.

Now, I ask all who hear me, why the learned men who are preaching salvation say that God created the heavens and the earth out of nothing? The reason is, that they are unlearned in the things of God and have not the gift of the Holy Ghost. They account it blasphemy in any one to contradict their idea. If you tell them that God made the world out of something, they will call you a [fool]. But I am learned, and know more than all the world put together. The Holy Ghost does, anyhow; and he is within me, and comprehends more than all the world; and I will associate myself with him.

You ask the learned doctors why they say the world was made out of nothing; and they will answer, "Don't the Bible say he created the world?" And they infer, from the word create, that it must have been made out of nothing. Now, the word create came from the word [*baurau*], which does not mean to create out of nothing; it means to organize—the same as a man would organize materials and build a ship. Hence we infer that God had materials to organize the world out of chaos—chaotic matter, which is element, and in which dwells all the glory. Element had an existence from the time He had. The pure principles of element are principles which can never be destroyed: they may be organized and reorganized, but not destroyed. They had no beginning, and can have no end.

I have another subject to dwell upon, which is calculated to exalt man. But it is impossible for me to say much on this subject. I shall, therefore, just touch upon it; for time will not permit me to say all. It is associated with the subject of the resurrection of the dead— namely, the soul, the mind of man, the immortal spirit. Where did it come from? All learned men and doctors of divinity say that God created it in the beginning. But it is not so. The very idea lessens man in my estimation. I do not believe the doctrine. I know better. Hear it, all ye ends of the world; for God has told me so; and if you don't believe me, it will not make the truth without effect. I will make a man appear a [fool] before I get through, if he does not believe it. I am going to tell of things more noble.

We say that God himself is a self-existent being. Who told you so? It is correct enough; but how did it get into your heads? Who told you that man did not exist in like manner upon the same principle? Man does exist upon the same principles. God made a tabernacle and put a spirit into it, and it became a living soul. [Referred to the old Bible.] How does it read in the Hebrew? It does not say in the Hebrew that God created the spirit of man. It says, "God made man out of the earth, and put into him Adam's spirit, and so became a living body."

The mind or the intelligence which man possesses is coequal with God himself. I know that my testimony is true; hence, when I talk to these mourners, what have they lost? Their relatives and friends are only separated from their bodies for a short season: their spirits which existed with God have left the tabernacle of clay only for a little moment, as it were; and they now exist in a place where they converse together the same as we do on the earth.

I am dwelling on the immortality of the spirit of man. Is it logical to say that the intelligence of spirits is immortal, and yet that it had a beginning? The intelligence of spirits had no beginning, neither will it have an end. That is good logic. That which has a beginning may have an end. There never was a time when there were not spirits; for they are co-equal with our Father in heaven.

I want to reason more on the spirit of man; for I am dwelling on the body and spirit of man—on the subject of the dead. I take my ring from my finger and liken it unto the mind of man—the immortal part, because it has no beginning. Suppose you cut it in two, then it has a beginning and an end; but join it again, and it continues one eternal round. So with the spirit of man. As the Lord liveth, if it had a beginning it will have an end. All the fools and learned and wise men from the beginning of creation, who say that the spirit of man had a beginning, prove that it must have an end; and if that doctrine is true, then the doctrine of annihilation would be true. But if I am right, I might with boldness proclaim from the housetops that God never had the power to create the spirit of man at all. God himself could not create himself.

Intelligence is eternal and exists upon a self-existent principle. It is a spirit from age to age, and there is no creation about it. All the minds and spirits that God ever sent into the world are susceptible of enlargement.

The first principles of man are self-existent with God. God himself, finding he was in the midst of spirits and glory, because he was more intelligent, saw proper to institute laws whereby the rest could have a privilege to advance like himself. The relationship we have with God places us in a situation to advance in knowledge. He has power to institute laws to instruct the weaker intelligences, that they may be exalted with himself, so that they might have one glory upon another, and all that knowledge, power, glory, and intelligence which is requisite in order to save them in the world of spirits.

This is good doctrine. It tastes good. I can taste the principles of eternal life, and so can you. They are given to me by the revelations of Jesus Christ; and I know that when I tell you these words of eternal life as they are given to me, you taste them, and I know you believe them. . . .

The greatest responsibility in this world that God has laid upon us is to seek after our dead . . . for it is necessary that the sealing power should be in our hands to seal our children and our dead for the fullness of the dispensation of times—a dispensation to meet the promises made by Jesus Christ before the foundation of the world for the salvation of man. . . .

You don't know me; you never knew my heart. No man knows my history, I cannot tell it; I shall never undertake it. I don't blame anyone for not believing my history. If I had not experienced what I have, I could not have believed it myself. I never did harm any man since I was born in the world. My voice is always for peace. I cannot lie down until all my work is finished. I never think any evil, nor do anything to the harm of my fellow-man. When I am called by the trump of the archangel and weighed in the balance, you will all know me then. I add no more, God bless you all. Amen.

HOW THE INCOME AND WEALTH ESTIMATES WERE MADE

GIVEN THE STRICT FINANCIAL SECRECY OF THE CHURCH OF JESUS CHRIST of Latter-day Saints and the difficulty of the task, how did this book come up with its account of the scope of the Mormon economic empire? Part of the answer is that reporter S. C. Gwynne was given more than routine access to inside church sources and acquired some official information on assets and internal operations as a starting point. Among others, he interviewed Presiding Bishop David Burton (in LDS parlance, the church's chief financial officer) and Rodney Brady, head of Deseret Management Corporation, which holds most of the church's subsidiary companies, its media holdings, farm and ranch system, life insurance company, and other interests. Brady, for example, discussed specific sales figures for Bonneville, the giant media holding company, and specific assets and capital figures for Beneficial Life, the $16 billion insurance company that is wholly owned by the LDS church. Richard Ostling also touched on finances in his interview with church President Gordon B. Hinckley. Finally, our research benefited from sources who necessarily must remain anonymous.

Though the church authorities steadfastly refused to provide aggregate numbers, certain things they said during the interviews turned out to be extremely useful. Most useful of all was Burton's remark that the tithe was "90 percent" of the church's income. Knowing the tithe, then, would indicate how much income the church makes from its other assets and also allow an estimate of the size of those earning assets. Presumably the other 10 percent would include only the income from church-controlled businesses that is actually paid to the church as dividends, rents, or royalties, not the total income of those commercial entities. Nor would such cash transactions reflect appreciation in asset values, which no doubt are very substantial but do not count unless an asset is sold and the gain actually realized.

Before turning to the several approaches that were used in this book, it should be stated that these can be only rough estimates. No one outside of the First Presidency, the Quorum of the Twelve, and the Presiding Bishopric knows the real aggregates. But there are ways to double-check an estimate, and where possible we used two different calculating techniques to estimate the size of the church's income and assets.

Broadly speaking, the church derives income from two sources: tithing, which Burton said provides by far the largest share; and income from church investments, including both stocks and bonds passively held and direct investments in ranching, media, financial, real estate, and other interests that the church owns. We were able to work from some individual numbers, such as the $172 million in revenue made by Bonneville Corporation. But there was no easy way to get at some of the other corporate revenue.

And there was no direct way at all to get at tithing figures. So to find an estimate we looked for the closest comparable denomination of some size with a commitment to both open records and tithing, in order to examine contributions from both U.S. and (vastly different) international memberships. We settled on the Seventh-day Adventist Church, which emphasizes tithing and perpetuates a similarly disciplined, close-knit fellowship. The worldwide memberships are similar (9.3 million for the Adventists and 9.7 million for the Mormons in 1996), although a far higher percent-age of Adventists live overseas.

In 1995, the last year for which complete Adventist numbers were avail-able, the average annual contribution per U.S. baptized member (neither denomination baptizes infants) was $989, and $77 per foreign member. There is a general consensus among observers that the Mormons place heav-ier emphasis on the tithe than do the Adventists and are more successful in harvesting it. For one thing, Mormons who do not tithe are not allowed inside temples, a central aspect of their religious life. Of course, the socioe-conomic status of the two groups would affect comparisons, both in the United States and overseas, but we lacked sufficient data to adjust for that.

Nonetheless, the situations are roughly comparable, and while a straight correlation between the tithing of one church and the other is almost cer-tainly inaccurate, we are convinced that the following projection errs on the conservative side. The U.S. Mormon membership multiplied by the average U.S. Adventist contribution would yield revenues of $4,903,875,402. The foreign Mormon membership multiplied by the foreign Adventist average of $77 would yield $364,651,749. The projected annual worldwide LDS membership contributions would thus be roughly $5.3 billion as of 1995. Interestingly, in 1991 the *Arizona Republic* ran similar equations based on giving in the Church of the Nazarene and came up with $4.3 billion, which, adjusted for inflation, is not far from our number.

For the Mormon Church to insist that the $5.3 billion is "greatly exag-gerated" would be to admit that it is far less efficient than the Adventist Church in pulling in the tithe. From what we know, that is something that few Mormons and hardly anyone in the wider religious community at large would believe. On the other hand, one unknown factor is the degree to which baptized LDS members on the rolls are inactive and noncon-tributing. Also, the LDS membership could include more children and nonworking spouses without income than that of the Adventists or other groups. As indicated, one knowledgeable source thought $4.25 billion would be a safer estimate, so the Adventist-based projection of $5.3 billion may be high. In any case, it is of the correct order of magnitude.

The next step, figuring out church income from investments, could then be taken according to the presiding bishop's ratio. If $5.3 billion in member contributions is 90 percent of revenues, by the reckoning provided us by Presiding Bishop Burton total revenues would be around $5.9 billion. Or by the more cautious reading of tithing income, it would be just under $5 billion. In either case, the numbers are likewise within the correct order of magnitude.

Estimating annual investment income at a total of $600 million allows us in turn to make at least a general stab at estimating the size of that portfolio. If we assume Mormons are competent enough managers to make a 10 percent return on assets after taxes (in the 1990s its stock portfolios would almost certainly be doing double that, balancing out whatever shortfalls there might be among the church's corporate investments), then a reasonable estimate for invested assets would be $6 billion. That estimate was corroborated by an informed source.

Looking just at investment portfolios, John Heinerman and Anson Shupe's 1985 *The Mormon Corporate Empire* estimated value at $954 million, probably correctly, based on the documents they had. The 1991 *Arizona Republic* estimate was "more than $1 billion." In addition, there are the direct investments: companies owned by Deseret Management such as Beneficial Life ($1.6 billion), Bonneville (probably $350 million or two times sales), commercial real estate investments around the country, and so forth. Compare our $6 billion estimate with the *Arizona Republic*'s estimate that as of 1991 total investment "easily exceeds $5 billion."

We have estimated ranches, farms, and accompanying real estate at $5 billion, though considering the amazing scope of such Mormon investments in the United States, that number is probably low too. Again, we have obtained independent corroboration of this estimate. Of course, it is hard to separate out land value from commercial value (of ranches, for example), and it is also hard to keep track, year in and year out, of how many farms and ranches are in the welfare system—and therefore nonprofit and nontaxed—rather than in the church's commercial realm.

Though the *Arizona Republic* listed a great many of these assets, by size and by value, it failed to get a reliable aggregate number. Heinerman and Shupe, whose information in this particular area seems rather good, estimated total farm, ranch, and commercial real estate holdings at $3 billion as of 1983. Our $5 billion is an inflation- and growth-adjusted equivalent of that number. Some examples suggest that this figure is probably low. For instance, consider just one piece of that empire, the 312,000-acre Deseret Ranch, prime real estate located just outside Orlando, Florida, near Disney World. Based on per-acre real estate prices published in the *Orlando Sentinel,* the value of that land in 1991 was $858 million, and it is probably much higher now. All told, we calculate that the church owns somewhere in the neighborhood of one million acres of farm and ranch land in the United States.

Our estimates for the value of LDS schools and miscellaneous other holdings is based on the insider numbers obtained in the early 1980s by Heinerman and Shupe. They estimate this number, the largest portion of which is BYU, at $836 million, which includes church and archival holdings as well as genealogical and historical properties. Because we had very little information about the value of these assets, our own estimate reflects the barest of increases over that number.

Now for the big numbers, which are in many ways the least remarkable and also the least meaningful. We have estimated the value of the church's meetinghouses, temples, and the land they are on at $18 billion. Once again, we have used "comparables" in our statistical database. In this case, a very close comparable to the LDS church is the Chicago-based Evangelical Lutheran Church in America (ELCA), with a U.S. membership of 5,190,000 and 10,995 local congregations as of 1995. The two denominations have similar demographics, and it would be fair to assume that the real estate holdings for religious use are roughly comparable. For 1995 the ELCA estimated the value of its congregational properties at just under $11 billion, providing the basis for our $12 billion in domestic Mormon Church properties. Though the number of foreign meetinghouses now equals or exceeds those in the United States, we have estimated this value to be only half the value in the United States, or $6 billion. That would include a type of building (temple) not found in the ELCA. Heinerman and Shupe estimated per-temple value of $13 million in 1983, and in 1996 the *New York Times* reported a cost of $18 million per temple.

The real estate holdings for religious use are among the most difficult to estimate, in part because the assets are so far-flung and numerous. Bishop Burton said that many meetinghouses cost well in excess of $2 million.

Similarly, a mission president said that the most expensive American chapel to date, due to high land prices, was the $8 million building opened in 1997 in the South Bronx; church sources told local media that $8 million was three times the national average cost for a chapel. If the Heinerman-Shupe estimate of $470,000 is taken as the average value of a meetinghouse (globally), then considering conventional commercial real estate price gains over the past fifteen years, the number now would easily exceed $1 million (much lower than one-third of the Bronx chapel's cost). But if we say that the average Mormon facility costs $1 million, then the global total is around $12 billion. The church does not release the exact number of meetinghouses, but Heinerman and Shupe estimated 6,802 in 1983, and the church says that it has been building about 350 new ones every year. This would mean that more than 12,000 additional meetinghouses had been built fifteen years later. Factoring in 1980s growth rates and considering that global commercial real estate has vastly outpaced inflation, the average value could be $1.5 million, for a total asset value of $18 billion. Of course, as President Hinckley correctly noted in his interview, all these properties are revenue-consuming, not revenue-producing. But it is also true that the construction of more temples and meetinghouses is an investment that reaps increased tithing revenue. Like the religious-use properties of any denomination, one can know what a facility cost at the time of construction, but it is hard to convert that to any true market value.

To be very conservative, since we do not have access to inside accounts and inventories, we would conclude that total LDS assets are in the range of $25–30 billion.

ENDNOTES

The following notes list major sources that were consulted for each chapter. They do not cite every fact or quotation. The notes have three purposes: to credit the superb scholars whose ideas and research we have borrowed; to provide guidance for those interested in further exploration of a topic; and to document sources for controversial facts and opinions. Most quotes without citations were part of the interviewing conducted for this book.

INTRODUCTION. A NEW WORLD FAITH

Michael Austin, "Mormon Stereotypes in Popular Fiction, 1980–1998," paper presented at the Sunstone Symposium, August 1, 1998.

Sir Arthur Conan Doyle, *A Study in Scarlet* (1887; reprint, London: Penguin, 1981), p. 93.

Mark Twain, *Roughing It* (1872; reprint, New York: Penguin, 1981), pp. 93, 138, 567–68.

Travel advice for the choir: Charles Jeffrey Calman, *The Mormon Tabernacle Choir* (New York: Harper & Row, 1979), p. 65.

Jan Shipps, "The Mormon Image Since 1960," paper presented at the Sunstone Symposium, August 1, 1998.

CHAPTER 1. SEALED WITH BLOOD

Quincy quoted: In Leonard J. Arrington and Davis Bitton, *The Mormon Experience: A History of the Latter-day Saints* (New York: Alfred A. Knopf, 1979), p. 71.

Smith's political frenzy in early 1844: D. Michael Quinn, *The Mormon Hierarchy: Origins of Power* (Salt Lake City: Signature Books/Smith Research Associates, 1994), pp. 123–124, 360–362. For sequence of all events in Nauvoo, see pp. 105–141.

Smith on religious sacrifice: Joseph Smith, Lecture 6 of "Lectures on Faith," *Doctrine and Covenants* (1835), sect.7, p. 60; reprinted in *New Mormon Studies* CD-ROM (Salt Lake City: Smith Research Associates/Signature Books, 1998).

The description of Nauvoo's political organization and economy is heavily indebted to Robert Bruce Flanders, *Nauvoo: Kingdom on the Mississippi* (Urbana: University of Illinois Press, 1975). Discussion of English converts and Parley Pratt quote, pp. 74–76; Nauvoo's charter, pp. 96–98; Nauvoo's use of habeas corpus, p. 99; Nauvoo's economy, pp. 144–178; Joseph Smith's store, p. 162.

Also see descriptions of life in Nauvoo in Arrington and Bitton, *The Mormon Experience;* and James B. Allen and Glen M. Leonard, *The Story of the Latter-day Saints* (Salt Lake City: Deseret Book Co., 1976).

For longer excerpts from Joseph Smith's "King Follett Discourse," see Appendix A.

Wallace Stegner on "chosen people": Wallace Stegner, *The Gathering of Zion: The Story of the Mormon Trail* (1964; reprint, Lincoln: University of Nebraska Press, 1981), p. 24.

Council of Fifty and Nauvoo political activities: Flanders, *Nauvoo*, pp. 292–294; and Quinn, *The Mormon Hierarchy: Origins of Power*, pp. 127–128, 643.

"I am above the kingdoms of this world": Smith quoted in Robert Bruce Flanders, "Dream and Nightmare: Nauvoo Revisited," *The Restoration Movement: Nauvoo Revisited*, rev. ed. edited by F. Mark McKierman, Alma R. Blair, and Paul M. Edwards (Independence, Missouri: Herald Publishing House, rev. ed., 1992), p. 148.

Chronology of events with Foster and Law: Quinn, *The Mormon Hierarchy: Origins of Power*, pp. 124–132, 137–141, 642–645. Also see description of events in Linda King Newell and Valeen Tippetts Avery, *Mormon Enigma: Emma Hale Smith: Prophet's Wife, "Elect Lady," Polygamy's Foe* (Garden City, N.Y.: Doubleday, 1984), 167–168, 177–178, 180–182; Fawn M. Brodie, *No Man Knows My History: The Life of Joseph Smith, the Mormon Prophet* (New York: Alfred A. Knopf, 1945), 340, 343, 368–375; Arrington and Bitton, *The Mormon Experience*, pp. 77–82; Allen and Leonard, *The Story of the Latter-day Saints*, pp. 191–193; Richard S. Van Wagoner, *Mormon Polygamy: A History* (Salt Lake City: Signature Books, 1989), pp. 63–71.

Crises between William Law and Joseph Smith in April and May, 1844: Quinn, *The Mormon Hierarchy: Origins of Power*, pp. 125, 126, 138.

Nauvoo *Expositor*, June 7, 1844; reprinted in *New Mormon Studies* CD-ROM.

Nauvoo city council activities related to the *Expositor*: Quinn, *The Mormon Hierarchy: Origins of Power*, p. 645; on the problem for Joseph Smith, see p. 139. Also see discussion in Dallin H. Oaks and Marvin S. Hill, *Carthage Conspiracy: The Trial of the Accused Assassins of Joseph Smith* (Urbana: University of Illinois Press, 1975), pp. 14–20.

Warsaw press hysteria: *Warsaw Signal* quoted in Roger D. Launius, *Joseph Smith III: Pragmatic Prophet* (1988; reprint, Urbana: University of Illinois Press, 1995), p. 20.

"I want Hyrum to live to avenge my blood": Smith quoted in Arrington and Bitton, *The Mormon Experience*, p. 79.

"I am going as a lamb": Smith quoted in Arrington and Bitton, *The Mormon Experience*, p. 80.

Testimony sealed with blood: Mary E. Lightner, "The Life and Testimony of Mary Lightner" (Salt Lake City: Pioneer Press, 1997), p. 103. Reprint of an address given at Brigham Young University April 14, 1905.

Press reactions to Joseph's death: Paul D. Ellsworth, "Mobocracy and the Rule of Law: American Press Reaction to the Murder of Joseph Smith," *BYU Studies,* 20, no. 1 (1979): 71–82; 1995 reprint E3–79.

Ghost town description of Nauvoo: Thomas L. Kane, *The Mormons* (1850), quoted in Steven Shields, *An Illustrated History of Nauvoo* (Independence: Herald Publishing House, 1992), pp. 7–8.

CHAPTER 2. BEGINNINGS: A VERY AMERICAN GOSPEL

On Isaac Bullard: see Brodie, *No Man Knows My History,* p. 12.

Millennial expectations in the nineteenth century: Nathan O. Hatch, *The Democratization of American Christianity* (New Haven: Yale University Press, 1989), p. 184. A good discussion of LDS millennialism can be found in Dan Erickson, *As a Thief in the Night: The Mormon Quest for Millennial Deliverance* (Salt Lake City: Signature Books, 1998).

Millerite size estimate: Michael O. Wise, *The First Messiah: Investigating the Savior before Jesus* (San Francisco: HarperSanFrancisco, 1999), p. 15.

Religion for the common people, Hatch, pp. 4ff. Elitist religion, Thomas O'Dea, *The Mormons* (Chicago: University of Chicago Press, 1957), pp. 8–10ff.

Joseph Smith's boyhood interest in Indians, Lucy Mack Smith, *Biographical Sketches* (1853), p. 85, reprinted in *New Mormon Studies* CD-ROM.

The canonized version of the First Vision is included in the LDS scriptures as part of the Joseph Smith "History of the Church" in the Pearl of Great Price. It was written in 1838 and differs in some details from an uncanonized version written in 1832. The earlier version speaks of one personage, the Son, appearing to Joseph; the canonized 1838 version has two personages. Some analysts say the later version supports Smith's emerging theology of a plurality of Gods, which became most explicit in his 1835 work on the Book of Abraham. The 1832 version of the First Vision is available in Dean C. Jessee, ed., *The Papers of Joseph Smith: Autobiographical and Historical Writings of Joseph Smith* (Salt Lake City: Deseret Book Company, 1989), vol. 1, pp. 6–7. In an editorial note to Smith's 1832 history, p. 1, Jessee writes, "This document is the earliest extant attempt to write a history of his life, and his only autobiographical work containing his own handwriting."

The magic and occult activities of Joseph Smith and his family are detailed and meticulously documented by D. Michael Quinn, *Early Mormonism and the Magic World View* (Salt Lake City: Signature Books, revised and enlarged edition, 1998).

Evidence of Smith family magic activities too well documented for Mormons to deny: Richard L. Bushman, "Treasure-seeking Then and Now," *Sunstone,* 11, no. 5 (1987): 5.

Alexander Campbell evaluation of the Book of Mormon: quoted in Richard L. Bushman, *Joseph Smith and the Beginnings of Mormonism* (Urbana: University of Illinois Press, 1984), p. 126.

O'Dea's naturalistic explanation of Joseph Smith: O'Dea, *The Mormons,* p. 24.

Sidney Rigdon July 4 "war of extermination" sermon quoted in Allen and Leonard, *The Story of the Latter-day Saints,* p. 123. Gov. Lilburn W. Boggs's retaliation with his Mormons "must be exterminated or driven from the state" order, quoted p. 127.

Haun's Mill Massacre description: see Alexander L. Baugh, ed., "Joseph Young's Affidavit of the Massacre at Haun's Mill," *BYU Studies,* 38, no. 1 (1999): 199.

Why were the Mormons so hated? Quinn, *The Mormon Hierarchy: Origins of Power,* p. 91. Arrington and Bitton, *The Mormon Experience,* pp. 62–63, 57–58.

CHAPTER 3. THE AMERICAN EXODUS

Inventory list for trek: B. H. Roberts, ed., *History of the Church of Jesus Christ of Latter-day Saints,* 2nd ed., rev. (Salt Lake City: Deseret Book Co., 1964), vol. 7, pp. 454–455; reprinted in Edwin S. Gaustad, ed., *A Documentary History of Religion in America to the Civil War* (Grand Rapids, Mich.: Eerdmans Publishing Co., 1993), pp. 361–362.

The description of preparations for the Great Trek is drawn from Allen and Leonard, *The Story of the Latter-day Saints;* Arrington and Bitton, *The Mormon Experience;* Leonard J. Arrington, *Great Basin Kingdom: An Economic History of the Latter-day Saints 1830–1900* (Cambridge: Harvard University Press, 1958); Leonard J. Arrington, *Brigham Young: American Moses* (New York: Alfred A. Knopf, 1985); Claudia Lauper Bushman and Richard Lyman Bushman, *Mormons in America,* Religion in American Life Series (New York: Oxford University Press, 1999).

Census for the trek: Bushman and Bushman, *Mormons in America,* p. 57; mid-May figure, Allen and Leonard, *The Story of the Latter-day Saints,* p. 221.

Sugar Creek and Winter Quarters descriptions: Arrington, *Great Basin Kingdom,* pp. 18–22; Bushman and Bushman, *Mormons in America,* p. 59.

Polk letter quoted in Arrington, *Brigham Young,* p. 130.

Description of Brigham Young: see Arrington, *Brigham Young.* Story of the shoes, p. 11.

The Saints' acceptance of Brigham Young as their leader: Stegner, *The Gathering of Zion,* p. 49.

The Mormon Battalion: Arrington and Bitton, *The Mormon Experience,* p. 99.

Description of the first wagon train to Utah: O'Dea, *The Mormons,* p. 80, and Arrington, *Brigham Young,* p. 130.

Young quote on entering the valley: O'Dea, *The Mormons,* p. 82, and Allen and Leonard, *The Story of the Latter-day Saints,* p. 247.

Description of the Young wagon train contingent: Arrington, *Brigham Young,* p. 157.

The Lucy Groves incident: Arrington, *Brigham Young,* pp. 157–158.

Emigration statistics: Arrington, *Brigham Young,* p. 172.

Mary Goble Pay diary quoted in Arrington and Bitton, *The Mormon Experience,* p. 134; see also 362n.

Military surplus: Arrington, *Great Basin Kingdom,* p. 199. Economic information of early Utah is drawn in large part from *Great Basin Kingdom.* Discussion of United Order of Enoch and cooperatives, pp. 293–349; quote on cooperatives, p. 338.

Smith claiming America for Zion: O'Dea, *The Mormons,* pp. 166, 171, 276.

The Utah War and "incongruity of comic opera," Arrington and Bitton, *The Mormon Experience,* p. 169.

Abraham Lincoln quoted in Arrington and Bitton, *The Mormon Experience,* p. 170.

Young's death described: Arrington, *Brigham Young,* pp. 398–401.

CHAPTER 4. POLYGAMY THEN AND NOW

Brigham Young's first reaction when introduced to the theology of plural marriage: Arrington, *Brigham Young,* p. 100.

Young interview with Horace Greeley: Arrington, *Brigham Young,* pp. 5–6.

Church reaction to Fawn Brodie: Richard S. Van Wagoner and Steven C. Walker, *A Book of Mormons* (Salt Lake City: Signature Books, 1982), pp. 29–33.

Lists of Joseph Smith's wives: Todd Compton, "Prologue: A Trajectory of Plurality: An Overview of Joseph Smith's Wives," *In Sacred Loneliness: The Plural Wives of Joseph Smith* (Salt Lake City: Signature Books, 1997), pp. 1–23.

Lawrence Foster on rationale for polygamy: Lawrence Foster, *Religion and Sexuality: The Shakers, the Mormons, and the Oneida Community* (Urbana: University of Illinois Press, 1984), pp. 150–151; also see Lawrence Foster, "Sex and Prophetic Power: A Comparison of John Humphrey Noyes, Founder of the Oneida Community, with Joseph Smith, Jr., the Mormon Prophet," *Dialogue: A Journal of Mormon Thought,* 31, no. 4 (Winter 1998): 76.

Early Mormon polygamy and Emma's reaction to the principle: Linda King Newell and Valeen Tippetts Avery, *Mormon Enigma: Emma Hale Smith: Prophet's Wife, "Elect Lady," Polygamy's Foe* (Garden City, N.Y.: Doubleday, 1984), p. 64.

Joseph Smith's approach to Mary Elizabeth Rollins Lightner: Newell and Avery, *Mormon Enigma,* p. 65.

The episode with Marinda Nancy Johnson in Kirtland: Donna Hill, *Joseph Smith: The First Mormon* (Garden City, N.Y.: Doubleday, 1977), p. 146.

The monogamous entry in the 1835 Doctrine and Covenants: Brodie, *No Man Knows My History,* p. 185; Quinn, *The Mormon Hierarchy: Origins of Power,* p. 623; Van Wagoner, *Mormon Polygamy,* p. 623.

Oliver Cowdery's excommunication: Compton, *In Sacred Loneliness,* pp. 38–40. Discussion includes Cowdery's reaction to Fanny Alger episode.

Joseph Smith defiance of the law to conduct illegal weddings: Quinn, *The Mormon Hierarchy: Origins of Power,* pp. 88–89.

Helen Mar Kimball marriage, Compton, *In Sacred Loneliness,* pp. 486–534; Joseph's pursuit, p. 499; her poem, p. 500.

Lucy Walker marriage: Compton, *In Sacred Loneliness,* pp. 457–472; Joseph Smith quote, p. 465.

Sarah Ann Whitney marriage: Compton, *In Sacred Loneliness,* pp. 342–363; the pretend ceremony as cover-up, p. 351.

The Lawrence sisters' marriages: Compton, *In Sacred Loneliness,* pp. 473–485; dispute over their inheritance, p. 478.

Eliza Snow episode: Compton, *In Sacred Loneliness,* p. 129; Newell and Avery, *Mormon Enigma,* pp. 133–135.

Nancy Rigdon episode: Van Wagoner, *Mormon Polygamy,* pp. 32–33; Emma's quote, p. 35; Newell and Avery, *Mormon Enigma,* pp. 111–113; Compton, *In Sacred Loneliness,* 239–240; Quinn, *The Mormon Hierarchy: Origins of Power,* pp. 112, 162, 492, 634.

Joseph Smith interpreting the Parable of the Talents: quoted and discussed in Compton, *In Sacred Loneliness,* p. 296.

Unorthodox sexual practices in other new religions: see Foster, *Religion and Sexuality,* pp. 130ff.

Possible influence of Emanuel Swedenborg: Quinn, *Early Mormonism and the Magic World View,* pp. 115, 153, 176, 217–219, 487n.

Book of Mormon and plural marriage: the *Encyclopedia of Mormonism* claims that Jacob 2:28–30 countenances polygamy when God commands it, though the average reader would not necessarily interpret the language of those verses as referring to post-biblical plural marriage.

Times and Seasons declaration of monogamy: quoted in Newell and Avery, *Mormon Enigma,* pp. 128–129.

Emma Smith receives her endowment: Newell and Avery, *Mormon Enigma,* pp. 140, 143.

The Lawrence sisters' inheritance: Newell and Avery, *Mormon Enigma,* p. 244.

Emma Smith's regret at giving permission for plural marriage: Newell and Avery, *Mormon Enigma,* p. 145.

Joseph Smith's loyalty to Emma: Newell and Avery, *Mormon Enigma,* p. 147.

Emma Smith's 1879 interview: "Last Testimony of Sister Emma," *The Saints' Herald,* 26, no. 19 (October 1, 1879): 1.

"Mormonism was referred to as the 'plague spot' in the Rocky Mountains": B. Carmon Hardy, *Solemn Covenant: The Mormon Polygamous Passage* (Urbana: University of Illinois Press, 1992), pp. 40–41.

United States v. Reynolds decision: Robert T. Miller and Ronald B. Flowers, "The Mormon Cases: Reynolds v. United States," *Toward Benevolent Neutrality: Church, State, and the Supreme Court* (Waco, Tex.: Baylor University Press, 1982), pp. 67–71.

John Taylor and plural marriage: quoted in Van Wagoner, *Mormon Polygamy,* p. 128.

Description of polygamists in hiding: Hardy, *Solemn Covenant,* p. 49.

"Celestial marriage": Hardy, *Solemn Covenant,* p. 54.

Joseph Smith prediction that "56 years should wind up the scene": Joseph Smith, *History of the Church,* 2:182; reprinted in *New Mormon Studies* CD-ROM.

Post-Manifesto plural marriages: D. Michael Quinn, *The Mormon Hierarchy: Extensions of Power* (Salt Lake City: Signature Books, 1997), pp. 182–183, 790–810; quote, p. 183; D. Michael Quinn, "On Being a Mormon Historian (and Its Aftermath)," 1981 speech reprinted in George D. Smith, ed. *Faithful History* (Salt Lake City: Signature Books, 1992), pp. 69–111; quote, p. 87.

Mormon Fundamentalism: discussion and Dorothy Allred Solomon quoted in Hardy, *Solemn Covenant,* p. 378.

Estimates of current polygamous sects: J. Gordon Melton, *Encyclopedia of American Religions* (Detroit: Gale Research Inc., 1993), pp. 622–27.

Feature story on current polygamy in Utah: Timothy Egan, "The Persistence of Polygamy," *New York Times Magazine,* February 28, 1999, pp. 51–55; quote, p. 55.

CHAPTER 5. REDEFINING THE KINGDOM OF GOD

"most despised large group": Martin Marty, *Modern American Religion: The Irony of It All: 1893–1919,* vol. I (Chicago: University of Chicago Press, 1986), p. 301.

The *New York Times* and women's suffrage: Bushman and Bushman, *Mormons in America,* p. 90.

Description of Martha Hughes Cannon: Bushman and Bushman, *Mormons in America,* pp. 94–95. Cannon interview quoted, Arrington and Bitton, *The Mormon Experience,* p. 230.

Edmunds-Tucker Act problems: Arrington, *Great Basin Kingdom,* pp. 360ff.; the Supreme Court decision, p. 375.

Senator Frederick T. Dubois quote on political tactics: Klaus J. Hansen, "The Metamorphosis of the Kingdom of God: Toward a Reinterpretation of Mormon History," *The New Mormon History: Revisionist Essays on the Past,* edited by D. Michael Quinn (Salt Lake City: Signature Books, 1992), p. 231.

LDS publications and attacks on anti-Mormons: Quinn, *The Mormon Hierarchy: Extensions of Power,* p. 261.

Woodruff journal quote: Arrington, *Great Basin Kingdom,* p. 377.

Manifesto a tactical maneuver: Hansen, "The Metamorphosis of the Kingdom of God," p. 230.

Church debt and tithing: D. Michael Quinn, "LDS Church Finances from the 1830s to the 1990s," *Sunstone,* 19:2, no. 102 (June 1996), pp. 17–28; table on p. 20.

Divestiture: Arrington, *Great Basin Kingdom,* pp. 407–408ff.

Rudger Judd Clawson as church accountant: see notes and comments by Boyd Payne and "Rudger Clawson's Report on LDS Church Finances at the Turn of the Twentieth Century," *Dialogue,* 31, no. 4 (Winter 1998): 165–179.

Great Basin economic discussion based largely on Arrington, *Great Basin Kingdom;* quote, p. 409. Post-statehood church investments: also see discussion in Allen and Leonard, *The Story of the Latter-day Saints,* pp. 468–472.

Discipline of B. H. Roberts and Moses Thatcher: Richard S. Van Wagoner and Steven C. Walker, *A Book of Mormons* (Salt Lake City: Signature Books, 1982), pp. 240–248, 367–370; see also Quinn, *The Mormon Hierarchy: Extensions of Power,* p. 351.

B. H. Roberts hearings in Congress: see Hardy, *Solemn Covenant,* pp. 248–253; quote, p. 253.

Reed Smoot Senate hearings: see Hardy, *Solemn Covenant,* pp. 251–283; also see Allen and Leonard, *The Story of the Latter-day Saints,* pp. 439–445 and Arrington and Bitton, *The Mormon Experience,* pp. 245–256.

President Joseph F. Smith's testimony in the Smoot Senate hearings: D. Michael Quinn, "LDS Church Authority and New Plural Marriages," *Dialogue,* 18, no. 1 (1985): 9–108; testimony quoted p. 97. [Note: all *Dialogue* articles before 1996 have been taken from the *New Mormon Studies* CD-ROM.] For remarks on testimonies of Apostles John Henry Smith and Marriner W. Merrill, see Hardy, *Solemn Covenant,* p. 254. This book's discussion of LDS post-Manifesto plural marriages is drawn largely from Quinn and Hardy.

Manifesto placed in Doctrine and Covenants in 1908: Hardy, *Solemn Covenant,* p. 297.

Woodruff's consultants about release of the Manifesto to the press: Hardy, *Solemn Covenant,* p. 139.

Post-Manifesto plural marriages: see appendix list in Hardy, *Solemn Covenant,* pp. 389–425; see also Quinn, *The Mormon Hierarchy: Extensions of Power,* pp. 808–809; Quinn on Ivins, p. 809.

Salt Lake Tribune on post-Manifesto polygamy: Hardy, *Solemn Covenant,* p. 288.

Description of anti-Mormon magazine articles: Hardy, *Solemn Covenant,* p. 289.

Discussion of LDS public relations: Allen and Leonard, *The Story of the Latter-day Saints,* pp. 472–475.

Deceit in the name of a higher good: Cowley quoted in Hardy, *Solemn Covenant,* pp. 373–374; see Quinn on "theocratic ethics" in *The Mormon Hierarchy: Origins of Power,* p. 112.

Importance of honesty: Hinckley's 1990 *Ensign* piece quoted in Hardy, pp. 363–364, 380n.

Federal investments in the Great Basin after statehood: Mark P. Leone, *Roots of Modern Mormonism* (Cambridge: Harvard University Press, 1979), p. 158.

Shift of kingdom paradigm: Thomas O'Dea, *The Mormons,* pp. 166, 171.

Waning of millennialism: Dan Erickson, *As a Thief in the Night: The Mormon Quest for Millennial Deliverance* (Salt Lake City: Signature Books, 1998).

Second coming of Christ "not far distant": Bruce R. McConkie, *Mormon Doctrine* (1966, 1979; Salt Lake City: Bookcraft, reprinted 1997), p. 693.

President Hinckley quote on the millennium: from interview with coauthor Richard N. Ostling.

CHAPTER 6. ALMOST MAINSTREAM

The black and Polynesian priesthood history is drawn substantially from *Neither White nor Black: Mormon Scholars Confront the Race Issue in a Universal Church,* edited by Lester E. Bush Jr. and Armand L. Mauss (Midvale, Utah: Signature Books, 1984), an anthology of articles, most of which originally appeared in the journal *Dialogue.* Another useful source is Newell G. Bringhurst, *Saints, Slaves, and Blacks: The Changing Place of Black People Within Mormonism* (Westport, CT: Greenwood Press, 1981).

Brazilian mission work mostly with white German-speakers: Bush and Mauss, *Neither White nor Black,* p. 152.

Accounts of the 1978 black priesthood revelation that were consulted include Leonard J. Arrington: *Adventures of a Church Historian* (Urbana: University of Illinois Press, 1998), pp. 176–183; Bruce R. McConkie, "The New Revelation on Priesthood," *Priesthood* (Salt Lake City: Deseret Book, 1981), pages 126–137; and D. Michael Quinn, *The Mormon Hierarchy: Extensions of Power,* pp. 13–17.

Merrill Bateman on the revelation: interview with coauthor Richard N. Ostling, Provo, Utah, June 1997.

Haight on the revelation: "Great Army Needed to Carry Message of Hope, Salvation," *Church News* supplement to *Deseret News,* Salt Lake City, April 13, 1996.

Kimball admonitions on dating and marriage: "Interracial Marriage Discouraged," *Church News* supplement to *Deseret News,* June 17, 1978.

Rewriting Book of Mormon in 1981 to change "white" to "pure": Quinn, *The Mormon Hierarchy: Extensions of Power,* p. 876. The phrase "white and delightsome" is in the original 1830 first edition (II Nephi xii, p. 117), which has different chapter numbers from today's edition and no verse numbers. This edition is available in the *New Mormon Studies* CD-ROM and in a photo-offset reproduction published in 1962 and 1995 by Wilford C. Wood (*Joseph Smith Begins His Work,* vol. 1 [Salt Lake City: Wilford C. Wood Publishers Press]. A photomechanical reproduction of the original edition has also been published by Jerald and Sandra Tanner (Salt Lake City: Utah Lighthouse Ministries).

Ordination of one or two blacks under Joseph Smith: Lester E. Bush Jr., "Whence the Negro Doctrine? A Review of Ten Years of Answers," in Bush and Mauss, *Neither White nor Black,* p. 196.

Claims that Smith verbally opposed black priesthood: Bush, "Whence the Negro Doctrine?" in Bush and Mauss, pp. 199–200.

Young to Snow, "the Lord had cursed Cain's seed": in Bush, "Whence" in Bush and Mauss, p. 198.

Young on the mark of Cain as black skin, Cain's descendants as "black, uncouth, uncomely . . ." and that Abolitionists cannot "alter that decree": *Journal of Discourses* 7 (October 9, 1859): 290. The *Journal of Discourses* was published by the LDS Church in Liverpool, England, from 1854 to 1886 as a semi-monthly periodical containing speeches of church leaders. All references to the *Journal of Discourses* in this book have been taken from the *New Mormon Studies* CD-ROM.

Young on black priesthood only after the final resurrection: *Journal of Discourses,* 2 (December 3, 1854): 143.

Young on God's penalty for miscegenation as "death on the spot": *Journal of Discourses,* 10 (March 8, 1863): 110.

Text of the First Presidency's 1949 statement on the "Negro Question" is found, among other places, in a book-length Mormon defense of the priesthood ban, John J. Stewart, *Mormonism and the Negro* (Orem, Utah: Bookmark, 1963). Bush's research indicates that book's 1951 date for the statement was in error.

On the church's civil rights era troubles: Armand L. Mauss, "The Fading of the Pharaohs' Curse: The Decline and Fall of the Priesthood Ban Against Blacks in the Mormon Church," in Bush and Mauss, *Neither White nor Black,* pp. 154–161.

Branding the LDS church as "a political and social cancer: Wallace Turner, *The Mormon Establishment* (Boston: Houghton Mifflin, 1966), pp. 228, 244.

Text of the 1969 statement from two counselors in the First Presidency: in Bush and Mauss, *Neither White nor Black,* pp. 222–224.

Race as factor in the 1978 revelation omitted in LDS high school text: *Doctrine and Covenants: Church History Seminary Student Manual* (Salt Lake City, Church Educational System, Church of Jesus Christ of Latter-day Saints, 1989), p. 304.

Newark, New Jersey, missionary advises "razoring out" skin color references in children's Book of Mormon reader: Jessie L. Embry, *Black Saints in a White Church: Contemporary African American Mormons* (Salt Lake City: Signature Books, 1994), p. 63.

McConkie "forget everything that I have said": in McConkie, "The New Revelation," *Priesthood,* p. 132.

Bruce R. McConkie lays out the traditional race theology in his *Mormon Doctrine:* see such articles as "Cain," "Caste System," "Ham," "Lamanite Curse," "Nephites and Lamanites," "Races of Men."

David Jackson incident: from Jackson telephone interview with coauthor Richard Ostling, April 1999; Armand Mauss interview with coauthor Richard Ostling at the Mormon History Association convention in Washington, D.C., May 1998; and documents provided by Jackson. See also "Mormons May Disavow Old View on Blacks" by Larry B. Stammer, *Los Angeles Times,* May 18, 1998; "*Los Angeles Times* Story on Blacks and the Priesthood: First Presidency Statement" (press release from LDS Public Affairs Department, May 18, 1998); "Mormon Leader Defends Race Relations" by Larry B. Stammer, *Los Angeles Times,* September 12, 1998.

The BYU survey of black Mormons is described throughout Embry, *Black Saints;* Embry summary quote, p. 234.

Eugene England's observations on BYU students: "Becoming a World Religion: Blacks, the Poor—All of Us," *Sunstone,* 21:2, no. 110 (June 1998): 49–60 (reprinted from *Exponent II*).

Mauss on "residue of racialist" teaching: address to Mormon History Association, Washington, D.C., May 23, 1998.

Mauss on "strictly human origin" of race ideas, "The Fading of the Pharaohs' Curse," in Bush and Mauss, p. 173.

Data on temples, missions, stakes, and memberships: *1999–2000 Church Almanac* (Salt Lake City: Deseret News, 1998).

Quinn on David M. Kennedy's function: Quinn, *The Mormon Hierarchy: Extensions of Power,* p. 406.

History and statistics on Church Security Plan: Julie Dockstader, "Six Decades Later, Welfare Program Still Restores Hope," *Church News* supplement to *Deseret News,* February 27, 1999.

The church's twentieth-century sociopolitical involvements are surveyed, among other places, in various articles in the *Encyclopedia of Mormonism,* edited by Daniel H. Ludlow (New York: Macmillan, 1992); throughout D. Michael Quinn; and in Wallace Turner, *The Mormon Establishment,* pp. 267–331. The details on Ezra Taft Benson came from Quinn, *The Mormon Hierarchy: Extensions of Power.*

CHAPTER 7. MORMONS, INC.

The financial reporting for this chapter was done by S. C. Gwynne, correspondent for *Time* magazine, expanded and updated from the *Time* cover story on Mormons published August 4, 1997. For a further explanation of sources and how the income and wealth estimates were made, see Appendix B.

Formal LDS church response protesting the financial reporting in the *Time* cover story: Bruce Olsen, managing director, Public Affairs Department, letter to the editor published in *Time* (August 25, 1997): 6.

N. Eldon Tanner interview on church silence toward financial disclosure: Robert Gottlieb and Peter Wiley, *America's Saints: The Rise of Mormon Power* (New York: G. P. Putnam's Sons, 1984), p. 98. The other book-length attempt to investigate Mormon finances is John Heinerman and Anson Shupe, *The Mormon Corporate Empire* (Boston: Beacon Press, 1985).

Quinn estimate on tithing revenue: *The Mormon Hierarchy: Extensions of Power,* p. 203.

CHAPTER 8. SOME LATTER-DAY STARS

The uniquely useful starting point for this chapter was listings of prominent twentieth century Mormons in many fields from Appendix 5 (chronology) in Quinn, *The Mormon Hierarchy: Extensions of Power,* pp. 746–898. The chapter was compiled from: coverage and interviewing conducted for this book; material provided by the LDS Church and the celebrities' representatives; and web sites. Also, approximately 100 articles among the many available on these personalities, in particular from: Associated Press archive, *Contemporary Authors, Current Biography, Fortune, Deseret News, Entertainment Weekly, Life, Leadership Library, McCall's, New York Times, New York Times Magazine, Newsweek, People Weekly, Publishers Weekly, Salt Lake Tribune, Sports Illustrated, Sunstone, Time,* and *USA Today.*

Senator Orrin Hatch interview in *Sunstone* 5:5 (September 1980): 52–57.

Columbia Journalism Review assessment of Mark Willes is by James B. Kelleher in March–April, 1999, p. 11.

Steve Young's football career is gauged by Allen Barra, "The Best Quarterback Ever," *New York Times Magazine*, January 11, 1998, pp. 28–29.

Critique of Stephen R. Covey: Alan Wolfe, "Capitalism, Mormonism, and the Doctrines of Stephen Covey: White Magic in America," *New Republic*, 218, no. 8 (February 23, 1998): 26–35.

CHAPTER 9. THE POWER PYRAMID

Hinckley's career is detailed in Sheri L. Dew, *Go Forward with Faith: The Biography of Gordon B. Hinckley* (Salt Lake City: Deseret Book, 1996).

Hinckley quotes: from interview with coauthor Richard N. Ostling, June 1997.

Problems with aged presidents are recounted most thoroughly in D. Michael Quinn, *The Mormon Hierarchy: Extensions of Power*, pp. 54–58.

Steve Benson in 1993 on senility of his grandfather, Church President Ezra Taft Benson: Quinn, *The Mormon Hierarchy: Extensions of Power*, p. 891.

The duties of various church offices are detailed in appropriate articles in the *Encyclopedia of Mormonism* and *Church Handbook of Instructions*. The latter is a restricted administrative document not available to the general public or church members.

Family relationships in the hierarchy: Quinn, *The Mormon Hierarchy: Extensions of Power*, pp. 163–197, 731–745.

Geographic spread of General Authorities: *1999–2000 Church Almanac*.

CHAPTER 10. FAMILIES FOREVER

Spencer Kimball quote on attracting a marriage partner: from *Doctrine and Covenants: Student Manual*, Religion 324–25 (Salt Lake City: Church Educational System, the Church of Jesus Christ of Latter-day Saints, 1981), p. 328. This is the current textbook for the college-level Doctrine and Covenants course.

Vern Anderson on the new *Church Handbook of Instructions:* Associated Press wire story December 5, 1998. Quotes of Presidents David O. McKay, Ezra Taft Benson, and Gordon B. Hinckley are from the Anderson story.

Biographer's single sentence on Gordon B. Hinckley's involvement in anti-ERA campaign: Dew, *Go Forward with Faith*, p. 371.

For full discussion of the LDS church campaign against the Equal Rights Amendment see D. Michael Quinn, *The Mormon Hierarchy: Extensions of Power*, pp. 373–402. On Hawaii and same-sex marriages, see pp. 402–406.

Same-sex marriage issue in Hawaii and Alaska: see Associated Press piece by Bruce Dunford on the wire October 24, 1998; AP wire piece by Ben DiPietro on November 4, 1998, including information about money from the Mormon church given to the campaign in Hawaii; Mormon church money given to the Alaska anti-gay marriage campaign is detailed in an October 17, 1998, AP wire story without a byline. Associated Press archives are searched by key words and bylines; original stories are untitled.

CHAPTER 11. A PECULIAR PEOPLE

The Word of Wisdom and *BYU Studies* episode: Leonard J. Arrington, *Adventures of a Church Historian* (Urbana: University of Illinois Press, 1998), p. 58.

Tangle over Word of Wisdom in *Letters of Brigham Young to His Sons:* Arrington, *Adventures,* pp. 119–121.

Joseph Smith and the Word of Wisdom: see Brodie, *No Man Knows My History,* pp. 166–167, 392. Brodie says Rigdon forced a vote to replace wine with water in the communion (p. 167). However, wine was replaced by water in the sacrament as of July 5, 1906, according to Thomas G. Alexander, *Mormonism in Transition: A History of the Latter-day Saints, 1890–1930* (Urbana: University of Illinois Press, 1986, 1996), p. 261.

The case of Steven Epperson at Brigham Young University: see "Report: Academic Freedom and Tenure: Brigham Young University," *Academe: Bulletin of the American Association of University Professors,* 83, no. 5 (September–October 1997): 62–63; see also Scott Abbott, "On Ecclesiastical Endorsement at Brigham Young University," *Sunstone,* 20:1, no. 105 (April 1997): 9–14.

"In kind" tithes: Arrington, *Great Basin Kingdom,* pp. 140–141.

Discussion of temple garments: Colleen McDannell, "Mormon Garments: Sacred Clothing and the Body," *Material Christianity: Religion and Popular Culture in America* (New Haven: Yale University Press, 1995), pp. 198–221.

CHAPTER 12. RITUALS SACRED AND SECRET

History of racial restrictions on temple activities and genealogy research, Quinn, *The Mormon Hierarchy: Extensions of Power,* pp. 819, 854–855.

The church's "name extraction" program for vicarious temple ordinances: Armand L. Mauss, *The Angel and the Beehive: The Mormon Struggle with Assimilation* (Urbana: University of Illinois Press, 1994), pp. 130–131.

Mormon vicarious baptisms for Jewish Holocaust victims: see "Church to Stop Baptizing Holocaust Victims," *Sunstone,* 18:3, no. 100 (December 1995). Also see Quinn, *The Mormon Hierarchy: Extensions of Power,* p. 893.

Church discipline for members who talk publicly about temple rituals: "Comments on Temple Changes Elicit Church Discipline," *Sunstone,* 14:3, no. 77 (June 1990): 59–60.

The discussion of the history and relationship of Masonry to the Mormon temple ritual is drawn largely from Michael W. Homer, "Similarity of Priesthood in Masonry: The Relationship Between Freemasonry and Mormonism," *Dialogue,* 27, no. 2 (Fall 1994): 2–113. Also see David John Buerger, *The Mysteries of Godliness: A History of Mormon Temple*

Worship (San Francisco: Smith Research Associates, 1994); Quinn, *The Mormon Hierarchy: Origins of Power*, pp. 113–115, 129–131, 491, 633.

Casting Satan for the endowment film: Buerger, *Mysteries of Godliness*, p. 169.

CHAPTER 13. TWO BY TWO

Ordination to the Melchizedek priesthood as indication of retention rates: Lawrence A. Young, "Confronting Turbulent Environments: Issues in the Organizational Growth and Globalization of Mormonism," in *Contemporary Mormonism: Social Science Perspectives*, edited by Marie Cornwall, Tim B. Heaton, and Lawrence A. Young (Urbana: University of Illinois Press, 1994), pp. 43–63.

The LDS church in Africa: see Peggy Fletcher Stack, three articles, *Sunstone*, 21:2, no. 110 (June 1998): 71–74.

Growth analysis: Rodney Stark, address and remarks at the Mormon History Association convention, Washington, D.C., May 22, 1998. Stark's predictions on LDS growth have been published in several essays and books, including "Modernization and Mormon Growth: The Secularization Thesis Revisited," in Cornwall, Heaton, and Young, *Contemporary Mormonism*, pp. 13–23. Jan Shipps's remarks are in response to the Stark address, the Mormon History Association convention, May 22, 1998.

CHAPTER 14. SAINTLY INDOCTRINATION

Student statistics provided by Brigham Young University.

The 1935 and 1973 studies showing conservative trends among Brigham Young University students: Mauss, *The Angel and the Beehive*, pp. 178–179.

Internal 1996 study of BYU students leaked to Associated Press: see "BYU Grads More Active Than Other University Attenders," *Sunstone*, 19:2, no. 102 (June 1996).

Description of schools in Kirtland, Nauvoo, and early Utah is drawn largely from Allen and Leonard, *The Story of the Latter-day Saints*, pp. 95–96, 158, 255, 276, 341, 453; quote, p. 158.

Seminary and institute statistics provided by the Church Educational System (CES).

Concern that CES programs have turned away from "intellectual articulation" to "indoctrination": Mauss, *The Angel and the Beehive*, p. 102.

CES materials in the early decades: Leonard J. Arrington, "Notes and Comments: The Founding of the L.D.S. Institutes of Religion," *Dialogue*, 2, no. 2 (Summer 1967): 140.

Evaluation of CES materials and the George Tanner journal remarks: Mauss, *The Angel and the Beehive*, pp. 97–98.

Student institute textbooks: *Book of Mormon Student Manual:* Religion 121–22 (Salt Lake City: Church Educational System, the Church of Jesus Christ of Latter-day Saints, 1989, 1996) and *Church History in the Fulness of Times: The History of the Church of Jesus Christ of Latter-day Saints* Religion 341–43 (Salt Lake City: Church Educational System, the Church of Jesus Christ of Latter-day Saints, 1989, 1993). Both are the texts in current use. For a scholarly study of Mountain Meadows see Juanita Brooks, *The Mountain Meadows*

Massacre (1950; reprint, Norman: University of Oklahoma Press, 1962, 1970 with a foreword and afterword by Jan Shipps).

Apostle Dallin H. Oaks, "Reading Church History," Ninth Annual Church Educational System Religious Educators' Symposium, August 16, 1985, Brigham Young University.

Student spy rings at BYU: Gary James Bergera and Ronald Priddis, *Brigham Young University: A House of Faith* (Salt Lake City: Signature Books, 1985), pp. 207–217; Quinn, *The Mormon Hierarchy: Extensions of Power,* pp. 68, 81–83, 86, 92, 95, 100–101, 113, 310; Bryan Waterman and Brian Kagel, *The Lord's University: Freedom and Authority at BYU* (Salt Lake City: Signature Books, 1998), pp. 12, 127, 169, 370; and D. Michael Quinn, "Ezra Taft Benson and Mormon Political Conflicts," *Dialogue,* 26 (Summer 1993): 50–55.

Basketball coach Roger Reid fired: "BYU Coach Fired After Errant Remarks About Church Leaders," *Sunstone,* 20:1, no. 105 (April 1997): 73.

Scott Abbott analysis of troubles at Brigham Young University: "One Lord, One Faith, Two Universities: Tensions between 'Religion' and 'Thought' at BYU," *Sunstone,* 16:3, no. 89 (September 1992): 15–23; and "On Ecclesiastical Endorsements at Brigham Young University," *Sunstone,* 20:1, no. 105 (April 1997): 9–14, esp. p. 11.

BYU firing of David P. Wright: "BYU Professor Terminated for Book of Mormon Beliefs," *Sunstone,* 12:3, no. 65 (May 1988): 43.

David P. Wright, "Statement," *Sunstone,* 12:3, no. 65 (May 1988): 44.

BYU firings of David Knowlton, Cecilia Konchar Farr, Brian Evenson, Gail Turley Houston: AAUP, "Academic Freedom and Tenure: Brigham Young University" (committee report), *Academe: Bulletin of the American Association of University Professors,* 83, no. 5 (September–October 1997): 52–71; for BYU's response to the report, see pp. 69–71.

Responses of Church President Gordon B. Hinckley and BYU President Merrill J. Bateman: interviews with coauthor Richard N. Ostling, June 1997.

Anonymous BYU insider essay: "Clipped and Controlled: A Contemporary Look at BYU," *Sunstone,* 19:3, no. 103 (September 1996): 611–72.

BYU hiring process leak to Associated Press: see "BYU Tightens Faculty Hiring Process," *Sunstone,* 16:8, no. 94 (February 1994): 79.

CHAPTER 15. FAITHFUL HISTORY

Recital of Oaks family history: U.S. Senate Committee on the Judiciary, *Hearings Concerning S. 2148, The Religious Liberty Protection Act of 1998,* testimony of Dallin H. Oaks, June 23, 1998. A copy of the full text of Oaks's testimony was released by the LDS public affairs division.

Re-enactment as an ingredient in ritualization of history: Davis Bitton, "The Ritualization of Mormon History," *The Ritualization of Mormon History and Other Essays* (Urbana: University of Illinois Press, 1994), pp. 171–187; quote, p. 143.

The seagull story: William G. Hartley, "Mormons, Crickets, and Gulls: A New Look at an Old Story," *The New Mormon History: Revisionist Essays on the Past,* edited by D. Michael Quinn (Salt Lake City: Signature Books, 1992), pp. 137–151; quote, p. 143.

Pioneer history as a cult in Utah: Stegner, *The Gathering of Zion*, p. 2.

Mormon consciousness of their own sacred history: Jan Shipps, *Mormonism: The Story of a New Religious Tradition* (Urbana: University of Illinois Press), pp. x, 222.

Martin Marty on sensitive historical issues in Mormonism: "Two Integrities: An Address to the Crisis in Mormon Historiography," in *Faithful History: Essays on Writing Mormon History*, edited by George D. Smith (Salt Lake City: Signature Books, 1992), pp. 169–188; quote, p. 174.

"Career apostates" Jerald and Sandra Tanner and scholarship noting comparisons of changes in Joseph Smith's History of the Church and Doctrine and Covenants: see D. Michael Quinn, "On Being a Mormon Historian (and Its Aftermath)," in Smith, *Faithful History*, pp. 69–112, esp. pp. 101, 104.

The allegedly dynamic and fluid quality of truth in Mormonism: Leone, *The Roots of Modern Mormonism*, pp. 204, 211.

Mormon teachers exhorted to present the acceptable faith-promoting view of history. Boyd Packer address: "The Mantle is Far, Far Greater Than the Intellect," reprinted in *BYU Studies*, 21, no. 3 (1981): 259–277. Ezra Taft Benson quote, p. 275; *BYU Studies* reprint P1–76b (1995). The speech was delivered August 22, 1981.

For a collection of essays expressing different views on how to approach church history: see Smith, *Faithful History*. Two essays are by articulate adherents of the conservative position: Louis Midgley, "The Acids of Modernity and the Crisis in Mormon Historiography," (pp. 189–225), and David Earl Bohn, "Unfounded Claims and Impossible Expectations: A Critique of New Mormon History," (pp. 227–261). Richard Bushman's essay in the volume, "Faithful History," (pp. 1–17) takes a moderate stance: "The enlargement of moral insight, spiritual commitment, and critical intelligence are all bound together" (p. 16). D. Michael Quinn would be an example of a "new Mormon history" scholar who attempts to combine the goal of objective scholarship and candor with taking faith claims seriously.

Discussion about the early church suppression of Lucy Mack Smith's *Biographical Sketches* in the original version: Shipps, *Mormonism*, pp. 91–107; quote, p. 106.

Quinn on simple honesty among scholars and deliberate suppression of evidence: see "Editor's Introduction," in Quinn, ed. *The New Mormon History*, pp. vii-xx, especially p. xiii. Also see Quinn's essay in Smith's *Faithful History*, p. 107.

Eugene Campbell 1981 remark to American Historical Association that authorities discourage sensitive faculty research at BYU: Hardy, *Solemn Covenant*, pp. 337, 353n.

Problems of Mormon historians including Fawn Brodie, Juanita Brooks, Linda King Newell, and Valeen Tippetts Avery: D. Michael Quinn, "150 Years of Truth and Consequences about Mormon History," *Sunstone* 16:1, no. 87 (February 1992): 12, 13, 14.

Church pressure successful in getting Warner Brothers studio to kill major film project on Mountain Meadows massacre: Quinn, *The Mormon Hierarchy: Extensions of Power*, p. 838.

Church dealings with forger Mark Hofmann: Linda Sillitoe and Allen Roberts, *Salamander: The Story of the Mormon Forgery Murders* (Salt Lake City: Signature Books, 1988); see prices paid, pp. 270, 540–543. Several books have been written about this sensational case; the best are Sillitoe/Roberts and Richard E. Turley Jr. *Victims: The LDS Church and the Mark Hofmann Case* (Urbana: University of Illinois Press, 1992). Turley presents something of an inside-church view; he is managing director of the LDS Church historical department.

BYU Studies fortieth anniversary editors ignoring journal's suspension in its first year over Leonard Arrington Word of Wisdom article: episode is described by Arrington in *Adventures of a Church Historian,* p. 58 (see Ch. 11 of this book). Essays by the journal's first two editors in its anniversary issue: Clinton F. Larson, "The Founding Vision of *BYU Studies, 1959–1967,*" and Charles D. Tate Jr., "*BYU Studies* from 1967 to 1983," *BYU Studies,* 38, no. 1 (1999): 10–13.

Apostle (later President) Howard Hunter assuring Leonard Arrington that the LDS church is "mature enough that our history should be honest": Arrington, *Adventures,* p. 14.

Cataloguing of *Great Basin Kingdom* in the church historian's office: Arrington, *Adventures,* p. 34; plans in the church historian's office in early Arrington years, pp. 93–94; Apostle Boyd Packer's complaints about the volume of Brigham Young letters: p. 119. Arrington's memoirs provide a detailed account of the church historian's office difficulties with the First Presidency and Quorum of the Twelve.

Ezra Taft Benson quote: Lavina Fielding Anderson, "The LDS Intellectual Community and Church Leadership: A Contemporary Chronology," *Dialogue,* 26, no. 2 (Spring 1993): 10.

Arrington's diary on problems of LDS intellectuals: Arrington, *Adventures,* p. 154; G. Homer Durham and the restructuring of the history department, pp. 160, 215; Strengthening Church Members Committee and student spying on Arrington at BYU, p. 193.

Restricting access to archives in the church historian's office in Salt Lake City and at Brigham Young University has been described by many researchers. For example, see D. Michael Quinn, *Early Mormonism and the Magic World View,* the 1998 revised and enlarged edition, p. 327.

The poignant ecclesiastical footnote to Leonard Arrington's career as church historian: Davis Bitton, "Ten Years in Camelot: A Personal Memoir," *Dialogue,* 16, no. 3 (Fall 1983): p. 19.

CHAPTER 16. THE GOLD BIBLE

"Were there really golden plates?" Brigham D. Madsen, "Reflections on the LDS Disbelief in the Book of Mormon History," *Dialogue,* 30, no. 3 (Fall 1997): 87–97; quote, p. 95.

Developing "plausibilities" for historicity of the Book of Mormon: John Sorenson, "Introduction," *An Ancient American Setting for the Book of Mormon* (Salt Lake City and Provo: Deseret Book Co./Foundation for Ancient Research and Mormon Studies [FARMS], 1996), p. xviii.

The Smithsonian Institution's Statement on the Book of Mormon: John L. Sorenson, "A New Evaluation of the Smithsonian Institution 'Statement Regarding the Book of Mormon,'" reprint SOR–93 from FARMS (1993); "Smithsonian Statement on the Book of Mormon Revised," *Journal of Book of Mormon Studies,* 7, no. 1 (1998): 77.

Alexander Campbell's 1831 critique of the Book of Mormon: quoted in Arrington and Bitton, *The Mormon Experience,* p. 33; appeared originally in the Painesville (Ohio) *Telegraph,* 15 March 1831.

View of Harold Bloom on Joseph Smith: *Omens of Millennium: The Gnosis of Angels, Dreams, and Resurrection* (New York: Riverhead Books, 1996), Smith compared to C. S. Lewis, p. 22; genius of Joseph Smith, p. 224.

Martin Marty's view of Joseph Smith: see Marty essay in Smith, *Faithful History,* pp. 186, 181. Jan Shipps develops the theme throughout her book *Mormonism.*

Rodney Stark and the rise of Mormonism: "Extracting Scientific Models from Mormon History," address at the Mormon History Association convention, May 22, 1998.

RLDS flexibility in evaluating historicity of the Book of Mormon: William D. Russell, "A Further Inquiry into the Historicity of the Book of Mormon," *Sunstone,* 7, no. 5 (September–October 1982): 20–27; quotes pp. 20, 26.

Orson Pratt on importance of the Book of Mormon as historical fact: S. Orson Pratt, "Divine Authenticity of the Book of Mormon," *Orson Pratt's Works* (Liverpool, 1851), p. 1.

Louis Midgley on importance of maintaining the historicity of the Book of Mormon: see Louis Midgley, "The Acids of Modernity," in Smith, *Faithful History,* p. 214.

Moderate view on historicity and the Book of Mormon: Blake Ostler, "The Book of Mormon as a Modern Expansion of an Ancient Source," *Dialogue,* 20, no. 1 (Spring 1987): 66–123, esp. pp. 66, 79, 100, 107–114.

Smith family activities in folk magic and the occult: see Quinn, *Early Mormonism and the Magic World View.* Quinn also discusses Smith's lack of formal education and the books and literary resources available to him as a youth and young man in upstate New York.

Importance of Joseph Smith's lack of education as factor in evaluating his authenticity as a prophet: Richard Bushman, *Joseph Smith and the Beginnings of Mormonism* (Urbana: University of Illinois Press, 1984), p. 124.

Shipps on the spiritual formulae and the Book of Mormon: see discussion in *Mormonism,* p. 23.

Contemporary materials on the Book of Mormon witnesses: Dan Vogel, ed., *Early Mormon Documents,* vol. 2 (Salt Lake City: Signature Books, 1998), pp. 288–293, 253–271.

Martin Harris and his vision of Christ as a deer: in Vogel, *Early Mormon Documents,* p. 271. These are from 1827–1828 interviews with John A. Clark, an Episcopal priest who had lived in Palmyra as a Harris contemporary. (Also, p. 271, in April 1831 two Ohio newspapers printed Harris's descriptions of Jesus and the devil, both of whom he had claimed to see.)

Stan Larson scholarship on the Sermon on the Mount and his forced resignation from the church translation department: see Stan Larson, "The Historicity of the Matthew Sermon on the Mount in III Nephi," in *New Approaches to the Book of Mormon: Explorations in Critical Methodology,* edited by Brent Lee Metcalfe (Salt Lake City: Signature Books, 1993), pp. 115–163; "Man Forced to Resign Over Translation Issue," *Sunstone,* 10, no. 9 (January 1986): 38–39.

Yale anthropologist Michael D. Coe on Book of Mormon archaeology: see Michael D. Coe, "Mormons and Archaeology: An Outside View," *Dialogue,* 8, no. 2 (Summer 1974): 40–54; quoted, pp. 40, 46.

Church President Joseph Fielding Smith's reluctance to locate Book of Mormon geography: Joseph Fielding Smith, *Answers to Gospel Questions,* compilation of 5 vols. (Salt Lake City: Deseret Book Co., 1998), vol. 2, p. 196.

Bruce R. McConkie's convictions that Hill Cumorah and the great battle took place in upstate New York: *Mormon Doctrine,* p. 175.

A recent defense of the traditional upstate New York for Book of Mormon geography: Duane R. Aston, *Return to Cumorah* (Sacramento, Calif.: American River Publications, 1998).

The story of Thomas Stuart Ferguson: Stan Larson, *Quest for the Gold Plates: Thomas Stuart Ferguson's Archaeological Search for the Book of Mormon* (Salt Lake City: Freethinker Press/Smith Research Associates, 1996).

A Mesoamerican geography for the Book of Mormon: see Sorenson, *An American Setting for the Book of Mormon.* Sorenson deals with anachronisms in the book, including silk, p. 232; Book of Mormon animals, pp. 288–299, proposing deer as a possible candidate for horse, pp. 295–296, 299.

A representative selection of conservative scholarly essays on the authenticity of the Book of Mormon is *Book of Mormon Authorship Revisited: The Evidence for Ancient Origins,* edited by Noel B. Reynolds (Provo: Foundation for Ancient Research and Mormon Studies, 1997). A representative selection of liberal essays on the authenticity of the Book of Mormon is Metcalfe, *New Approaches to the Book of Mormon.*

B. H. Roberts on the authenticity of the Book of Mormon: B. H. Roberts, *Studies of the Book of Mormon,* edited and with an introduction by Brigham D. Madsen and with a biographical essay by Sterling M. McMurrin (Urbana: University of Illinois Press, 1985), pp. 21, 250.

Sterling McMurrin charge that there was an attempt to suppress publication of the Roberts study: see Ron Bitton, "B. H. Roberts Book Stirs Controversy," *Sunstone,* 10, no. 9 (January 1986): 36–38.

Testimony to faith in the Mormon scriptures: Daniel C. Peterson, "Editor's Introduction: Traditions of the Fathers," *FARMS Review of Books,* 9, no. 1 (1997): xxvi.

CHAPTER 17. DISCOVERING "PLAIN AND PRECIOUS THINGS"

Price of the mummies and papyri: H. Donl Peterson, *The Story of the Book of Abraham: Mummies, Manuscripts and Mormonism* (Salt Lake City: Deseret Book Co., 1995), p. 6.

Joseph Smith on beginning to translate the hieroglyphics: Joseph Smith, *History of the Church,* vol. 2, p. 235; reprinted in *New Mormon Studies* CD-ROM.

Reaction of William S. West, early Ohio Gentile, to Joseph Smith's Book of Abraham: "A Few Interesting Facts Respecting the Rise, Progress and Pretension of the Mormons" (pamphlet), 1837; quoted in Stan Larson, *Quest for the Gold Plates,* pp. 89, 122, n17.

Scholarship of Théodule Devéria: Stan Larson, *Quest for the Gold Plates*, pp. 102, 126. Controversies related to Egyptologists' analysis of the fragments in connection with the Book of Abraham are detailed in *Quest for the Gold Plates;* also see Charles Larson, *By His Own Hand Upon Papyrus: A New Look at the Joseph Smith Papyri* (Grand Rapids, Mich.: Institute for Religious Research, 1992).

Analyses of leading non-Mormon Egyptologists of the Book of Abraham papyri: John A. Wilson, "The Joseph Smith Egyptian Papyri: A Translation and Interpretation: A Summary Report": *Dialogue,* 3, no. 2 (Summer 1968): 68–85; Richard A. Parker, "The Joseph Smith Papyri: A Preliminary Report": *Dialogue,* 3, no. 2 (Summer 1968): 85–88; Klaus Baer, "The Breathing Permit of Hôr: A Translation of the Apparent Source of the Book of Abraham," *Dialogue,* 3, no. 3 (Fall 1968): 109–133.

Reaction of British Museum Egyptologist I. E. S. Edwards to Joseph Smith's *Egyptian Alphabet and Grammar:* Stan Larson, *Quest for the Gold Plates,* pp. 93, 129.

Analysis of Mormon Egyptologist: Stephen E. Thompson, "Egyptology and the Book of Abraham," *Dialogue,* 28, no. 1 (Spring 1995): 160.

Stan Larson on the papyri as a catalyst for Book of Abraham inspiration, telephone interview with coauthor Joan K. Ostling, April 1999.

Columbia University historian Richard Bushman on authenticity of the Book of Abraham, interview with coauthor Richard N. Ostling, June 1997.

Klaus Hansen on the effect of the Abraham problems: Klaus Hansen, "Reflections on the 'Lion of the Lord,'" *Dialogue,* 5, no. 2 (Summer 1970): 110.

Church Educational System scholar on Egyptologists: H. Donl Peterson, *The Story of the Book of Abraham,* pp. 249, 252.

Joseph Smith's Civil War predictions: Dan Erickson, *As a Thief in the Night: The Mormon Quest for Millennial Deliverance* (Salt Lake City: Signature Books, 1998), pp. 75–77.

Witness David Whitmer as dissident: "An Address to All Believers in Christ" (1887), reprinted in *New Mormon Studies* CD-ROM.

Joseph Smith's use of the Bible: Philip L. Barlow, *Mormons and the Bible: The Place of the Latter-day Saints in American Religion* (New York and Oxford: Oxford University Press, 1991), p. 43.

Joseph Smith, "There are many things in the Bible which do not, as they now stand, accord with the revelations of the Holy Ghost to me" (1843): Smith quoted in Robert J. Matthews, "The Role of the Joseph Smith Translation in the Restoration," *Plain and Precious Truths Restored: The Doctrinal and Historical Significance of the Joseph Smith Translation,* edited by Robert L. Millet and Robert J. Matthews (Salt Lake City: Bookcraft, 1995), p. 40.

Joseph Smith's translation of *elohim* and the grammar of his Hebrew tutor, Rabbi Joshua Seixas: Michael T. Walton, "Professor Seixas, the Hebrew Bible, and the Book of Abraham," *Sunstone,* 6, no. 2 (March–April 1981): 41–43.

Analysis of the doctrinal influence of the Joseph Smith Translation: Robert J. Matthews, "The 'New Translation' of the Bible, 1830–1833: Doctrinal Development during the Kirtland Era," *BYU Studies,* 11, no. 4 (1971), reprint M7–71, pp. 420–422.

Influence of Boyd K. Packer and Bruce R. McConkie on the Mormon edition of the Bible: Barlow, *Mormons and the Bible,* pp. 206, 208, 210.

McConkie's headnote for Romans 4: Barlow, *Mormons and the Bible,* p. 212.

McConkie on higher criticism: Barlow, *Mormons and the Bible,* p. 188.

Proselytizing and public relations a reason to keep use of the King James Version: cf. Joseph Fielding Smith, *Answers to Gospel Questions,* vol. II, p. 207; Matthews, "Questions and Answers Pertaining to the Joseph Smith Translation," in Millet and Matthews, *Restoring Plain and Precious Truths,* p. 178.

Best ancient manuscripts of the Bible: Emanuel Tov (of Hebrew University, Jerusalem), "Textual Criticism: Old Testament," and Eldon Jay Epp (of Case Western Reserve University) "Textual Criticism: New Testament," in *Anchor Bible Dictionary,* edited by David Noel Freedman, vol. 6 (New York: Doubleday, 1992), pp. 393–412, 412–435.

Joseph Fielding McConkie's views on the problems of "premeditated mischief" on the part of the "great and abominable church" deliberately damaging the Bible: Joseph Fielding McConkie, "Restoring Plain and Precious Truths," in Millet and Matthews, *Restoring Plain and Precious Truths,* p. 32.

Problems in Mormon biblical scholarship, and most modern Mormons' lack of familiarity with the Bible: Barlow, *Mormons and the Bible,* pp. 224, 226.

A choice of world view: testimony of Kevin Christensen, "Paradigms Crossed," *FARMS Review of Books,* 7, no. 2 (1995): 181–182.

CHAPTER 18. "HOW GOD CAME TO BE GOD"

President Gordon B. Hinckley on whether God was once a man: Hinckley quoted in "Mormons Inc." *Time* (cover story), August 4, 1997. *Time* reported (verbatim text): "On whether his church still holds that God the Father was once a man, he sounded uncertain, 'I don't know that we teach it. I don't know that we emphasize it . . . I understand the philosophical background behind it, but I don't know a lot about it, and I don't think others know a lot about it.'" (The interview was also used for PBS-TV *NewsHour with Jim Lehrer* aired July 18, 1997.) At the October 4, 1997, General Conference Hinckley complained such things were "incompletely reported."

Time reader Luke P. Wilson, executive director of the Institute for Religious Research, wrote the First Presidency to ask whether the Hinckley quote was accurately reported in *Time.* F. Michael Watson, Secretary to the First Presidency, responded in a letter dated September 3, 1997, "The quotation you reference was taken out of context. The statement was made in response to a question about the actual circumstances and background surrounding remarks given during the funeral services of a man named King Follett, not the doctrine of exaltation and the blessings that await those who will inherit the celestial kingdom." This book's coauthor Richard N. Ostling had conducted the Hinckley interview in question for *Time.* The full transcript of the relevant excerpt is as follows:

Q. Just another related question that comes up is the statements in the King Follett Discourse by the Prophet.

A. Yeah.

Q. About that, God the Father was once a man as we are. This is something that Christian writers are always addressing. Is this the teaching of the church today, that God the Father was once a man like we are?

A. I don't know that we teach it. I don't know that we emphasize it. I haven't heard it discussed for a long time in public discourse. I don't know. I don't know all the circumstances under which that statement was made. I understand the philosophical background behind it. But I don't know a lot about it and I don't know that others know a lot about it.

The 1901 exchange between B. H. Roberts and the Jesuit priest Rev. Cyril Van Der Donckt: B. H. Roberts, *The Mormon Doctrine of Deity: The Roberts-Van Der Donckt Discussion,* with a foreword by David L. Paulsen (Salt Lake City: Signature Books, 1998). Paulsen's foreword evaluates Roberts's status as the preeminent Mormon intellectual in Mormon history. Roberts list of three basic "complaints" traditional Christians have against the Mormon doctrine of God, p. 11.

Mormons valuing "plainness of doctrine": Thomas O'Dea, *The Mormons,* p. 30.

Roberts explicating Mormon theology: B. H. Roberts, *The Mormon Doctrine of Deity,* see esp. p. 85 (on Genesis), pp. 18–19 (Christology; Incarnation not a unique event).

Apostle John A. Widtsoe on the concept of a limited deity: John A. Widtsoe, *Rational Theology* (Salt Lake City, 1915), pp. 23–24; quoted in O'Dea, *The Mormons,* pp. 123, 273.

Discussion of Sterling M. McMurrin's analysis of Mormon thought is drawn largely from his "Philosophical Foundations of Mormon Theology," lecture published as a University of Utah Press pamphlet, 1959, pp. 5–31.

Apostle James Talmage in support of McMurrin's definition of miracle: see David L. Paulsen, "Comparative Coherency of Mormon (Finitistic) and Classical Theism," Ph.D. diss., University of Michigan, 1975), p. 73.

Liberal Mormons on the theology of God: see Eugene England, "On Spectral Evidence," *Dialogue,* 26, no. 1 (Spring 1993): 145–147; England, "Perfection and Progression: Two Complementary Ways to Talk about God," *BYU Studies,* 29 (Summer 1989): 37; both essays have been reprinted in Eugene England, *Making Peace: Personal Essays* (Salt Lake City: Signature Books, 1995). See also Blake Ostler, "The Mormon Concept of God," *Dialogue,* 17, no. 2 (Summer 1984): 65–93. Ostler writes, "Rejection of absolute omniscience is consistent with Mormonism's commitment to the inherent freedom of uncreated selves, the temporal progression of deity, the moral responsibility of humans, and consequential denial of salvation by arbitrary grace alone," p. 79.

Moral theology in Mormonism: Kim McCall, "What Makes Right Acts Right and Wrong Acts Wrong?" *Sunstone,* 6, no. 6 (November 1981): 27–32. The response of B. Bruce Lindgren, "Nothing More Than Superman," appeared as a letter in *Sunstone,* 7, no. 2 (April 1982): 4.

The "omni" issue in Mormon theology: Roberts, *The Mormon Doctrine of Deity,* p. 126; O'Dea, *The Mormons,* p. 124.

David L. Paulsen on the Mormon theology of God: "Comparative Coherency of Mormon (Finitistic) and Classical Theism," esp. pp. 67, 73–79. England on balancing absolutist descriptions against the concept of a God who is progressing: "On Spectral Evidence," pp. 145–146. Ostler on finitist deity: "The Mormon Concept of God," pp. 91–93.

Historical development of Mormon theology: Thomas G. Alexander, "The Reconstruction of Mormon Doctrine from Joseph Smith to Progressive Theology," *Sunstone,* 10, no. 5 (May 1985): 8–19.

God theology in Joseph Smith's Lectures on Faith: Joseph Smith, lectures 5 and 6 (1834–35) of "Lectures on Faith," *The Essential Joseph Smith,* from the *Latter-Day Saints Messenger and Advocate,* with Sidney Rigdon (Kirtland, Ohio, May 1835), 8:122–26; reprinted in *New Mormon Studies* CD-ROM.

Robert Millet's argument on Joseph Smith's God doctrine: Robert L. Millet, "Joseph Smith and Modern Mormonism: Orthodoxy, Neo-orthodoxy, Tension, and Tradition," *BYU Studies,* 29, no. 3 (1989): 49–68; quoted, pp. 51, 58.

Stephen Robinson quoting C. S. Lewis: see "LDS Doctrine Compared with Other Christian Doctrines," *Encyclopedia of Mormonism,* pp. 399–402, quote p. 402. The quote is from Lewis, *Mere Christianity* (New York: Macmillan, 1958), p. 160.

Deification in Lewis: C. S. Lewis, "The Weight of Glory," *The Weight of Glory and Other Addresses* (New York: The Macmillan Company, 1949), pp. 14–15.

Claim that C. S. Lewis taught that man becomes as God: Robert L. Millet, *The Mormon Faith: A New Look at Christianity* (Salt Lake City: Shadow Mountain/Deseret Book Company, 1998), p. 176.

Argument that C. S. Lewis is not a Mormon in embryo: see Evan Stephenson, "The Last Battle: C. S. Lewis and Mormonism," *Dialogue,* 30, no. 4 (Winter 1997): 43–69.

C. S. Lewis's awareness of the Book of Mormon and his assumption that Joseph Smith wrote it: see Lewis, "The Literary Impact of the Authorized Version," in *Selected Literary Essays,* edited by Walter Hooper (London: Cambridge University Press, 1969), p. 136.

Lewis on man as having no luminosity of his own but only as a mirror reflecting God: C. S. Lewis, *The Four Loves* (New York: Harcourt, Brace and Co., 1960), p. 180. The "savage" in relation to anthropomorphic conceptions of God, as quoted by Stephenson, "The Last Battle: C. S. Lewis and Mormonism," pp. 66, 69.

C. S. Lewis as orthodox Anglican: see Lewis essay "Christian Apologetics" in *God in the Dock: Essays on Theology and Ethics,* edited by Walter Hooper (Grand Rapids, Mich.: William B. Eerdmans Co., 1970), p. 90. Selection of Lewis quotes on the nature of God is from *Letters to Malcolm: Chiefly on Prayer* (New York: Harcourt, Brace & World, 1963, 1964), pp. 13, 21, 22, 73.

Greek philosophy and the early church fathers: G. L. Prestige, *God in Patristic Thought* (1936; reprint London: S.P.C.K., 1959), p. xiv. John Meyendorff, *Catholicity and the Church* (Crestwood, N.Y.: St. Vladimir's Seminary Press, 1983), p. 38.

Mormon appeal to Eastern Orthodox similarities and early church fathers in support of "deification" doctrine: see Daniel C. Peterson and Stephen D. Ricks, "Comparing LDS Beliefs with First-Century Christianity," *Ensign,* 18, no. 3 (March 1988): 6–11.

Eastern Orthodoxy and Mormon deification doctrine: see Timothy Ware, *The Orthodox Church* (1963; reprint, London and New York: Penguin Books, 1993), p. 232. Also quoted is letter from Bishop Ware dated March 30, 1999, in authors' possession.

Mormon deification doctrine and the early church fathers: see Philip Barlow, "Unorthodox Orthodoxy: The Idea of Deification in Christian History," *Sunstone*, 8, no. 5 (September 1983): 13–19; quoted, pp. 13, 16; Robert Millet, "What We Believe," devotional speech at Brigham Young University, February 3, 1998. BYU reprint, p. 4, 5; Stephen Robinson, *Are Mormons Christians?* (Salt Lake City: Bookcraft, 1991), p. 61.

"The gulf is never bridged between Creator and creature": in Prestige, *God in Patristic Thought,* p. 75.

Mormon deification church doctrine and early church fathers as seen by Yale scholar Jaroslav Pelikan: see Pelikan, *Christianity and Classical Culture: The Metamorphosis of Natural Theology in the Christian Encounter with Hellenism,* Gifford Lectures at Aberdeen 1992–1993 (New Haven: Yale University Press, 1993), pp. 295, 318, 330–333. Also, letter from Pelikan dated February 18, 1999, in authors' possession.

Pelikan discussion of Athanasius: Jaroslav Pelikan, *The Christian Tradition: A History of the Development of Doctrine,* vol. 1, *The Emergence of the Catholic Tradition (100–600)* (Chicago: University of Chicago Press, 1971), p. 206.

Quotations from early church fathers on the definition of God: taken from the Ante-Nicene Fathers reprinted on the *Christian Classics Ethereal Library: 1998* CD-ROM produced by Harry Plantinga (Wheaton, Ill.: Wheaton College, 1998). Athanasius, "Ad Afros, 7:39, 40; "De Decretis," 3:11:69; Irenaeus, "Against Heresies, Book I–XXII:1:275, 279; 4: XXXVIII:1, 3, 4.

Rev. Thomas Hopko, interview with coauthor Richard N. Ostling, April 1999.

CHAPTER 19. ARE MORMONS CHRISTIANS? ARE *NON*-MORMONS CHRISTIANS?

A gracious Mormon/Evangelical debate: Craig L. Blomberg and Stephen E. Robinson, *How Wide the Divide?: A Mormon & an Evangelical in Conversation* (Downers Grove, Ill.: InterVarsity Press, 1997). The Eugene England evaluation is from the manuscript of a review scheduled for a forthcoming issue of *BYU Studies.* The Richard J. Mouw critique is from "Can a *Real* Mormon Believe in Jesus?" *Books and Culture,* Vol. 3, No. 5 (September–October 1997): 11–13. Also see Francis J. Beckwith, "With a Grain of Salt: Assessing a Mormon-Evangelical Dialogue," *Christianity Today,* November 17, 1997, pp. 57–58. A forthcoming issue of the *FARMS Review of Books* is to evaluate *How Wide the Divide?,* including a major critique by Blake Ostler.

Examples of hostile behavior by both Mormons and non-Mormons: Blomberg in Blomberg and Robinson, *How Wide the Divide?,* pp. 22–23.

"A bit like asking if African Americans are human": remark by Philip Barlow during panel discussion on "Are Mormons Christians?", Sunstone Symposium, Salt Lake City, July 31, 1998.

Speeches at Brigham Young University before the Southern Baptist convention in Salt Lake City: Apostle Boyd K. Packer, "The Peaceable Followers of Christ," Church Educational System Fireside, February 1, 1998, transcript provided by LDS *Church News;* Robert L. Millet, "What We Believe," devotional delivered February 3, 1998, reprint from *Brigham Young University Speeches: 1997–98.*

Presbyterians on Mormonism: see Presbyterian Church (U.S.A.) assessments: "Presbyterians and Mormons: A Study in Contrasts" (Louisville, Ky.: Office of Theology and Worship, Presbyterian Church [U.S.A.], 1990). See also *Journal of the 207th General Assembly* (Louisville, Ky.: Presbyterian Church [U.S.A.], 1995), Overture 95–50.

Are Mormons Christians? View of Stephen E. Robinson, *Are Mormons Christians?,* p. 34. View of ex-Mormon author Charles Larson, *By His Own Hand Upon Papyri,* p. 189.

For a Mormon scholar's interpretation of the early church: see Hugh Nibley, *Mormonism and Early Christianity* (Salt Lake City: Deseret Book Co., 1987). On the apostles' "complete indifference," see pp. 168–208; on Christians altering evidence of their history, see pp. 109–322.

Bruce R. McConkie on apostasy of non-LDS churches: *Mormon Doctrine,* pp. 45–46, 171, 352, 525, 593, 628–629.

President Gordon B. Hinckley on relations with other churches: interview with coauthor Richard N. Ostling, June 1997.

Competing strands within Mormonism on how to interpret such core doctrines as sin, grace, atonement; the apparent drift of some Mormon writers toward pessimism on the nature of man: see O. Kendall White, *Mormon Neo-Orthodoxy: A Crisis Theology* (Salt Lake City: Signature Books, 1987); quoted, pp. 174–175. An extended negative review of the White book: Louis Midgley, "A Mormon Neo-Orthodoxy Challenges Cultural Mormon Neglect of the Book of Mormon: Some Reflections on the Impact of Modernity," *FARMS Review of Books,* 6, no. 2 (1994): 283–334; quoted, pp. 283, 285, 317.

Apostle Dallin Oaks on Mormon theology of eternal progression and the LDS view of Adam's fall, "The Great Plan of Happiness," address given October 3, 1993, at General Conference and published in *Ensign,* 23, no. 11 (November 1993): 73, 74.

Defining a Mormon doctrine of the atonement: see Keith E. Norman, "Toward a Mormon Christology: Are We Disciples to the Christ of History or the Christ of the Creeds?" *Sunstone,* 10, no. 4 (April 1985): 19–25. See also Peggy Fletcher [Stack], "Going My Way: An Interview with *Newsweek*'s Kenneth Woodward," *Sunstone,* 5, no. 5 (September–October 1980): 32–39, quoted p. 36. Fletcher's interview of Woodward in *Sunstone* was in response to Woodward's article, "What Mormons Believe," *Newsweek,* September 1, 1980, pp. 68, 71. Woodward had interviewed Truman Madsen for the *Newsweek* piece; the full transcript of the portion of the interview relating to the doctrine of the atonement, not quoted in *Newsweek,* was included in the *Sunstone* piece. For a good discussion of subtleties in the Mormon doctrine of the atonement, see Eugene England, "That They Might Not Suffer: The Gift of Atonement," *Dialogue,* 1, no. 3 (Autumn 1966): 140–155.

The relation of faith and works: McConkie on the "perverted" Church of England Articles of Religion, *Mormon Doctrine,* p. 107; James Talmage on the "most pernicious doctrine," in

Articles of Faith, p. 107. See *Encyclopedia of Mormonism* articles on "Enduring to the End," "Gospel of Jesus Christ," "Grace," and "Works."

Adam theology according to Apostle Bruce R. McConkie, as quoted in Robert Millet, "The Man Adam," *Ensign,* 24, no. 1 (January 1994): 13. McConkie source is *The Mortal Messiah: From Bethlehem to Calvary,* 4 vols. (Salt Lake City: Deseret Book Co., 1979–81), p. 4:125; see also Conference Report, April 1985, p. 10.

Adam theology according to B. H. Roberts: see Roberts, *The Mormon Doctrine of Deity,* p. 42.

Brigham Young on Adam-God and blood atonement: see *Journal of Discourses,* vol. 1, p. 50 and vol. 4, p. 53; reprinted in *New Mormon Studies* CD-ROM.

Is Mormonism Christian? Jan Shipps on the question: Shipps, *Mormonism,* pp. 148–149. Church President Gordon B. Hinckley on the question, address at General Conference, April 4, 1998, "We Bear Witness of Him," published in *Ensign,* 28, no. 5 (May 1988): 4.

CHAPTER 20. RIVALS AND ANTAGONISTS

Literature on the Church of Christ (Temple Lot) is available from its headquarters: 200 South River Boulevard, Independence, MO 64051. The estimate of "200 plus factions" appears in its periodical, *Zion's Advocate,* 75, no. 7 (July 1998): 134.

Catalog of Joseph Smith–related denominations: J. Gordon Melton, *Encyclopedia of American Religions,* 5th ed. (Detroit: Gale Research, 1996), pp. 561–585.

A fully detailed account of the 1844 succession crisis and subsequent schisms is found in Quinn, *The Mormon Hierarchy: Origins of Power,* pp. 143–263. Quinn appendices also provide a chronology, and biographies of the personalities.

Good overview of RLDS history in Roger D. Launius, *Joseph Smith III: Pragmatic Prophet* (Urbana: University of Illinois Press, 1988) and *Our Legacy of Faith: A Brief History of the Reorganized Church of Jesus Christ of Latter Day Saints* (Independence, Mo.: Herald Publishing, 1991). See also Roger D. Launius, "The Reorganized Church, the Decade of Decision, and the Abilene Paradox," *Dialogue,* 31, no. 1 (Spring 1998): 47–65, an article which analyzes statistical decline and recent problems in the RLDS.

RLDS reassessment of Mormon polygamy history: see Richard P. Howard, "The Changing RLDS Response to Mormon Polygamy: A Preliminary Analysis," *Restoration Studies III,* edited by Maurice Draper (Independence, Mo.: Herald Publishing House, 1986), pp. 145–162.

Interviews with RLDS historian Mark A. Scherer and RLDS Church President W. Grant McMurray conducted by coauthor Joan K. Ostling, Independence, Mo., October 1998.

Richard Price's conservative RLDS activity: see Roger D. Launius and Linda Thatcher, eds., *Differing Visions: Dissenters in Mormon History* (Urbana: University of Illinois Press, 1994), pp. 319–343.

RLDS doctrinal and scriptural changes: Louis Midgley, "The Radical Reformation of the Reorganization of the Restoration," *Journal of Book of Mormon Studies,* 2, no. 2 (Fall 1993): 132–163.

Reference work on cults: *The Directory of Cult Research Organizations: A Worldwide Listing of 752 Agencies and Individuals* (Trenton, Mich.: American Religions Center, 1996).

Career of Jerald and Sandra Tanner: see Lawrence Foster, "Career Apostates: Reflections on the Works of Jerald and Sandra Tanner," *Dialogue,* 17, no. 2 (Summer 1984), on Ehat dispute, pp. 47–48. Also see Wallace Turner, *The Mormon Establishment* (Boston: Houghton, Mifflin Co., 1966), pp. 249–256; and Arrington, *Adventures of a Church Historian,* pp. 63–64.

CHAPTER 21. DISSENTERS AND EXILES

The events surrounding the "September Six" cases, other church disciplinary hearings, and Brigham Young University controversies of the 1990s, were described in numerous articles in the Associated Press, *Deseret News, Dialogue, New York Times, Salt Lake Tribune,* and *Sunstone;* and in *The Lord's University: Freedom and Authority at BYU* by Bryan Waterman and Brian Kagel.

Lavina Fielding Anderson's compilation on one hundred-plus repression examples, her protest against the church's "internal espionage system," and the account of her own firing from *Ensign,* appear in her article "The LDS Intellectual Community and Church Leadership: A Contemporary Chronology," *Dialogue,* 26, no. 1 (Spring 1993): 7–64.

Child abuse lawsuits: three articles by Paul McKay in the *Houston Chronicle:* "Mormons Caught Up in a Wave of Pedophile Accusations," May 9, 1999; "Church Shunned Sex-Abuse Study," May 10, 1999; and "Mormon Psychologist's Recanting About Church Flaw Puzzles Some," May 10, 1999. See also documentation for various cases in *Case Reports of the Mormon Alliance,* compiled and edited by Lavina Fielding Anderson and Janice Merrill Allred as volumes published annually since 1995 and distributed through Signature Books.

Text of the First Presidency statement and church public relations comment on the Strengthening Church Members Committee: *Sunstone,* 16:2, no. 88 (August 1992): 63.

Gordon B. Hinckley speaking against prayer to "our Mother in Heaven": *Sunstone,* 15:4, no. 83 (September 1991): 69–70.

In 1996, three years after his excommunication, D. Michael Quinn let it be known publicly that he is homosexual, but that issue played no part in his years of difficulty with LDS officials. He took no leadership role in the Mormon homosexual movement but has published a book about the history of same-sex behavior among Mormons: *Same-Sex Dynamics Among Nineteenth-Century Americans: A Mormon Example* (Urbana: University of Illinois Press, 1996).

On the Deborah Laake case: see Newell G. Bringhurst, "Fawn M. Brodie and Deborah Laake: Two Perspectives on Mormon Feminist Dissent," *John Whitmer Historical Association Journal,* 17 (1997): 95–112.

LDS ecclesiastical law on church discipline is contained in the *Church Handbook of Instructions:* Book 1 (Salt Lake City: the Church of Jesus Christ of Latter-day Saints, 1998 [in effect January 1, 1999]), pp. 91–108.

On Sterling McMurrin criticized by apostles and shielded by President David O. McKay: see Sterling M. McMurrin and L. Jackson Newell, *Matters of Conscience: Conversations with*

Sterling M. McMurrin (Salt Lake City: Signature Books, 1996), pp. 196–199.

"Restrained skepticism": G. Wesley Johnson, editorial preface to inaugural issue of *Dialogue,* 1, no. 1 (Spring 1966): 6.

Stewart Udall's letter to the editor on race: *Dialogue,* 2, no. 2 (Summer 1967): 5–7.

The LDS racial history research was published as Lester E. Bush Jr., "Mormonism's Negro Doctrine: An Historical Overview," *Dialogue,* 8, no. 1 (Spring 1973): 11–49; also reprinted in booklet form by *Dialogue.*

On Lester Bush, Apostles Mark Peterson and Boyd K. Packer, BYU vice president, and Bill Marriott and *Dialogue*'s black priesthood article: Lester E. Bush Jr., "An Historical Overview of My 'Historical Overview,'" paper prepared for the Mormon History Association convention, Washington, D.C., May 23, 1998, and read for him in his absence.

Scott Kenney's prospectus for the new magazine: see *Sunstone,* 1, no. 2 (Spring 1976): 6.

Text of First Presidency and Quorum of the Twelve statement on "recent symposia": *Sunstone,* 15:4, no. 83 (October 1991): 58. Apostle Boyd K. Packer's follow-up warning quoted in "Church Issues Statement on 'Symposia,'" same edition, pp. 58–59.

On Boyd K. Packer's 1993 "three dangers" speech: "Elder Packer Names Gays/Lesbians, Feminists, and 'So-Called' Scholars Three Main Dangers," *Sunstone,* 16:6, no. 92 (November 1993): 74–75.

President Gordon B. Hinckley on feminists: from interview conducted by coauthor Richard N. Ostling, June 1997.

On the Sonia Johnson case: Alice Allred Pottmyer, "Sonia Johnson: Mormonism's Feminist Heretic" in Launius and Thatcher, *Differing Visions: Dissenters in Mormon History,* pp. 366–391.

On reduced autonomy for the church women's auxiliary: Jill Mulvay Derr, Janath Russell Cannon, and Maureen Ursenbach Beecher, *Women of Covenant: The Story of Relief Society* (Salt Lake City: Deseret Book, 1992), pp. 340–346.

On the chain of command for the Relief Society, male ward clerks, and situations where women are allowed to bless and to pray: Lavina Fielding Anderson, "A Loss of Certitude About Where Women Fit," *Sunstone,* 6, no. 6 (November 1981): 12–16.

On Claudia L. Bushman and Laurel Thatcher Ulrich disinvited, Hawkins dismissal, and other complaints: "Limitations on the Academic Freedom of Women at Brigham Young University," statement from BYU chapter of American Association of University Professors, March 1996.

"When our leaders speak, the thinking has been done": Ward Teachers' Message, *Improvement Era,* June 1945, p. 354, and President George A. Smith's apology, cited in Quinn, *The Mormon Hierarchy: Extensions of Power,* p. 830.

N. Eldon Tanner, "When the prophet speaks the debate is over" in *Ensign* (August 1979): 2–3, cited in Quinn, *The Mormon Hierarchy: Extensions of Power,* p. 872.

Ezra Taft Benson in 1980 on the Living Prophet over dead prophets: speech delivered February 26, 1980, "Fundamentals in Following the Prophet," quoted in Jerald and Sandra

Tanner, "The Mormon Purge," pamphlet published by the Utah Lighthouse Ministry, Salt Lake City, 1993, pp. 58–59.

On college students' manual saying the Lord will never lead Living Prophet astray: Quinn, *The Mormon Hierarchy: Extensions of Power,* p. 397.

On Apostle M. Russell Ballard in 1994, "We will not lead you astray; we cannot": Quinn, *The Mormon Hierarchy: Extensions of Power,* p. 368.

Affirmation member's plea to disciplinary council on homosexuality: provided to the authors by the member after his excommunication.

Boyd K. Packer, "The Mantle Is Far, Far Greater Than the Intellect," speech delivered at the Fifth Annual Church Educational System Religious Educators' Symposium, Brigham Young University, August 22, 1981; reprinted in *BYU Studies,* 21, no. 3 (1981): 259–277; *BYU Studies* reprint P1–76b (1995).

Dallin H. Oaks, "Reading Church History," speech delivered at the Ninth Annual Church Educational System Religious Educators' Symposium, Brigham Young University, August 16, 1985.

Text excerpt of James E. Faust statement after September Six excommunications: "Keeping Covenants and Honoring the Priesthood," *Sunstone* 16:6, no. 92 (November 1993): 70.

Text of First Presidency and Quorum of the Twelve statement after the September Six excommunications: *Sunstone,* 16:6, no. 92 (November 1993): 72.

Eugene England reflecting on BYU: "An Interview with Eugene England," *Student Review,* (April 10, 1998): 10–11.

Armand L. Mauss feeling "increasingly marginal": Armand L. Mauss, *The Angel and the Beehive,* pp. xii-xiii.

CHAPTER 22. MORMONISM IN THE TWENTY-FIRST CENTURY

Analysis of intellectual and future trends by Thomas O'Dea: *The Mormons,* pp. 222–263.

Rodney Stark's projections on Mormon growth: Rodney Stark, "The Rise of a New World Faith" (1984), reprinted with an updated postscript in *Latter-day Saint Social Life: Social Research on the LDS Church and Its Members,* edited by James T. Duke (Provo, Utah: Religious Studies Center, Brigham Young University, 1998), pp. 9–27.

Michael Evenden reviewing Tony Kushner drama: *Sunstone,* 17:2 (September 1994): 55–64.

Ex-Mormon Walter Kirn short story: "Mormon Eden," *The New Yorker* (June 9, 1997): 88–97.

Jan Shipps on changing status of Mormonism in American culture: "The Mormon Image Since 1960," paper presented at the Sunstone Symposium, August 1, 1998.

On Brazilian retention: Mark Glover, cited by Newell G. Bringhurst in "The Image of Blacks Within Mormonism as Presented in the *Church News*," *American Periodicals,* 2 (Fall 1992): 120. The anonymous ex-missionary's account was posted on the www.exmormon.org web site.

On black South African retention: Peggy Fletcher Stack, "African Culture Presents Challenges for Mormon Converts," *Salt Lake Tribune,* April 4, 1998, reprinted in *Sunstone* 21:2, no. 110 (June 1998): 73.

On black retention in Columbia and Greensboro: Heidi Swinton, "Without Regard for Race," *This People* (Summer 1988): 19–23, cited in Bringhurst, "The Image of Blacks Within Mormonism."

Sociologists on membership retention: Tim B. Heaton, "Vital Statistics," *Encyclopedia of Mormonism,* p. 1527; Lawrence A. Young, "Confronting Turbulent Environments: Issues in the Organizational Growth and Globalization of Mormonism," in *Contemporary Mormonism: Social Science Perspectives,* pp. 55–61; Young on "indigenous expression" in Latin America, p. 60.

Listing of twenty-three scholarly studies showing "ludicrous" forced correlation overseas: Armand L. Mauss, *The Angel and the Beehive,* pp. 206, 213–214.

Current Order of LDS Presidential Succession in the Quorum of the Twelve:

After Monson and Packer, the order of seniority by which other current Apostles are in line for automatic succession to the presidency is as follows (with age as of January 1, 2000, in parentheses):

L. Tom Perry (77)—Born in Utah; Utah State University finance degree; U.S. Marine in the Pacific theater during World War II; formerly vice president and treasurer of a Boston department store chain.

David B. Haight (93)—Born in Idaho; attended Utah State; Navy commander in World War II; formerly mayor of Palo Alto, California, district manager of a retail chain, mission president in Scotland, and assistant to the president of Brigham Young University.

James E. Faust (79)—Born in Utah, University of Utah law graduate; served in the Air Corps during World War II; formerly a Salt Lake City attorney, Utah state legislator, and president of the Utah Bar Association; Second Counselor in Hinckley's First Presidency since 1995.

Neal A. Maxwell (73)—Born in Salt Lake City; University of Utah master's degree; formerly a political science professor and executive vice president at that university and the church commissioner of education.

Russell M. Nelson (75)—Born in Salt Lake City; M.D. from University of Utah and Ph.D. from University of Minnesota; formerly a cardiovascular surgeon and medical researcher, and president of the Society for Vascular Surgery.

Dallin H. Oaks (67)—Born in Utah; BYU alumnus, University of Chicago law graduate who clerked for Chief Justice Earl Warren; formerly University of Chicago law professor, president of Brigham Young University, and Utah supreme court justice.

M. Russell Ballard (71)—Born in Salt Lake City; descendant of the martyred Hyrum Smith; attended University of Utah; formerly in automotive, realty, and investment businesses, and mission president in Canada.

Joseph B. Wirthlin (82)—Born in Salt Lake City; University of Utah business degree; formerly president of a Utah trade association and member of the Sunday School general presidency.

Richard G. Scott (71)—Born in Idaho; engineering degree from George Washington University with postgraduate work in nuclear engineering at Oak Ridge, Tennessee; formerly worked to develop military and private nuclear reactors.

Robert D. Hales (67)—Born in New York City; University of Utah alumnus with Harvard M.B.A.; U.S. Air Force jet pilot; formerly a business executive and mission president in England.

Jeffrey R. Holland (59)—Born in Utah; BYU alumnus, with master's and doctoral degrees from Yale; formerly a director of college institutes, president of Brigham Young University, and the church commissioner of education.

Henry B. Eyring (66)—Born in Princeton, N.J.; University of Utah alumnus, with master's and doctoral degrees from Harvard; the church commissioner of education and formerly president of Ricks College.

On retrenchment: Mauss: *The Angel and the Beehive*, pp. 77–176.

FOR FURTHER READING

Following is a selected list for readers interested in pursuing the subject of Mormonism. It is not a list of all works consulted in researching this book.

ENCYCLOPEDIA

Ludlow, Daniel H., ed. *Encyclopedia of Mormonism: The History, Scripture, Doctrine, and Procedures of the Church of Jesus Christ of Latter-day Saints.* 5 vols. New York: Macmillan, 1992. Nearly 800 articles by LDS scholars, plus the LDS scriptures. Brigham Young University professors are prominent among the writers. Authoritative, but not always candid on delicate issues.

DENOMINATIONAL DATA

1999–2000 Church Almanac, Deseret News 1998. PO Box 1257, Salt Lake City, UT 84110. Biographies of present and past General Authorities, statistics, detail on each U.S. state and foreign nation, temples, history, auxiliaries, other data, some curious omissions. Published biennially.

BOOKS

(See endnotes for other works cited.)

Scriptures

The "Standard Works"

The Book of Mormon, The Doctrine and Covenants, The Pearl of Great Price. 1 vol. ed. Salt Lake City: Church of Jesus Christ of Latter-day Saints, 1981.
The Holy Bible: King James Version. Salt Lake City: Church of Jesus Christ of Latter-day Saints, 1979. With standard explanatory notes and cross-references to the other Standard Works.

Joseph Smith's "New Translation" of the Bible. Independence, Mo.: Herald Publishing House, 1970. RLDS owns the copyright to the Joseph Smith Translation. This edition has parallel columns of the Smith and King James Versions.

Secondary Works

Barlow, Philip L. *Mormons and the Bible: The Place of the Latter-day Saints in American Religion.* New York and Oxford: Oxford University Press, 1991. An intellectual and cultural history, by a Mormon, based on his 1988 doctoral thesis for Harvard Divinity School.

Larson, Stan. *Quest for the Gold Plates: Thomas Stuart Ferguson's Archaeological Search for the Book of Mormon.* Salt Lake City: Freethinker Press/Smith Research Associates, 1996. Story of the search for archaeological support for the Book of Mormon; includes material on the Book of Abraham papyri. By a former employee of the LDS translation department who holds a Ph.D. in New Testament studies from the University of Birmingham, England.

Metcalfe, Brent Lee. *New Approaches to the Book of Mormon: Explorations in Critical Methodology.* Salt Lake City: Signature Books, 1993. A collection of essays by liberal scholars who doubt the literal historicity of the Book of Mormon.

Reynolds, Noel B., ed. *Book of Mormon Authorship Revisited: The Evidence for Ancient Origins.* Provo, Utah: Foundation for Ancient Research and Mormon Studies, 1997. A collection of essays by conservative Mormon scholars defending the historicity of the Book of Mormon. Essays include literary analysis.

Roberts, B. H. *Studies of the Book of Mormon.* Edited and with an introduction by Brigham D. Madsen and a biographical essay by Sterling M. McMurrin. Urbana: University of Illinois Press, 1985. Controversial work by the General Authority considered the dominant Mormon intellectual of the early twentieth century. These studies were withheld from publication in Roberts's lifetime.

Sorenson, John L. *An Ancient American Setting for the Book of Mormon.* 1985; reprint, Salt Lake City and Provo: Deseret Book Company and Foundation for Ancient Research and Mormon Studies, 1996. An attempt to find a plausible setting in Mesoamerica for the Book of Mormon.

Doctrine

Blomberg, Craig L., and Stephen E. Robinson. *How Wide the Divide?: A Mormon and an Evangelical in Conversation.* Downers Grove, Ill.: InterVarsity Press, 1997. Dialogue on four topics of theological disagreement. Critics on both sides have said that the two authors softened their points of contention too much to be accurate, but the debate is interesting and the tone is gracious.

Gospel Principles. Salt Lake City: Church of Jesus Christ of Latter-day Saints, 1997. Basic doctrine as presented in official adult Sunday school manual and approved by the Correlation Committee.

McConkie, Bruce R. *Mormon Doctrine.* 2nd ed. Salt Lake City: Bookcraft, 1979. A classic best-seller among Mormons (seventeen printings by 1997), though the author, an apostle, is a hard-line conservative and often controversial (for example: "Racial degeneration, resulting in differences in appearance and spiritual aptitude, has arisen since the fall.").

McMurrin, Sterling M. "The Philosophical Foundations of Mormon Theology." 1959; reprint, Salt Lake City: University of Utah Press, 1979. Lecture published as a pamphlet.

———. *The Theological Foundations of the Mormon Religion.* Salt Lake City: University of Utah Press, 1965. A very sophisticated liberal explication of Mormon thought.

Millet, Robert. *The Mormon Faith: A New Look at Christianity.* Salt Lake City: Shadow Mountain/Deseret Book, 1998. A presentation of Mormon doctrine by the BYU dean of religious education, intended as an appealing introduction for non-Mormons.

Roberts, B. H. *The Mormon Doctrine of Deity: The Roberts–Van der Donckt Discussion.* With a foreword by David L. Paulsen. 1903; reprint, Salt Lake City: Signature Books, 1998. Debate between Roberts and a Catholic priest over the nature of God.

———. (1) *The Truth, the Way, the Life,* edited by John Welch. Provo, Utah: *BYU Studies,* 1994.

———. (2) *The Truth, the Way, the Life,* edited by Stan Larson. San Francisco: Smith Research Associates, 1994.

Controversial doctrinal work withheld from publication in Roberts's lifetime and published simultaneously by two houses in 1994 after a dispute over whether the church or the Roberts family owned the copyright.

Robinson, Stephen. *Are Mormons Christians?* Salt Lake City: Bookcraft, 1991. A discussion of the perennial question, aimed at a Mormon audience.

Talmage, James E. *A Study of the Articles of Faith.* Salt Lake City: Church of Jesus Christ of Latter-day Saints, 1890, 1913, 1924, 1960. A classic doctrinal statement by an apostle.

White, O. Kendall. *Mormon Neo-orthodoxy: A Crisis Theology.* Salt Lake City: Signature Books, 1987. Argument from a liberal Mormon perspective that some late-twentieth-century Mormon thinkers have reacted to a crisis culture in a manner resembling Protestant neo-orthodox theologians, emphasizing sin, depravity, and man's dependence on an absolutist God, thereby straying from traditional Mormonism.

General Histories

Allen, James B., and Glen M. Leonard. *The Story of the Latter-day Saints.* Salt Lake City: Deseret Book Co., 1976. A one-volume history aimed at an LDS audience, a project of the church historical department.

Arrington, Leonard J., and Davis Bitton. *The Mormon Experience: A History of the Latter-day Saints.* New York: Alfred A. Knopf, 1979. A one-volume history aimed at a non-Mormon audience, produced by the church historian Arrington and his colleague Bitton.

Hansen, Klaus J. *Mormonism and the American Experience.* Chicago: University of Chicago Press, 1981. A study of the relationship between American society and Mormon intellectual and cultural development.

O'Dea, Thomas F. *The Mormons.* Chicago: University of Chicago Press, 1957. Still a classic study by a non-Mormon, with good theological analysis.

Shipps, Jan. *Mormonism: The Story of a New Religious Tradition.* Urbana: University of Illinois Press, 1985. By a leading non-Mormon expert; particularly good at grasping the Mormons' own sense of their sacred history.

Biographies

Arrington, Leonard J. *Brigham Young: American Moses.* New York: Alfred A. Knopf, 1985. Well-written biography by a scholar who is an admirer and knows how to write a good story.

Brodie, Fawn M. *No Man Knows My History: The Life of Joseph Smith, the Mormon Prophet.* New York: Alfred A. Knopf, 1945. Well-written and researched, and groundbreaking when published, but criticized by many Mormons because it fails to take Smith's faith claims seriously and has a negative, polemical tone.

Bushman, Richard. *Joseph Smith and the Beginnings of Mormonism.* Urbana: University of Illinois Press, 1984. Well-researched interpretation by a Mormon scholar who is a Columbia University history professor. Bushman is currently working on a full career biography of Joseph Smith that will be a major contribution to Mormon studies when published.

Hill, Donna. *Joseph Smith: The First Mormon.* Garden City, N.Y.: Doubleday, 1977. By a believing Mormon and something of a rival to the earlier Brodie biography.

Launius, Roger D. *Joseph Smith III: Pragmatic Prophet.* Urbana: University of Illinois Press, 1988. Informative biography of the LDS prophet's son, who became the leader of the Reorganized Church.

Newell, Linda King, and Valeen Tippetts Avery. *Mormon Enigma: Emma Hale Smith: Prophet's Wife, "Elect Lady," Polygamy's Foe, 1804–1879.* Garden City, N.Y.: Doubleday, 1984. A well-researched and -written book on Joseph Smith's wife, with a clear and fair analysis of the controversial elements affecting their marriage and the early Mormon Church.

Specialized Topics in Mormon History

Alexander, Thomas G. *Mormonism in Transition: A History of the Latter-day Saints, 1890–1930.* Urbana: University of Illinois Press, 1986, 1996. Study of the ecclesiastical, political, economic, and cultural adjustments the LDS had to make in the decades after Utah's statehood.

Arrington, Leonard. *Adventures of a Church Historian.* Urbana: University of Illinois Press, 1998. Candid memoir of a loyalist LDS intellectual, including the troubles of the church history department.

———. *Great Basin Kingdom: An Economic History of the Latter-day Saints, 1830–1900.* Cambridge, Mass.: Harvard University Press, 1958. A classic in Mormon studies.

Bergera, Gary James, and Ronald Priddis. *Brigham Young University: A House of Faith.* Salt Lake City: Signature Books, 1985. A history of conflict between religious authorities and intellectual life at Brigham Young University.

Brooks, Juanita. *The Mountain Meadows Massacre.* With a foreword and afterword by Jan Shipps. Norman: University of Oklahoma Press, 1962, 1970. Most interesting as a study of the church's difficulty dealing with the aftermath of the massacre.

Buerger, David John. *The Mysteries of Godliness: A History of Mormon Temple Worship.* San Francisco: Smith Research Associates, 1994. LDS ritual history.

Bush, Lester E., Jr., and Armand L. Mauss, eds. *Neither White nor Black: Mormon Scholars Confront the Race Issue in a Universal Church.* Midvale, Utah: Signature Books, 1984. Mostly articles from *Dialogue;* out-of-print, but the full text is available on the *New Mormon Studies* CD-ROM.

Compton, Todd. *In Sacred Loneliness: The Plural Wives of Joseph Smith*. Salt Lake City: Signature Books, 1997. A carefully documented study of all the polygamous marriages of Joseph Smith.

Flanders, Robert Bruce. *Nauvoo: Kingdom on the Mississippi*. Urbana: University of Illinois Press, 1965, 1975. Particularly good at analyzing the economics of Nauvoo; by an RLDS scholar.

Hardy, B. Carmon. *Solemn Covenant: The Mormon Polygamous Passage*. Urbana: University of Illinois Press, 1992. A careful study of post-Manifesto polygamy problems and the LDS transition to a monogamous culture.

Mauss, Armand L. *The Angel and the Beehive: The Mormon Struggle with Assimilation*. Urbana: University of Illinois Press, 1994. An excellent analysis of Mormon cultural changes in the last four decades of the twentieth century.

Quinn, D. Michael. *Early Mormonism and the Magic World View*. Revised and enlarged edition. Salt Lake City: Signature Books, 1998. Well-documented history of the folk magic and occult culture associated with Joseph Smith.

———. *The Mormon Hierarchy: Origins of Power*. Salt Lake City: Signature Books/Smith Research Associates, 1994. *The Mormon Hierarchy: Extensions of Power*. Salt Lake City: Signature Books/Smith Research Associates, 1997. Well-researched and scrupulously documented pair of volumes on history of the church leadership, by a former BYU history professor.

Smith, George D., ed. *Faithful History: Essays on Writing Mormon History*. Salt Lake City: Signature Books, 1992. A thoughtful collection of essays that ranges from very conservative (Louis B. Midgley) to moderate (Richard L. Bushman, Leonard J. Arrington) to liberal (D. Michael Quinn) and includes non-Mormons (Martin Marty and others).

Stegner, Wallace. *The Gathering of Zion: The Story of the Mormon Trail*. New York: McGraw-Hill, 1964. Reprint, Lincoln: University of Nebraska Press, 1981. The Utah trek, told by a non-Mormon master storyteller.

Van Wagoner, Richard S. *Mormon Polygamy: A History*. Salt Lake City: Signature Books, 1989. A solidly researched history of polygamy from its LDS beginnings to the present-day "fundamentalists."

Waterman, Bryan, and Brian Kagel. *The Lord's University: Freedom and Authority at BYU*. Salt Lake City: Signature Books, 1998. A study of controversies from 1988 to 1998 at Brigham Young University and the well-publicized firings of several professors. The authors were both student editors at BYU.

Wilkinson, Ernest L., and W. Cleon Skousen. *Brigham Young University: A School of Destiny*. Provo, Utah: BYU Press, 1976. Official centennial history of BYU.

Critics

Tanner, Jerald, and Sandra Tanner. *Mormonism—Shadow or Reality?* Salt Lake City: Modern Microfilm Company/Utah Lighthouse Ministry, 1987. Self-published and frequently updated book by Salt Lake City's best-known former Mormons.

White, James R. *Is the Mormon My Brother?: Discerning the Differences Between Mormonism and Christianity*. Minneapolis: Bethany House Publishers, 1997. Written largely as a response to Blomberg and Robinson, *How Wide the Divide?*, this is a fairly articulate analysis of theological differences as seen from an Evangelical perspective.

PERIODICALS

BYU Studies. Brigham Young University, 403 Clyde Building, Brigham Young University, Provo, UT 84602. A quarterly intellectual journal supporting the LDS faith. http://humanities.byu.edu/BYUStudies/homepage.htm.

Church News. PO Box 26368, Salt Lake City, UT 84126. A weekly tabloid supplement to the *Deseret News* published by the LDS church. http://desnews.com/cn.

Dialogue: A Journal of Mormon Thought. PO Box 20210, Shaker Heights, OH 44120. An independent quarterly with scholarship from various perspectives, including liberal LDS viewpoints. http://www.dialoguejournal.org.

Ensign. Church Magazines, 50 East North Temple Street, Salt Lake City, UT 84250. The church's official English-language adult magazine since 1971; published monthly, with General Conference issues in May and November.

FARMS Review of Books. PO Box 7113, University Station, Provo, UT 84602. A semiannual of the Foundation for Ancient Research and Mormon Studies; defends the LDS faith against all critics and assesses pro-LDS writings. http://www.farmsresearch.com.

Journal of Book of Mormon Studies. Another semiannual from FARMS; see *FARMS Review of Books.*

Journal of Mormon History. PO Box 581068, Salt Lake City, UT 84258-2068. The semiannual of the Mormon History Association. http://www.mhahome.org.

Sunstone. 343 North Third West Street, Salt Lake City, UT 84103-1215. An independent magazine that includes liberal LDS viewpoints. Web site to be established soon.

CD-ROMS

GospeLink. Salt Lake City: Deseret Book, 1998. A two-disc "reference library" with hundreds of LDS inspirational books, scriptural reference works, selected issues of the onetime church magazine *Improvement Era* (but not *Ensign,* the church magazine since 1971), and some other periodicals; from the LDS Church's publishing house.

Infobase Library. Salt Lake City: Bookcraft, 1998. A three-disc set from the LDS publisher with a concordance of *Ensign* articles (but not the full issues), *BYU Studies, Church News* 1988–98, official teachings and discourses of LDS prophets, the *Encyclopedia of Mormonism,* Bruce McConkie's *Mormon Doctrine,* the collected works of Hugh Nibley, and hundreds of other conservative titles published by FARMS, Bookcraft, Brigham Young University, and other church-related houses.

New Mormon Studies. Salt Lake City: Smith Research Associates/Signature Books, 1998. Indispensable easy-to-use tool for a serious Mormon studies researcher, from an independent publisher. Includes a wealth of primary-source historical books, documents, and periodicals (including such items as the *Nauvoo Expositor,* Ethan Smith's *View of the Hebrews,* original texts of the Mormon scriptures, and other materials), as well as the full serials of the independent contemporary Mormon journals *Dialogue* and *Sunstone.* The disc also includes much of the best independent Mormon studies scholarship: eighty titles from Signature Books and nineteen from the University of Illinois Press.

MORMON WEB SITES

Denominational

The Church of Jesus Christ of Latter-day Saints (official): http://www.lds.org.

Family Search: http://www.familysearch.org. Official Internet genealogy site maintained by the LDS Church to help members and nonmembers trace ancestors. At its 1999 inauguration the site charged no fee and listed nearly 400 million names.

All About Mormons: http://www.mormons.org. Unofficial but seeks to be "consistent with official church teachings"; much of its material is not available on the church's own web site. Operated by LDS members John and Jenny Walsh.

MormonNET: http://www.mormon.net. Similar to All About Mormons—unofficial and self-described as "pro-Mormon." Operated by church member John Hays.

Reorganized Church of Jesus Christ of Latter Day Saints (official): http://www.rlds.org.

Restoration.org: http://www.Restoration.org. Information and links on other Restoration denominations as well as the LDS and RLDS Churches; operated by John Hajiceck of Independence, Missouri.

Educational

Brigham Young University (official): http://www.byu.edu.

Book Publishers and Related Materials

Deseret Book Company: phone 1-800-453-4532; http://www.deseretbook.com. Owned by the LDS Church.

Signature Books: phone 1-800-356-5687; http://signaturebooksinc.com. Independent, includes liberal Mormon scholarship.

News

Associated Press: http://wire.ap.org. AP's Salt Lake City bureau closely follows LDS news. AP's archive on TheWire offers stories from the past two weeks free, and back to July 1997 with free search but a fee for retrieval.

Deseret News: http://desnews.com. Church-owned daily in Salt Lake City. Archive available.

Salt Lake Tribune: http://sltrib.com. Salt Lake City's non-LDS daily; closely follows LDS news. Archive available.

Defense of Mormons (Apologetics)

Foundation for Ancient Research and Mormon Studies (FARMS): http://www.farmsresearch.com. Affiliated with Brigham Young University.

Scholarly and Historical Information Exchange for Latter-day Saints (SHIELDS): http://www.shields-research.org. Includes materials criticizing the Tanners.

Foundation for Apologetic Information and Research (FAIR): http://www.fair-lds.org.

Criticism of Mormons

There are dozens of web sites operated by critics of the LDS religion. Among the more interesting:

Mormonism Research Ministry: http://www.mrm.org. Links to forty-five other sites. Operated by Bill McKeever of El Cajon, California.

Mormons in Transition: http://www.irr.org/mit. The web site of the Institute for Religious Research, Grand Rapids, Michigan, with numerous documents available online.

Recovery from Mormonism: http://www.exmormon.org. A web site for ex-Mormons, Christian and otherwise, and those questioning their faith; operated anonymously; with an e-mail newsgroup.

Utah Lighthouse Ministry: http://www.utlm.org. Operated by Jerald and Sandra Tanner of Salt Lake City, with links to twenty-three other sites.

ABOUT THE AUTHORS

RICHARD N. OSTLING, an Associated Press religion writer, was previously a writer and senior correspondent with *Time* magazine, where he authored two dozen cover stories about religion. He has also covered the field for the CBS Radio Network and PBS's *NewsHour with Jim Lehrer.* He has received the two major honors in religion coverage, the Supple and Templeton Awards, and is a past president of the Religion Newswriters Association. Ostling is a Phi Beta Kappa graduate of the University of Michigan and holds master's degrees from George Washington University (in religion) and Northwestern University's Medill School of Journalism, which named him a charter member of its Alumni Hall of Achievement.

Freelance writer and editor JOAN K. OSTLING is the coauthor of *C. S. Lewis: An Annotated Checklist of Writings About Him and His Works* and has written numerous articles. She was formerly a college English and journalism teacher, a newspaper reporter, and a writer-editor with the U.S. Information Agency. She earned a B.A. degree in political science and writing from Wheaton College in Illinois, an M.A. in political science from the University of Illinois, and an M.A. in English from the University of Maryland; she has completed coursework for the Ph.D. in English at New York University.

The Ostlings are the parents of two adult daughters and live in Ridgewood, New Jersey.

INDEX

Trinity, 298, 305–7
Twain, Mark, *Roughing It,* xxii
twenty-first century Mormonism, 372–85

Udall, Morris, 135, 136
Udall, Stewart, 134–35, 361
Ulrich, Laurel Thatcher, 367
United Order of Enoch, 51
University of Utah, 226, 276
Utah, 5, 16, 157, 162–63, 379; Mormon
    move to, 5, 20, 37–55, 226, 242, 247,
    286; statehood, xviii, xxiii, 53, 71,
    78–79, 83, 91. *See also* Mormonism
    and Mormon Church; Salt Lake City
Utah Expedition, 53–54
Utah Jazz, xx, 138, 198
Utah War (1857–58), 53–54, 246

Van Buren, Martin, 6
Van Der Donckt, C., 297
Van Noy, Nathan, 203–10
Vassal, Bruno and Cari, 162–64; Cayr
    Vassel, 200
volunteer labor, Mormon, 119, 127, 137,
    159, 163, 181–83, 211–12
voting, 76–77, 82–83

Walker, Lucy, 62–63
wards, 154, 155–56, 196, 227
Ware, Timothy (Bishop), 311, 423
War of 1812, 8
Warsaw Signal, 18
welfare system, 114, 124, 126–29, 179–80
West, settlement of, xviii, 7, 8, 38–55
White, O. Kendall, Jr., 324–25
Whitesides, Lynne Kanavel, 356, 364
Whitmer, David, 26, 34, 239, 266,
    287–88, 337, 338, 349
Whitney, Sarah Ann, 63
Wight, Lyman, 337, 339

Wilkinson, Ernest, 232
Willes, Mark, 138
Winter Quarters, 40–41, 43, 44, 240
Wirthlin, Joseph B., 431
women, Mormon, 76–77, 233; BYU fac-
    ulty, 237; childbirth, 45, 46; dissenters
    and exiles, 351–71; endowment, 195;
    family values, 159–72; feminists,
    296–97, 356, 364–68; missionaries,
    210, 241; in politics, 135; polygamy,
    56–75, 76–90, 167, 230, 248–52; in
    priesthood, 344, 356, 357, 364; suf-
    frage, 76–77
Woodruff, Wilford, 72, 79, 84, 87–88,
    246, 248, 284
Woodward, Kenneth L., 328–29, 425
Word of Wisdom, 176–78, 183, 254
works and salvation, 316–17, 329–30
World War I, 91
World War II, 111
worldwide population growth, Mormon,
    214–19, 374–75
Wright, David, 293, 358
Wyoming, 71

Young, Brigham, xvii, xxii, 3–5, 33,
    41–55, 77, 79, 92, 119, 139, 154, 177,
    180, 230, 240–41, 242, 246, 252, 262,
    284, 338, 349, 370, 379; childhood,
    41–42; death, 55; leadership, 42–55,
    247, 250–51, 338; move to Utah,
    39–55; as polygamist, 57–59, 64, 66,
    69, 70, 248; racial policies, 100–101;
    Smith and, 42–43, 55
Young, Lawrence A., 378–79
Young, Steve, 131, 139–40

Zion's Cooperative Mercantile Institution
    (ZCMI), 51–52